THE
OPENING
OF THE
CANADIAN
NORTH

MORRIS ZASLOW

THE OPENING OF THE CANADIAN NORTH

1870-1914

The Canadian Centenary Series

McClelland and Stewart Limited
Toronto/Montreal

0-7710-9072-2

The Canadian Publishers
McClelland and Stewart Limited
25 Hollinger Road, Toronto 374

For material in the illustration sections of this book, acknowledgement is made to the following sources:

THE GEOLOGICAL SURVEY OF CANADA for Coppermine River Eskimos packing overland to Great Bear Lake.

J. B. TYRRELL COLLECTIONS, UNIVERSITY OF TORONTO, for Men at work on Claim 42, Hunker Creek, Yukon; steamer *Tyrrell* coming into the wharf at Dawson.

ONTARIO ARCHIVES for interior of Algoma Iron Works; Hollinger Mine; Cobalt, Ontario; Silver Islet Mine buildings; Indians awaiting signing of Treaty No 9.

PUBLIC ARCHIVES OF CANADA for departure of Stefansson party, Collinson Point, Alaska; Capt Bernier's proclamation of sovereignty, Melville Is.; cleaning whalebone; Canadian Arctic Expedition ship *Karluk*; Skidegate Village, B.C.; Indians at Qu'Appelle Industrial School; police post, Chilkoot Pass.

UNITED CHURCH OF CANADA ARCHIVES for Grand Trunk Pacific Railway track, Tête Jaune Cache; part of Dawson, Yukon.

Every reasonable care has been taken to trace ownership of copyright material. Information will be welcome that will enable the publisher to rectify any omission.

Printed and bound in Canada by
THE HUNTER ROSE COMPANY

A History of Canada

W. L. Morton, EXECUTIVE EDITOR

D. G. Creighton, ADVISORY EDITOR

VOLUMES STARRED ARE PUBLISHED

CONTENTS

The Opening of the Canadian North

MAPS

Courtney C. J. Bond, CARTOGRAPHER

ILLUSTRATIONS

Facing Page 116

Laying track on the Grand Trunk Pacific Railway – Grand Trunk Pacific track arriving at Tête Jaune Cache, B.C. – Temporary bridge, Grand Trunk Pacific Railway – Interior, Algoma Iron Works, Sault Ste Marie, Ontario – Hollinger Mine buildings, Timmins, Ontario – Cobalt, Ontario – Belgo-Canadian Pulp and Paper Company – Coppermine River Eskimos packing overland to Great Bear Lake – Departure of the Stefansson party, Collinson Point, Alaska – Capt Bernier's proclamation of sovereignty, Melville Island – Cleaning whalebone on the ship *Belvedere* – Canadian Arctic Expedition ship *Karluk*

Facing Page 180

Council of Hudson's Bay Company commissioned officers – Commissioner's residence, Dawson, Yukon – Rampart House on the Porcupine River – Hudson's Bay Company store, Fort Vermilion, Alberta – Silver Islet mine buildings – Indians awaiting signing of Treaty No 9 – Skidegate village, B.C. – Indians at Qu'Appelle Industrial School – Men at work, Claim 42, Hunker Creek, Yukon – N.W.M.P. post, Chilkoot Pass – Steamer *Tyrrell* arriving at Dawson wharf – Bear Creek dredge at work – Part of Dawson city, Yukon.

The Canadian Centenary Series

Half a century has elapsed since *Canada and Its Provinces*, the first large-scale co-operative history of Canada, was published. During that time, new historical materials have been made available in archives and libraries; new research has been carried out, and its results published; new interpretations have been advanced and tested. In these same years Canada itself has greatly grown and changed. These facts, together with the centenary of Confederation, justify the publication of a new co-operative history of Canada.

The form chosen for this enterprise was that of a series of volumes. The series was planned by the editors, but each volume will be designed and executed by a single author. The general theme of the work is the development of those regional communities which have for the past century made up the Canadian nation; and the series will be composed of a number of volumes sufficiently large to permit adequate treatment of all the phases of the theme in the light of modern knowledge.

The Centenary History, then, was planned as a series to have a certain common character and to follow a common method but to be written by individual authors, specialists in their fields. As a whole, it will be a work of specialized knowledge, the great advantage of scholarly co-operation, and at the same time each volume will have the unity and distinctive character of individual authorship. It was agreed that a general narrative treatment was necessary and that each author should deal in a balanced way with economic, political, and social history. The result, it is hoped, will be an interpretive, varied, and comprehensive account, at once useful to the student and interesting to the general reader.

The difficulties of organizing and executing such a series are apparent: the overlapping of separate narratives, the risk of omissions, the imposition of divisions which are relevant to some themes but not to others. Not so apparent, but quite as troublesome, are the problems of scale, perspective, and scope, problems which perplex the writer of a one-volume history and are magnified in a series. It is by deliberate choice that certain parts of the history are told twice, in different volumes from different points of view, in the belief that the benefits gained outweigh the unavoidable disadvantages.

Professor Zaslow's book has a special significance for the Centenary Series, because it completes the trilogy of volumes devoted to the theme of the North in Canadian history within the Series as a whole. The first was that of Professor T. J. Oleson, *Early Voyages and Northern Approaches*, the second that of Professor E. E. Rich, *The Fur Trade and the Northwest to 1857*, Volume XI. The term "North" in the Series has meant the unoccupied and unsettled, sometimes even the unclaimed, territory beyond the area of organized Canada. So it was in the first two volumes. Now Professor Zaslow has accomplished the formidable task of presenting in one volume a coherent account of the penetration by trader and missionary, and of the formal, legal occupation by government of all northern and Arctic Canada to the Polar Sea. (Indeed, so forbidding has the task proved that an additional volume is to follow to bring the history of the Canadian North down to recent times.) The present book, however, completes the story of the formal incorporation of the North into the Canadian polity. It is a story dominated by no man and no set of men, by no great company, and certainly not by the government, or the public, of Canada. The greater therefore is Professor Zaslow's achievement in bringing its main features and their telling details into one on-going narrative and analysis, under the grand and ultimately convincing theme of the gradual evolution of Canada's special skills in surveying and policing, of the slow seeping outward of its second, and perhaps its greater frontier, the North.

W. L. MORTON,
Executive Editor.
D. G. CREIGHTON,
Advisory Editor.

PREFACE

The Opening of the Canadian North

Canadians fail to recognize, or often forget, that they are essentially a northern people. Nowhere is this more apparent than in the way historians have so often treated the creation of the transcontinental state in 1870-71 and its subsequent development as simply the westward extension of central Canada. Actually, much of Canada's development since 1870 has followed a northwesterly or northerly direction, which has posed special problems and given a unique flavour to the Canadian experience. But notwithstanding the importance or the uniqueness of this aspect of the nation's development, little thought or systematic study has been devoted to it to date. It is hoped that this volume, in which the course, character, and problems of northern expansion constitute the central subject of enquiry, will kindle greater interest in this side of Canadian history, many large features of which still remain to be adequately investigated.

This book deals with the opening of the Canadian North, but it should be recognized that what constitutes "the North" has itself undergone considerable change since 1870. In the immediate post-Confederation period, anything beyond Lake Nipissing was termed "North." When Canada secured the new territories in 1870, it conferred the name "North-West Territories" on them, including in that description country as far south as the forty-ninth parallel – which, indeed, crosses Ontario and Quebec at the admittedly northerly levels of Cochrane, Abitibi, Lake St John, and Gaspé. Only after 1912 was the name (revised by then to "Northwest Territories") confined to those parts of Canada lying beyond the sixtieth parallel. It is impossible, therefore, to speak of the opening of the Canadian North without looking first into the expansion to the prairie region. Such an approach is all the more valid since "North-West" and "North" are more than geographical expressions. They also constitute a process: the advance of frontiers and frontier experience from the rear of the Province of Canada to the prairie northwest, then gradually northward along several fronts to the northern coasts of Canada and the islands beyond. Such frontiers were of many kinds – of societies, cultures, and administrations, as well as of industries and people.

Most of the activities described on the succeeding pages occurred in the broad coniferous forest band that stretches across the continent north of the St Lawrence Lowlands and the prairie region, or in the treeless tundra farther north. The latter region is universally defined as "Arctic," but what single word can most appropriately be applied to the broad band of transitional forest? Geographers have come increasingly to employ the term "Middle North" for this important forested belt, and for convenience, this practice will be followed here. Spellings of names of organizations and institutions also have changed over time. In such cases the terminology appropriate to the time referred to will be used, though references to geographical features will follow present-day usages. Every effort has been made to reproduce quoted material accurately, misspellings included, and to avoid obtrusive editorial insertions or corrections.

Many persons and institutions over a long period helped me to pursue the studies represented by this book. I offer grateful thanks to the universities of Toronto and of Western Ontario for study leaves and lightened teaching loads for part of the time this work has been in progress. A fellowship awarded by the Nuffield Foundation in 1960-61 enabled me to spend a sabbatical year in congenial surroundings and to utilize the facilities of the British Museum, the Bibliothèque Nationale, and other libraries and archives. The Canada Council extended a summer study grant in 1960 and a subsequent grant to help with research and typing. The Rockefeller Fund and the Canadian Social Science Research Council provided earlier grants in connection with my doctoral dissertation, out of which this present study has grown. Staff members of many libraries, archival institutions, and government departments in England, France, the United States, as well as across Canada, frequently extended help beyond the normal course of duty. I am especially grateful to many of my students for term papers, reports, and theses that cast light on many previously dark corners; for invaluable observations and insights during discussions; and for perceptive criticisms of drafts of the manuscript. William G. Attwell was employed as research assistant in the summer of 1968, while Miss Pauline Laurin and Mrs Louise Weyerman assumed the main burdens of typing. The maps were prepared with his usual professional competence by Courtney C. J. Bond. Like other writers for this series, I must acknowledge a profound debt to Professor W. L. Morton for his unfailing courtesy, tolerance, and encouragement in the face of many disappointments during the prolonged gestation of this manuscript. Finally, for her assistance, as well as her patience and understanding over long periods of familial neglect, I offer heartfelt thanks to my long-suffering wife, Betty.

MORRIS ZASLOW

CHAPTER 1

Canada Enters on the Northwest

1870 – 1885

While the attention of the world was fastened upon the European struggles by which the German Empire was forged and Rome was secured as the capital of the Kingdom of Italy, across the Atlantic one of the largest transfers of territory in all of recorded history was being effected, virtually unnoticed. In four brief years after its inception in 1867, the Canadian Confederation burst beyond its narrow frontiers astride the lakes and the River and Gulf of St Lawrence and lunged across the breadth of the continent, westward to the shores of the Pacific and northward to the icy coasts of Hudson Bay and the Arctic Ocean. Following successful negotiations with the Colonial Secretary and the Hudson's Bay Company, the Canadian government prepared to receive Rupert's Land and the North-Western Territory into the Dominion before the end of 1869. After a delay occasioned by the winter's happenings at Red River, the transfer was actually implemented on July 15, 1870. By that time, negotiations had commenced in Ottawa between Canadian ministers and British Columbia delegates, and on July 20, 1871, that colony also entered the union, rounding out an expansion that added some 2,500,000 square miles to the area of Canada. In return for a cash and land settlement with the Hudson's Bay Company, guarantees of the property and civil rights of the existing inhabitants of Red River, and promises of generous fiscal terms and transcontinental railway communication to the British Columbians, the Dominion of Canada suddenly was transformed into one of the world's largest states, mistress of half a continent.

But the new acquisitions were more noteworthy for their physical extent and their latent resources than for their existing level of development. The sole commodities from the region to figure in external commerce were furs and other products of the hunt, as well as placer gold from the rivers of the Pacific slope. The territory was home to some 150,000 nomadic aborigines and to small numbers of white men, many of them transient, engaged

1

in prospecting, fur-trading, fishing and whaling, or the saving of souls. Here and there, at intervals, small settlements had grown up, almost invariably around important posts of the fur trade. Only in two small districts had settlement progressed beyond the level of the isolated community: in the very centre of the continent, separated from Canada by 1,200 miles of forests and rocks; and on the shores of the distant Pacific, 1,500 miles farther west. But although the Red River Settlement and southern British Columbia could be described as regional societies and polities, on the eve of their union with Canada neither held many more than 10,000 inhabitants. *The Great Lone Land, The Wild North Land* – such were the succinct characterizations that the British soldier, W. F. Butler, selected for the titles of his two excellent accounts of travel through parts of the region in 1870 and 1872-73.

In fact, this empty, undeveloped quality of the country northwest of Canada constituted its main attraction to Canadians. Their drive to secure the territories had been dictated to a considerable degree by the increasing inability of the Province of Canada to present opportunities for growth comparable to those offered by the neighbouring United States. The American westward movement, particularly after 1850 when railways began laying open the trans-Mississippean west and California and Oregon beckoned along the Pacific coast, made it imperative for British North Americans to match this advance by expanding west into the territories of the British Crown. Not to do so would expose those lands to the danger of being overwhelmed by the United States and would condemn the people of Canada to their present narrow limits and to a lower standard of living than their neighbours. Expansion became a national duty for Canada, a commitment with destiny.[1]

Already Canada faced a crisis because its most attractive lands had been occupied, and what remained seemed incapable of drawing immigrants to the country or holding the natural increase of its present population. Alarm was being felt at the growing numbers of Canadians taking up residence in the United States. The Commissioner of Crown Lands, Joseph Cauchon, reflected this concern in his very able report for 1856. After dutifully detailing the virtues of such regions as Lake St John and the St Maurice valley, he went on to describe the exhaustion of settlement land "in the great western Peninsula of Upper Canada, which has hitherto been the chief receptacle of immigration to this Province,"[2] and proceeded to devote a large part of his report to the "Red River and Saskatchawan (sic) Country" on the grounds that only there could lands be found for Canada's sons and immigrants, comparable to those previously available in the province, or as attractive as those currently offered in the western United States.

Upper Canadians hoped, and Lower Canadians feared, that northwestward expansion would ensure the ascendancy of Anglo-Canadians over the

French, while ambitious Toronto businessmen dreamed of developing strong commercial ties with the region. People began studying travel accounts and scientific reports of the Northwest, spoke of transcontinental railways and other developmental projects, and developed contacts with the region through fur-trade personnel, missionaries, and the few Canadians who had lived, or were living, there. The government came out against the Hudson's Bay Company's application for a renewal of its licence to the North-Western Territory and staked its own claim to be regarded as the company's successor in Rupert's Land. It subsidized a direct communications link with Red River and sent two expeditions of S. J. Dawson and H. Y. Hind in 1857 and 1858 to survey a route from Fort William to Fort Garry and to report on the agricultural and other resources of the region west of Lake Superior and the prairies beyond. The expansion of Canadian economic activities in the northwesterly direction was further indication of the drive, as the Toronto *Globe* pointed out in an editorial of October 22, 1864:

> We look upon every fresh discovery of mineral wealth upon the northern shores of Lakes Huron and Superior as of immense importance in reference to the question of North-western extension. . . . If, by means of the mines which are being opened along the coast, settlements can be formed and roads constructed, we shall attain to that much desired object, the bridging over of the gaps of rough and partially barren country which lie between us and the fertile prairies of North-western British America. Progress is being made in this direction, and every discovery of ore gives it an impetus. The formation of lumbering establishments on the Georgian Bay, the projection of new mines near the Ste. Marie river, the extension of the settlements at the Sault, the opening of copper and lead mines at the upper end of the lake, the permanent establishment of the steamer route to Fort William, are all steps in the right direction.

By 1864, after frustrating delays, Canada had set its feet along the road that led to the acquisition of the Northwest. Among other things, the Great Coalition of 1864 brought about a workable compromise on the subject of westward expansion. The Conservatives, French and English, ceased to delay or block the movement, while the Clear Grit party finally acceded to the necessity of settling the proprietary claims of the Hudson's Bay Company and assuming the other burdens associated with expansion. By filling the best land of the Province of Canada, its people had been forced into accepting the responsibilities of expansion and of nationhood. In their search for a frontier, Canadians discovered a nation. Now they had to explore and organize the territory they inherited from the Hudson's Bay Company and the Crown.

There was more to integrating the new domains into Canada than proclaiming sovereignty over them, more than building roads or railways to

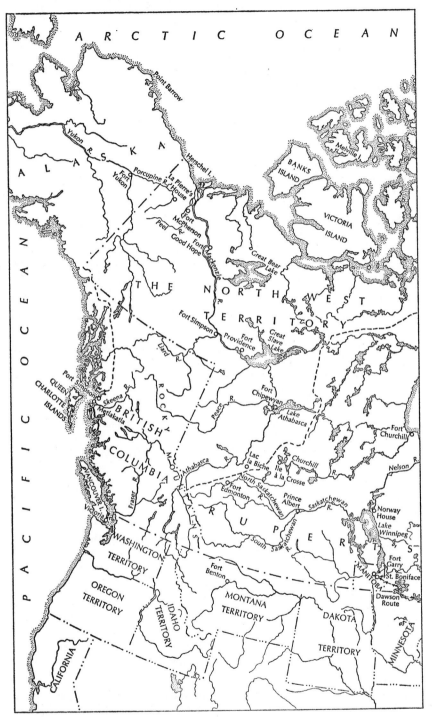

British North America

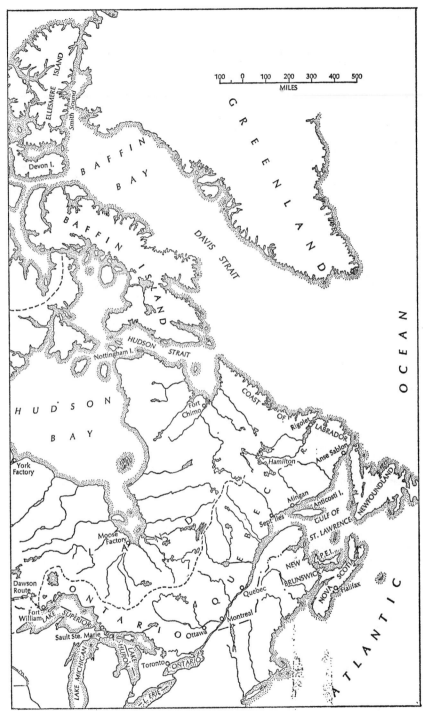

in 1869-70

overcome the great distances, more even than planting there the society and institutions of eastern Canada. For the territory was no empty void to be shaped *de novo* to the will of the Canadians. Though it was scarcely developed at all by European standards, it possessed both a firmly rooted economy utilizing such resources as the inhabitants were capable of exploiting, and social patterns based on the tribal organization of the native peoples and their interaction with the few traders and missionaries who lived among them. The contemplated peaceful conquest and redirection of the region would require profound social and cultural adjustments from the original inhabitants.

Reconciling these existing patterns with those that Canada proposed to introduce did not seem to present any difficulties as regards the two centres of white settlement, since these were already committed to the modern order, though in widely differing ways. Moreover, both the Red River Settlement and the Crown Colony of British Columbia, in growing up in the midst of large aboriginal populations, had evolved two contrasting approaches to the problem of white-Indian relations. Red River was the product of a slow fifty-year development from a simple fur-trading and agricultural establishment to a variegated collection of distinct economic, religious, and social strands. Pre-eminent among the factors on the social side was the large, well-organized Métis community, and on the economic side, the still-important fur trade. Rather than evolving or imposing a common nationality to subsume the identities of the several groups, there had grown up among most of the 12,000 inhabitants a group collectivity, coupled with a sense of community based on attitudes of mutual tolerance, of refraining from kindling animosities that might embitter future good relations among groups.

Furthermore, though the colony was given a governing council and an administration appointed by the Hudson's Bay Company, its government was characterized by a primitive system of taxation and public finance, a makeshift array of courts, few land titles, rudimentary surveys and limited public improvements, educational and welfare services provided by the churches, and the almost complete absence of a law-enforcement agency or security system. Thus the settlement presented a balance between the permissiveness, disorganization, and conservatism of the old order characteristic of its large native sector; and the elements of the new, represented by the fur-traders and missionaries, the transplanted Scots farmers, and the rising professional and commercial class.

British Columbia, in place of the pattern of wide ethnic and cultural diversity of Red River, presented (in its shrunken post-gold-rush state) the aspect of a fairly homogeneous colony of some 8,500 persons of European extraction and outlook, who belonged to a common social and material tradition and followed similar patterns of work. They were characterized by the same materialistic, acquisitive, competitive drives, the same skills and tastes, and the same concepts of state and society appropriate to people of a western European heritage of the time. The Indians were at least four times as numerous as the whites, but they were brushed aside and excluded from any part of the life of the settled colony; they were regarded as a sector of casual labour and a social and moral problem of drunkenness, prostitution, and disease. Yet though they were excluded, they were not treated as enemies. The colonial administration kept a firm grip over white and Indian alike to prevent or punish breaches of the peace by either side.

For, in contrast with Red River, the colony had an effective, modern system of government, with a legislative assembly elected by the settlers, and a bureaucracy drawn initially from the British colonial service. Firm control was instituted over the scattered parts of the colony by a system of judges, circuit courts, and regional administrators, while military expeditions made forays into the Indian country as required. An impressive system of public works considered necessary for the colony was undertaken, and in the process, a large debt was created. Systems were promulgated for disposing and developing land and other natural resources, municipal institutions were established to enable ratepayers to provide for local improvements, a public school system was organized, and the churches and Hudson's Bay Company were reduced to the status of private corporations.

It seemed a foregone conclusion that Canada would embrace the British Columbian pattern in providing for her new possessions, and set aside as unworkable and undesirable the Red River pattern, which attempted to reconcile and harmonize the old order with the new. For after all, the Dominion government's objective was to institute in the new territories a homogeneous economic and social order, like that of British Columbia. Moreover, the new Dominion was propelled in that direction by the experience of its predecessor, the Province of Canada, which served in large measure as its administrative laboratory. The leading figures in the federal government brought with them to the larger stage the attitudes and experience derived from dealing with the problems of the frontiers of the former Province. A large part of the administrative staff concerned with frontier development in the Province, as well as some of the agencies, were transferred to the national arena for the express purpose of carrying out on a grander scale the same programs of directing immigration and investment into the attractive lands of the Northwest.

Of particular significance for any program of frontier development was the system, bequeathed by Britain, that the Province of Canada had evolved to deal with the Indians. Unlike France or Spain, where the Indian was unequivocally regarded as a subject of the Crown, some British colonies had gradually adopted the view that the Indian was initially possessed of aboriginal title to his tribal territory. It was therefore necessary to negotiate with him for the relinquishment of this title and the acceptance of the authority of the Crown. These negotiations resulted in treaties under which the Indian's natural right to close his territory to the increasingly powerful white settlers – a dubious prospect at best – was exchanged for a secure, unquestioned ownership of some part of the original tribal territory, under a covenant that thereafter became legally binding upon all subjects of the Crown and protected the Indians' reserves from encroachment with the full sanctions of the state.

Besides these reserves, payments in goods and money were made to individuals or to bands. The Indians could follow their traditional life on the Crown lands that were not appropriated to other purposes, but it was anticipated they eventually would abandon their nomadic existence to make their way in the white-dominated society of the future. To help with this transition, further undertakings regarding educational and other aids were made. Moreover, besides the treaties, special legislation – the Indian Act – was enacted governing the status of the Indians. This gave them a position of dependence as wards or clients of the state while holding out the opportunity, if they so desired, of exchanging this special status through a process of enfranchisement to one of full citizenship.

Most of southern Upper Canada had been "surrendered" in this fashion by 1836, when Lieutenant-Governor Sir Francis Bond Head decided to take a leaf from the United States government's book and remove the Indians to Manitoulin Island or "elsewhere towards the northwest," since the greatest kindness to "these intelligent, simple-minded People, is to remove and fortify them as much as possible from all communication with the Whites."[3] Though the policy was quickly reversed, some cessions remained in effect, notably that of the Saugeen peninsula adjoining the Canada Company's grant of the Huron Tract. Later, in 1849, the intrusion of mining operations into the country north of Lakes Huron and Superior touched off a so-called Michipicoten War, when the Indians of that locality seized the property of the Quebec and Lake Superior Mining Company at Mica Bay to force the government to some action on their behalf. W. B. Robinson was sent in 1850 to negotiate a treaty of surrender for the territory north of Lakes Huron and Superior, and the Indians received tribal annuities of £600 and £500 respectively, with promise of more – possibly even as much as £1 per head per annum – if the government's revenue from the ceded territory sufficed. A dozen years later, a cession of most of Manitoulin Island was secured by the Commissioner of Crown Lands, William McDougall, to ease the land hunger of Upper Canada farmers. The period of the Union also saw the Indians of Lower Canada placed on a footing similar to those of

Upper Canada, even though no treaties of surrender, on the British model, were signed. Reserves were granted in the Timiskaming, Ottawa, St Maurice, and Lake St John regions, and there were small sums available for education and relief for certain of the bands. Such aspects of Indian policy as the treaties system, annuities payable in cash instead of goods, registered reserves, band trust funds, special Indian legal status, enfranchisement, and state-aided education and training through the instrumentality of missions were developed and refined in the Province of Canada, to become, in turn, the basis for Indian administration in the new territories.

Once arrangements with the Indians had been effected, surveys became essential to prepare the land for development and to receive settlers. Naturally enough, the first surveys were of an exploratory nature. Thus, in the future Muskoka and Haliburton country, expeditions in the 1820's and 1830's traced the watercourses; then between 1847 and 1857, other parties worked over the territory to locate roads that were likeliest to lay open the useful resources of the district. By the end of this period, instructions were being issued to demarcate the boundary lines of the various townships, following which came subdivision into concessions and lots. The progress of surveys into the district north of Lakes Huron and Superior illustrates these same phases, and also demonstrates the northwesterly advance of Canada. After exploring the potentially arable sections between Lake Nipissing and Sault Ste Marie in 1855, the land surveyor A. P. Salter was instructed in the following year to run a base line from Lake Nipissing to Lake Superior. Next, other surveyors drew meridian lines from this base line at eighteen-mile intervals, which formed the lateral boundaries of townships. In 1859 and 1860, subdivision surveys were underway in strategic localities like Sault Ste Marie, Garden Island, and the head of Lake Superior. A significant departure for the future was the adoption in these surveys of the United States system of 36-square-mile townships subdivided into 640-acre (square-mile) and 160-acre (quarter-section) segments, rather than the Upper Canadian system of surveys aligned with the fronting lake, river or road, and subdivided in multiples and fractions of one hundred acres.

The period of the Province of Canada coincided with the rise of the science of geology, from which would evolve another type of survey and an organization that would play a long and distinguished part in the unfolding of Canada's northern frontiers. Following a petition of the Natural History Society of Montreal in 1841 and inspired by the example of Michigan, where the appointment of Douglas Houghton as state geologist had contributed mightily to the development of the copper-mining industry, the legislature voted £1,500 for geological surveys of Canada. The following year the Province secured William E. Logan, a Montreal-born Edinburgh-educated practical mining man, and the Geological Survey of Canada was inaugurated. During the next dozen years, Logan and his assistant, Alexander Murray, ranged over nearly every section of Canada from Gaspé to the head of Lake Superior. This had such effect that a select committee of the legislature in 1854 paid the following tribute: "In no part of the world has there been a more valuable contribution to geological science for such a small outlay (hardly more than £20,000 in all)."[4] Such complaints as the committee expressed were all to Logan's credit – inability to meet the demand for reports; the lack of maps and plates; the scarcity of technical and interpretative conclusions such as Logan gave in papers to learned journals; the survey's collections still lying in packing cases in Montreal. The committee's recommendations were to print up to 20,000 copies of the reports, open the museum and library, speed up exploration and reporting on rich mineral localities, increase the staff and furnish it with topographical survey parties so the geologists could devote themselves entirely to their proper work of drawing the geology on prepared base maps. The committee, under the chairmanship of the versatile John Langton, concluded its report by recommending an increase in expenditure from £2,283 to £6,000 to expand the work of the survey.

The confidence of the legislature proved justified. The work of the survey ranged ever farther afield – to Manitoulin Island and the Lake Nipigon district on the west, and to Anticosti, Lake St John, and the Moisie River in the east. The efforts of Logan and Murray were supplemented by explorations by J. Richardson and young Robert Bell, the latter initiating over forty years of work with a study, in 1857, of the fauna of the Saguenay basin. On the technical side, the brilliant chemist and mineralogist, T. Sterry Hunt, was joined in 1856 by a palaeontologist, Elkanah Billings. Thanks mainly to Logan's participation in the exhibitions in London in 1851 and Paris in 1855, the Geological Survey of Canada gained a world-wide reputation, and Logan received a knighthood. The expansion of Canada in 1870-71 gave the Geological Survey a tremendous new field in which to operate and achieve even greater distinction.

In the administration of its natural resources, the Province of Canada also developed important policies and agencies that were to provide a basis for similar programs in the Northwest and in the provinces of Quebec and Ontario. These varied from a negligent, defective program for mining lands, to a progressive conservation-minded approach to the fishery that even included fish hatcheries. But of particular relevance for the future development of the Northwest were the Province of Canada's activities respecting forest and agricultural lands. After much thought on appropriate regulations for the important timber industry, a system of selling berths by public auction was instituted in 1859 that became generally practised thereafter. The successful bidder paid a bonus at the time of sale, dues based on timber cut, and an annual ground rent of 50 cents per square mile. To discourage speculation, the ground rent was progressively increased each year the berth was not worked. The problem of reconciling the lumberman's desire to enjoy the exclusive use of woodlands with the farmer's wish to cultivate the soil continued unsolved. The superior voting power of the settlers, and the general view that the public interest was best served by placing the maximum number of settlers on the land usually prevailed, with the result that land was brought under the plough that would best have been left to the lumberman. A few enlightened persons were just then beginning to suggest the obvious solution – to classify the land and allocate it to particular uses.

Two major questions arose in connection with disposing of land for agricultural purposes: whether it should be sold in large blocks to colonization interests; and whether it should be given away free to bona-fide settlers. When the Canadas were united in 1841, there was a strong prejudice against large-scale grants, but a system of selling townships at a rate of 50 cents per acre was authorized in 1859. One sale of ten townships (403,125 acres) was made in Haliburton County in 1860, but the company had no great success in settling a very difficult area, part of which is today included in Algonquin Park. The land-grant colonization company, however, was destined to enter upon a new chapter of chequered history in the Northwest after 1870.

Having passed through a long period of giving lands away, the united Province had grown eager to sell its remaining lands, if it could. A nominal price of $1 per acre by instalments, or 70 cents for cash, was set, though sometimes the price was lowered (to 20 cents, for instance, for lands in the District of Algoma) to encourage settlement of the remote areas. Collections were lax and foreclosing was difficult. An all too frequent occurrence was that settlers would clear off the timber before their instalments came due and would then abandon the farms, defrauding the Province of timber dues and the limit holder of his rightful property, offering unfair competition to the law-abiding lumberman, and ruining the lots for future settlers. Accordingly, to bring the situation under control, settlers were permitted to cut timber from their lots under licence, provided they paid the regular dues on any timber they sold.

By the 1850's opinion was turning once more to the policy of making free grants to attract settlers. In 1853, free 100-acre grants were offered to settlers along the colonization roads for fulfilling certain settlement requirements and maintaining their share of the road in good repair. The sentiment for giving free homesteads to bona-fide settlers continued to grow, the contention being that the colony was amply repaid by the value of the land brought into production. Three provinces had instituted free homesteads by 1872, and the adoption of such a law by the United States in 1862 made it a foregone conclusion that the system would be followed in the Northwest, for competitive reasons if no other.

Canada also gave thought to developing a system of mining regulations to protect the public interest as well as to encourage mining development. The initial policy in 1846 granted exploration licences in the Huron-Superior country to British subjects on payment of a £150 fee. With the discovery of a mineral deposit the finder was entitled to stake a five-mile by two-mile claim, within which he could purchase land at four shillings an acre, the fee becoming part of the payment. Because of complaints against the high initial payment, in 1853 the exploration fee was reduced to £25 and the size of the reserved lot to 400 acres. But the program soon was discredited as a failure, because it did not foster a mining boom comparable to that in nearby Michigan. Complaints continued, with greater justice, that the system played into the hands of wealthy friends of government who sold out to companies that lacked the will or the experience to exploit their holdings, thus keeping the best mining lands of the Province out of the hands of those who would develop them. Consequently, in 1860, the Province turned about and, copying Michigan, proposed hereafter to sell 400-acre locations at a fixed price of $1 per acre to any applicant. Ore mined was to be subject to a 2½ per cent royalty, but even this was abolished in 1865. Ontario retained this incredibly lax sale policy for more than twenty years after Confederation, though it did impose a 2 cents per acre annual land tax in the District of Algoma to hit at the speculating interests that had successfully purchased the best mining lands and then kept them closed to development.

A firm tradition of organization and development of frontier lands and their resources had thus been established in the expanding Province of Canada. Another facet of that tradition was governmental assistance to development through the provision of public works and other aids, the most obvious example being the ambitious colonization-roads program begun in 1852-53. In Upper Canada a series of roads was built extending north into the back concessions of Frontenac, Addington, Hastings, Peterborough, Victoria, and Simcoe counties, intersected by east-west roads (the Ottawa and Opeongo, Monck, and Peterson roads), to lay open the great Huron and Ottawa tract to settlement. A similar program was instituted in Lower Canada, principally in the Eastern Townships, Gaspé, and the Lake St John district. Somewhat later the road network was extended northward through the Muskoka district to Parry Sound and towards Lake Nipissing, eventually to link with the similar roads being constructed in the region north of Lake Huron for the new settlements there. Again, to assist the lumber industry, the Department of Public Works, at a cost of over one million dollars, built and maintained a large system of timber slides. Most were on the Ottawa, which carried over half the timber produced in the Province, but other slides were built on the Saguenay, St Maurice, and Trent river systems. Unlike the colonization roads, the timber slides produced revenue in the form of dues which came close to paying an adequate return on the government's investment.

Strangely, the Province of Canada seemed reluctant to participate in the building of a Sault Ste Marie canal to assist the development of mining in the Lake Superior country and to open the route to the west. A canal could have been built on the Canadian side more easily and cheaply than on the American side, but while Canada delayed, a canal was finished on the American side in 1855. Canadians used this canal on sufferance, and sometimes faced humiliation, as in the case of the Wolseley Expedition to Red River in 1870. Railways, of course, were an obvious case for state aid in view of the immense material benefits they offered for the opening of frontier areas. However, since Canada was already deeply involved in assisting railways in the settled portions of its territory, the Province was unlikely to offer further assistance for lines of questionable financial solvency, however desirable they might be as development roads. Nevertheless, in 1866 a committee on northern mining conditions did recommend that land grants in alternate blocks be offered to encourage the building of a railway north of Lakes Huron and Superior. Here, again, was an important precedent for the future, for securing the all-important link to bind the new Dominion from sea to sea.

II

In assuming control of the new territories in 1870-71 the Canadians might have been prepared with agencies and programs based on their past experience of developing the frontiers of the Province of Canada. Yet given the years of yearning to expand to the Northwest, the government of Canada had made surprisingly little effort to study or understand the existing situation there, or to adapt its policies to the peculiar circumstances of that region. The uprising in Red River was a monument to its lack of foresight, and almost certainly would never have occurred had the government not been blind to local realities. But no matter—Manitoba was erected into a province of sorts, the inhabitants were appeased, and the authority of the Dominion was established. As for the bulk of the acquisition of 1870, which was speedily organized as the North-West Territories,*

---

* In the spring of 1906 this spelling was changed officially to "Northwest," the present form. Between 1893 and 1906 "North-West" was often rendered as "North-west," but to avoid complications, that intermediate variant form is not used here.

Canada seemingly learned nothing from the experience at Red River. The bland assumption that the territory, having been paid for (and conquered by) the Dominion, ought to be used for the primary benefit of eastern Canada, continued to characterize her governance of the Northwest. "The Dominion has purchased the whole of the North-West, and it belongs to Canada," was how Macdonald expressed it.[5]

Canadian institutions were imposed on the Northwest in rigid and unimaginative fashion, both by the Conservatives and by the Liberals who replaced them in power in Ottawa for part of the 1870's. Both governments tended to see the Northwest as an area whose resources should be used for the purposes of the Dominion—to ease the burdens of the eastern taxpayer, and to afford opportunities for friends of government. Macdonald's indolence and political opportunism led him to neglect the region badly, while the Liberal administration of Alexander Mackenzie tended to be too Ontario-centred, too indecisive, and too inhibited by fears of expense to provide adequately for its needs.

Both administrations jealously guarded their authority over the region and both exercised too much control from afar. Records were centralized in Ottawa (or occasionally, Winnipeg), where easterners seemed to have the advantage over residents of the Northwest in securing lands or other grants or appointments. Decisions, even on minor matters, had to be made in Ottawa by people out of touch with the situation, often after inexcusably long delays. Little initiative was allowed the residents through their elective institutions, in marked contrast with the considerable degree of local autonomy that newly organized territories possessed under the United States. Both Dominion governments of the era were immovably committed to the same objective: the older civilization of Indian and half-breed, with its hunting, fur-trading and freighting economy, should be thrust aside, the Northwest should be settled as quickly as possible and stamped with the social, cultural, and political institutions of Canada. The new settlers, along with national communication facilities, would ensure that the territory became truly integrated into the national fabric. The outbreak of the North-West Rebellion of 1885 was a result of fifteen years of such administration, and also the last struggle of a dying order. The comparative ease with which the rebellion was suppressed only accelerated the process of cultural displacement already well under way in the Northwest, and hastened the advance of the southern part of the territories towards the patterns of Ontario-style Canadian society.

Above all, in proceeding to the goal of integrating the Northwest into Canada, the governments failed to pay sufficient heed to the urgent problem of the rapidly changing Indian and half-breed societies. Canadians continued to regard the native population in the light of eastern Canadian experience, notwithstanding warnings like those of S. J. Dawson, the explorer, that "They are very different from the timid and cringing creatures who are now the sole representatives of the Indian Race in the back settlements of Canada."⁶ A sense of superiority pervaded their outlook towards Indians and Métis, in the latter case aggravated by religious animosities heightened by the uprising of 1869-70. The native way of life was inherently inferior to that of the white settler, they believed. At best an anachronism, at worst an enemy to orderly progress towards civilization, it must be eradicated without mercy. Archbishop Taché complained about this attitude: "Common lumbermen, fishermen, sailors, &c., as a class, are much more rough in their manners, and have no more idea of thrift than most of the half-breeds of the plains. They are, however, never represented as being in a semi-barbarous state, nor as semi-savage. Farming, although so desirable, is not the sole condition in the state of civilization."⁷

For generations the Plains Indians had been successful migratory hunters of bison, elk, and antelope, dwelling in light, portable, and easily erected conical skin tents. In the eighteenth century they acquired the horse, which, with the bison, became the material foundation of their civilization. The buffalo hunts yielded sufficient food to permit the Indians to remain together in great camps for a large part of the year. The horse gave mobility for war as well as for the hunt, so that the plains became convulsed by swift, sanguinary inter-tribal raids. The Plains Indians were trained in co-operative action and tended to be organized along military lines into tribes and confederacies, numbering thousands of individuals. Their relative self-sufficiency and powerful tribal organization made them proud, difficult, though essential, clients for the fur trade, since the northern operations of the trade depended on the pemmican they furnished in return for firearms, liquor, and other goods.

Confederation came at a time of extreme crisis in the Northwest. The entire balance of Indian life on the prairie and parkland was in question because of the diminution in the buffalo and game through the indiscriminate use of firearms and poison, the depredations of unscrupulous traders, and the uprooting of the generations-old equilibrium among peoples. The great smallpox epidemic of 1870, which spared none of the native peoples, further weakened and demoralized the Blackfoot Confederacy. The tribes of the southwest found their lands invaded by fugitive Sioux and Piegans from the United States, by the expanding Crees on the north and northeast, by Métis moving westward from Red River, and, behind them all, the American frontiersmen and the thin stream of Canadian pioneers. By 1873, American whiskey-traders had established ten posts on Canadian territory and nearly a hundred Indians were killed in drunken brawls in a single year. In May, 1873, the worst crime of all was perpetrated in the

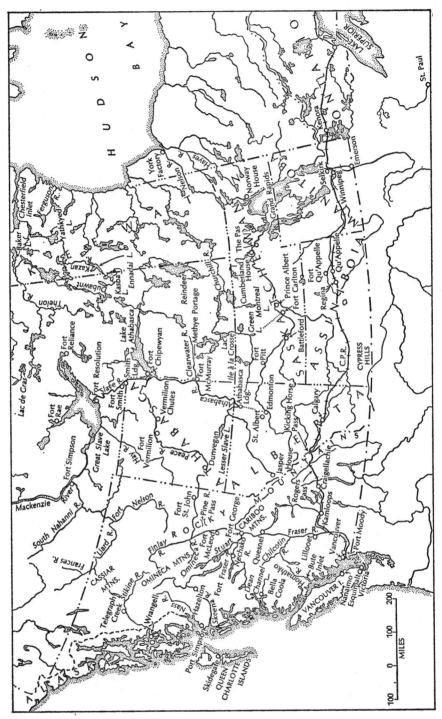

The Canadian West, 1870-94

Cypress Hills: twenty-two Assiniboines were massacred after being plied with drink by American whiskey-dealers.

Such depredations gave urgency to the calls for some show of Canadian force to bring the west under control, either the military, as in the American west, or a police organization. Colonel P. Robertson-Ross, commander-in-chief of the Canadian militia, proposed a plan that was, in the main, eventually accepted—a police force to garrison the frontiers, enforce customs regulations, and protect the natives. Incidentally, he counselled adopting the famous red tunic on the grounds that the Indians associated the colour with British authority from the Sixth Regiment of Foot's sojourn at Red River, 1846-48. The North-West Mounted Police came into being in 1873, made their historic ride across the prairie from Winnipeg in the spring of 1874, then took up the work of patrolling the frontier. Their arrival drove off law-breakers and ensured that the Americans who remained conducted themselves in orderly fashion. The main early role of the police, however, was to deal with the large numbers of desperate Indians searching for the vanishing buffalo herds along the border. One M.P. was even prompted to enquire: "What are they for but to look after the Indians?"[8] However, as the Indians sullenly retired to their reserves away from the border, the police began redeploying in the Saskatchewan valley to watch the explosive mixture forming there of restless Indian bands, colonies of Métis squatters, and new Canadian settlements.

For the regular control of Indian affairs after Confederation, the Dominion government, charged with this responsibility throughout Canada by the British North America Act, extended the operations of its Indian Affairs Branch. The branch therefore found its task of dealing with the approximately 34,000 Indians of eastern Canada quadrupled by the addition of 34,000 Indians between Lake Superior and the Rockies, 36,000 in British Columbia, and an assumed 26,000 in the northern parts. Indian Affairs fell to a new ministry, the Secretary of State for the Provinces, which became entrusted with most federal concerns in the North-West Territories until these were handed over in 1873 to the Department of the Interior. There, for practical purposes, it remained for the next sixty years, even though in 1880 the branch was elevated to the status of a separate department. Following the death of William Spragge, the deputy superintendent since 1862, the position was filled by Lawrence Vankoughnet between 1874 and 1893, and by Hayter Reed from 1893 to 1897.

Following the British colonial and Upper Canadian tradition, seven treaties were signed between 1871 and 1877 with the Indian peoples of the region from Lake Superior to the Rocky Mountains, and from the International Boundary to beyond the line of the North Saskatchewan River, embracing the whole of the territory of immediate interest to farm settlers.

The signing of these treaties was an almost annual affair in the mid-seventies, conducted with all the ceremony that either side was capable of, with ample food for the hordes of hungry Indians, festive dances, and gleeful traders waiting to harvest the unaccustomed cash windfall. In each case the Indians received large reserves for their bands, calculated on the basis of 640 acres per family of five. A small cash gratuity was paid upon signing, and an annuity of $5 per head, with suits, medals, and somewhat higher annuities for councillors and chiefs. Every band received gifts of twine and ammunition, while bands that were prepared to begin farming received livestock, seed, and implements. Schools were provided for, and in one instance (Treaty No. 6 at Carlton and Fort Pitt), a further promise of $1,000 for provisions for three years after the reserves were taken up was agreed upon. There was also another clause, at which the Minister of the Interior and Parliament took great alarm: "That in the event hereafter of the Indians comprised within this treaty being overtaken by any pestilence, or by a general famine, the Queen . . . will grant to the Indians assistance of such character and to such extent as Her Chief Superintendent of Indian Affairs shall deem necessary and sufficient to relieve the Indians from the calamity that shall have befallen them."[9]

The government's commitment to provide for the Indians was almost immediately put to the test, and not for the signatories of Treaty No. 6 alone. With the disappearance of the buffalo, the government was forced to distribute large quantities of flour and beef to save thousands of Indians from starvation. Insufficient as these aids were to relieve the physical hardships of those days of transition, and although given with bad grace, they nevertheless provided concrete evidence of the vague but real moral obligation of the state under the treaties towards the Indian signatories.

At first the Indians carried on their former nomadic existence, but as the bison diminished in numbers, desperate Indians became a serious threat to the property and persons of the few white settlers, while the government was put to extraordinary expense supplying them with rations. Accordingly, every effort was made to induce the Indians to cease their wanderings and move to their reserves where, being divided into smaller bands, they would be easier to control and less of a menace to the settlers. Besides, it was anticipated, once the reserves had been taken up, the Indians would adopt the agricultural way of life, become self-sufficient, and less of a burden on government. In the summer of 1882 the Indians were urged to quit the Cypress Hills, and a cold, starving winter completed the persuading. Big Bear, the last major holdout, took treaty, and during 1883 the last bands reluctantly moved to their various reserves.

Thus began the long task of leading "the Indian people by degrees to mingle with the white race in the ordinary avocations of life."[10] An administrative machinery was established consisting of commissioners, regional superintendents, treaty agents, local agents responsible for large reserves or for groups of smaller reserves, farm instructors, and inspectors. With the signing of Treaty No. 7, the North-West Superintendent, David Laird, felt the time opportune for a new departure. In 1877, in line with the desire to turn the Indians into cultivators, the government supplied seed and farm instructors to the bands in the Qu'Appelle district. By 1879 farming agencies were established for seventeen reserves, the policy being to subsidize the instructors to operate farms adjoining the reserves while they trained Indians in the work, and at the same time inspected and advised them on their farming operations. As early as 1878 there was talk of subdividing the reserves into lots and establishing schools on the reserves with teachers who stressed farming or ranching in their instruction.

The results seemed favourable at first, delighting and even surprising the officials. In 1880 the Department of Indian Affairs permitted itself the confident hope "that the majority of the bands will, in the course of a few years, be self-supporting."[11] Two years later it announced that

> the advanced condition of the Indians, settled upon reserves in several localities in the Territories, admitted of the closing during the past season of the Instructors' farms in those localities. The object for which they were established, namely: the practical exemplification to the Indians of the manner in which farms should be managed, has been attained. It is hoped that, next autumn, the Indians in several other localities will be sufficiently advanced to admit of a similar change being effected.[12]

But these hopes proved illusory, and the closing of the instructors' farms was at once an economizing move (part of the headlong curtailment of aid that contributed largely to the Rebellion of 1885), and a recognition that the system was not succeeding in its purpose, but in most cases was merely resulting in a farm privately operated by the instructor. The Indians did not take readily to either the routine or the (to them) menial work of farming. They were too easily discouraged and too impatient to see results, and the transition to the farming life was attended by innumerable difficulties.

Schools were promised in the treaties and the Indians seemed most eager to secure them. As the pledge came to be implemented, however, the federal government merely continued the old course of the Province of Canada and handed the religious denominations a monopoly of Indian education. By 1874 the Indian Affairs Branch, with fine impartiality, subsidized three Anglican, three Methodist, and three Roman Catholic schools in the territories, and in succeeding years extended annual grants to many other day schools, usually as a lump sum of $200 or $300, or occasionally as a per-capita rate of $12 per pupil. But these schools did not seem to equip their pupils for civilized life as the authorities saw it. Hence, as early as 1879, the government contemplated establishing a few industrial schools to train children in agricultural and mechanical arts, with a view to making them eventually self-supporting. Three such schools were built at Battleford, Qu'Appelle, and High River, and went into operation in 1882 and 1883. These, too, were under denominational control, with the expenses being entirely assumed by the government. In 1893, however, the government began paying the administering churches per-capita grants ($115 to $140 per pupil) and leaving the management to maintain the schools from these sums.

By the late 1880's the missions also began to indicate a preference for boarding as against day schools as a way of keeping children under the educative influence of the schools and thereby changing the Indian way of living. Boarding schools, being on or near the reserves, also were less unpopular with the parents, as they were not entirely deprived of contact with their children. Less emphasis than in the industrial schools tended to be placed on trades like carpentry, and more on agriculture and domestic science, which were believed to be more in keeping with the Indians' life on the reserve. The missions received per-capita grants at a lower rate, from $50 to $60 per pupil in attendance. The government unquestionably secured instruction more cheaply than if it had to provide facilities of its own, and no doubt economy was a large factor in the decision. But it was not always to the government's advantage, as Sir John Macdonald himself pointed out in 1884. The churches, he said, "insisted that as they raised the missionary funds in their own denominations, and had charge of these Indians and their schools, they should select the teachers without reference to the Department."[13] Under the direction of the churches, and starved for proper financial backing from federal authorities, Indian education remained on a low level, retarding the upward progress of the Indian.

The Métis, numbering some 15,000 persons in the prairie and parkland at the time of Confederation, and made formidable by their cohesive sense of nationality, as the events of 1869-70 and 1885 showed, constituted a separate but equally grave problem. Their Catholic faith, their semi-nomadic style of living, and their role in the troubles of 1869-70, made them objects of enmity and scorn to many Canadian settlers. Few of the new settlers, or the government in Ottawa, for that matter, were prepared to accept them as they were, or to concede their customs. The Anglo-Saxon, Protestant, farming way was to be the standard for the western prairies; and the Métis were to have the opportunity to secure land under these rules through the magnanimity of their conquerors. For the Métis of Manitoba, the Dominion government was prepared to issue scrips that would

extinguish their aboriginal claims. But, as in so many other matters, implementation left much to be desired. Beginning in 1875, a Half-Breed Land
and Scrip Commission began allocating land scrips at a rate of 240 acres
per head for "children of the half-breed heads of families," and as an after-
thought four years later, another 160 acres for the parent or guardian. A
reservation of 1,400,000 acres of Manitoba land was set apart, but proved
insufficient; thereafter the claims of some of the children and most of the
parents were settled by $160 and $240 cash scrips. Hardly a quarter of
the land grants were taken up, and most of those were sold very cheaply
to land speculators or to incoming settlers. Then, and afterwards, the
scrips were traded at a discount and the proceeds squandered, while a class
of "half-breed scrip millionaires" was created "whose fortunes were built
upon the dispossession of a group of men who were victims of their own
ignorance, their weakness and their ill-adaptation to the new economy."[14]

And still there remained many Métis with similar claims, residing outside Manitoba and clamouring for comparable treatment. Some of these
had taken the Indian treaty, especially when the passage of years pyramided
the small annuities into a sizeable back pay. Very belatedly, on March 30,
1885, the eve of the North-West Rebellion, a new commission was appointed "to make an enumeration of the Half-breeds resident in the North-
West Territories of Canada, previous to the 15th day of July, 1870," and
to issue scrips for 160 or 240 dollars or acres as requested.[15] The distribution of this new largesse (only 25 per cent of the applicants insisted upon,
or were compelled to take, the land scrips) was extremely protracted, becoming, in the final stages, a parallel operation with the signing of new
Indian treaties. Officials, bewildered by the numbers involved and the duration of the process, were prone to suspect that some of the Métis had collected more than once, but it would appear that the claims were carefully
checked. More to the point was the gradual relaxing of the conditions, as
when Métis were allowed to resign from Indian treaties they had joined,
supposedly after their Indian agents had certified they could support
themselves off the treaty without government assistance. Western businessmen, quick to appreciate the value of placing scrips in the hands of the
Métis, exerted themselves to expand the reckoning, as in 1889, when a
campaign was launched to bring the children born between 1870 and
1885 into the calculations. In 1900 these efforts bore fruit, and a new
commission was appointed to deal with this class of claimant.

More serious than the question of their aboriginal claim was the matter
of status. The Métis did not automatically inherit the special status evolved
for the Indians. Instead, the Métis were legally classed from the outset as
full citizens, entitled to all the privileges but also all the obligations of the
citizen. While many were fully capable of living on an equal footing in a

white society, many others proved completely at a loss and were hampered, rather than aided, by their status of equality. For them, the protections and guarantees of the Indian treaties and the Indian Act would have been preferable, as many clergy and administrators recognized at the time. But it was impractical to offer the Métis any sort of special status in view of the considerable attainments of many of their number, and the sensitivity and pride of the group as a whole. As members of the community, Métis were permitted to take up homesteads under the same conditions as other settlers, or to secure title to lots they had settled in various parts of the Northwest. Following Quebec practice, these holdings were long strips of land extending back from the rivers, rather than the square, quarter-section lots of the official plan. While some settlements, for example, St Albert, eventually received special surveys, the government was tragically remiss in not providing special surveys with sufficient rapidity. Only in the autumn of 1884 was a beginning made to meet these complaints.

The greatest problem, however, was the inability of many Métis to cope with the rapidly changing economic and social environment. In Manitoba their pastures and woods were being encroached upon by incoming settlers, and many Métis, plagued by debts or tempted by ready cash, turned over their farms to the newcomers. Freighting opportunities were also diminishing in Manitoba, though those to the Saskatchewan River settlements and the northern posts continued to increase for some years to come. Métis began migrating westward to the older settlements of St Albert, Lac la Biche or Lac St Ann; others settled at formerly good buffalo-hunting localities like the Qu'Appelle valley, Wood Mountain, Battle River, or Cypress Hills. And especially they formed new communities in the Fort Carlton district, like St Laurent (1871), Duck Lake (1878), and Batoche (1881), peopled mainly by disgruntled fugitives from Manitoba. But still the nomadic life beckoned. As long as they could engage in free trade or freighting goods for their livelihood, they continued to neglect the farms that they were supposed to be proving up as homesteads. Their crops were put in hastily and unskilfully and were harvested in slipshod, unsystematic fashion, so that yields were low and winters of hardship frequent. After his 1889 tour of inspection the Deputy Minister of the Interior, A. M. Burgess, quit the Saskatchewan valley most pessimistic over the prospects of the Métis. No one could suggest any solution for their problem. Soon freighting would be a thing of the past, and with it would vanish a major source of their livelihood. They lacked experience as farmers, and because they did not take readily to discipline, they would not make satisfactory labourers or domestic servants. Grants were only a temporary relief and would not solve the problem finally or satisfactorily. Some form of tutelage was necessary for those unable to fend for themselves, he felt, but the others should be ordered either to accept the responsibilities of citizenship, including earning their own living, or be treated as wards of the government.

For many of the Métis the only answer seemed further flight into the still unsettled wilderness where they could fish and hunt without interference. As Father Morin reported,

> Our poor half-breeds continue to desert our colonies and to take the direction of the north. This poor child of the prairie cannot submit to the exigencies of civilization; our customs and our laws are burdensome to him, and he frees himself by abandoning his native country for the depths of the solitude of Athabaska and the Mackenzie.[16]

III

Stabilizing the native population was the negative side of the Canadian program for the development of the west. On the positive side, it was essential to prepare the land for settlement, recruit immigration from outside, furnish easy access to the territory, and establish a governmental framework to provide for the needs of the resulting community. This last consisted, under the North-West Territories Act of 1875, of a lieutenant-governor and an appointed five-man council, to be supplemented by elected members returned from districts containing 1,000 eligible voters within an area no larger than 1,000 square miles. The council was to become a fully elective legislative assembly when the number of its elected members reached twenty-one. Unfortunately, it had very little power, since most administrative functions were carried out by agents of federal government departments, or by the lieutenant-governor in his capacity as agent of the Dominion government. It received very little income either from Ottawa or from territorial sources, its ordinances were frequently disallowed in Ottawa, and it lacked sufficient power to establish municipal institutions capable of managing the affairs of the widely scattered communities. In sum, it echoed the weaknesses of federal control of the Northwest—the unwillingness to delegate authority or to encourage significantly the growth of local autonomy.

For most of its administrative tasks in the Northwest the Dominion relied primarily on the many-branched Department of the Interior, inaugurated on July 1, 1873; and in particular on its Dominion Lands Branch, which had been established two years earlier, on March 7, 1871, to perform the continuing surveying and resources management functions. The department also oversaw the territorial governments, the national parks, and, at various times, Indian Affairs, the Geological Survey, the North-West Mounted Police, and the immigration service. Besides the headquarters' staff in Ottawa, the Dominion Lands Branch comprised a large number of local agencies in the Northwest, notably Crown lands and timber agencies in Winnipeg, Prince Albert, Edmonton, or Calgary, under the general supervision of the commissioners of Crown lands in Winnipeg. Other government agencies also had their representatives and offices throughout the territories.

Preparing the west for settlement entailed a survey operation that has hardly ever been matched. In a celebrated estimate of March 1, 1872, Colonel J. S. Dennis, the first surveyor general, calculated the lands under the control of the Dominion in the Northwest as 1,412,304,000 acres, divided into five great categories, as follows:[17]

1. Unavailable for cultivation, being the portion of the great American Desert, which extends into British Territory	50,000 sq. mis.	32,000,000 acres
2. Prairie country, the greater part of which is unsurpassed for agricultural purposes, with occasional groves and belts of timber	120,000	76,800,000
3. Timbered land, with occasional large prairies (as in the Peace River District) adapted for growth of wheat and other cereals. Possesses abundance of timber	466,225	298,384,000
4. Belt lying outside of No. 2 and 3, (or agricultural zone proper), in which potatoes, barley and grasses may be successfully cultivated. Sufficiently supplied with timber	928,200	594,048,000
5. Rock and swamp, barren lands, in which the timber growth extending up from the south gradually disappears. Fur producing region.	642,300	411,072,000

Dennis had initiated the survey operations in Red River in the autumn of 1869 before the transfer date, and it was while he was engaged in this premature work that the uprising of the Métis occurred. The delay enabled the land-survey system to be modified in line with that of the United States, on the advice of Lieutenant-Governor Archibald of Manitoba, so the familiar six-mile-square township divided into thirty-six square-mile sections of 640 acres, and these into 160-acre quarter-sections, was adopted. The survey of Manitoba was recommenced in 1871, and authority was granted in 1874 to extend the survey of meridians and base lines all the way to the Peace River district. The difficulties were reduced when the telegraph became available in the later seventies, for it became possible to make more accurate astronomical observations on which to base the system. By 1877 the special survey group had extended the Third Meridian (106° W) to the North Saskatchewan River. In 1883 the Fifth Meridian (114° W) was extended from Edmonton to the Peace River district, and the Sixth Meridian (118° W) was located there. Every twenty-four miles, beginning at the International Boundary, base lines were run in an east-west direction to serve as centre lines for tiers of four townships measured off due west from each meridian, as well as east from the Principal Meridian (97° 27' 28" W). Next came block outline surveys, which marked off twelve-mile-square segments containing four townships, followed by sub-division surveys that divided these into sections and quarter-sections. Special survey parties were delegated to deal with settlements, Métis lands, Indian reserves, and the like. Inspectors checked the work, and constant revision was needed to replace destroyed markers and correct errors in the original surveys. Since each survey was also a reconnaissance of the ground covered, much information was secured for purposes of planning and publicity.

Even granting the comparative ease of surveying the prairie and park-land, the pace was phenomenal. In the record year, 1883, 119 survey parties subdivided 1,221 townships (27,000,000 acres) as well as traced 11,300 miles of township lines—results that the official report later claimed "probably stand unrivalled in the history of land subdivision in any country."[18] That season's work practically completed the surveying of the Fertile Belt, the prairie region south of the North Saskatchewan River. Four years later, when over 70,000,000 acres had been subdivided, the deputy minister congratulated himself that at last the survey work of the Dominion Lands Branch was "reduced to what I presume may be re-garded as their normal proportions."[19] The historian of surveying in Canada has paid this tribute to the work:

> That pattern of land division, so reminiscent of the checkerboard, is the visible signature of one of the great civil engineering triumphs of all time. The system of survey of which this panoramic tapestry is a striking by-product, constitutes one of the most outstanding accomplishments of the Canadian government in early post-Confederation years. As an example of a uniform plan of survey over an immense area the project is unsurpassed for precision of execution, permanence of marking and absence of sub-sequent litigation over property boundaries.[20]

Thus the area of the Fertile Belt of the transfer agreement with the Hudson's Bay Company was made ready for occupation by settlers and developers, and the process of transforming the almost empty acres into a vigorous offshoot of western European civilization could begin. Allocation of the land to users could now proceed according to the policies of the directing authority. These, in the main, reflected the experience of the former Province, modified by the need to match conditions in adjacent territories and states to attract a fair share of immigrants to the Canadian Northwest, and by the current position of a once land-poor government suddenly grown land-rich beyond imagining. For individual settlers, a system of 160-acre homesteads was established, together with provisions for purchasing additional land. The lumbermen were provided for by a system of auctioning off timber berths, and the commercial fishermen by the gradual extension of the inland fishing regulations. Disposal of mining lands followed the prevailing system of leases and outright sale of valuable resources under conditions that were highly favourable to the speculator. The nature of the country dictated some departures, drawing mainly on the experience of the American west, such as grazing leases to aid the development of a ranching industry for which parts of the country were so obviously well suited, and regulations to promote the construction of irrigation works. Reserving part of the land for the support of education also followed an American policy, though it had Canadian antecedents in the clergy reserves of notorious memory. The administration offered large reserves and grants to colonization societies or companies, few of which met their commitments; it fulfilled its undertakings to the Hudson's Bay Company, and to the Indians for reserves under the treaties; and it made a beginning of allocating land for national park purposes.

Above all, the Dominion made huge grants of western lands, aggregating 31,783,654 acres, for railways. Some were for comparatively short lines to provide for particular sections of the Northwest, but most were for the all-important rail link with the outside world. This enterprise, the Canadian Pacific Railway project, was to be a major preoccupation of federal governments between 1871 and the completion of the line on November 7, 1885, at Craigellachie, British Columbia. The railway was viewed as the sole hope for the development of the Northwest, and consequently it was argued that the cost should be shouldered by that region from its ample lands, or from the proceeds of the sale of those lands. Actually, the railway's developmental role was important for Ontario and British Columbia as well as for the prairies, while the material benefits redounded largely on eastern metropolitan centres, notably Montreal. Furthermore, the railway had a much wider, grander purpose for the nation as a whole—to unify the state, secure its defence, and help construct an integrated economic system. Evidence that the government regarded the railway in this wider context may be seen from the markedly higher priority in governmental concerns that railway matters commanded as against the needs of the few, disfranchised inhabitants of the Northwest.

Nevertheless, the railway's role was also of vital concern for the development of the Northwest. This is underscored by the way the settlers hung on every action and rumour associated with planning and building the railway, and marked its progress by vigorous land rushes and speculating orgies, or, alternately, by moods of deflation, despondence, and resentment. Besides, the surveys in connection with the route added much useful information about the potentialities of the region and advertised these to the public at large. In the Northwest these surveys ranged from the International Boundary all the way to the Peace River district, and featured the work of geologists like G. M. Dawson, R. G. McConnell, Robert Bell, and J. B. Tyrrell, the botanist John Macoun, and a succession of railway explorers and location engineers. The Peace River district alone was the subject of five separate investigations between 1871 and 1879.[21]

Exploring and surveying, in fact, were the main preoccupations of the chief engineer, Sandford Fleming, throughout the seventies, for much still needed to be learned about the engineering and economic aspects of the country in connection with determining the route of the Canadian Pacific Railway. Fleming himself had no great difficulty in reaching his own conclusions; even before he and the Reverend G. M. Grant made their interesting journey across the continent in 1872, Fleming had announced that the railway should enter British Columbia by way of the Yellowhead Pass. He ruled later that the prairie region should be approached from the east by way of Rat Portage (now Kenora) at the outlet of Lake of the Woods, the line to cross the Red River at Selkirk, the head of navigation for Lake Winnipeg and the Saskatchewan River system beyond, twenty miles below Winnipeg. West from Selkirk he envisaged a route that proceeded northwestward across the narrows of Lake Manitoba to the Swan River district, then on to Yellowhead Pass, crossing the South Saskatchewan twelve miles north of present-day Saskatoon, and the North Saskatchewan some thirty miles upstream from Edmonton. Between 1874 and 1876, the telegraph line was built along this route from Red River to Edmonton, a distance of 807 miles.

In fixing on this route Fleming was not without many critics and challengers. British Columbians were strongly interested in the pass selected, since this would largely determine the route followed through their province. The Yellowhead Pass route favoured the railway proceeding by way of the Fraser River to the delta and Burrard Inlet. That was not at all to the liking of the Vancouver Islanders, who wanted a line that crossed to Vancouver Island from Bute Inlet on the mainland. This would become feasible if a more northerly pass, particularly the Pine Pass southwest of the Peace River district, was chosen. The Peace River Pass could also be used for this, though that might be even more in keeping with a still more northerly ocean terminus in or near Port Simpson. There was also the matter of the quality of the regions that would be traversed by the various routes, as well as the engineering aspects of the passes themselves. Pressure from British Columbians, the support of Fleming's assistant engineer Marcus Smith, and glowing reports concerning the fertility of the Peace River district, explain why the northern alternatives were examined so many times. The new Conservative government had the question investigated once more in the summer of 1879, following which the decision for the Yellowhead route was reaffirmed, and Fleming pronounced the matter settled:

> The location of the railway being now definitely fixed and contracts awarded on the line to Burrard Inlet, there is no longer any necessity, in the interest of the railway for continuing examinations in the northern districts. Many years must elapse before the great areas of available lands between Manitoba and the mountains are fully occupied, and by this period the capability of the Peace River District will have been tested.[22]

This was where matters stood on October 21, 1880, when the federal government signed a contract with a syndicate of leading Canadian businessmen to complete the railway, turning over to it the sections of the line built or put under contract, as well as the results of Fleming's ten years of surveys costing $4,166,187 in all. The new owners, from considerations of economic factors rather than the engineering criteria that shaped Fleming's decisions, immediately decided to scrap the Saskatchewan-Yellowhead Pass route and build directly westward to the mountains. Parliamentary approval was secured to adopt a more southerly route that was at least one hundred miles inside Canada. The new alignment was selected in 1882 through the "sea of mountains" to Kamloops by way of the Kicking Horse Pass of the Rockies, the recently discovered Rogers Pass, and the Eagle Pass. When the track entered British Columbia at the end of 1883, the Northwest was furnished with a line of railway across the southern part of the prairies via Winnipeg, Regina, Calgary, and Banff that linked the region with Great Lake navigation at Port Arthur.

It is doubtful whether a more important decision could have been made as far as the course of the future development of Canada was concerned. The choice of the southern route contributed to the making of the North-West Rebellion in 1885. Furthermore, the adoption of this southern route across the prairies (and, to a lesser degree, similar decisions in northern Ontario and British Columbia), meant that the Canadian Pacific Railway did not have anything like the effect it might have had on the northward advance of Canada's frontiers. In the Northwest it actually diverted the course of settlement, investment, and attention away from the northward-facing settlements of the Saskatchewan valley (Prince Albert, Battleford and Edmonton) with their links with the fur trade and the older civilization of the great sub-Arctic forest belt. Canadians' attentions became focussed now on the empty farmlands and ranchlands of the south that drew their settlers from eastern Canada, the United States, and Europe, and looked eastward rather than northward. The "Northwest," for practical purposes, became replaced by the "West," and for twenty years Canada's primary developmental task became to people the southern agricultural prairies, establish its institutions there, and integrate its economy and society into those of Canada as a whole. Until that task was well on the way to completion, the North would have to mark time.

CHAPTER 2

Along the Pacific Frontier

1871 – 1896

When British Columbia entered Confederation, the province was quite as under-developed as were the territories immediately east of it. Most of the 8,576 whites, 1,548 Chinese, and 462 Negroes[1] were concentrated in a corner of the vast expanse – in southeastern Vancouver Island and along parts of the Fraser River between the delta and the Cariboo gold field. The forty thousand or so Indians were more widely distributed about the province, but even they were mainly settled along the coastal inlets and a few river valleys. The task of government was to make the rich resources of British Columbia the basis for a wealthy, populous, progressive province. Unlike Manitoba or the North-West Territories, this was primarily the responsibility of the provincial legislature, not that of the Dominion government. True, the latter assumed control over trade, shipping, sea fisheries, Indian Affairs, geological surveys, and undertook the commitment of providing adequate communications with the rest of Canada. British Columbia, however, as a functioning province, retained wide powers of local self-government that enabled it to maintain and extend its institutions and fix the direction and pace of its internal growth. The province owned and regulated the natural resources of its territory, and its governments accepted corresponding responsibilities towards the land and the people.

To develop even so rich a land required strenuous efforts from both levels of government as well as full co-operation between them. The Dominion was concerned with securing the transcontinental railway; solving the marketing problems of a province largely excluded by high tariff walls from the nearby United States, and by distance from trading with the Atlantic world; and providing for the needs of the large Indian population, comprising about 80 per cent of the inhabitants of the province. In these areas the Dominion's programs were of vital concern to the province, but the province did not always feel that distant federal governments understood or heeded its views and interests. Indeed, in its dealings with British Columbia, Ottawa seemed unable to make sufficient allowance for the peculiar characteristics of the province's situation. But British Columbia had a legislature with its mandate from the people, which, besides implementing the province's programs, could serve as a forum from which to criticize and challenge actions of the Dominion government.

A unique and important feature of British Columbia was the position occupied by the large, advanced, and threatened Indian population. The prodigal riches of sea and forest along the coast gave rise to a highly developed Indian society and civilization centred in relatively permanent villages along the tidal rivers, where there was food enough to sustain the largest, most prosperous aboriginal populations in the territories added to Canada. Their villages were rows of lodges with beams of solid cedar trunks and walls of thick cedar planks; each lodge was capable of containing several hundred guests. In fifty-foot dugouts they braved ocean storms in search of seal or whale and in the conduct of trade or war. Their carved and painted pillars and "totem poles," ornate boxes, baskets, ornaments and jewels, ceremonial attire, and tattooing displayed a high degree of artistic skill, and their commercial and social relations revealed a considerable measure of sophistication. They possessed a strong sense of property, with wealth measured in blankets, boxes of eulachon grease, ceremonial masks and costumes, ornaments of rare copper, stone, and shell, and especially human slaves, over whom ownership conferred complete powers of life and death. They even developed an ingenious method of establishing credit for future consumption by means of a system of potlaches. Their society was organized into an elaborate system of tribes, clans, and houses, and included many gradations between head chief and slave, property accumulation being the chief agency of social mobility.

Nearly a century of contacts with white traders, and latterly with a few Anglican and Roman Catholic missionaries, had brought the Indians some of the white man's goods and techniques, as well as exposed them to the ravages of alcohol and disease, those almost inevitable adjuncts of unregulated contact. The Indians and their societies had grown highly demoralized, and their numbers were reduced by perhaps two-thirds from pre-contact times. But still they remained a major element in the security and future prosperity of the province. Consequently, although constitutional responsibility for the Indians passed to the Dominion under the Terms of Union, provincial governments were bound to be vitally concerned over the management of Indian relations.

Almost immediately after Confederation, a major disagreement over Indian reserves disclosed fundamental differences between the philosophies and the approaches of the two governments in the field of Indian policy. Clause 13 of the Terms of Union enjoined that "a policy as liberal as that hitherto pursued by the British Columbia Government shall be continued by the Dominion Government after the Union," while the province agreed to convey tracts of land to the Dominion for use as Indian reserves "of such extent as it has hitherto been the practice of the British Columbia Government to appropriate for that purpose," with the Colonial Secretary arbitrating any disagreements.[2] The Dominion discovered, with considerable surprise, that no real effort had ever been made to secure a surrender of the Indian title to the soil, and that the colony had never granted Indians more than ten acres per family, as contrasted with the eighty-acre standard prevalent in the old Province of Canada or the 640-acre standard being instituted in the North-West Territories. On March 21, 1873, the province was ordered to surrender land for reserves on a basis of eighty acres per family of five. Having expended the considerable sum of $54,000 upon British Columbia's Indians in 1872 and 1873, the Dominion government also felt justified in observing, "This liberality of the Dominion Parliament stands in marked contrast with the policy previously pursued towards the Indians by the Local Government."[3] Challenged in the Commons, Prime Minister Mackenzie reiterated the charges that the Dominion spent more on the Indians of British Columbia in a single year than the province had done in all its history, and that provincial niggardliness was responsible for a serious threat to law and order by Indians concerned for the security of their land.

British Columbia members replied that the colony had given the Indians all the land they needed and could put to good use, and grumbled that the Dominion had no right to indulge its philanthropic feelings towards the Indians with land belonging to the province. G. A. Walkem, the attorney general, issued a lengthy rebuttal against the Dominion's harsh condemnation of the province simply because British Columbia had not had the foresight to anticipate or copy the Canadian approach towards the Indian. In contrast with the federal policy of isolating Indians in a state of tutelage by concentrating them upon reserves, in British Columbia, Walkem said, "the Natives were invited and encouraged to mingle with and live amongst the white population with a view of weaning them by degrees from savage life, and of gradually leading them by example and precept to adopt habits of peace, honesty and industry." In his next sentence, however, he was forced to confess, while putting the best face on it, "It is true that this step was not unattended with some of the well-known evils which are unfortunately inseparable from the attempted fusion of savage and civilized races, but these defects it was believed would in time have been largely removed by the application of proper remedies."[4] As for the accusation of niggardliness, Walkem detailed various expenses – from punitive expeditions to Queen Victoria Day celebrations – to demonstrate the colony's serious concern with native affairs. The limited outlays on education he defended on the grounds that it was desired first to "reclaim the Natives from their savage state and teach them the practical and rudimentary lessons of civilized life."[5] The colonial policy, he asserted, was "based on the broad and experimental principle of treating the Indian as a fellow subject."[6] He accused the Dominion of ignoring the physical and economic conditions of the country and the Indians' way of life, and pleaded for a realistic policy that took these factors into account. There was no need, he said, to transform the vast majority of Indians into agriculturalists, for three-quarters of the native population could safely be left to follow their traditional way of life merely by reserving to them their fishing stations, fur-trading posts and settlements, future town-sites and, in mountainous areas, setting apart the most suitable hunting localities as wildlife preserves. Those Indians who wished to become cultivators or ranchers could apply for land upon similar terms with whites, while others could carry on as workers in the lumber or fishing industries where they already formed a valuable segment of the labour force. Walkem also raised the important question of the province's reversionary interest – that when land handed over to the Dominion no longer was needed for Indian reserves (because of the diminution, extinction, or emigration of the Indian population), it should not be retained by the Dominion government but should revert to the province.

The views expressed in this exchange coloured the relations of Dominion and province for succeeding decades. The two governments hovered on the brink of an agreement on a system of reserves based on twenty acres per family, but British Columbia refused to consider enlarging the reserves already granted, while the Dominion rejected the alternative of resuming all the existing reserves and starting afresh. When in 1876 the problem was turned over to a three-man reserves commission on which both parties were represented, a further disagreement arose because the commissioners requested that the province buy out white settlers located upon land desired for reserves. The commission agreed on a policy of many small reserves to enclose the various tribal habitats, burial grounds, fishing stations, and cultivated lands, and upon the province's reversionary right to lands no longer required for reserves. After it was dissolved for reasons of economy in 1878, Gilbert M. Sproat, the joint commissioner, carried on alone. The work continued until 1910 under Sproat's successors, Peter O'Reilly, a county court judge who had been retired from the service of the colonial government on pension at Confederation, and A. W. Vowell, a former gold commissioner and later Indian superintendent. Gradually the enormous task of assigning reserves, often to reluctant bands, was finally completed. O'Reilly surveyed numerous reserves along the Pacific coast, on the Queen Charlotte Islands, and on the Nass and Skeena rivers in 1881-82. By 1892, when the process was extended to New Caledonia in the northern interior, a total of 778 reserves, averaging less than 1,000 acres apiece, had been assigned.

The awarding of these reserves was accompanied by hostility on the part of white settlers as well as Indians. By 1884 the province was complaining that too much good land had been, and was being, granted to Indians, and was urging that they be given, instead, "wild lands equally suitable for the purpose for which they require them."[7] Demands were voiced for the province to take up the reserves and sell the land to white settlers, with the money going to an Indian educational fund or similar purpose. As the numbers of Indians declined and the average acreage per family rose above the amount originally agreed upon, calls went out for the province to resume the excess under its reversionary right. In effect, the province stood to benefit from the diminution of its large native population.

In the face of provincial hostility, the federal machinery for Indian administration was slow to become established throughout British Columbia. In 1871 the Dominion appointed Dr I. W. Powell as Indian superintendent, and established a three-man Indian board, including Joseph Trutch, the lieutenant-governor, to advise the federal government on local conditions. The board, having proved ineffectual, was abolished in 1876 and the two Indian superintendencies of Victoria and Fraser River were taken under direct Ottawa control. Not until the imbroglio over reserves was settled did the Dominion appoint six Indian agents (1881), two for the southern interior, one for the lower Fraser River, two for Vancouver Island, and one for the Kwakiutl along the coast. New agencies were established at Lillooet and Skeena in 1883 and arrangements were made for others at Babine and the Kootenay. The Skeena district was particularly troublesome. The Indians of Metlakatla rejected the Dominion's agent, and in 1887 a provincial commission of enquiry into the disorders in the area recommended that two agents be sent to the Nass and Upper Skeena districts, but warned, "It is useless to send among them second-rate, ill-paid men . . . the agent should be a man of character, of good presence and of refined mode of life, one in fact, whom the Indians could look up to in every respect."[8] Nevertheless, by the early nineties, twenty years or more after Confederation, most parts of the province had been furnished with these essential officials.

Other matters continued to perplex the relations of Dominion and province – particularly the province's frequent and sometimes petty complaints at having to spend money maintaining law and order in cases where Indians were exclusively, or largely, involved. When troubles arose on the Skeena River in the 1880's, each government endeavoured to throw the responsibility and expense for maintaining order upon the other. The commission of enquiry which the province appointed in 1887 recommended that the province take over the entire management of Indian affairs to put an end to the confusion over control and overcome the weaknesses of supervision from afar. At the height of this disagreement, the province even forbade Indian agents the use of provincial courts, jails, or police.

While the two governments quarrelled over native policy, the Indian himself did not remain entirely passive in the face of governmental indifference and neglect and the increasing encroachment by white settlers upon his ancestral domain. During the 1870's and 1880's, the Indian began to appear as a protagonist in his own right, supported in his claims by well-wishers, among whom certain missionaries held high place. For years some bands refused to accept reserves on the ground that the land was theirs in any case. The provincial commission of 1887-88 was met with demands for compensation for lands required for settlement and for other trespasses by whites, by refusals to accept any of the machinery of the Indian administration, and by threats to move to Alaska unless the Indians received the treatment they wanted. The commissioners concluded that these disrespectful attitudes arose from the religious affiliation of the spokesmen, the three disaffected centres being Canadian Methodist missions, though they imputed the origin of the unrest to the serious disruption in 1881 between Anglican authorities and their missionaries at Metlakatla.[9]

This intermingling of mission politics with the complicated issues of Indian control arose naturally from the prominent place the missionaries held in the advancement of the British Columbia tribes – a place that owed much to the well-publicized success in Indian work of William Duncan, the first, most celebrated Protestant missionary along the northern coast. Duncan, while still a student-in-training, had been sent out by the Church Missionary Society, a Church of England organization, when the opportunity arose to place a missionary aboard a warship proceeding to the North Pacific station. By October, 1857, he had commenced work at Port Simpson, in the remote, relatively isolated Skeena district. He underwent many trials in the first difficult years, living in the midst of a barbaric camp of two thousand Tsimshean Indians, menaced by prestige-conscious chiefs, his life threatened by the medicine societies. But he persisted with his school for children and adults, until at last his preaching won a respectful audience and he made a few devoted converts. Gradually Duncan reached the conclusion that the only way of permanently elevating the Indians was to establish a colony in an environment free from contaminating influences, and in 1862 he led four hundred followers to Metlakatla, some twenty miles from Port Simpson.

Despite his clerical sponsorship, his main concern was the temporal one of effecting a social and cultural revolution among his Indian followers. Metlakatla was administered by a governing council and appointed constables; the inhabitants paid taxes and contributed their work to individual and communal projects. To train his Indians in habits of industry and the ways of business, Duncan developed new lines of economic endeavour, purchased a schooner, set up a community store, and opened an export trade independent of the Hudson's Bay Company. The symbol of his success was the erection, entirely with Indian labour, of the largest, finest church north of Victoria, capable of seating eight hundred people.

Within a few years, reports of Duncan's experiment were being broadcast around the world by way of the publications of the Church Missionary Society. His work appeared to prove that the Indians could be rescued from the seemingly inevitable spiral of disease, degradation, and extinction. Other native peoples along the Pacific coast began clamouring for similar missions, and other Anglican clergymen strove to duplicate the Metlakatla experiment, as did the Methodists, led by a flamboyant enthusiast, the Reverend Thomas Crosby, who stepped into Duncan's original station of Port Simpson. Colonial governors and Canadian governors general visited Metlakatla, and Duncan was called on to advise both governments. His experiment lent credence to the provincial thesis that the Dominion's policies of wardship and large reserves were not necessarily appropriate for British Columbia's Indians, though Duncan himself was equally critical of the province's parsimony with grants and lands, and its seeming indifference to misdeeds by whites against Indians.

Unfortunately, religious troubles disrupted the happy idyll. The increasingly bitter competition among Anglicans, Methodists, and Roman Catholics along the coast and in the interior kindled new rivalries among Indian factions and heaped discredit on the missionary endeavour. Furthermore, Duncan became caught up in a long, angry clash with his superiors over doctrinal and policy questions. The issue terminated with his taking himself and his followers out of the Church of England, and out of Canada, too, to found a New Metlakatla one hundred miles farther north, on Annette Island, Alaska.

William Duncan's primary goal was to educate British Columbia's Indians to the point where they would be able to make a full contribution to the progress of the burgeoning new province from a position of equality. He had shown that, in many ways, British Columbia presented a unique opportunity, for the situation lacked the emergency quality characteristic of the prairies. In British Columbia only a small fraction of the territory was exploitable by the new settlers, and so most of the province could safely be left to the original inhabitants. The natives could continue to draw adequate sustenance from the seemingly inexhaustible supplies of fish, game and fur, and forest products. Alternatively, these resources could become the foundation for new extractive industries in which the Indians could obtain useful, valuable employment alongside white co-workers.

In addition, their village society, relatively high level of sophistication, and industrious work habits meant they were educable to the demands of the new civilization to a greater degree than were the more nomadic, less advanced bands of the prairie or forest. As elsewhere, however, the federal government failed to perceive any challenge or opportunity, and merely extended to British Columbia the easy, cheap, and politically safe method of subsidizing mission schools. In 1874 small grants were paid for three day schools – one Catholic, one Anglican, one Methodist – at St Mary's, Metlakatla, and Nanaimo. By 1880 the number had swelled to seven, and by 1896 the number of subsidized Indian day schools had risen to twenty-three. The program of industrial schools, which was well suited to the needs and capabilities of the coast Indians and which Dr Powell recommended as early as 1872, did not go into effect until 1891. Of the four opened in that year, two, at Kuper Island and Metlakatla, were for the northwest coast Indians.

In other ways, too, the British Columbia Indians began to move towards accepting the norms of white society. Tattooing, labrats and nose ornaments, slavery, and polygamy were virtually eradicated by police action or because of social or religious pressures, and survived only in remote places. The same held true of the liquor trade, as the enforcement of federal regulations began to take hold. As Dr Powell reported:

> A great blow has been given to the abominable whiskey traffic, by the operation of the recent Federal liquor law. Some well-known and extensive vendors have been mulcted in the utmost penalty prescribed by the law; and the procuring of large quantities of Indian liquor in Victoria, as heretofore with facility, has received a wholesome check; and the example has proved most beneficial in restraining other evil doers.[10]

Indians began to adopt single-family dwellings, to favour the white style of dress, to cultivate gardens and raise livestock, and to measure property in dollars instead of coppers, slaves, and blankets.

The spectacular art of carving memorial columns or totem poles that had come into vogue around the 1840's began to decline during the 1880's because of missionary disapproval. A carver of Skidegate recalled in his old age one such cultural turning-point:

> Most people, when I was young, wanted to have their own totem poles. But when the Rev. Mr. Crosby, the missionary, arrived in his boat in 1884, he stopped the people and threatened them with jail, if they wanted to raise totems. And he had a number of converted Skidegates wear police uniforms. It was at that time that the Skidegates began to build white man's houses here. . . . The old-timers among our people, who were used to the old style, did not care for the new buildings.[11]

Traditional carvings and head-dresses of the earlier civilization also came under the ban. The Indian agent for Babine reported the effect of a visitation in 1893 by the Roman Catholic Bishop of New Westminster, A. Dontenwill, that "caused the destruction by fire of those ceremonial paraphernalia, which still bound the inhabitants of two villages to the customs and ideas of prehistoric days and prevented them from entering into the spirit of full civilization."[12]

Another aspect of the native civilization that became an object of particular concern of government as well as missionaries was the potlach. Dr Powell described one held in an apparently impoverished camp at South Saanich, near Victoria, in 1875:

> Some three thousand Indians, from neighbouring Tribes had assembled there as guests, and were now at the height of enjoyment; and I was astonished at the great display of wealth which met the eye on all sides. A platform, some two hundred yards in length, had been erected, on which were piled blankets, clothing, etc., in unlimited quantities. I saw three members of one family (brothers) give away 3,500 blankets, no doubt the savings of many years, (at the expense of many privations during the interval) carefully kept for the occasion. Goods to the value of some $15,000 were distributed ere the affair ended.[13]

The potlach was opposed on economic and social as well as on moral grounds. The time spent attending potlaches kept many Indians from useful productive labour and their children from schooling and training. Potlaches kept the Indians from developing orderly habits, caused them to impoverish themselves and invest their surpluses in consumables like blankets or flour rather than in land, boats, or other capital equipment that would have bettered their economic position. Futhermore, Indian agents reported, they were supported only by the older men who had repayments due them, and by traders who profited from supplies purchased and consumed. Young men did not really desire to become involved in the self-perpetuating system of obligations.

Potlaches were an inconvenient survival from the pre-industrial epoch, and hence antagonistic to the individualistic, commercial economy that white men considered the sole route to progress. The potlach, like other customs, fell before the prevailing Protestant ethic. In 1884 an amendment to the Indian Act declared it a misdemeanour, subject to a jail penalty of from two to six months, to engage in, assist, or encourage a potlach.[14] While the enforced disappearance of such customs and art-forms may have ended certain undesirable practices, it also deprived the Indians of honoured means of self-expression and did much to undermine the self-confidence every people needs to survive. This their well-meaning directors failed to comprehend in their bland assumption that native practices automatically ran counter to moral and doctrinal precepts, if not to the law of the land.

Thanks to pressures of these sorts, missionaries and Indian agents could report the appearance of a new progressive native society that showed gratifying tendencies of conforming to the white man's standards. "The Indians of this agency are industrious and energetic in their efforts towards advancement in civilized acquirements, possess considerable intelligence and mechanical skill which they turn to good account. . . . Each year affords additional evidence of their self-control; and instances of intemperance and open profligacy are becoming rare," wrote the agent for the northwest coast in 1896.[15] From Babine, agent R. E. Loring reported:

> The women, formerly mere "beasts of burden," are now tidy housekeepers, able to cook, bake good bread, sew, knit and mend, [and are] being treated by their husbands with due consideration. It is pleasing to observe, on a Sunday, families coming to church well dressed, plainly conscious of their moral elevation. A general improvement in all the Indians and their surroundings, in comparison with former years, is especially commented on by people even after a short absence from here.[16]

Another agent reported that with the ending of potlaches, quite a number of Indians had money in the bank, and were taking well to work; he rated 30 per cent as "quite industrious," 40 per cent fairly industrious "in their own way," and 20 per cent "indolent."[17]

Equally impressive were their communal achievements. The commissioners touring the northwest coast in 1887 reported the settlements as having streets, sidewalks, street lamps, storey-and-a-half houses in regular alignment, extensive schools, and fine church buildings. At Port Simpson they noted, in addition, a modern cemetery, with "many costly marble monuments" (a latter-day successor to the totem pole that presumably met with the Reverend T. Crosby's approval), a well-conducted orphanage, and a Temperance Hall. Besides the by-now traditional fire brigades and brass bands, there were native municipal councils, policemen, teachers, and lay preachers on the Metlakatla model pioneered by Duncan.[18]

Unfortunately, for all these outward signs of progress, the population statistics of British Columbia's Indians continued to record a downward trend after 1870, though unquestionably it was far less than the precipitate decline of the two previous decades. According to figures quoted by Dr G. M. Dawson of the Geological Survey, the Haida population of the Queen Charlotte Islands fell from 6,593 in 1841 to below 2,000 by 1878. The Indian Affairs statistics are quite unreliable for the early years, but they show an unmistakable decline from the 35,000-40,000 mark during the seventies (the remnant of the aboriginal population that may have been as high as 125,000 in the early nineteenth century) to just 25,068 in 1896, slightly below the figure Governor Douglas had given forty years before for Vancouver Island alone. Tuberculosis, smallpox, measles, whooping cough, as well as social diseases, continued to take their toll. As Chief Justice Matthew B. Begbie explained:

> They rear small families and the children often die. Accidents do much in such small adventurous societies; private quarrels do much, whisky and dissipation wear them to an early death, and sap the powers of reproduction; but the great devastators have been their cruel tribal wars, and, much worse, small-pox and measles. Vaccination has made a stand to secure them against the former; but measles are nearly as deadly, and even vaccination is as severe a malady with them as measles among Europeans. Eruptive disorders seem to overcome their constitutions. Wars have immensely diminished of late; there are deadly private quarrels; few tribal war expeditions.[19]

To a considerable extent what Dawson reported of the Haidas held true for the province as a whole:

> They are not long-lived, though grey-haired men and women may occasionally be seen. Pulmonary diseases accompanied by spitting of blood, and blindness generally caused by a species of opthalmia, are not uncommon; and other diseases incident to a life of exposure tend to reduce the term of life, as they do among all the aborigines of the continent. Besides these, however, and much more fatal, are diseases introduced among them since contact with the whites. Great numbers of the Haidas, with all the other tribes of the coast, have been cut off by small-pox, both during their periodical visits to Victoria and after their return to their native islands. This disease is with them almost certainly fatal, and I could learn of a single instance only in which recovery had occurred. Owing to the complete demoralization of the Haidas since contact with the whites, and their practice of resorting to Victoria and other places, where they maintain themselves by shameless prostitution, veneral diseases are extremely common and destructive.[20]

Similarly, Commissioner O'Reilly, who visited the islands in 1882, observed the many abandoned, decayed villages and the tendency of the young people to migrate to the towns. He "was particularly struck, when visiting the several villages, by the small number of children."[21] Dawson was optimistic for the future, however, for he felt the Queen Charlotte Islanders had finally reached a turning point. Henceforth, he hoped, their number would begin to rise as they began participating in the coming development of the forest and fish resources of their island home.

II

Of all the threats posed to the native population by the white man's desire to develop and put to use the natural wealth of British Columbia, the most serious was in the fishery. For ages the bountiful marine resources had sustained the numerous, advanced aboriginal populations. But these same resources presented attractive opportunities to white men, and largely at the Indians' expense. The white men and the Indians met as partners and associates in the fur trade; in mining, forestry, and agriculture, for the most part, they functioned on different levels and in separate locations. In the fishery, however, they were competing directly in the same localities and for the same resources. Little thought was given to whether the resource could sustain the demands of the technically efficient, white commercial fishermen working to supply limitless world markets, let alone the demands of both groups. Even less, except by Duncan, was any thought given to the possibility that the Indians already living there might fulfill the commercial producers' role, thus ensuring the Indians' future and making the entry of outsiders to exploit the fishery largely redundant.

Instead, in keeping with the *laissez-faire* attitudes of the time, a commercial fishery was encouraged to grow up in the region, under conditions of little or no regulation, harvesting the rich resources of the coasts and rivers of northern British Columbia for markets mainly in Britain or (despite high tariff barriers) in the United States. At first the fish was salted, smoked, or canned for export; marketing of fresh fish had to await the establishment of cheap, speedy rail communications after 1885, though as early as 1878 halibut was being shipped, packed in ice, to San Francisco. The most significant economic development of the period was the rise of a salmon-canning industry, which, like the gold rushes, moved up the coast from California to Alaska in a twenty-year span, beginning in 1864. The industry was started by local interests on the Fraser River and was well established there by 1876 when the first cannery went into operation on the Skeena. Seven years later, besides a dozen canneries on the Fraser, there were six canneries on the Skeena, two on the Nass, and one apiece at Smith Inlet, Rivers Inlet, and Alert Bay. Though the numbers fluctuated in response to business conditions, output tended to increase as the industry spread north, until, by 1895, forty-seven canneries were in operation (thirty on the Fraser alone) and production had increased fifty-nine times over in less than twenty years. Increasing quantities of halibut also were being taken, and the prized eulachon (candlefish) grease was being refined and sold commercially.

As the fate of the American fishery was vividly demonstrating, depletion of prime canning varieties like the sockeye was an ever-present threat unless exploitation was controlled, particularly since more efficient equipment was constantly being introduced. By the late eighties, operators were placing large seines off the mouths of the rivers and installing small steamers to deliver the catch to the canneries. There was no regulation of the fisheries under the colony, and only after 1877, when the Dominion Fisheries Act went into effect, was a belated effort launched to curb the most flagrant abuses. The regulations were gradually adjusted to meet the particular conditions of the Pacific coast fishery. Those instituted in 1890 suspended fishing operations two days each week, prohibited barring more than one-third of a river with nets, and ordered canneries to secure their supplies only from the tidal sections of the rivers. Seines could only be placed in specific areas. The number of boats fishing a particular river was restricted, and fish quotas were established for canneries. Pollution of the waters by sawmills and the reckless disposal of fish offal by the canneries were also to be controlled.

Enforcement, however, was a different matter, particularly in the north. An annual inspection trip was all that the northern rivers received until 1889, when fishery guardians were assigned specifically to the Skeena and Nass rivers. Even then, lack of men and equipment made effective action difficult. In 1892 one guardian complained about the futility of trying to oversee activities in the Grenville Channel as well as in forty-five miles of fishing grounds on the Skeena with only a rowboat. It was also contended that strict enforcement of the regulations was undesirable because the Canadian fishery would be placed at a disadvantage relative to that of the United States, where laxity was the universal rule. Other American influences were seen in the unwelcome activities of American fishermen just outside the three-mile limit off the Fraser estuary, poaching in unpoliced Canadian waters like the Queen Charlotte Islands, and the establishment of a virtual monopoly over the halibut fishery through tariffs and a buyers' cartel. (The shoe was on the other foot in the case of the fur seal hunt, in which Victoria firms began participating as early as 1876, and, in one year alone, 1894, took 94,474 skins.)

The swift rise of the commercial fishery raised the problem of the Indians' role in this new industry. The administration recognized that the Indians enjoyed aboriginal rights in the fishery and conceded that commercial exploitation should not interfere with these rights. But when regulations were adopted to control the commercial operators, the Indians were also expected to comply, something that the proud, property-conscious Indians would not concede. They refused to take out fishing licences, and they regarded the regulations as infringements on their age-old fishing rights. At Nass Harbour in 1888 one fishery guardian was informed by the chief of Kincolith that the river belonged to his people, that whites should pay licences to fish upon it, and that their dues were rightfully the property of the Indians. Magnanimously the chief offered the guardian one-half of what he collected and ordered him "to inform the Government to that effect, which I respectfully take this method of doing," the guardian added.[22]

The rise of the commercial fishery was not wholly disadvantageous to the Indians. The canneries were primarily interested in the earlier runs of sockeye salmon and largely left the others for the Indians. The regulations were actually designed to ensure that some portion of the fish eluded the canners and escaped to rivers where they might be taken by Indians for their own needs. Commercial operations gave the Indians the opportunity to sell the excess of their catch and provided employment for the men in fishing and the women in making nets or as cannery workers. Many canneries supplied Indians with boats and nets to fish for them under contract. At Metlakatla, the Indians for several years operated a salmon cannery as a community enterprise. The fur seal hunt gave numbers of Indians the opportunity to share in the chase on a partnership basis.

But increasingly, as capital equipment became more significant, the Indians were passed over and displaced. Chinese labourers proved more reliable cannery employees. Seal fishery captains claimed white men were easier to handle and, with experience, better hunters, so by 1893 Indians were occupying only one-third of the places on the schooners. White men came increasingly to dominate the fishery through their technical skill, their greater energy, their more efficient capital equipment. No effort was made to secure a privileged position for the Indians in the harvesting of the marine wealth of their homeland. Instead, the provincial government exerted itself to recruit Newfoundlanders, Norwegians, and Scottish crofters to settle the coast and participate in the fishery, while Japanese fishermen began entering the province for the same purpose. A great new industry was being founded, but the central material prop of the North Pacific Indian civilization was being undermined.

The other major industry to attract white men into the Indian tribal territories of northern British Columbia, this time to the valleys and plateaus of the interior, was placer mining. Of itself, such activity did not interfere with the livelihood of the Indians, and might even have aided them economically. But the prospectors, scattered far and wide about the region, sometimes harmed the morals of the Indians with whom they came in contact, and occasionally were the cause or object of quarrels and crimes. A missionary like Duncan dreaded the passing of prospectors up the Skeena into the interior as almost certain to imperil his work, while the government had to be ready to uphold the law and prevent disputes between prospectors and Indians from erupting into violence. However, in spite of the many opportunities for serious trouble, the prospectors were able to go about their business with few untoward incidents. The lack of any great new discovery considerably limited the disruption of Indian life by the mining industry.

The only important placer gold discovery during the seventies and eighties occurred in the spring of 1872 in the Cassiar district. Henry Thibert, who had left Minnesota to prospect on the Mackenzie in 1869, found rich gravel on Thibert's Creek, a feeder of Dease Lake. His three-man party was quickly joined by several hundred prospectors attracted from other locations, particularly from Omineca in the western headwaters of the Peace River system, where disappointingly poor results followed a brief revival of the field in 1870-72. More paying gravel was soon found on Dease and McDame creeks, and by the summer of 1874, 1,400 men had entered the area, the villages of Laketon and McDame were taking shape, and $1,100,000 of gold was mined. Production began falling off in 1876, and no new large finds were made, even though prospectors ranged far up the Liard River to a mysterious Sayyea Creek somewhere around Frances River. For the next dozen years the district continued downhill, yielding a total of $4,300,000 to the end of 1880.

The Cassiar gold field followed the same pattern as dozens of earlier placer camps. It began with discoveries rich enough to offset the very high cost of supplies, laboriously hauled in over roadless terrain, and quickly attained full development. Transportation facilities were improved by governmental expenditures on trails, roads, and bridges, and the decline in costs of supplies brought down the expense of mining. With improved access to the area, too, heavier equipment could be brought in to inaugurate more economical hydraulic mining methods and such further transportation improvements as a steamboat on Dease Lake. But soon the richest gravels were worked out to the point where white men could no longer earn wages from their claims. Chinese miners, with their lower standard of living, often purchased marginal claims and worked them for a further period until the return was too meagre to satisfy even their modest wants. By 1879 the three creeks were nearly worked out, "affording at present, with but few exceptions, no profitable employment to white men, and but an indifferent and uncertain means of livelihood to the indefatigable efforts of the Chinese."[23] By 1884 the entire camp produced ony $101,600 in gold and the mining population, half of it Chinese, had fallen to 180 men.

The Cassiar was largely a summertime camp and idle during the long, severe northern winters. Not until the opening of the Yukon mine field in the following decade was any appreciable amount of wintertime mining carried out. The Cassiar miners found their best operating period to be the early spring, before the heavy freshets washed over their workings. In the autumn most would depart for outside, either to the Stikine so as to be ready for an early start the following year, or to Victoria. This departure was chiefly due to the scarcity and high cost of food, though beginning in the summer of 1877, some cereals and vegetables were grown locally, inaugurating yet another industry. But the birth of agriculture also indicated the decline in gold-mining; in the boom years men had been too busy mining or prospecting to farm, and all food had been imported.

From the mid-eighties onward, the Yukon country began to figure more prominently as a centre for prospecting and placer mining. This was in spite of the fact that its northerly location made for a very short summer season indeed, and increased transportation costs and other expenses proportionately. In 1878, however, an American, Henry Holt, led the way to a backdoor entry into the area from the south – from the fiord-like Lynn Canal over the Chilkoot Pass. The Chilkoot Indians had long used this route in their role as middlemen between the Tlingits of the coast and the Stick Indians of the interior, and had kept it a jealously guarded monopoly; now and henceforth they gained their recompense through working as porters over the pass. By 1887, when James J. Healy, in the early seventies a leader in the Whoop-Up country north of Montana, established a post at Dyea at the head of Lynn Canal, this route was in common use; and in 1892, with the backing of Chicago capital, Healy established a North American Transportation and Trading Company, with its own supply steamer on the upper Yukon and posts as far down as Circle City, Alaska. As northern mine fields like Cassiar and Juneau declined, more and more miners made their way farther north to the Yukon country. From thirty men active there in 1882, the number reached three hundred by 1887 and five hundred by 1894-95.

As elsewhere, work was restricted at first to working the surface gravels in the brief summers, but a way was found to mine the lowest levels nearest the bedrock, potentially the best-paying gravel of all. The method entailed thawing the frozen gravel by wood fires, removing the softened gravel and repeating the process until the shaft, deepened by about a foot a day, reached bedrock, after which a tunnel was carried across the valley by the same method, and along the paystreak, if one was found. This kind of underground operation proceeded better in winter than in the summer; through the winters the miners piled up the laboriously dug gold-bearing gravel for washing the following summer. The rise of a substantial year-round white population working on the creeks created a problem of food supplies in the winters and added to the trading companies' business. The Yukon miners were experienced men who knew how to look after themselves: "Old miners have learned from experience to value health more than gold and they therefore spare no expense in procuring the best and most varied outfit of food that can be obtained."[24] They were highly mobile, with every report or rumour of a strike bringing unsuccessful prospectors running from all corners of the country. Interest shifted from river to river in the Canadian Yukon and neighbouring Alaska.

Year by year the gold produced from the creeks on the Canadian side increased – from $40,000 in 1891 to $250,000 in 1895 and $300,000 in 1896 – as did miners' confidence that the country was rich indeed and before long would become the locale of a major strike, such as those of the Cariboo or California.

Besides the fur trade, the fishery and placer mining were the only commercial activities carried on to any extent in the northern parts of the province, notwithstanding the obvious plenitude of other resources. Why should anyone go far afield when so much rich, productive forest stood ready for cutting practically within sight of shipboard in Burrard Inlet or the lower Fraser River? The logging industry gradually expanded along the coasts of Vancouver Island and along the routes of the railways of the interior on the mainland, but in more remote locations the forests for many years only met local needs for firewood or construction materials, and fed frequent forest fires. Greater governmental attention was paid to promoting agricultural settlement, for it was hoped that the arable land would draw permanent settlers to build up the province. The province made every effort to encourage this goal by instituting an easy land-granting system that was fairly comparable to those of adjacent states. The initial regulations allowed a settler a pre-emption lot of 320 acres (160 acres in districts nearest the coast) at a price of $1 per acre, subject to four years' official residence and his making improvements to the value of $2.50 per acre on the holdings. These were eased in some areas by reducing the residence period to two years and eliminating the purchase price. The local demand for farm produce encouraged settlement in the southwestern corner, where the province accordingly carried out township and subdivision surveys in line with the American system. Ranching was extensively practised in the interior, for cattle and horses enjoyed a dependable market in the mining camps and ports, the herds being capable of moving long distances from the Okanagan or Chilcotin districts to railhead, or coastal port, or distant mining camp.

A problem related to bringing the resources of the region into practical use was the concession by the province under the Terms of Union, in return for an annual grant of $100,000, of an important tract of land for a Railway Belt – the territory twenty miles on either side of the Canadian Pacific Railway "along the line of Railway throughout its entire length in British Columbia."[24] The early difficulties were over location, since the Dominion delayed making its formal decision on the route until 1878, keeping would-be developers in a state of uncertainty. After the selection was agreed on, the Dominion instituted the regulations and machinery of the Dominion Lands administration to manage and dispose of the resources of this district. Now further difficulties arose over mineral rights, parts of the tract already committed to other uses, and conflicting land-management policies. And in 1883 the Dominion also received the right to select a 3,500,000-acre tract in the northeastern corner of the province. Under the complicated arrangement, the Dominion agreed to provide an Esquimalt to Nanaimo Railway and pay for the graving dock at the former point as compensation to the Vancouver Islanders, who were disappointed at not having the transcontinental railway extended to the island. In 1906 the Dominion eventually selected its tract – an area known as the Peace River Block, extending west from the Alberta boundary on either side of the Peace River, which it retained to 1930.

During the seventies in particular, efforts were made to evaluate the economic potential of much of the interior, mainly in connection with the Dominion government's investigations of the Pacific railway route. In trying to keep pace with the ubiquitous gold-seekers, the colony had opened up the Kootenay, Columbia, Fraser, Thompson, and Peace River districts in the interior for mining development. Some explorations were also carried on in conjunction with road and railway projects, such as Walter Moberly's explorations through the Gold and Selkirk mountain ranges that certainly discovered the Eagle Pass and possibly the pass subsequently reported and named by Major A. B. Rogers; or the exploration projected in 1864 by Alfred Waddington from Bute Inlet via the Chilcotin country to Quesnel that ended tragically with the massacre of his men by Indians.

After British Columbia entered Confederation, the province's interest was mainly to encourage settlement of accessible areas, and there was only an occasional examination of country like northern Vancouver Island for possible future development. A certain amount of exploratory work was carried out by the Geological Survey of Canada, working in conjunction with the railway surveys and on its own. The survey conducted investigations of some northern parts of the province like the Queen Charlotte Islands, and examined the Liard River from its source to its mouth in 1887. Mainly, though, it was the work over a period of ten years of the Canadian Pacific Railway surveys that produced the majority of studies of the large segment of the province lying between the Fraser and Skeena rivers.

These were more than engineering surveys, for to help determine potential traffic it was necessary to evaluate the resources of the regions traversed. First they concentrated on possible routes between Yellowhead and Howse passes and points along the Fraser River between Kamloops in the south and Fort George in the north. Then, to find an easier way through the Coast Range than the difficult one the Fraser River offered, Sandford Fleming turned his attention to the country between the Fraser and the coast north of Burrard Inlet. Studies were made of the feasibility of routes from Lillooet to Howe Sound; via the Chilcotin and Homathco or Nazko rivers to Bute Inlet; via the Bella Coola to North Bentinck Arm; or from Fort George via the Salmon and Blackwater rivers to Dean Channel (the way by which Mackenzie had reached the Pacific overland from Canada in 1793). Furthermore, in response to groups interested in having the route proceed through the Peace River district, Marcus Smith, Fleming's deputy, ordered a series of explorations, directed by H. J. Cambie in 1879, 1880, and 1881, of the routes between the Peace River district and Fort George, Fort Fraser and Hazelton, and from the last to the mouth of the Skeena.

Still, knowledge of the potentialities of such districts meant little unless means were provided for settlers to move their produce to markets. Their location made it possible to begin developing the resources of the islands, inlets, and mouths of the major rivers without any great delay. But travel and transportation inland at once came up against the difficulties of mountainous, rocky terrain, dense rain forests, and turbulent rivers that, in spite of their faults, provided the best means of communication. The Fraser was a major artery; steamer services had been established up to Yale in the gold-rush days, and on its middle section, from Soda Creek to Quesnel, by the early sixties. Steamers had also been placed on the Thompson River as early as 1866 to serve traffic to and from the southeastern part of the province. In the summer of 1871 the transportation entrepreneur G. B. Wright took a steamer up the Fraser, Nechaco, and Stuart rivers to ply the lakes above Fort St James. This voyage was made to investigate the possibility of accommodating traffic entering the Omineca district by way of the Skeena River. The region, at the western headwaters of the Peace, was the locale of a gold rush between 1868 and 1872. The Cassiar rush also resulted in the introduction of steamboats in 1874 between Wrangell, Alaska, and Telegraph Creek on the Stikine, "by all odds the most dangerous stream for river navigation in the province."[26] A small steamer was also installed on Dease Lake, the machinery for which was brought in over the trail from Telegraph Creek. The difficult Skeena was served after 1890 by the Hudson's Bay Company's steamer *Caledonia*, making Hazelton, its terminus, the main point of departure for Omineca and other northern districts. An unwelcome stowaway on the first trip was the common housefly, which established itself so quickly by 1893 in the Hazelton district that "Now this pest is all prevailing."[27]

Away from the rivers, the task involved constructing trails and roads through very difficult country. The colony had gone heavily into debt building roads to the gold fields to assist the miners. The resulting roads – from Yale to Barkerville in the Cariboo, and over the mountain ranges from Hope to the Kootenays – continued in use, impressive monuments to the herculean efforts of those first years, until they were supplanted by railways. The province continued to be called on to improve trails to aid the development of new mining districts or to permit ranchers to drive their herds to markets. The progress of the mining industry was vitally dependent on such improvements, for cheaper transportation meant that lower grade ores could be mined economically and that the scale of the mining operation could be enlarged. Improved techniques followed, and determined how long the camp could carry on. The province even developed an eight-hundred-mile trail from Quesnel to Dease Lake in 1874, over which three hundred head of cattle were driven from the Cariboo to the mining camp in the following year. An expedient adopted for a time was the issuing of charters to individuals to build roads in return for a provincial subsidy and the right to levy tolls for a period of years on traffic carried over the roads. The province almost always had to take these over, either because they were badly built, or because of users' complaints against the high tolls. The entrepreneur was frequently reimbursed for his expenses, and sometimes he received a little extra for his trouble. Captain William Moore, who built and improved the trail from Telegraph Creek to Dease Lake in 1873-74, was bought out in 1875 at a 25 per cent bonus, after which the road became part of the regular system of the province, managed by a district roads superintendent who attended to maintenance and possible extensions.

Railways were the real answer for developmental problems, since they made it feasible to establish base metal mining, lumbering, agriculture, and other industries serving more than purely local markets. British Columbians looked at the planned transcontinental line for its effects on meeting local developmental needs as well as for its broader functions of guaranteeing the future of some ocean terminus and unifying the country from sea to sea. The Dominion government's first contract to build part of the Canadian Pacific Railway in British Columbia was with Andrew Onderdonk. It was for a 127-mile section between Yale, the head of navigation on the lower Fraser, and Savona's, near Kamloops on the North Thompson River, which also served the local function of overcoming the difficult portages around the unnavigable section of the Fraser River. Later Onderdonk received another contract for the section from Yale to the western terminus, Port Moody, on Burrard Inlet. These sections were built at government expense, and when completed were turned over to the Canadian Pacific Railway as part of the Dominion government's agreement with the syndicate. The completion of the line in late 1885 promoted the fuller development of the Railway Belt and of more remote districts on either side of the line, of the Kootenay and Okanagan districts on the south, and of the Cariboo, Fraser, and Chilcotin districts farther north. By 1896 the Canadian Pacific had been supplemented by other railways across the southern part of the province, while the districts along the border were linked with American railways from the south. The arrival of the railway was reflected by the construction of smelters at points along the lines, the opening up of copper, silver, and lead mines in the Kootenays and other districts along the border, and the beginnings of lumbering and farming. The Canadian Pacific, concerned over the drain of the traffic and trade of this region to Spokane and other cities, was on the verge, in 1896, of commencing the Crowsnest Pass and Kettle Valley railways to win the traffic of the region for itself and its trade for Canada. Irrigation works were also beginning to be constructed to transform the arid valleys of the interior from ranches into prosperous fruit and vegetable farms, while dyking and drainage schemes were being worked out to increase the area of cultivation of the lower Fraser district.

The usual social and political institutions were introduced in regular settled parts of British Columbia, but were almost non-existent in the bulk of the province, where elaborate administrative arrangements were not yet required. A few provincial police constables were stationed in districts like the upper Skeena to uphold the law and keep the peace between miners and Indians. For new mining districts, where more services as well as better control were required, the province continued the system instituted in the days of the Fraser gold rush: a gold commissioner was appointed to serve as the administrative and judicial arm of the provincial government in Victoria. In his capacity of district government agent he issued mining licences, processed timber, land, and mining applications, regulated the gold-mining industry, supervised other government employees in charge of public works or law enforcement, tried minor legal suits by virtue of his appointment as stipendiary magistrate, reported to the government on conditions and recommended courses of action. Men like P. O'Reilly or A. W. Vowell, who served in a succession of districts from Wildhorse in the Kootenay to Cassiar in the north, became quite skilled in maintaining a semblance of authority. They met the needs of the camps expeditiously and held their judicial powers in reserve, though they did not shrink from vigorous action whenever they felt the miners needed to be shown "that matters were to be on a different footing as they are in American mining camps."[28] They enjoyed considerable latitude in arranging for the construction of trails and lock-ups, and were given subsidies to encourage miners to explore for new placer deposits and the like. A small regional bureaucracy would develop, such as the two recorders, two constables, roads overseer, and customs collector stationed at Cassiar at the height of the rush.

This obviously temporary system of local government was made necessary by the impermanence of many mining districts and by the province's limited means. Even more, it reflected the long-standing fears of the government of allowing a group of miners, particularly from the American west, to establish some kind of regional authority. A measure of local organization and a good deal of co-operative action – to determine local rules respecting land and water rights, working conditions, to provide public facilities, settle disputes, and petition government for various kinds of assistance – were essential to the proper functioning of a mining camp. The government's fear was that if the miners were left too much alone, they would provide for their own needs by establishing *de facto* squatter governments on the model of the traditional miners' meetings that had been evolved in the western United States. Since the authorities did not want such organizations petitioning to Washington or getting ideas of constituting themselves into governments, the gold commissioners watched the miners' meetings closely and turned them into orderly vehicles for expressing local needs and for calling for governmental action. In Omineca and Cassiar, miners' meetings were occasionally called, sometimes at the instance of the gold commissioner, to deal with matters in which a wide measure of public support was desirable. The meetings were well advertised, elected a chairman and secretary, kept minutes, and concluded their deliberations by passing resolutions which were forwarded to the proper authority – the government in Victoria.

The province also was forehanded in providing remote districts with representation in the provincial legislature, even though this was far from deserved in terms of population. It was considered important to have a member to act as the main channel of communication between the government and the people of such districts to make their wishes known and secure appropriations to help meet the needs of their district. The system of regional district agents combining a wide range of administrative functions continued to characterize local administration in view of the segmented nature of the mountainous province.

The system was far more flexible than that adopted by the Dominion in the Northwest. The federal government assigned officers to carry out particular administrative functions in local areas (though many functions often had to be gathered into the hands of a single agent, such as a police officer). Whereas the lack of an effective liaison between the national and local levels of administration produced innumerable tensions in the Northwest, in British Columbia the hiatus between regional and local levels was very successfully overcome by the gold commissioner. He also filled an important time gap – between the beginnings of the settlement and the introduction of regular channels of communications and authority.

Another significant difference with the prairie west was over the control of natural resources. The gold commissioner could function effectively since he was the agent of the resource-owning and resource-granting authority. In the North-West Territories, however, even when a regional government was constituted, it still lacked authority in the most vital areas of local concern and was quite powerless to deal effectively with local problems. Thus it was not against the innocuous, powerless territorial government that the North-West Rebellion was waged, but against the apparatus of remote control provided by the Dominion government.

In another important phase related to northern development the province had to restrict its role to spurring the Dominion government to action. This was in the field of Canadian-American relations, notably over national boundaries. Almost from British Columbia's entrance into Confederation, provincial spokesmen pointed to the importance of an early definitive settlement of a boundary that barred almost half the province from direct access to the Pacific Ocean. There were complaints that the access by way of the Stikine River, granted by the Treaty of Washington in 1871, was unnecessarily restrictive, and was so administered as to make it difficult for British Columbia interests to establish regular contacts across the Alaska Panhandle with the northern parts of the province. It was contended that Canada was losing considerable amounts of customs duties, while Canadian businesses were losing $300,000 worth of trade from these districts to Americans. Fears were also expressed that the delays in negotiating a definitive boundary settlement could lead to Canada's being deprived of valuable territory. Partly as a result of such representations, a conventional boundary was established along the Stikine River in 1878, but British Columbians' disquietude continued, intensified by disputes over the Bering Sea seal fishery; and by the nineties, over access to the Yukon district and the boundary at the passes and the 141st meridian – the next frontier of the North.

CHAPTER 3

Traders and Missionaries in the Middle North

1870 – 1896

For a quarter-century after 1870-71, while Canadians remained preoccupied with developing the prairie district, life in the great forested region farther north continued with few alterations, particularly in the life of the indigenous population. There were only minor changes in the numbers of white men living and working in the region, or in those major institutions of the region, the fur trade and missions. But fur-traders and missionaries, by leading the inhabitants increasingly to adopt the trade goods and market economy of the modern age along with its Christian doctrines and code of morality, were, in spite of themselves, the instruments and harbingers of coming developments. While they educated and trained a few of the original inhabitants, they also assisted increasing numbers of white men to travel about the region inspecting the land and its people – an indispensable first step to any further development of the region. Furthermore, by their calls for help to discharge their own important functions, and by speaking out on behalf of a voiceless people for greater governmental aid, the clergy and fur-traders were instrumental in drawing Canada to extend its authority over a primitive land. It is therefore fitting that the roles of these two major forces in the life of the region should be examined here in some detail.

For the Hudson's Bay Company, the period after 1870 was one of retreat and transformation as it gradually became adjusted to the momentous changes of the sixties, when increasing competition began to affect trading results, and control over the labouring force was greatly weakened. The field officers, the aristocrats of the fur trade, had been angered and demoralized by these changes, and especially by the sale of the company to the International Financial Society in 1863 and then the surrender of its original charter in 1869 – the compensation in both cases going exclusively to the shareholders. Their morale had to be restored, and operations had to be redirected so that the company would function efficiently as a private corporation under Canadian law in a land marked out for rapid settlement. Accordingly, while the H.B.C. maintained its posts in the new towns of the prairies district, these gradually became general stores, serving mainly a white clientele. Credit advances to Indians and Métis had to be curtailed as the bison disappeared and the numbers of fur-bearing animals declined, but the H.B.C. began to develop a system of cash trading, striving to capture windfalls like treaty payments, or government contracts to supply survey parties, the police, or rations for destitute Indians. Along the Canadian Pacific Railway, from Sudbury to Vancouver, sales shops were opened in the new railway towns. In older centres of settlement the posts began stocking the varied requirements of a wage-earning or self-employed white society, and officers embarked upon other opportunities for profitable business – for example, flour and saw mills, or shipping operations.

Surpassing the British shareholders' hopes of profits from the fur trade was their desire to realize on the Hudson's Bay Company's large real estate holdings in the Fertile Belt. The "speculators in civilization" who had bought out the original investors in 1863 had pinned their faith on making large profits from the sale of the vast acreages of Rupert's Land. Even though the property of the H.B.C. was greatly reduced by the transfer agreement of 1869, they still were convinced their shrunken estate would yield a princely return. But settlers were few, and good land was cheap or free to homesteaders, so for many years the large acreages retained by the Hudson's Bay Company – some 6,689,000 acres in all – were more a source of expense and trouble than revenue. For a time, in 1875-76, the H.B.C. considered selling back its lands to Canada for £550,000, a price Prime Minister Mackenzie had negotiated with the committee. But the Canadian cabinet proved unwilling to accept the bargain,[1] and so the H.B.C. was compelled to retain its lands. Eventually these afforded gross receipts – in the years 1894-1930 alone – of sixty million dollars.[2] More encouraging at first were the returns from the sale of urban real estate. These involved acreages surrounding the H.B.C.'s original trading posts, notably the 500-acre tract at Fort Garry, from which, as Winnipeg boomed, the company, by 1882, stood to derive revenue in excess of the £300,000 it had received for surrendering the charter. But in the long depression that followed, the trading-post lands became almost as unprofitable as the real estate scattered in 480- and 640-acre units across the prairies. To manage its lands, the H.B.C. looked to its agents, the officers of the fur trade, particularly those in charge at centres that held good possibilities of developing into cities in the near future. The officers, being excluded from sharing in the profits of this side of the operations, were unwilling to assume this added responsibility until, under a new Deed Poll which went into effect in 1871, it was made part of their duty to serve the company in all its activities.

Reluctantly, the shareholders accepted the unpalatable fact that for the foreseeable future they would have to depend on the fur trade for their dividends. One solution was to improve the trading operation, particularly by reducing the costs of inland transportation, the largest single operating expense. Hence, great hopes were placed on investments in steamboats, wagon roads, and portage tramways to improve the efficiency and profitability of the northern fur trade. Besides, drastic reform of the transport system was imperative in view of the deterioration in the available labour force. As Roderick Macfarlane, chief factor in charge of Athabasca district, urged in 1873:

> I have in previous communications pointed out that *Boat Work* was about being *played* out, and I again beg to reiterate the statement, with the further request that no time be lost in putting *steam* on the Athabasca and MacKenzie Rivers. A relative subject of grave importance is that of *Servants*. . . . I must not conceal from you that bad as the present lot are, in some respects, we cannot even by offering increased pay, have them replaced by better or as good hands from Red River, and that it will therefore be advisable to grant good terms to those we now have in Athabasca, and also introduce steam as quickly as possible, & thus enable us to dispense with a number of servants at present absolutely required for our District Transport business.[3]

The Hudson's Bay Company was already participating in the transportation revolution under way in the American midwest since the 1850's that saw railroads approaching the headwaters of the Red River and a steamboat placed on the river itself in 1859. As these communications improved, the H.B.C. changed its mode of operating by making Winnipeg rather than York Factory its principal transportation base for the Northwest. The historic supply route by way of Hudson Bay and the Hayes and Nelson rivers was gradually abandoned during the seventies, and the large depots of York Factory and Norway House declined to simple trading posts serving their local districts.

Instead, the H.B.C. gained control of the shipping on the Red River and Lake Winnipeg, and after 1870, developed the Saskatchewan River into its main supply route for the northern and western districts. Large shallow-draft steamers like the *Northcote* were built on the Saskatchewan above the Grand Rapids to navigate that river all the way to Edmonton. To improve the transfer of freight around the rapids, the H.B.C. had a tramway built in 1876 by Walter Moberly, the last spike being driven by Lady Dufferin, wife of the governor general. Though at first there were difficulties in managing the steamers, the system proved effective, laying down heavy cargoes at posts like Carlton or Edmonton at a fraction of the cost of the former York boats or of freighting by cart overland. Besides, the steamers earned revenue for the company as public carriers. However, by 1883 the railway had become a more convenient supply medium than the steamboats for the Saskatchewan valley posts and the country beyond. From Regina, Qu'Appelle, and Calgary, Red River cart brigades, wagons, and stagecoaches hauled freight and passengers to Prince Albert and Edmonton until railways reached these points as well. From these new railheads, river steamers continued for some years to serve the intermediate Saskatchewan River settlements and the posts in the lower Saskatchewan district like Cumberland House or The Pas.

To improve the access from the North Saskatchewan to the northern districts, it was necessary to develop overland trail connections with the rivers and lakes of the Churchill, Athabasca, and Peace river systems. A useful cart road was in operation over the long Methye Portage (Portage la Loche) by 1874, improving access between Prince Albert or Carlton and the Athabasca River below Fort McMurray. An alternative route via Lac la Biche Mission and Horse River had a brief trial but was abandoned as too difficult. During the early 1880's Edmonton increasingly became the principal supply base from which traffic moved north over an improved hundred-mile trail to Athabasca Landing. Posts in the western part of the Peace River, heretofore served by boat brigades from Fort McMurray and Fort Chipewyan, also began to be supplied from Edmonton and Athabasca Landing. From the western end of Lesser Slave Lake, reached by ascending the Athabasca, a wagon road was built to the Peace River at the site of the future town of Peace River. Part of the trade of these Peace River posts was also carried on with the Hudson's Bay Company's western department in British Columbia from the Fraser at Fort George, across Giscombe Portage and thence down the Peace River system.

The culmination of the H.B.C.'s efforts was the placing of steamboats on the rivers of the Mackenzie basin between 1883 and 1887. Three shallow-draft boats – *Athabasca* (for the navigable sector above and below Athabasca Landing), *Grahame* (for the lower Athabasca, Slave, lower Peace rivers and Lake Athabasca, centred at Fort Chipewyan), and *Wrigley* (for the Slave and Mackenzie rivers and Great Slave Lake) – were put in service to supply the entire waterway down to the Arctic Ocean. Another portage tramway was constructed at the Grand Rapids of the Athabasca to facilitate the transfer of freight and passengers by scows between the end of the *Athabasca*'s route and the start of the *Grahame*'s at Fort McMurray.[4] The trail around the Slave River rapids between the new settlements of Smith's Landing and Fort Smith also was improved into a passable wagon road. The great waterway was thus rendered easily accessible, making it possible to import bulky foodstuffs and other supplies, and greatly improving the Hudson's Bay Company's financial results for the northern districts. From this northern artery other side routes continued to be operated by boat crews and packers. Among these was one from Fort McPherson through the mountains via the Peel, Bell, Rat, Porcupine, and Yukon rivers to those westernmost trading posts, La Pierre House, Rampart House, and Fort Yukon. Another, operated for a few years during the 1860's and sporadically afterwards, led from Fort Norman or Fort Good Hope to Fort Anderson on the Anderson River, and was the H.B.C.'s first serious effort to conduct a trade especially for the Eskimos of the central Arctic. Other services were extended east from the main waterway to Lake Athabasca and Great Slave Lake points, and west up the Liard River to Fort Liard and Fort Nelson. Away from the Mackenzie basin, the H.B.C. operated other inland transport systems for its own trade and for such commercial traffic as offered. The facilities ranged from the H.B.C.'s steamboat on the Skeena to the traditional boat brigades inland from the James Bay posts of the company's southern department. The Canadian Pacific Railway changed the trade and traffic patterns of some of these after 1885, but others, like the brigade that travelled the length of the Rupert River to supply the post on Lake Mistassini, remained unaffected. The company thus provided the only practical means of commercial transport for half of Canada, an inestimable aid to improving access to, and establishing control over, the undeveloped Middle North.

By improving its transportation facilities in northern Canada, the Hudson's Bay Company was able to reduce its expenses, its dependence on unsatisfactory, expensive labour, and expand the quantities of supplies entering the region. Unfortunately, this was not an unmixed blessing, for competitors also were enabled to penetrate the strongholds of the fur trade. As early as 1867 one trader had observed that the inaccessibility of the northern districts was one of the company's greatest sources of strength.[5] With the establishment of considerable mercantile concerns in the settlements along the North Saskatchewan, competition became acute in the district adjoining that river and far beyond it. Firms like Stobart and Eden, John A. McDougall (afterwards McDougall and Secord), or Norris and Carey, developed their own networks of client trappers and traders among the Métis and Indians. What Fort Garry had been in earlier years, Edmonton now became – a centre of free trader operations, where fur was disposed of to the Hudson's Bay Company or its rivals. These were drawn from considerable distances – from Jasper House (which the company finally abandoned in 1884), from Fort Chipewyan (where Colin Fraser, the son of Sir George Simpson's Highland piper, had his post), and from points even farther afield, where Edmonton-based traders opened posts of their own. J. Hislop and E. Nagle commenced operations at Fort Rae and Fort Resolution during the winter of 1893-94, instituting a firm which, under the later name of Northern Trading Company, was to survive through various changes of ownership down to 1939. Chief Factor Julian Camsell complained that their inroads forced the cost of furs up, and added gloomily that "They talk of going on to Good Hope & Norman if so the prices of the whole District will be demoralized."[6]

Victoria was an even more serious source of competition, particularly since European and American fur-buyers came there regularly for fur seal skins and sometimes would pay as much as 15 per cent over the prices prevailing in London for other furs. When this happened, the Hudson's Bay Company agents could not afford to bid and had to let the fur go to their rivals. Their firm's practice of disposing of all its fur at semi-annual London auctions simply made it impossible to compete in such cases. With Victoria as their base for supplies and markets, independent traders were able to challenge the H.B.C. practically anywhere in British Columbia. On the Skeena a major opponent was William Cunningham, Duncan's one-time mission helper; in the Cassiar it was the mail contractor Rufus Sylvester, "a very generous man, an extravagant trader."[7] A succession of free traders – the Elmore brothers, William Cust, "Twelve Foot" Davis – made their way from the Fraser into the Peace River district and invaded the H.B.C.'s historic trading preserves, drawing furs all the way from the country adjoining Great Slave Lake to their posts along the Peace River. The managers in Athabasca tried the usual tactics: increasing the prices paid for furs, improving the selection of trade goods, sending flying parties to intercept Indians on their way to trade with the interlopers, and, as a last resort, buying out their rivals. But such tactics only brought peace for short intervals; the retiring concerns were succeeded by younger men like Allie Brick, son of the Reverend J. G. Brick, and J. K. Cornwall, another progenitor of the Northern Trading concern.

In British Columbia and the regions north of the prairies the company fought its competition by economic means; but it had to retire from Alaska as a result of the transfer of that land to American sovereignty. From the 1840's a post was operated at Fort Yukon, at the junction of the Yukon and Porcupine rivers, well inside Alaskan territory. Fort Yukon was extremely difficult to supply from the Mackenzie River, but it was highly lucrative. Following the transfer of Alaska, however, an American expedition under Captain C. W. Raymond took possession of the fort in 1869, and the Hudson's Bay Company sold its Alaskan interest to a member of the soon-to-be-formed Alaska Commercial Company. A new post, Rampart House, was established on the Porcupine River, and the Fort Yukon Indians were induced to move their trapping ground to the vicinity. The H.B.C.'s withdrawal from Fort Yukon had the effect of opening the upper Yukon to Alaska-based trading interests. N. L. McQuesten, whose competition in the upper Mackenzie district had been bought out, reappeared in the Yukon in

1873 with a new partner, Arthur Harper. With the support of the Alaska Commercial Company, they founded the trading post of Fort Reliance in 1874. Then they separated, and McQuesten built posts at the mouth of the Stewart River and Fortymile River in partnership with A. H. Mayo, while Harper and Joseph Ladue established others at Fort Selkirk and Sixtymile River. These trading centres, supplied by an annual steamer from St Michael's, served the trappers and traders as well as the growing number of prospectors drawn into the Yukon district by indications of placer gold.

Worse than the competition of rival traders was the serious economic depression and the change in fashion away from furs like marten and mink and toward long-haired furs like beaver and lynx. The moderate declines that set in after 1874 reached catastrophic depths and remained there for a decade after 1884. At the same time, fur receipts fluctuated downwards, partly because of over-trapping resulting from the competition for furs, but mainly because of the increasing scarcity of game as firearms became more readily available to native hunters. In the years after 1887, food shortages began to be felt more widely and to recur more frequently, causing the trappers to devote themselves to hunting sufficient food for their families, and to pay less attention to trapping. The years of scarcity made it necessary for the company to import more provisions, increasing its own operating expenses, and to extend larger advances to trappers and more relief.

The food shortages were by no means confined to the native population; at times the white men resident in the North, particularly fur-traders and missionaries, went on very short rations too. The Hudson's Bay Company therefore bent greater efforts at making its northern trading districts as self-sufficient as possible through securing larger catches of fish. Posts along the route of the caribou migrations were encouraged to provide meat for other centres, and those in appropriate situations expanded local farming and herding activities. By the 1890's the H.B.C., like the missionaries, was encouraging the establishment of a stable agricultural economy, centred at Fort Vermilion, to serve as a convenient source of food for the forts farther north.

The principal responsibilities for trading operations throughout the vast area of the fur forest still devolved upon the H.B.C.'s commissioned officers, for the most part Highland Scots, among whom the occasional Englishman or Canadian seemed almost an interloper. Theirs was often a hard apprenticeship in terms of outdoor travel, hunting, and even physical combat with unruly natives or recalcitrant company servants, and of heavy responsibility for their subordinates' acts as well as their own. The plaintive plea by Chief Trader Donald Ross, with which he concludes the diary of his trip of 1874 from Fort Dunvegan to Methye Portage with his district's winter trade, is a commentary both on this and on the inadequacies of the brigade transport system:

The main object I had always in view was to try and render our Returns
in good order . . . but in a long voyage many unavoidable accidents will
happen; at the same time there are many careless characters in the Boats
who will not tell when a package gets wet, as it does not effect them
personally and the person in charge cannot be everywhere. Nor is it fair
and just to make the officer in charge of the Brigade responsible for every
loss that may be sustained. There are various ways in which furs may be
hurt or destroyed; some may be damp or greasy when packed, and how is
this to be known by anyone except the packer?[8]

Still, there were offsetting benefits, both material and honorific. Officers
received allowances of tea, flour, sugar, candles, etc., and indented for
luxuries like books and photographic equipment that were imported at very
reasonable prices. They enjoyed periodic leaves and, by the standards of the
time, a good pension arrangement. As heads of the trading and transportation of their districts they were virtually uncrowned monarchs, possessing
very considerable powers over their native clients or their employees. In
many ways, too, they were recognized as eminent personages and were consulted by governments, commissioned as justices of the peace, or appointed
to the territorial council or to the Dominion Senate. Scientific organizations
like the Smithsonian Institution in Washington approached them with
requests to furnish animal and bird skins, eggs, rocks, native artifacts,
weather readings, and anthropological reports; and many museums and
libraries in the United States, Britain, and Canada were greatly indebted to
their endeavours. Some, like Bernard R. Ross or Roderick Macfarlane, were
recognized as authorities and were invited to memberships in the great geographical and scientific societies of their day. At Fort Simpson, Fort Chipewyan, York Factory – to name three centres – museums and libraries were
established through the patronage of well-disposed officers, to the constant
surprise and delight of visitors. They were hosts to many distinguished
visitors and travellers in the sub-Arctic forests, and went out of their way
to assist them in their journeys and to extend lavish hospitality.

However, the commissioned officers found their work increasingly bewildering and distasteful, and, with good reason, felt their days were
numbered. Their incomes failed to come up to the levels of the 1850's or
1860's, so money worries plagued officers who had children to be educated
abroad, wives and young families living "outside" for reasons of health, or
grown sons and daughters to launch into the world. At many isolated posts
loneliness was a serious psychological problem, fortifying some – Donald A.
Smith spent thirteen years in barren Labrador before blazing forth on his
meteoric financial and political career – but driving others to excessive
reliance upon the bottle. Veteran officers felt they knew their districts best
and resented the increasing regulation of their freedom of action by inspect-

ing officers and fur-trade commissioners. They complained bitterly against shortsighted, penny-pinching economies that caused them to lose trade to their opponents, or at the failure of their superiors to sanction buying out dangerous competitors. The stricter system of accounting designed to give realistic financial pictures of every post – a necessity if the trade was to survive – was resented as an interference and a prying into their domestic arrangements. Furthermore, the bookkeeping methods of the district office in Winnipeg were widely distrusted. Officers complained that prices of goods for which they indented were inflated so as to swell the profits of the Winnipeg store. Traders also alleged that they were regularly charged for goods – notably liquor – which they never received, and that they were constantly hampered by shortages of important goods that were intercepted by traders situated nearer the supply centre.

Adding to the uneasiness of the officers, and the underlying cause for most of their complaints, was their suspicion of the company headquarters in London, where efforts were continually being made to reorganize operations, notably through developing the retail store trade. In 1882 the directors sought specialists "of a very different kind from that to which most of the Company's officers had been specially trained."[9] The old traders, set in their ways, were sceptical. There had been frequent complaints against the management of Chief Commissioners Donald A. Smith (1870-1874) and James A. Grahame (1874-1884), but at least they had been fur-trade officers who had risen in the ranks, understood the problems of the fur trade, and could command the confidence of their fellow officers. However, in 1884 Grahame was replaced by Joseph Wrigley, a former president of the Huddersfield Chamber of Commerce, who was to manage the trade of the settling districts "on proper commercial principles."[10] Wrigley struggled against hard times, competition, low prices, and the indifferent support of the fur-trade officers, until, in 1891, he retired, a victim to the continued poor results in terms of dividends. For his successor, the London directors chose C. C. Chipman, a former secretary to Sir Charles Tupper.

Appointed in a time of crisis, Chipman's main concern was retrenchment and the reorganization of the trading structure. Soon officers were complaining of his petty economics, the despotic tone of his instructions or commands, and the cruel treatment meted out to veteran officers who, it was charged, were being goaded into resigning to replace them with low-salaried clerks. The chief commissioner continued his way, reducing working expenses by £10,000 a year and lowering the expenses of management by bringing many posts under the direct control of Winnipeg. But though the Hudson's Bay Company withdrew from some sections, there also were drives to expand trade into previously neglected corners, for example in the Stikine, Skeena, and Cassiar districts, at the same time

(1893) as other posts in the Porcupine River district – Rampart House and La Pierre House – were being closed. So fierce was the attempt to blanket every section of the fur country that frequently agents from two districts found themselves competing with one another.

The period of Chipman's commissionership also saw the completion of a long campaign to reduce the special status and position of the fur-trade officers under the historic Deed Poll, which made the officers partners rather than employees, sharing 40 per cent of the profits of the fur trade. The system, instituted in 1821, was unsuited to the new conditions of operations as the H.B.C. began to move into selling real estate and ordinary shop trading, and as large capital investments and tight control and supervision became essential if the fur trade was to survive the widespread competition and dangerously low prices. Nor was the Deed Poll satisfactory from the standpoint of the traders, for it did not produce sufficiently large or dependable incomes. In 1865 it had been necessary to guarantee to the officers for the five succeeding years a minimum of £275 per chief trader's unit share, or £550 for the higher grade of chief factor.

The new Deed Poll of 1871, which bound the officers to engage in any type of operations undertaken by the Hudson's Bay Company, also instituted five levels of officers to share in the profits pool, and increased the company's control over appointments, retirements, and pensions. These last were a special subject of concern. In 1871-72, after bitter negotiations, the officers accepted £107,000 as full settlement of their retirement interests to date, and a new pension fund was set up under the Deed Poll of 1871. Several of the officers thus were able to quit the H.B.C., while those who remained were able to draw on their credits during the lean years that followed. For after the five-year guarantee expired, a small loss was incurred on outfit 1875 (i.e., on the operations for the year 1875-76) and the officers received no pay whatever. When the results of outfit 1876 were similar, the H.B.C., to keep up the officers' morale, offered £100 per share, finding the money from the officers' new pension fund. Outfit 1877 was very little better; the officers' entitlements would have amounted to only £32 per share. The H.B.C. therefore agreed to pay the officers a minimum of £150 per share for the five outfits of 1877-1881 inclusive. The agreement continued in succeeding years, but was increased to £200 per share in 1886. Finally, in 1893, when the results for outfit 1891 had been received, the company abolished the profit-sharing system once and for all in favour of a straight salary. Bookkeeping and recording procedures were greatly simplified by ending the necessity to keep separate accounts for every year's trade, or to differentiate between the fur trade and other business operations. By 1895 the fur-trade accounts disappeared from the annual report, and the commissioned officers, a declining group, were merely salaried employees under the firm control of the London headquarters and the Winnipeg-based commissioner. Between 1899 and 1908, through the good offices of the governor, Lord Strathcona (the former Donald A. Smith), considerable sums from land profits were earmarked as a provident fund to provide pensions not merely for forty or fifty commissioned officers but for the more than seven hundred full-time Hudson's Bay Company employees in Britain and Canada. The historic councils of the fur-trade officers – which had been convoked only intermittently after 1870, and then attended only fitfully – were terminated in 1887 with a meeting at the Queen's Hotel, in Winnipeg.[11] For a few years longer commissions continued to be issued – the last in 1905 – to employees whose term of service began before 1870. But another historic link with the Hudson's Bay Company's past was severed with the abolition of the Deed Poll, and something of the glamour of being a senior employee of the Hudson's Bay Company ended.

By 1896 the H.B.C. had achieved an amazing revolution of its corporate structure, administrative system, and operations. In 1870 it had been the effective ruler of most of the new lands acquired by Canada, and Canadian authority could be exercised only with the support and consent of the fur-trade baronage. Now its officers were little more than salaried employees, small cogs in a larger machine, and the H.B.C. much like any other commercial organization operating under the authority of Canada. Within the settled and settling districts of the Dominion, its operations fell into the common mould – landowner and operator of general stores and large department stores, whose fur-buying departments were reduced to a secondary position. Only in the northern forests did something of the old system and authority survive. Though some posts had been abandoned because of changing supply routes or in the face of too-strong competition, across the heartland of the fur-trading kingdom, from Labrador to Peel River, the Hudson's Bay Company continued its fur-trading and transportation activities, fighting competition by its superior resources, efficient management, reformed organization, and, especially, by the skills of its servants and the long-ingrained loyalties of its native clients.

II

When Canada gained the new territories, Christian missionaries were working in much the same areas as the fur trade, though in far smaller numbers. However, as more missionaries took up stations their influence rapidly increased. Two of the four denominations active in the Middle North before 1870 – the Presbyterians and Methodists – were sustained by co-religionists in the Province of Canada. The Presbyterians, whose work was primarily with families that had moved to the region, were represented by congregations at Red River, Prince Albert, and in British Columbia. The Methodists, in contrast, were interested mainly in native missions, continuing an early association that began in Upper Canada, moved to the country north of the upper Great Lakes in the 1830's, and entered the Northwest in 1840 in association with the British Wesleyan Methodist Society. Though the Reverend James Evans, the mission superintendent, perfected his system of Cree syllabic script while serving at Norway House, the joint program soon collapsed. The work was taken over completely in 1854 by the Canada Conference, which reorganized the missions, expanded the work, and shifted the emphasis to the region east and south of Fort Edmonton.

More widely extended than these were the operations of the Roman Catholic and Anglican missions, backed in large measure by powerful religious societies in France and England. The Roman Catholic mission was started at Red River in 1818 by regular clergy from Lower Canada, but after 1841 members of the Oblates of Mary Immaculate (O.M.I.), a powerful French religious order, began to predominate. Anglican work, which was also started at Red River in 1820, was supported by a variety of evangelical organizations in Britain, notably the Church Missionary Society. From 1822 onward, the society supplied clergy and funds for the North-West America Mission, and in 1856 it inaugurated the North Pacific Mission by sending out William Duncan. Private gifts made it possible to endow two bishoprics, Rupert's Land (1849) and Columbia (1859), whose incumbents directed operations in the two sees. Roman Catholic activities were also organized along hierarchical lines, beginning with prefectures and apostolic vicariates headed by bishops appointed to sees *in partibus infidelium*, and eventually advancing to regular bishoprics as the country became more settled. The Roman Catholic jurisdictions by 1870 included the bishoprics of St Boniface (1851) and Vancouver's Island (1847), and the apostolic vicariates of Athabaska-Mackenzie and British Columbia.*

Fierce denominational rivalries were the order of the day in this early period, and sometimes led to feverish rushes to open new districts, like the race down the Mackenzie in 1858-59 between Archdeacon James Hunter of Rupert's Land and Father Henri Grollier, O.M.I. The Roman Catholics were better equipped for this competition – apart from the presumed ad-

---

* Before 1902 "Athabasca" was the spelling followed by the Hudson's Bay Company, the Anglican missions, and the government, while others, notably the Roman Catholic missions, employed "Athabaska." In 1902 "Athabaska" was made the official spelling by decision of the Geographic Board of Canada, but this was reversed in 1948 and the spelling returned to "Athabasca." This is the form followed here, except in the case of the vicariate.

vantage the Anglicans may have enjoyed by virtue of the support of the Hudson's Bay Company's English directorate. Oblate priests outnumbered the Anglican clergymen, and also had the advantage of being aided by lay brothers who performed many necessary tasks and freed the priests for religious duties, and by the Sisters of Charity, or Grey Nuns, a Canadian order that opened convents to meet some of the educational and charitable needs of their districts. The Anglicans could supplement their work to a smaller degree by employing their families and training their most apt pupils to serve as schoolmasters, catechists, or, eventually, ordained ministers. Unlike the Oblates, who were ordained clergy expressly trained for missionary work, some of the Anglican missionaries were laymen, more were clergymen drawn from charges in England, and only a few had been trained specifically for missionary work at the C.M.S. College in England or at St John's College in Red River. As a rule, the Catholic clergy were also more zealous and energetic than their opponents, and were able to devote years to contacting new bands, or to spend forty and even fifty years at a single station. Since they were pledged to poverty, their missions also required far less money or supplies to sustain them than did those of the Protestant churches.

Furthermore, the Roman Catholics' approach to the work seemed more likely to bring about successful results. Protestant missionaries envisaged an exacting role for their converts, believing that they had to achieve their own salvation through a lengthy process of private study, reflection, prayer, and inner revelation, culminating in baptism. Roman Catholics, however, conceived of salvation as requiring not only the efforts of the candidate, but priestly intercession as well. Consequently, they placed great stress on the sacerdotal succession and upon the careful selection, training, and ordination of priests. Baptism was not so much a culmination as a necessary preliminary to achieving salvation. Protestant missionaries complained that itinerant priests baptized with undue haste to "stake their claim," but they were not above pursuing the same tactic to protect their interest against encroachments by rival clergy.[12]

The more limited role in which Roman Catholic clergy cast their native adherents, the stress upon religious observances and ceremonies, the colour and pageantry of the ritual, were better suited to the particular situation than were the vaguer concepts of personal revelation and spiritual regeneration taught by the Protestant missionaries. Possibly the Oblates' many advantages in the competition for adherents bore some relationship to the markedly greater readiness of Protestant missionaries to undertake social and economic experiments for the purpose of raising their followers' material, as well as their spiritual and moral, condition.

The arrival of settlers to the prairie lands of the Northwest also transformed the religious life of that region. Pioneer clergy of the period of transition merged the first few white settlers with their existing congregations, and did what they could to ease the shocks of the sudden passing of the age of the buffalo hunter and trapper, and the advent of that of the rancher, homesteader, and townsman. Increasingly, however, religious work became differentiated along the lines of the two societies. As the numbers of white settlers grew, they progressed from a missionary stage of religious activity to one of regular church membership, forming largely self-supporting congregations organized in regular parishes, presbyteries, conferences, or dioceses. At the same time religious work with the native population, now largely segregated on their reserves, continued in the category of missionary operations. It therefore often came under different church divisions and agencies than those that served the remainder of the population. Now that the Indians were largely stopped from their nomadism, mission activities on the reserves tended to fall into regular routines. Churches, chapels, and convents began to be built in considerable numbers. Furthermore, the missions also operated government-subsidized schools and hospitals – activities that in the other society were by this time largely secular in character and in some degree subject to local control – further segregating the native people from the wider community.

In the northern forests, however, missionaries continued in their earlier role, attempting to supply the temporal wants as well as the spiritual needs of nomadic native bands. As the presence of the Dominion government began to be felt, the missionary found himself serving as an intermediary between the primitive population and the new authority. Also, a gradual social and cultural transformation was under way, even in these remote districts, and the missionary had to assume the main responsibility for helping the Indian achieve his proper place in a world that was changing around him.

For the missions, the years before 1870 had been a time of beginnings in the northern forest belt; after 1870 came a period of consolidation, expansion, and competition. The Canada-based Presbyterian and Methodist churches, preoccupied with their existing congregations and wracked by internal dissensions, could play only a relatively minor role in the Middle North. Not until their various sects had been united to form two strong churches were the Presbyterians and Methodists able to set their missionary activities on a proper footing, under the management of superintendents and boards. Even then their efforts were mainly centred on the prairies and the coast of British Columbia, districts where the native populations were sedentary from age-long practice, or had become divorced from nomadism by the economic, social, and administrative changes since 1870. Furthermore, traditions of congregational autonomy, self-supporting congregations, and the rotation of ministers among churches hampered these denominations from mounting the expensive, long-term campaigns required to achieve successful results among the native populations of the northern woodlands. Consequently, this region was largely pre-empted by the Catholic and Anglican churches, except where the Methodists had previously established themselves.

The episcopal, hierarchical structure of the Roman Catholic and Anglican churches, in fact, played a large part in their success in this field. The heads of their missions were bishops of international religious communities, who could place their problems before the highest councils of their faiths and appeal for assistance to the faithful of many lands. They could thereby secure more support beyond what was available from the communicants of the Canadian churches to aid missionary efforts in the more remote parts of the country. Moreover, the principal means of the Roman Catholic and Anglican churches for expanding the work was through forming new dioceses headed by bishops. Such a step had a way of giving new impetus and greater effectiveness to their missionary efforts, so the gradual enlargement of the episcopates was more than a formality.

In 1870 there had been only two Anglican sees in the entire west: Rupert's Land, under Bishop Robert Machray (1865-1904), extending from James Bay to beyond the Mackenzie delta, and Columbia, under Bishop George Hills (1859-1892), embracing the area of British Columbia. In 1872 the part of Rupert's Land surrounding James and Hudson bays was erected into the diocese of Moosonee. In 1874 the district drained by the Saskatchewan rivers was established as the diocese of Saskatchewan, and the immense territory between Methye Portage and Alaska as the bishopric of Athabasca. Ten years later Athabasca was again divided, the portion south of 60° retaining that name, and the remote northern portion becoming the new diocese of Mackenzie River. Later still, in 1891, when it became apparent that the work in the Yukon country was difficult to regulate or expand, the diocese of Selkirk (later named Yukon) was split off from Mackenzie River. In 1902 Moosonee was also divided, the territory west of James Bay becoming the diocese of Keewatin. Farther south, Algoma had been carved from the archdiocese of Toronto in 1873. Finally, Columbia also was divided in 1879, the northern part of British Columbia becoming the diocese of Caledonia.

The Roman Catholic church followed the same process at a somewhat slower pace. The diocese of St Boniface was decentralized by setting up apostolic vicariates of Athabaska-Mackenzie in 1862, and of British Columbia in 1863. In 1871 the prairies west of Manitoba became the bishopric of St Albert, from which the apostolic vicariate of Saskatchewan was erected in 1891. The northern apostolic vicariate of Athabaska-Mackenzie was divided in 1901 into two vicariates, Athabaska in the south and Mackenzie in the north. Finally, in 1908, the apostolic prefecture of Yukon was created, embracing Yukon Territory and British Columbia north of 54°. This does not cover all the complexities of the Roman Catholic hierarchical system. Many bishops, bearing titles of distant places in partibus, also served apprenticeships as coadjutors to other bishops before becoming responsible for the direction of bishoprics or vicariates in their own right.

For the Church of England, in particular, the establishment of a new diocese was a great impetus to expand and enlarge its operations. Since an endowment fund (usually £10,000) had to be raised to cover the bishop's salary and other basic fixed costs, this became the first task of the new bishop, and the occasion for as much publicity and support as could be mustered. Religious foundations and societies or private benefactors were canvassed, the public was appealed to through the religious press, and the bishop or one of his missionaries undertook deputation work – a round of visits, addresses, and meetings with church groups. Their skill in this all-important task varied. At one extreme was W. C. Bompas, first bishop of each of Athabasca, Mackenzie River, and Selkirk, too diffident and retiring to undertake a task that would take him back into sophisticated society, and so, as a result, was continually hampered in the field by financial difficulties. Bishop John Horden of Moosonee, by contrast, was quite successful in the role of "mitred mendicant." Bishop John McLean of Saskatchewan ("Saskatchewan Jack") ranked as a veritable marvel; of his deputation in England, one who had to follow him commented, "Before him was the Garden of Eden and behind him a howling wilderness."[13]

The English church was the mainstay of the fund-raising activities, though efforts were made to get the Canadian church to lend greater support. In 1872 the Archbishop of Canterbury proclaimed an annual Day of Intercession for Foreign Missions. The Church Missionary Society, besides contributing a large part of the original endowment, continued to support many of the missionaries. As late as 1895 it was supporting forty-nine clergymen, five laymen, and eleven ordained Indians in its two Canadian mission fields at a cost of £18,000. Its aid, however, was intended only for work among the native population, and dioceses were informed they must find other means for carrying on among the newly settled European communities. The society also disclaimed any responsibility for financing Indian congregations, except as a last resort.[14] Other Anglican societies and religious foundations assisted missionary, educational, and other work among pioneer white settlers, though here again special organizations had to be devised to serve the religious needs of the impoverished and scattered communicants.

The deputation work and other publicity was a principal means for securing regular and continuing material assistance essential for the missionary work in northern Canada, and for recruiting clergy, missionaries-in-training, lay readers, catechists, schoolmasters, farmers, and artisans to staff the operation. It produced the money to build churches and mission houses, purchase Bibles and prayer books, print translations, and collect and forward useful parcels of clothing, drugs, and books for the missionaries and their congregations. More personnel were brought in to help with the work of itinerating, to staff permanent stations and schools, and to open new churches. The clergy of the new diocese were organized into a synod (which also included prominent laymen) to discuss past work, present needs, and future plans. One clergyman could be assigned to serve as diocesan secretary, and an archdeacon or two might be appointed to supervise the work in a remote portion of the diocese. Thus the establishment of the new diocese automatically placed the operation under more effective local oversight and control, while the greater means permitted the work to move into activities like hospitals, training colleges, industrial farms, gardens, ranches, lumber mills, and steamboats to make the work more efficient.

The Roman Catholic effort was not quite so dependent on the erection of new dioceses, for it was based mainly on the sustained support of powerful missionary organizations, pre-eminent among them being the Oblates of Mary Immaculate, reinforced by the Grey Nuns and other orders of teaching sisters, with convents and orphanages at Ile à la Crosse (1860), Lac la Biche (1862), St Albert (1863), Fort Providence (1867), Fort Chipewyan (1874), Prince Albert (1883), Edmonton (1888), and Lesser Slave Lake (1894). The considerable number of lay brothers – twenty-nine men in Athabaska-Mackenzie alone (1890) – laboured merely for their keep, with the same devotion as the missionaries, as hunters and fishermen, farmers, lumbermen, builders, boatmen, and dog-team drivers. The vicariate thus could build chapels and churches at little expense, inaugurate its own system of water transport, and cultivate large farms to provision the northern missions and convents.

Staffing was easier for the Roman Catholic bishops, since missionary and teaching orders provided so much of their personnel, and supplied replacements as needed. Among the Anglicans, however, recruiting and retaining the services of almost every single worker in the missions was the bishops' personal concern. Hence their expressed preference for Canadian-born agents, whom they found better suited to the conditions of the work and likelier to stay in the field. Bishop Bompas was not alone in his concern lest the Church Missionary Society discriminate against Canadian personnel, and in his wish to see great native participation in the work:

> It seems desired to make a marked distinction between Native & European Missionaries. But I hold that we are all of us now *Canadians* here & there-

fore none of us properly Europeans; nor can the Mission Agents properly be termed Natives though they may have mixture of Indian with European blood in their ancestry. I believe it was agreed some time since in this country that English & Country born Missionaries should stand pari passu & that as far as possible we should do away with distinctions of race.[15]

Small wonder, in view of the need. When Bompas became Bishop of Athabasca in 1874, he had five missions for a region as large as western Europe, only three of which (Forts Chipewyan, Simpson, and McPherson) were conducted by ordained clergy, the other two (Fort Norman and Rampart House) being under schoolmasters and catechists. By dint of strenuous efforts he added two new establishments at Fort Vermilion and Fort Dunvegan in the Peace River district, and to represent the Church of England on Great Slave Lake stationed a minister at Fort Rae and a schoolteacher at Hay River. The bishop himself frequently had to fill in at threatened centres or for clergy on leave. In the more restricted diocese of Mackenzie River he was able to concentrate exclusively upon the Mackenzie and Yukon sectors, so that by the end of the eighties his staff north of 60° included eight clergy and four schoolmasters and catechists, operating ten missions. By contrast, the Roman Catholic personnel of the same region at that date comprised twelve Oblates, seven Grey Nuns, and thirteen lay brothers, operating eighteen missions and stations. Little wonder that in the competition waged in this portion of the North, the victory should go in the main to the Roman Catholics.

The competition between the churches, expressed in endless itinerations between posts and camps, races to steal marches on one another, hasty baptisms to establish claims over Indians and Eskimos, and denigrating the motives and characters of their rivals, were features of the religious picture in much of northern Canada in the final third of the nineteenth century. No doubt competition speeded up and increased the facilities provided for the inhabitants, but it also created divisions within bands, undermined established lines of authority, and sometimes encouraged appeals to unworthy motives that heaped discredit upon the work of organized religion.

In the east the positions of the two churches had become fairly stabilized by 1870. The Anglicans, entrenched along the coasts of Hudson and James bays, maintained a series of establishments at inland points to "guard the frontier from Roman Catholic encroachment,"[16] and served inland nomadic bands like the Naskapi of Labrador by occasional visits to the remote posts at which they traded. In Ungava, a notable mission to the Eskimos, begun in 1859, was carried on with great success by the Reverend E. J. Peck, who commenced at Little Whale River in 1876. Bishop Horden of Moosonee was equally successful at his seat of Moose Factory and the stations to the west, principally because of his skill in raising funds, his effective use of native-born clergy (notably Archdeacon Thomas Vincent and the Reverend John Sanders) trained at St John's College, Winnipeg, or at his own school in Moose Factory, his promotion of translations of texts into Cree and Eskimo, and the active support of the Hudson's Bay Company agents in the area. Competing Roman Catholic missionaries had to make their way north from the St Lawrence and Ottawa. Occasionally they sallied as far as the bay itself, though not until 1892 did they open a permanent mission there. The Montagnais of interior Labrador were their converts, however, through the labours of missionaries stationed along the North Shore.

East of Lake Winnipeg and north of the North Saskatchewan River, denominational rivalries followed the lines established earlier by the missionaries from Red River or from Canada. Important Anglican establishments in several main centres between Lake Superior and Lake Winnipeg and along the Saskatchewan River were staffed in considerable measure by locally trained clergy from Red River or from Emmanuel College, which Bishop McLean established in 1883 at Prince Albert. The removal of Indians from York Factory to Split Lake in the 1890's because of the changed fur-trade pattern, caused an Anglican mission to be opened there to serve them. Here, too, were found important Methodist missions, like those of Berens River (directed by the prolific writer the Reverend E. R. Young), Norway House, and Oxford House north of Lake Winnipeg, and in the Saddle Lake district along the North Saskatchewan, where the outstanding Indian missionary, the Reverend H. B. Steinhauer, worked. The Oblates had stations of their own in nearly all the districts from Lake Superior to St Albert, and were unopposed at Ile à la Crosse and other fur-trade centres of the little-travelled territory stretching north to Lake Athabasca.

The main centre of missionary rivalries was in the Arctic watershed of the Athabasca, Peace, Slave, and Mackenzie rivers. Operations had only been commenced in 1858 along the Mackenzie River proper, but by the mid-sixties both churches were strongly entrenched along the waterway and were struggling to gain the ascendancy in remote sections. In the next thirty years, the Anglicans strengthened and extended their work in this northwesternmost part of Canada, thanks in large measure to the successful ministry of the Reverend Robert McDonald, who continued to serve the Kutchin, Loucheux, or Tukudh at Fort Yukon, Rampart House, and Fort McPherson for more than forty years after 1862. Oblate missionaries from Fort Good Hope passed through to Fort Yukon in 1862-63 and again in 1872, but their projected Alaska mission, west of McDonald's mission to the Tukudh, came to naught. After six years of indifferent success at Fort McPherson, the Oblates withdrew, taking their Loucheux converts with them to a new community along the Mackenzie at Arctic Red River, which replaced Fort Good Hope as their "farthest north" mission (1896).

Neither church had much success with the Eskimos of the western Arctic until the Reverend I. O. Stringer, a Canadian from Wycliffe College, Toronto, went to live and work among them in 1894.

Along the Mackenzie and Liard rivers and Great Slave Lake, the Anglicans failed to repeat their successes among the Loucheux and Eskimos. Despite vigorous efforts by Bishops Bompas and W. D. Reeve of Mackenzie River, the few, mostly short-term Anglican workers could not match in numbers or in permanence the Oblate missionaries, who gradually won control over the Mackenzie River settlements. The Anglicans only maintained themselves at Fort Simpson (the Anglican episcopal seat where an Oblate mission was opened after 1894), and at Hay River, where the school and mission were opened in 1892 under the Reverend T. J. Marsh. The Indian religious census for 1896 reported 3,520 Roman Catholic to 830 Anglican Indians in the Mackenzie, Great Slave, and Liard districts.

The Church of England was even less successful with the Indian and Métis populations of the Athabasca district, although Bishop Bompas and his successor in Athabasca, Bishop R. Young, tried to establish strong positions at Fort Chipewyan and in the Peace River district. Incidentally, seventeen years before Frederick Jackson Turner enunciated his frontier hypothesis, Bompas reported an interesting example of advancing frontiers in this district:

> In Peace River it is singular to observe that there is already an incoming population removing from the Sascachewan plains who are thrust westward by the old inhabitants of Manitoba migrating to the plains, these being in their turn displaced by immigrants from Canada and elsewhere. Thus the several parts of the country are likely gradually to fill up and I think the Ecclesiastical provision already made is intended in God's providence to meet coming changes.[17]

In 1876 and 1878 Bompas opened two missions with an agricultural emphasis, both manned by Canadians, at Fort Vermilion and Fort Dunvegan. Bishop Young transferred his seat to Fort Vermilion and opened new missions in the Lesser Slave district, while the Oblates had major establishments (nearly all including convents) at Fort Chipewyan, Fort Vermilion, Lesser Slave Lake Settlement, and Lac la Biche, in addition to their numerous smaller missions and outposts. In this district, the 1896 census listed only 194 Anglican Indians against 3,056 Catholic Indians.

In British Columbia, the Roman Catholics were almost completely successful among the Indians of the interior, from the Kootenays to the upper Skeena and Fraser (where the prolific writer and scholar, the Reverend A. G. Morice, laboured for many years). The Church of England, plus a powerful Methodist incursion, dominated the North Pacific coast and enjoyed some success in expanding inland in central and northern British Columbia. Notwithstanding the disruption of the Anglican work occasioned by Duncan's secession from the Church of England and his removal to Alaska, the Protestants continued to monopolize the North-West Coast Agency. The Anglican work continued to centre among the coast settlements, while Bishop William Ridley of Caledonia, Duncan's principal adversary, pushed the work inland to Hazelton and other centres in the upper Skeena country. The Methodist entrance into the North Pacific in 1873 was led by the dynamic, emotionalist spellbinder, the Reverend Thomas Crosby, who developed an entire missionary district within ten years. Centred at Port Simpson, it comprised ten different missions, operated by three ordained ministers and six native assistants, and had sixteen preaching points. Copying Duncan's model, Crosby organized new villages complete with hospitals and native-owned saw mills and other industries at Port Simpson and Bella Bella. The Methodist schools received government aid on the basis of an enrolment of 1,020 pupils attending an industrial school for boys and six day schools.

For the missionary in this period of active proselytization, life was exceptionally difficult, entailing travelling under most trying conditions and constant living among trading posts and Indian bands that undermined the missionaries' physical and mental health. There were the hardships of spending long periods in distant, unknown places and separation from relatives and friends. Bishop Lofthouse of Keewatin reported that when his daughter was born, "there was neither doctor nor nurse to be had, the missionary as usual being both," and later how "the parting from an only child, as in our case, constituted one of the greatest trials of our missionary life."[18] Missionary wives faced added frustrations – cooking for visitors who appeared at all hours of day and night, cleaning and combing children, training Indian girls as domestics, doing without the many comforts of civilization, helping as teachers, nurses, and at Sunday services, and worrying about their own and their families' health and future. Few occupations were more demanding: the missionary had to be physician, teacher, judge, social worker, preacher, translator, linguist, biblical scholar, anthropologist, public lecturer, fund-raiser, and trainer of other clergy. Not a few succumbed to drowning, freezing, disease, hunger, and murder, and many were worn out before their time. Yet, though many, unable to withstand these ordeals, left the service, the true missionary found the rewards far in excess of the hardships and risks.

Associated with the work of spiritual and moral conversion of the native population and of particular significance for the future development of the region was the task of "civilizing" them, of improving their material conditions so they might enjoy what the missionaries felt to be more meaningful lives, and be more easily dealt with. As Bompas wrote, "in these desolate wilds the gospel must be known by its fruits & that by teaching the Indians to cultivate their land we may win their hearts to seek God's grace for their souls also to produce fruits of righteousness. A Missionary here ought to be either a school teacher, a farmer or a doctor, or else endeavor to combine all three with the preaching of the gospel."[19]

The primary goal of ensuring the physical survival of the Indian inhabitants inspired missionaries to give as much medical aid and relief as their limited means permitted. Frequently they had to treat ailing Indians or vaccinate entire bands against smallpox, so practical medicine became an increasingly important part of the missionary's training. Many missions included facilities for medical treatment, and sometimes a hospital, as at Kincolith and Metlakatla in the North-West Coast Agency, a region of heavy rainfall where the mortality rate from tuberculosis and associated diseases was extremely high.

Schools were an integral part of the missionary task of religious instruction, and a first component of a permanent mission. Government grants for Indian schools were a commitment under the Indian treaties, and missionaries working beyond the treaty limits began to apply for the same aid. The Department of Indian Affairs apparently made no difficulties about offering them the same grants – typically from $150 to $300 a year for day schools and $72 per pupil per annum for residential schools. As early as 1880 aid was being extended to the Grey Nuns' schools at Forts Chipewyan and Providence, then outside treaty, and the number of assisted schools grew steadily until, by 1896, the list also included the principal mission centres of the Mackenzie waterway, along the Hudson and James bay coasts, and even in the remote Yukon district. A few of the subsidized schools were residential and industrial schools, following the tendency, as soon as means permitted, of adopting this mode of operation. In their health, relief, and educational activities, the northern missions were moving into the welfare field as allies and precursors of the federal government's Department of Indians Affairs. Equally, by financing some of these activities, the government was underwriting the work of the churches in the welfare field, and sustaining their position in relation to the Indians and vis-à-vis rival denominations as well.

Many missionaries resembled William Duncan in seeing their goal as assisting the native to attain an improving standard of living and greater security from want as a necessary means of making him a better Christian. Bishop Bompas, who acknowledged his indebtedness to Duncan, instituted a program of mission farms in the Peace River district, to which he sent workers with farming experience in Canada and arranged for farm machinery, milling equipment, and livestock to be imported there. At Fort Vermilion he placed E. P. J. Lawrence as schoolmaster, farm instructor, and eventually, farm agent, to assist the Reverend A. C. Garrioch, while at Fort Dunvegan George Garrioch took charge of a mission farm. The Reverend J. Gough Brick, who went to Fort Dunvegan in 1880, soon returned to eastern Canada, and raised enough money to bring back a railway carload of machinery. This he transported from Calgary to a new site along the Peace River – Shaftesbury Settlement, near the modern town of Peace River – there to commence the agricultural conquest of that district, though not by, or for, the native people. A more pertinent and successful approach to the problems was that of the Reverend H. B. Steinhauer, the Methodist missionary at Whitefish Lake, who encouraged each native family to develop a small farm from which it could live in relative comfort, and induced the men to assume the unaccustomed roles of cultivators and labourers.

The many-sided, industrial enterprise of Metlakatla was feasible only in a physical and human setting like that of the North Pacific coast. There it was copied by similar experiments in organizing village communities, building homes, streets, and public buildings, and establishing industries. Other Anglican and Methodist missionaries followed suit until it seemed that social engineering and developmental programs, rather than the saving of souls, were becoming the main goals of missionary endeavours. This was brought home forcibly to the Reverend James Woodsworth, superintendent of missions for the Methodist Church, when he visited Port Simpson in 1894 and heard Indian appeals for a preacher "who would build them a cannery, or a steamboat, or a sawmill, or do something else to help them along material lines."[20]

The missionary had other effects upon the development of the Canadian North, particularly by transmitting a knowledge of the region and its people to the outside world. The early missionary was something of an explorer, in a position to report on geographical features of little-known country, as Father E. Petitot did by virtue of his trips about Great Slave Lake, between Great Slave and Great Bear lakes (many of the lakes in this area owe their names to him), and from Great Bear Lake and Fort Good Hope north to the Arctic coast. Without instruments, he still was able to fill in many of the blank spaces on Franklin's map of the region by reckoning his position as he moved about in his travels.[21] Again, since the success of missionary labours depended on a mastery of Indian languages and a correct understanding of Indian psychology and social anthropology, missionaries made serious attempts to master these sciences. Great efforts were devoted to translating the scriptures, prayer books, and other sacred writings into many native tongues. In setting these languages into writing (an extremely important step in the acculturation of the Indian), most missionaries adopted the simple alphabet the Reverend James Evans had devised at Norway

House. Missionaries also recorded the customs of vanishing native societies and made important linguistic, ethnological, and anthropological studies. Sometimes their work reflected the writer's lack of training in these sciences, the primitive conditions under which he had to work, and, occasionally, his over-active imagination in reading into Indian ways correlations with Chinese, Hebrew, or primitive Christian antecedents. But, making due allowances, the missionaries produced an extremely important contribution to the dissemination of scientific knowledge of northern Canada.

More important still was their role in publicizing their work and the needs of the Canadian North in Europe, eastern Canada, and the United States. Among the duties of Anglican missionaries – and those of other denominations as well – were "To keep a journal of his proceedings and to forward the Church Missionary Society, from time to time, . . . extracts from it containing matters of interest or importance."[22] They prepared reports for religious journals, wrote pamphlets and books about their work, and frequently addressed influential church groups and public bodies on the characteristics of the country and its people. The reportorial side of the missionary endeavour advertised the potentialities of the region and heightened the public's awareness of the natural resources and possibilities for settlement in the region. In particular, the fantastic wealth of forest and sea along the North Pacific coast and the arable soils of the Peace River district were held out as inducements for would-be settlement and were important factors in encouraging the occupation of these regions by settlers from eastern Canada and Europe. In the case of the Reverend J. G. Brick, at least, the missionary impulse even seems to have been eclipsed by the urge to become an agricultural pioneer, like so many of those missionaries, half a century before, who had picked their way through the mountains to Oregon as the advance wave of an earlier manifest destiny.

CHAPTER 4

The Dominion Government Moves into the Middle North

1870 – 1896

The completion of the Canadian Pacific Railway ended a first great phase of Canadian expansion, rounding out the political extension of the Dominion from sea to sea. The immediate task became to develop the rich farmlands and coal fields of the prairie region as well as the forests and fertile valleys of the Pacific slope. In the meantime the forested lands farther north could remain as they were – the habitats of nomadic Indian bands following their generations-long patterns of precarious survival, and being directed safely (as far as the white men were concerned) by missionaries and traders bringing them a knowledge of the benefits of the white man's goods and economic system, the virtues of his morality, and the consolations of his religion. Some day, no doubt, the forested lands would attract the attentions of lumbermen, farmers, and miners. In 1873 Capt W. F. Butler had predicted that "It will yet be found that there are ten acres of fertile land lying *north* of the North Saskatchewan for every acre lying south of it."[1] But surely all that lay far in the future; the present frontiers offered opportunities and challenges enough to engage the energies of Canadians for generations to come.

Still, a few Canadians harkened back to that earlier Northwest – the forested belt beyond the western prairie and parkland. One such man was John C. Schultz, the *bête noir* of the Métis and Hudson's Bay Company government of Assiniboia in the troubled years before the transfer of Rupert's Land. The years had not dealt very kindly with him. By 1888, at the comparatively early age of forty-eight, Schultz was plagued by illnesses and drained by pernicious anaemia.[2] But he retained the same pioneering urge that had drawn him to Red River in 1860 as a young man of twenty. On March 27, 1888, he rose from his place in the Canadian Senate – to which he had been called in 1882 after eleven years as an M.P. for Manitoba – to suggest that the time was opportune for investigating the resources of the lands north of the Fertile Belt between Hudson Bay and the Rocky

Mountains. A Senate committee of the previous year had heard much favourable testimony concerning the actual and potential food-producing qualities of the regions beyond the North Saskatchewan River. In the light of the wonderful progress of Manitoba since 1870, was it not desirable to evaluate the resources of the territories farther north and consider possible governmental policies of development and control?

Despite some criticisms that such an investigation was premature, Schultz received his committee "to inquire as to the value of that part of the Dominion lying north of the Saskatchewan watershed, east of the Rocky Mountains and west of the Hudson Bay, comprising the Great Mackenzie Basin – its extent of navigable rivers, lakes and sea coast, of agricultural and pastoral lands, its fisheries, forests and mines."[3] Over the next two months, the committee amassed a considerable volume of testimony from many witnesses – officers of the agricultural, meteorological, and geological branches of the federal government, Anglican and Roman Catholic missionaries, Hudson's Bay Company officers, businessmen of Prince Albert and Edmonton, and a student or two of the Northwest, like the celebrated J. W. Taylor of Winnipeg. To these, as well as to a large number of correspondents inside the region, the committee addressed a series of ninety questions on navigation and communications, resources of arable or pastoral land, forests, minerals, fish and game, and native conditions and problems. Under the beneficent influence of such testimony, Senator Schultz's health and strength revived, as did his political fortunes, for soon he was appointed lieutenant-governor of Manitoba and of the District of Keewatin.

The final report of the Senate Committee on the Great Mackenzie Basin produced many enthusiastic predictions that were to echo in publicity releases during the next forty years. It drew attention to the extent of navigable waterways afforded by the Hudson Bay and Arctic coasts, by the Athabasca, Peace, Slave, and Mackenzie rivers and the connecting lakes. It estimated there were 860,000 square miles of pastoral land and 316,000 square miles on which wheat could be grown. The Peace River country, in particular, was singled out for much favourable comment. The report referred to the wildlife resources of fish, marine animals, and fur-bearing species, observing that " the region in question is the last great fur preserve of the world, . . . all the finer furs of commerce being found there, and the sales in London yearly amounting to several millions of dollars."[4] It spoke enthusiastically about the potential mineral wealth – a 150,000-square-mile auriferous region in the headwaters of the Peace, Liard, and Peel rivers, deposits of copper, salt, coal, and of petroleum "so extensive as to justify the belief that eventually it will supply the larger part of this continent."[5] In a mood of unparalleled optimism, the report even concluded that "the capabilities of this extent of country in our own continent exceeds in extent of navigation, area of arable and pastoral lands, valuable fresh water fisheries, forests and mines and in capacity to support population" a comparable extent of Europe, embracing the Scandinavian countries, Germany, and Austria, as well as parts of Britain, France, and Russia.[6]

But along with such optimism went the thought that some extension of governmental authority over the region was necessary to safeguard the national interest. The report suggested that efforts should be made to raise a revenue from the fur trade and from the American whaling ships – with the added purpose of regulating the catches and protecting the resources from extinction. It is also proposed a Crown reserve over the petroleum beds in a 40,000-square-mile area bounded by the Peace and Athabasca rivers, lest a property of incalculable value be lost to the nation:

> The evidence submitted to your Committee points to the existence in the Athabasca and Mackenzie Valleys of the most extensive petroleum field in America, if not in the world. The uses of petroleum and consequently the demand for it by all nations are increasing at such a rapid ratio, that it is probable this great petroleum field will assume an enormous value in the near future and will rank among the chief assets comprised in the Crown domain of the Dominion.[7]

The report also expressed the desire for early mapping and sounding of the Arctic coastline and the western outlets of the Mackenzie River to find the channel from the Arctic Ocean to the lower Mackenzie that would best render that region accessible by the sea from Canada's Pacific coast ports.

The report was acclaimed by politicians and friendly newspapers in Canada and Britain. While the committee was sitting, London papers were commenting on the testimonies as indicating Canada's potentialities, and in Toronto, the *Daily Mail* urged that another committee be appointed to study ways of turning the wealth of the region to account. To outward appearances, however, the committee was an exercise in propaganda that acquired some plausibility from the speed with which earlier pessimistic views about the prairie west were being overturned. Still, it did inspire the Dominion government to undertake further investigations, and numerous railway promoters to hasten to secure charters for possible railways to or into the area. The report remained a valuable source of information about the country for many years to come. And, after all, it was not all that premature. In just ten years a city would be rising far to the north near the 64th parallel beside an obscure river whose name was anglicized as Klondike; within fifteen years civilization would be preparing to spring forward from the prairies adjoining the Canadian Pacific Railway into the lands beyond the North Saskatchewan River, towards the farmlands of the Peace and the rich petroleum deposits of the Athabasca.

As the report indicated, various governmental agencies were devoting considerable attention to these regions, chiefly as explorations that yielded descriptions and maps to assist future development, rather than as any overt exercise of authority or control. Pre-eminent in this role was the Geological Survey of Canada, and to a lesser extent, the Topographical Surveys Division of the Dominion Lands Branch. The topographer's task was to relate the physiographic features of an area by astronomical and ground measurements to previously determined reference points; the geologist's to map the rock formations with a view to ascertaining their relationships with one another. Ideally, the geologist's work could go forward much more rapidly and satisfactorily if an accurate base map of the topography was available, but not enough topographical work was being done by other services – federal or provincial – to keep pace with the Geological Survey's needs. Hence the survey reluctantly began employing topographers for its own map-making needs, eventually in 1909 setting up its own topographical division. The fact that two major government organizations were thus engaged in mapping the northern waterways and reporting on conditions and resources did not produce much duplication of effort, but it did contribute to jealousies and, at times, strained feelings between the personnel of the two agencies.

The expansion of Confederation, which followed close after the appointment in 1869 of an Englishman, Alfred R. C. Selwyn, as successor to the great Sir William Logan, vastly enlarged the Geological Survey's area of operations. In addition to its normal operations, it was immediately called to help with locating the Pacific railway. This entailed exploring the districts tributary to the first-favoured route via the Saskatchewan River and Yellowhead Pass, as well as examining the Peace and Athabasca districts, the Peace River and Pine River passes through the Rockies, and routes across central British Columbia to various harbours. Later, when the present route was adopted, its officers examined the drift-covered prairies, the coal-rich southern passes of the Rockies, and the metal-bearing mountain ranges of southern British Columbia.

Yet, as if this was still not enough, in 1877 the economy-minded Liberal government enacted that the survey should also be responsible for the description and classification of natural and human history phenomena encountered during the work in the field.[8] In the process, the survey's geological museum was transformed into a natural history museum, out of which was to grow the present-day National Museum of Canada. The survey in 1881 was transferred from Montreal to Ottawa, bringing it more directly within the normal framework of the Canadian civil service, and under the nominal oversight of the Department of the Interior. It was felt, too, that the survey would be able to take advantage of, and assist, the work of other branches of government and be better able to advise Parliament and government upon matters affecting Canada's far-flung domain.

Hence the officers of the Geological Survey became naturalists as well as geologists, and their reports came to reflect this trend. For example, the "Report of Progress for 1878-79" contained two admirable sections on the Haida Indians and their vocabulary, the product of G. M. Dawson's survey of the Queen Charlotte Islands in 1878. The museum collection grew apace, and the staff came to include men in fields other than geology, like Dr John Macoun, the self-trained botanist who joined the survey as an assistant director in 1882. Survey officers became the foremost travellers and explorers in Canada's history, traversing the rivers and coasts of the North, collecting specimens, reporting upon the soil, vegetation, fish and game, the living conditions of the native inhabitants, engineering problems and developmental possibilities. All this was in addition to their regular duties of surveying and mapping the geological and physical features of the country, for they usually had to make their own base maps as a first step to evaluating the geology. The winters were spent in Ottawa recording and analyzing their findings in the light of a rapidly progressing science, preparing reports, giving lectures, writing newspaper articles, and contributing to the learned journals. The officers were prominent members of the Royal Society of Canada and other Canadian and international scientific societies and organizations. Through its displays at the great international exhibitions of the period – Philadelphia, 1876; Paris, 1878; London, 1886; Chicago, 1893 – the Geological Survey contributed greatly to making Canada's resources known abroad to powerful capitalists and men in public life, as well as to humble families looking for new homes across the seas.

Much of the excellent work and high prestige of the survey was a reflection of its extremely able personnel, for staff appointments were entirely in the hands of the director. One of these, Robert Bell (1841-1917), has been called "the father of place names in Canada."[9] He had been introduced to the collecting of rocks and plants of the Ottawa valley by his father, a Presbyterian minister and a respected friend of Sir William Logan, and had worked for the Geological Survey during Logan's time. Although a gifted traveller and naturalist, a ready speaker and prolific writer, he lacked both the temperament for accurate painstaking work, and the scientific background in geology of one expressly trained for that purpose. Personally ambitious, he aspired to the directorship both as a personal vindication, and to keep the generalist, exploratory side of the work, in which he excelled, uppermost.

George M. Dawson (1849-1901) was a complete antithesis. Overcoming, or compensating for, a physical deformity that left him hunchbacked and almost a dwarf in stature, he sought out, rather than avoided, hardships, and performed great feats of travel. A son of Principal J. W. Dawson of McGill, he had been a gold medalist of the Royal School of Mines in London, then had made his reputation as geologist and botanist on the boundary survey of the 49th parallel in 1872-75, before entering the Geological Survey. He was thorough, scholarly, intelligent, and polished, and represented Canada creditably at various semi-diplomatic missions in connection with the Alaska boundary and Bering Sea seal fishery questions. His many publications were thoughtful, learned contributions of remarkable versatility and unvarying excellence.

To these two giants were added a succession of very able young men, among them R. G. McConnell, J. B. Tyrrell, A. P. Low, D. B. Dowling, and A. C. Lawson, who were to make great names for themselves as explorers and scientists. Nor should the supporting scientific staff who studied the specimens the exploring geologists brought back and built up the survey's museum collections be overlooked.

Such was the organization that bore the brunt of studying, mapping, describing, and publicizing Canada's northland. Dr. Bell conducted an impressive series of explorations year after year, mainly reconnaissances of an enormous tract of country surrounding Hudson Bay. In the course of these explorations, he mapped virtually every major river, from the Nottaway on the east to the Churchill on the northwest. He pioneered in the maritime exploration of Hudson Bay and the Arctic islands, accompanying Canadian government expeditions as geologist, naturalist, and physician to Hudson Bay in 1884 and 1885, and to southern Baffin Island in 1897. He spent several seasons examining the district between the Ottawa and Lake of the Woods, concentrating especially on Sudbury and the country west of it, and served on the important Royal Commission on the Mineral Resources of Ontario. He worked in western Canada as early as 1873, first on the prairies, then in the Athabasca River region on an examination of the bituminous sand deposits (1882), and, finally, in 1899 he conducted the first exploration of Great Slave Lake for the survey. A truly great explorer, Robert Bell could hardly be excelled in his ability to traverse and map rapidly a little-known territory and assess its potential from the practical point of view.

G. M. Dawson could not equal Bell's record in terms of distances traversed and areas explored, though his contribution to Canadian discovery was as great in its way, and to geological science, greater. Assigned to British Columbia for most of his years with the survey, in his many notable explorations he worked out the intricate geology of the mountain ranges, plateaus, and valleys, and studied the mineralization and economic factors affecting mining development. In 1879 he made an important reconnaissance between the mouth of the Skeena and Edmonton via the Pine River

Pass and the Peace River district. Increasingly, as far as his many administrative and diplomatic duties permitted, he concentrated his attention on the Kootenay and Okanagan mining districts.

One of Dawson's assistants was R. G. McConnell (1857-1942), a young McGill graduate whose long, distinguished career culminated with his appointment as Deputy Minister of Mines in 1914. In 1887 Dawson and McConnell embarked on a most remarkable geological exploration, primarily to examine the situation in the Yukon district. The party entered the region from Wrangell, by way of the Stikine River, down Dease Lake and River to the Liard. Here the explorers separated, McConnell continuing eastward down the Liard while Dawson ascended it to Frances Lake, crossed to Pelly River, ascended the Lewes to its headwaters, and crossed the Chilkoot Pass to reach the Pacific coast on September 20, 1887, after a journey that enclosed a *terra incognita* of some 60,000 square miles.

McConnell's party found its way down the Liard over long, difficult portages around precipitous, narrow canyons within whose confines the river whirled and boiled as it forced its way eastward through the Cordillera. Once this section was overcome, the remainder of the journey to Fort Simpson on the Mackenzie River was simple. After wintering at Fort Providence, McConnell departed down the Mackenzie, across to Fort Yukon in Alaska, up the Yukon to its source, and over Chilkoot Pass, completing a remarkable 4,200-mile journey of valuable geological reconnaissance and survey. Other noteworthy journeys of exploration followed, including an inspection in 1889 of the marshy terrain north of Lesser Slave Lake, bounded by the Peace and Athabasca rivers, principally to examine petroleum occurrences; and another of the Finlay and Omineca rivers, the headwaters of the Peace River west of the Rockies, in 1896.

Thus, year after year the geological map of Canada was being augmented, and remote districts were examined, mapped, and reported on by competent naturalist-scientists. But vast stretches remained unexplored and untravelled. In an address of March 7, 1890, "On Some of the Larger Unexplored Regions of Canada," Dawson listed sixteen such areas on the mainland of Canada, aggregating one million square miles in all.[10] Two of the largest regions were investigated in 1893: the west coast of Hudson Bay north of Fort Churchill, and the Labrador peninsula.

Joseph B. Tyrrell (1858-1957), the future mining executive and amateur historian, had worked mainly on the prairies and the foothills region of Alberta, then along the margin of the Canadian Shield between Lake Winnipeg and Lake Athabasca. In 1893, assisted by his brother, James W. Tyrrell, he explored the Keewatin country, north from Lake Athabasca to the Thelon River, into a land of scattered groves of stunted black spruce and tamarack. The Dubawnt River bore them east, north, then east again across the Arctic tundra until at length they reached the head of Baker Lake. They continued to Chesterfield Inlet, then along the Hudson Bay coast to Fort Churchill. This last section proved the most arduous of all. Winter had set in, their canoes were unusable because of the ice along the bay shore, the party had little food or fuel, and the men's clothes were in tatters. However, they reached Fort Churchill on October 19, then completed the journey in short, gradual stages on snowshoes and by dog team, arriving at Lower Fort Garry, whence a telegram was despatched to Ottawa on New Year's Day, 1894: "Complete success; crossed barren grounds; explored Chesterfield Inlet and west shore of Hudson Bay."[11] Altogether the brothers had travelled 3,200 miles beyond the railways, and had surveyed 770 miles of lakes, 272 miles of rivers, and 360 miles of coastline. A by-product of this expedition was James W. Tyrrell's celebrated account, published in 1897, *Across the Sub-Arctics of Canada*.

In the following year, J. B. Tyrrell made another trip to the Barrens, this time from DuBrochet post at the north end of Reindeer Lake. He was accompanied by R. Munro-Ferguson, aide-de-camp to the governor general, the Earl of Aberdeen. The party crossed to Kasba Lake, descended Kazan River, surveying parts of Lakes Ennadai and Yathkyed, then portaged to Ferguson River (named after Tyrrell's companion), which flowed into Hudson Bay at latitude 62°. A difficult journey along the shore of Hudson Bay, similar to that made in 1893, brought them to Fort Churchill, and overland to Selkirk, Manitoba. This journey included 815 miles of newly surveyed routes between Reindeer Lake to Hudson Bay.

Meanwhile, on the other side of Hudson Bay, another momentous exploration was under way, the work of Albert P. Low (1861-1942), who made northern Quebec and the Ungava district his particular sphere of operations from 1884. In that year he participated in a joint expedition to Lake Mistassini with a veteran land surveyor, John Bignell, who was to make a topographical survey for Quebec. The operation was a miserable fiasco; Bignell complained about Low's alleged insubordination, while Low charged that Bignell was making no serious effort to execute the survey. When Bignell proposed to winter at Fort Mistassini – the intended point from which the geological survey was to commence – and to postpone his survey of the lake until spring, Low, angered by the delay and alarmed at the waste of survey funds, journeyed back to Ottawa to lay his complaint at the feet of Dr Selwyn. Quebec withdrew from the program, and Low was authorized to make the survey on behalf of the Dominion government. He completed the traverses of Lake Mistassini in June and July, 1885, disproving the rumours that the lake was as large as one of the Great Lakes, then traced Rupert River down to James Bay and returned to Ottawa by way of Moose Factory. Later he examined the islands off the east coast of Hudson and James bays and the major rivers emptying into them from the rolling, rock-ribbed, lake-studded Labrador plateau.

For the traverse of Labrador in 1893, Low returned to Lake Mistassini, crossed to the Eastmain River, ascended to its source, then descended the Ungava, or Koksoak, River to Fort Chimo, passing a succession of canyons, rocky ledges, and massive iron-bearing formations *en route*. At Fort Chimo the party boarded the Hudson's Bay Company's steamer *Eric* for Rigolet and took up winter quarters at the company's post of Northwest River, from which point supplies were placed in readiness for surveys west up the Hamilton (now Churchill) River. On May 3 the party reached the Grand Falls (now Churchill Falls) where the river "falls two hundred feet in less than four miles rushing along in a continuous heavy rapid," then, narrowed to less than a hundred yards, "sweeps downwards with huge waves over a number of rocky ledges preparatory to its plunge of three hundred feet, as the Grand Falls, into a circular basin about two hundred yards wide at the head of the cañon below."[12] Above the falls, the party conducted journeys in several directions from Sandy Lake, through country incredibly rich in iron-bearing rocks, then made their way south to the Gulf of St Lawrence on August 22, 1894.

They had traversed 5,660 miles, surveyed 2,039 miles of it, and for the first time accurately determined the courses of three great rivers – the Eastmain, Koksoak, and Hamilton. Low felt the country was not entirely forbidding, though he had to report distress and starvation among the natives during the winter of 1892-93 because of forest fires and the failure of the caribou to follow their usual migration routes. An important scientific finding of Low's and Tyrrell's expeditions was information on the size and movements of the great ice sheets that had formerly overlain Labrador and Keewatin. Together, the two explorations represented the most significant advance to date in the understanding of the glaciation of most of Canada. From the economic standpoint, Low's major discovery was the massive beds of iron-bearing rocks along the Koksoak and upper Hamilton river basins:

> . . . a great and hitherto unknown area of Cambrian rocks, extending north-north-west from north latitude 53° to beyond the west side of Ungava Bay. . . . Their chief economic value is due to the immense amount of bedded iron ore found along with them. The ores are chiefly specular and red haematite, together with beds of siderite or carbonate of iron. Thick beds of fine ore associated with jasper, were met with in many places, on both the Ungava and Hamilton Rivers; and the amount seen runs up into millions of tons. Owing to their distance from the seaboard, these ores at present are of little value, but the time may come when they will add greatly to the wealth of the country.[13]

Low's expedition was perhaps the most dramatic single illustration of the great practical achievements of the Geological Survey in the period, leading, as it has done under favourable economic and technological conditions, to the modern iron-mining and hydro-electric power industries that are transforming the face of this "land that God gave to Cain." But one can hardly exaggerate the cumulative effects of the scores of surveys that extended across the continent from Hamilton Inlet to Fort Yukon, from the Great Lakes to Fort Chimo, Baker Lake, and Fort McPherson. Most were economical, hasty reconnaissances that could only give accurate data regarding the narrow strips of territory adjoining the routes actually travelled. Still, most major water courses of the Canadian North were mapped during Selwyn's directorship. A fairly good general idea was secured of the geological structure of the country, the boundaries of the main geological and physiographic regions, the districts most favourable to the occurrence of the various metallic minerals and mineral fuels, and the economic problems in the way of their early development. In keeping with the broadened functions of the survey, its officers had reported upon the whole range of physical features – soil, climate, forest and plant cover, wildlife, waterpowers, travel routes – and upon the settlements and the inhabitants of the country traversed. Through their published reports and papers and the specimens they collected for the museum or for the various exhibitions, the Geological Survey did more than any other organization or group of persons to make the resources of northern Canada known to the government and to the public in Canada and the world over. By dispelling so much of the ignorance of the potentialities of northern Canada, they prepared the way for future advances of Canada's mining, forest, and farming frontiers. That their work did not go unnoticed was indicated by the many honours heaped on the officers by leading scientific societies in Canada and other lands, as well as by Parliament's according the Geological Survey the status of a department of government in 1890.[14]

Parallelling the role of the Geological Survey in the areas outside the Fertile Belt, though on a much smaller scale at this time, was the Dominion Lands Branch, whose topographical surveyors had been responsible since 1871 for running meridians, base lines, and township outlines and subdividing the land into section and quarter-section units for easy disposal to homesteaders and others. As Otto J. Klotz, a future assistant chief astronomer and founder of the systematic magnetic survey of Canada, said, they "devoured . . . the whole country with instrument and chain."[15] But the work of surveying and subdividing the prairies was rapidly completed, and little additional effort was needed to lay the groundwork for a future resumption of subdivision surveys on the grand scale if and when settlement began to move beyond the prairies.

The township lines running north from the Fertile Belt reached the Peace River district in 1883 when William Ogilvie, a noted explorer and future commissioner of the Yukon Territory, extended the Fifth Meridian north to the Athabasca River, while W. T. Thompson located the Sixth Meridian in the Peace River district, ran the Twenty-first Base Line westward, and outlined a few townships in the prairie section of the district. However, the surveyor general, Edouard Deville, discontinued township outline and subdivision surveys in favour of exploratory surveys of principal waterways, which were in need of accurate surveying in any case. Accordingly, in 1884, Ogilvie proceeded on a survey down the Athabasca River from Athabasca Landing to its mouth, then up the Peace River to Dunvegan (a total of 1,050 miles), while Klotz surveyed the Saskatchewan and Nelson rivers from Prince Albert to York Factory (850 miles). Later, in 1888, Thomas Fawcett linked these two surveys by mapping the waterways between Frog Portage on the Saskatchewan and Fort McMurray. In addition, Fawcett and others mapped the Lake of the Woods-Winnipeg River-Lakes Winnipeg and Winnipegosis system, as well as water routes as far east as Albany River, the northern boundary of Ontario.

In 1887 Ogilvie was sent to the Yukon district in conjunction with the Dawson-McConnell survey, his assignment being to locate the Alaska boundary (the 141st meridian) along the Yukon and Fortymile rivers. A few years previously, in 1883, a vainglorious United States Cavalry lieutenant, Frederick Schwatka, had floated down the Yukon River on a raft from its source to its mouth, giving most of the physical features along the waterway inappropriate names, some of which they still retain. In his slipshod way, he placed the boundary twelve miles too far west – a matter of considerable importance in view of the subsequent discovery of gold along the Fortymile in the vicinity of the border. Travelling without the permission of the Canadian government or the backing of his own government, he publicized his journey so effectively that Congress ultimately accorded him the honour of an official report.[16] Ogilvie mapped the route into the Yukon district by way of the Chilkoot Pass and the Yukon River, and also reported another pass, the White Pass, which was to become the principal way into the country. He wintered in the Yukon, locating the 141st meridian boundary at the Yukon and Fortymile rivers by observations of the transits of the moon. Though working under extremely primitive conditions, and in very cold weather that affected his chronometer, he was only 218 feet in error. In the following year the American surveyors J. H. Turner and J. E. McGrath checked his observations and ascertained the boundary at the Porcupine River farther north. Ogilvie also surveyed townsites and mining claims, advised prospectors on Canadian mining regulations, and suggested better mining methods. In 1888 he followed the

Yukon, Porcupine, Peel, Mackenzie, and Slave River route to Fort Chipe-wyan, which he had located on his previous survey. His route was the reverse of McConnell's, except that the geologist had had to contend with the difficult Liard. Nevertheless, Ogilvie's feat was compared to those of Livingstone and Stanley in "energy, enterprise and intrepidity."[17] The Royal Geographical Society awarded him its Murchison Medal, and a grateful Parliament made him an unprecedented $5,000 grant in recognition of his services.

After tracing the Ontario boundary north from Lake Timiskaming to James Bay, and then surveying along the coast to the mouth of the Eastmain River in 1890, Ogilvie returned to the Northwest in 1891 to survey the lower Liard and Fort Nelson rivers. From Fort Simpson he ascended the Liard, Fort Nelson, and Sikanni Chief rivers, crossed overland to Fort St John, and returned by way of the Peace River and the overland trail to Lesser Slave Lake. In his two major explorations Ogilvie had carefully mapped the waterways of the Mackenzie and Yukon basins, and assembled a great deal of accurate information regarding the possibilities of this north-western frontier region. It is doubtful whether Canada has ever been served by so able and devoted a group of public servants as the men of the geological and topographical surveys in the final quarter of the nineteenth century.

II

Basic to any development of the forested region of the Canadian North was the provision of transportation facilities. These were on many levels, each appropriate to a particular stage of resource utilization. Thus the level represented by the voyageur's canoe or the prospector's pack train permitted primitive economic developments like fur-trading or placer mining, whose transport needs were reckoned in hundredweights. Steam-boats and wagon roads, by making it possible to move small tonnages, opened the region to the efforts of pioneer farmers, lumbermen, commercial fishermen, or oil-well drilling crews. To enable the territory to achieve its full economic potential, railways capable of hauling hundreds of thousands of tons cheaply in and out of the region on a year-round basis were re-quired. Such is the familiar relationship between transportation facilities and regional development, but the details – economic and social costs and benefits, timing, and political implications – present an infinitude of varia-tions on the theme.

By the early eighties, the mid-continental transportation revolution had materially improved access into the northern forests. The completion of the Canadian Pacific Railway across the southern prairie in the years

1881-83, followed by branch railways to Prince Albert and Edmonton, brought these bases into effective, year-round contact with the outside world. Furthermore, the Hudson's Bay Company's relay of steamboats on the Mackenzie waterway permitted several hundred tons of freight to be shipped each year by the flat-bottomed, shallow-draft vessels to serve or establish limited industries in the region, or enable travellers to pay short summer visits there.

But the distance still had to be overcome between the settlements along the Saskatchewan River and Fort McMurray, the real terminus of the northern navigation. Beyond Fort McMurray water transports could proceed all the way to the Arctic with only a single portage, or by the Peace River west to the Rocky Mountains with a single three-mile portage at Vermilion Chutes. From Prince Albert, Carlton, or Fort Pitt, the Hudson's Bay Company experimented with forwarding freight to Fort McMurray via the rivers and lakes of the upper Churchill River system to Portage la Loche and the Clearwater River. However the portage, despite work done on it in the seventies, still was very arduous, while the Clearwater River was difficult navigation. Increasingly Edmonton began to be used as the forwarding base, and the steamer on the upper Athabasca was intended mainly for this purpose. The one-hundred-mile wagon trail from Edmonton to Athabasca Landing became the gateway to the Mackenzie valley. In January, 1884, the company arranged to forward four hundred cart-loads of freight from Calgary to Edmonton, three hundred loads to go to Athabasca Landing for distribution to the northern districts. The awakening of the hopes for a dazzling metropolitan future for Edmonton, based on its northern hinterland, is revealed as early as March 10, 1883, by this editorial in the *Edmonton Bulletin*:

Although Edmonton is situated near the northwestern limit of the fertile Saskatchewan country . . . north of it, and far greater in extent, reaching to the Arctic ocean, along the eastern base of the Rocky mountains stretches the country of which the rivers Athabasca, Peace, Liard and their great united stream the Mackenzie, with their thousands of tributaries and the enormous lakes drained by them, form the highway. A region having double the area of the four original provinces of Canada. A region of resources as diversified as its extent is great; two thousand miles in length by five hundred in breadth. The timbered regions of the Athabasca, the farming lands of Peace river, the gold bearing Liard, the fur country of the Mackenzie, the salt deposits of the Great Slave or lower Peace river, the petroleum beds of the lower Athabasca, the fisheries of the mighty lakes all will have to seek some point on the Saskatchewan as their outlet and market. To possess the trade of such a country, when developed, must build up a great city, and what place more likely to possess that trade than Edmonton? . . . It is on the certainty of possessing the trade of this immense region that the more brilliant prospects of Edmonton are principally founded, and that they are well founded does not admit of the shadow of a doubt.

Overland transport also was being improved in western Athabasca. Not content with the Hudson's Bay Company's trail from the western end of Lesser Slave Lake to the upper Peace River, the citizens of Edmonton pressed for a direct trail to the Peace River country. The Senate committee of 1888 even received a letter urging construction of a road from Edmonton via the Peace and Pelly rivers all the way to the Yukon, to develop a series of potential mining districts along the route. However, none of these grander plans was implemented. The trail to Athabasca Landing continued to be improved, as was the portage trail around the rapids on the Slave River, where ox-cart brigades handled the transfer to the lower river. As late as 1896, however, post office routes – a good measure of current transportation practicalities – only offered service beyond the Saskatchewan River from Battleford to Onion Lake, and from Edmonton northwest to Rivière qui Barre, north to Morinville, and northeast to Lac la Biche.

The improved access to the North was indicated by the numbers of tourist visits to the region, and its mention in the first Baedeker guide to cover Canada (1894). Several noteworthy visits already had indicated the possibilities of the route. J. W. Taylor's youngest daughter Elizabeth, who made the trip to Peel River in 1892 to indulge her many interests as artist, botanist, ornithologist, and naturalist, was impressed by the botanical diversity of the Far North:

> Only a few miles south of the Arctic Circle, but no one would imagine the high latitude from the vegetation near the post . . . The air was filled with the perfume of roses, those beautiful northern roses with stem, leaf, and flower of almost equal fragrance, the showy yellow flowers of the arnica, the northern gallium, the beautiful rose like flower of the Dryas, blue columbines, bilberries, cranberries, red and black currants and gooseberries, great spikes of rose colored fireweed and the raspberry, cloudberry, Siberian asters, the fleabanes, pink and Arctic, and the large blue lupine, Labrador tea, wild parsley or parsnip, and pink and purple vetches, and the yellow, the false asphodel, a number of grasses.[18]

The region became more accessible, too, to game hunters and scientists as well as ordinary travellers. The Earl of Lonsdale's party came in 1888 to hunt polar bear and muskox, departing for the Pacific by way of Peel River and Rampart House. Warburton Pike used the steamboats to travel to Great Slave Lake in 1889 on a hunting trip that had for its climax the slaughter of a small, tight cluster of muskoxen at Lac de Gras, north of Great Slave Lake. Later, in 1892, he presented the Geological Survey museum with "a magnificent example of the Wood Buffalo (*Bison Americanus*, var.) . . . the only specimen of the kind known to be preserved in any museum."[19] Other hunters after muskox and wood bison included Henry Toke Munn, Caspar Whitney, and Frank Russell. Russell, a young naturalist from the University of Iowa, traversed the country in the years 1893 to 1895 "to obtain specimens of the larger arctic mammals, especially muskox," and incidentally, "to pick up everything else that I could lay my hands on."[20] He wintered at Fort Resolution in 1893-94, shot his muskox (which he described as like shooting sheep)[21] in the Coppermine River area, spent the winter of 1894-95 at Fort McPherson, went to Herschel Island in the autumn of 1895, and left with his booty by whaling ship to San Francisco. With him went another traveller, the Count de Sainville, who had gone down to Fort McPherson in 1889 and, during a lengthy sojourn, made a notable exploration of the Peel River. Russell's hundreds of skins, feathers, trophies, and artifacts eventually reached Iowa City in good shape, testimony to the excellence of the Hudson's Bay Company's transportation system beyond Lake Winnipeg.

Other motives besides shooting muskox or bison drew white men into the forested country north of the prairies. Whitney encountered two white trappers at Fort Resolution in 1893-94. Prospectors, those most footloose of adventurers, made their way into the region from west of the Rockies, seeking placer ground along the Peace River. In the early nineties there was a prospectors' rush to the upper Saskatchewan River and gold dredges were introduced at Edmonton, but the rush soon died out from lack of success. In view of the optimistic reports based on widespread indications of oil and bituminous sand, petroleum was another topic of interest, though inadequate transportation facilities inhibited serious activity. Petroleum regulations promulgated on December 18, 1890, authorized entry to lands merely upon submission of an affidavit that the applicant "verily believes that petroleum exists on the location applied for," but title or rights to purchase land were withheld unless the applicant succeeded in bringing in a paying well within five years. The Geological Survey started the work by drilling a 1,700-foot well at Athabasca Landing in 1895, followed in 1897 by two more wells, at Pelican Rapids along the Athabasca closer to the bituminous sands outcrops, and at Victoria, downriver from Edmonton. These failed either to reach an oil-bearing formation or to go through the entire sedimentary succession to the Precambrian basement.

Two more extractive industries were beginning to approach the region from the south. Forestry remained tied to the Saskatchewan River drainage basin, with mills at Prince Albert and Edmonton geared to local and district markets. (Far ahead of the lumbermen, however, raced the forest fires, blamed mostly on careless travellers.) The commercial fishery, being better equipped to deal with the transportation problem, was somewhat farther advanced than the lumbering industry. Lake Winnipeg and other large lakes of Manitoba had been fished commercially since the 1870's, to the point where evidences of depletion by 1890 were causing serious concern. The arrival of railways to Prince Albert and Edmonton, capable of transporting fish to the Chicago market, led commercial operators to begin fishing the lakes near these centres, typically in winter when fish could be hauled in sleighs to the railhead.

The farmlands of the Peace River district attracted much attention and a few settlers. The missionary and fur-trader farmers at Dunvegan and Fort Vermilion were joined by more settlers, who also took up farms on the open prairie country away from the river and started ranches on the more remote Spirit River and Grande Prairies. The question of whether or not the region was a good farming district still was unresolved; boosters generalized from the few successful farms along the Peace River valley, critics from the disappointing results of the few farms on the plateau. G. M. Dawson, at the one extreme, reported in 1879-80 that the region contained over 20,000 square miles of arable land, fully as good as that of the Edmonton district, capable of producing 300 million bushels of grain per annum.[22] Ogilvie, who examined the region in 1884 and 1891, on the other hand, concluded his review with, "I regret that I have to present such an unfavourable account of a region of which much has been said and written. . . . It may be that when the necessities of settlement require it, early seeding and early varieties of grain may materially alter conditions, but at present I would advise no one to think of farming there except in the river bottom, in which there are flats extensive enough to locate a few score homes."[23]

The coming of white men in large numbers to the prairies and in much smaller numbers to the northern forests added to the problems of the Indian and Métis inhabitants of the land beyond the North Saskatchewan. Those Indians who received reserves beyond the North Saskatchewan River were able for some time to continue their former lives of fishing, hunting, and trapping. When they moved on the reserves they tended to turn to raising cattle and horses, and after the first few years of sometimes killing for food the cattle stock provided by the Indian administration, they began to show results, marketing their surplus cattle and hay to the police and others. The quality of the stock was low, but ranching did appear a particularly suitable industry:

> The efforts of the Indian Department in the direction of encouraging cattle raising amongst all bands of Indians, are meeting with marked success. . . . The work suits the Indians better also, as they can only cut hay when there is no hunting, and the non-hunters can remain at home during the season and feed the cattle. Farming is too steady and monotonous work for them, although some have fine fields.[24]

Gradually these northern reserve Indians began putting in crops, and some even began to show a change of outlook that caused Agent John Ross of Saddle Lake Reserve to rejoice: "they are displaying more thrift, and the former custom of sharing with their neighbours and of giving feasts when their supplies were in a flourishing condition, has nearly altogether ceased, and they now put in practice the maxim of 'every man for himself.' "[25]

An interesting experiment was undertaken for the Métis in 1896 by the renowned Father Lacombe. A group settlement was to be formed on four townships adjoining the Saddle Lake Indian Reserve, in which each family would have its own home farm and be able to use the fish, wildfowl and fur resources, hay meadows, and timber, while private donations and government aid would provide the church, public hall, school, mill, and equip the more indigent settlers. Father J. B. Morin was hopeful that the situation would enable the Métis to progress at their own rate of speed: "I do not doubt that with a wise administration and a more than ordinary share of patience on the part of the director, the plan of redemption of the half-breeds, termed *the dream of Father Lacombe*, will succeed."[26] Unfortunately, the effort soon languished because of a lack of sufficient initial capital and an inability to recruit sufficient Métis, so the reserve began accepting French-Canadian settlers, who made the Métis uncomfortable, further hampering the experiment.

There was not the same urgency as on the prairies for government to become involved with the Indians farther north, for the land was not desired for farm settlement and the natives' way of life was not likely to be threatened for some time to come. But the government was not even well informed about their condition. The same figures for the Indians north of the existing treaties were published every year for most of the eighties: Peace River district, 2,038, Athabasca district, 8,000, Mackenzie district, 7,000, or a total of 17,038 persons. Then, suddenly, in the early nineties, more accurate, detailed, realistic – and amazingly different – figures became available, mainly from information provided by missionaries: upper (really lower) Mackenzie, 400, eastern Athabasca, 881, lower (really upper) Mackenzie, 2,058, Great Slave Lake, 1,915, Liard River, 377, Athabasca district, 1,331, Peace River district, 893, Lesser Slave Lake, 1,212, or 9,073 persons in all. Thus, though the later estimate, if anything, embraced a wider area than the former, its figures were barely half those of the earlier, crude estimates.

The discrepancy not only reflected improved knowledge of the northern Indians; it verified a belief that the northern Indians had declined in numbers, even though the terrible events had mainly occurred a quarter of a century or so before the figures were revised. A study of the Peel River district indicates that the Indian population there was swept by a series of epidemics from 1852 to 1872 (mumps, scarlet fever, measles, smallpox) that reduced the 337 Loucheux of the post to 164 persons in 1871, many of them newcomers from Fort Good Hope and Alaska.[27] After the great smallpox epidemic, the number of Indians held steadier, but the surviving population was greatly weakened by the considerable increase in tuberculosis and similar diseases. These were more prevalent because of the dietary change brought about by greater consumption of bacon and flour, the increasing use of wooden cabins, and the diminution in game resources, attributed mainly to the use of improved guns in hunting and, in some areas, to white intruders. There were also frequent reports of starvation among the northern Indians in the eighties. The sufferings of the native people began to demand an increasing degree of governmental intervention.

In the meantime, the Dominion was proceeding with its plans for organizing the North-West Territories, though most of its arrangements had greater geographic than administrative significance. On the east, the Dominion in 1876 separated off a District of Keewatin, which included the country claimed by the Dominion between Ontario and Manitoba on the west, and north of Manitoba all the way to the Arctic Ocean.[28] The boundaries of Keewatin – the most frequently changed of any in western Canada – fluctuated according to the successes of the two neighbouring provinces in securing accessions to their territory, while a wedge of country west of Lake Winnipeg and south of the Saskatchewan River was also annexed to the District of Saskatchewan. Keewatin had no real administrative life, however. The lieutenant-governor of Manitoba was lieutenant-governor of Keewatin as well, but the district had no council to legislate for it.

In contrast, in 1875 the North-West Territories Act (38 Vict., Chap. 49) had established an indigenous government for that region, with a lieutenant-governor empowered to legislate "by and with the advice and consent of the Council of the North-West Territories" in certain fields of local jurisdiction, but always within the framework of parliamentary legislation and subject to disallowance of any ordinance within two years. But how far the authority of this legislative council, and later assembly, extended remained undetermined. On May 8, 1882, the government by order in council established four districts from the southern part of the North-West Territories, "for the convenience of settlers and for postal purposes." Three of these were south of the Eighteenth Base Line (near the fifty-fifth parallel) – Assiniboia, Saskatchewan, and Alberta, which occupied the region between Manitoba and Keewatin on the east and British Columbia on the west. The fourth, Athabasca, extended from the Athabasca and Slave rivers west to British Columbia and from the northern boundary of Alberta to the Thirty-second Base Line, about ten miles south of the sixtieth parallel.[29] The three southern districts were represented in the council and assembly, were governed by its legislation, administered by its civil servants, paid taxes to it, and received services from it. But Athabasca was neither represented nor taxed by the territorial legislature, nor were the four later provisional districts established by the order in council of July 26, 1895 – Ungava, Franklin, Mackenzie, and Yukon. That order in council also extended Athabasca east to the boundary of Keewatin and north to the sixtieth parallel. However, the lieutenant-governor of the North-West Territories exercised some jurisdiction over these outside districts by appointing justices of the peace for Athabasca, while small amounts of territorial funds were spent on trails that extended into Athabasca, and a beginning was made to subsidize mission schools for educating non-Indian children all the way to Fort McPherson (Anglican) and Fort Providence (Roman Catholic) in the District of Mackenzie.

On the other hand, the Dominion government, which could legislate for all or any part of the North-West Territories, differentiated between the three settled territories controlled by the assembly in Regina, and the unorganized northern districts. A good example was the liquor question. The North-West Territories Act of 1875 prohibited the manufacture or importation of alcoholic beverages except with the written authority of the lieutenant-governor. But after years of complaints, Parliament in 1891 authorized the assembly to legislate on the liquor question "in so far as they apply to the territories comprising the several electoral districts noted in the schedule to this Act."[30] Thus the operation of any new legislation was confined to the three settled districts, while the older prohibitionist legislation continued for the Districts of Athabasca and Keewatin. Parliament also superseded the assembly's game legislation in 1894 by specifically enacting a separate system of game laws for the unorganized districts. Later, too, in 1898, the Dominion averted a possible confrontation over the control of the Yukon District by establishing it as a separate Yukon Territory.

The Dominion government, with its manifold responsibilities, gave the unorganized territories only very slight consideration. Collectors of customs were appointed, the meteorological service began supplying instruments to certain missionaries to aid in securing information on the Canadian climate, the steamboats on the various waterways became subject to inspection and licensing, but rarely, apparently, were they examined. As for the Indian administration, the government's growing concern was indicated by its offering grants to certain schools outside the treaty limits on the same basis as those assisted under the treaties, and reimbursing fur-traders for some of their expenditures on Indian relief. There was talk of new treaties to include the Indians farther north, particularly those of the Peace River district where, as Ogilvie reported in 1884, the Beaver Indians were dying out, while other Indians, Métis, and white settlers were moving in. But no treaty was to be made for the northern Indians until 1899, twenty-two years after the last treaty with the prairie Indians.

More tangible evidence of federal concern was the extension of the Dominion's control over the wildlife resources, partly out of concern for the native welfare. In 1891 an inspector of fisheries was appointed for the North-West Territories, and plans were made to enforce the regulations through part-time fishery overseers for thirteen districts, among them Lac la Biche, Ile à la Crosse, Stanley, Cumberland House, and The Pas, to enforce the close season and other regulations, license commercial operators, and secure records of catches. These northern districts provided the bulk of the catch, so they were most in need of patrolling, even though "The protection of the valuable fisheries of these outlying districts is very expensive."[31] Lac la Biche was a particular problem, for the large Métis population fished the lake quite extensively and followed wasteful methods like securing their main catch from the spawning fish, thus seriously undermining the lake's potential. Inspector F. C. Gilchrist reported that conservation practices were necessary to preserve the resource for the natives' benefit. He did not, however, express any great concern about the fish resources that were used only for local needs in districts farther north.

But it was a different matter with fur and game in view of the advent of white trappers and free traders who were not always concerned about desirable practices. In addition, the status of two rare game species – the wood bison and the muskox – threatened with extinction by sportsmen hunters and pelt buyers, was causing anxiety. The Unorganized Territories' Game Preservation Act of 1894 (57-8 Vict., Chap. 31) prohibited hunting wood bison until 1900, and established annual close seasons on muskox, other game animals, fur-bearing species, and birds. The act was aimed mainly against transients and newcomers, though the inhabitants had to comply with the conditions regarding the wood bison and muskox. Outsiders required permits to take bison or muskox and could only set aside the regulations in emergency. The use of poison, or running muskox and other game with dogs, was prohibited. Violations were to be tried before judges, justices of the peace, police officers, or game guardians, with fines and confiscations for penalties, and enforcement in the hands of appointed game guardians.

These pieces of legislation, added to the enforcement of the criminal law, the Indian Act, and other statutes, pointed to the need for an effective government presence in the unorganized districts, which obviously meant more work for the North-West Mounted Police. Since their formation in 1873, the police had confined their efforts mainly to the prairie and parkland, with only occasional patrols into the woodlands beyond. These were increasing in frequency after 1888 to points like Ile à la Crosse, Montreal Lake, Green Lake, Meadow Lake, Lac la Biche, Athabasca Landing, along the Jasper trail or the lower Saskatchewan River. Some of their purposes were to assist Indian agents on treaty payment tours, protect Hudson's Bay Company traders, investigate a murder or – most difficult of all – bring out a lunatic for trial or treatment. The most common reason for the presence of the Mounted Police, however, was in connection with the importation or manufacture of alcoholic beverages. There were patrols in 1889 to Grand Rapids to control liquor being smuggled into the Saskatchewan country from Manitoba, and to Lac la Biche to check home-brewing. In 1890 Inspector Begin visited York Factory to appoint a local justice of the peace to control local brewing and other illegal practices; in 1891 he made a similar trip to Lac Seul, in Keewatin, to visit reserves in connection with the enforcement of liquor prohibition under the Indian Act and to appoint a local justice of the peace; and he visited Cumberland House in 1892. He recommended police detachments for York Factory, Oxford House, The Pas, Grand Rapids, and other places, but these were rejected for lack of manpower, although a detachment was set up for three years at Cumberland House in 1892 to help with protecting the fisheries.

Following Parliament's invitation to the North-West Territories to legislate on the liquor question, the territorial assembly instituted a liquor licensing ordinance, permitting local boards to regulate the manufacture, import, and sale of liquor. Since the District of Athabasca, like other parts of the unorganized North-West Territories, remained under the federal prohibition legislation, preventing the spread of liquor into the North suddenly became an acute matter. A summer police detachment was placed at Athabasca Landing in 1892, and for four years no fewer than ten policemen were stationed along the route. While staff permitted, men were deployed to check the traffic at Athabasca Landing, at the mouth of Lesser Slave River proceeding to the Peace River district, and at the Grand Rapid transfer-point downstream of goods bound for the Mackenzie region. In 1896, however, for economy reasons, the effort had to be limited to the inspection by the Athabasca Landing detachment. The concern to protect the wood bison caused patrols to be extended in the winter of 1896 for the first time into the District of Mackenzie. Thus the police were increasingly being drawn farther into the forested northland of Canada.

This new northern role for the police was exemplified even more by a dramatic advance into an entirely different area of concern, the upper

Yukon River basin. Here, in the extreme northwestern corner of the Dominion, the North-West Mounted Police opened a glorious new chapter of its history that brought greater renown than ever before. Ever since the joint survey of Dawson, McConnell, and Ogilvie in 1887-88, concern had been felt by the government in Ottawa over the monopolization of the region by American miners and traders. Ogilvie at that time advised the government to refrain from imposing regulations on the district that might conflict with the customs of the American prospectors, and to harmonize its mining regulations with those of the Americans. As for administration, in typical Canadian fashion,

> Generally, my advice was that, as the country was in a very unsettled state, and our mining laws, so far as known, unsatisfactory to the miners, even of our own nationality, any attempt to take charge of affairs on our side of the line would hinder prospecting by driving most of the prospectors to the American side, and they would stay there till something very rich was discovered in Canada, and that the chance of this would be put back by our action, if we entered with authority then. . . . It was decided to allow things to stand as they were for awhile, but I was directed to keep my eye on the region, and whenever I thought it time to take possession to notify the Department.[32]

Accordingly, the miners continued to be left alone to regulate their affairs pretty completely by miners' meetings, able to be called by any miner with a grievance or problem requiring adjudication. The meetings were held under an elected president and appointed secretary (the camp recorder in most cases), usually in a saloon, and so long as the camp was small and its members known to one another, judgements appear to have been equitable. As the camps grew larger and more heterogenous, the assurance of fair treatment declined; sometimes personal popularity influenced decisions, and meetings perpetrated injustices or decided verdicts on frivolous grounds. Ogilvie found them completely unsuitable for ascertaining questions of fact or of right. Though the miners' meetings were not universally popular, they were accepted by the majority, and there would have been widespread resentment had Ogilvie attempted to interfere with their decisions.

By 1893 the scale of activity in the Yukon had reached the point where some permanent assertion of Canadian authority seemed desirable. From Juneau, where he was engaged on a joint survey of the Canada-Alaska boundary, Ogilvie warned that it now was "time we were moving in the matter of establishing authority over the Yukon . . . or we might, if the work were delayed, have to face annoyances if not complications through possession, without protest from us, by American citizens."[33] Bishop Bompas also wrote to the Superintendent of Indian Affairs and to the Minister of the Interior in 1893 appealing for a detachment of police to protect the Indians from corrupting influences. C. H. Hamilton, manager of the North American Transportation and Trading Company at Fort Cudahy, was another complainant against the lack of legal authority and the dangers of mob rule. His appeal was particularly valuable, since he represented an important American enterprise in the Yukon.

As a result, the government sent Inspector Charles Constantine and Staff-Sergeant Charles Brown to the Yukon to investigate the situation. Constantine spent about two months (July-August, 1894) in the district, entering by way of Dyea and the Chilkoot Pass and departing by river steamer to St Michael's. He reported that although the whites and the Indians were peaceable and co-operative, the area was a sort of "no man's land" and required forty-five to fifty police to control the several hundred miners. He singled out as necessitating police action the need to control liquor consumption and gambling, collect customs' duties, enforce Canadian laws, and discourage the miners' committees arrogating to themselves powers of enforcing law and order. He collected $3,248 in customs' duties and $485 for the Department of the Interior, then left Brown to winter in the district while he returned to report to the government. The upshot of Constantine's and Ogilvie's representations was that Constantine, assisted by Inspector D. A. E. Strickland, returned to Forty Mile during the spring of 1895 at the head of a specially selected force of twenty police. The detachment proceeded immediately to erect an imposing camp, "Fort Constantine," comprising a guardroom, barracks, staff-sergeants' and officers' quarters, a surgeon's office, hospital, and office building, arranged in the form of a square, like police posts on the prairies. Ogilvie also was sent back to the Yukon to continue and extend the demarcation of the boundary and to carry out other land surveys as required.

Constantine arrived on July 24, 1895, just two days before the Yukon District was created by Dominion order in council. His main task was to impress the fact of Canadian authority on the gold-miners of the Yukon and to establish the principle of the authority of the Crown over that of squatter sovereignty. There was a normal amount of grumbling at having to pay taxes to Canada, but the money was collected without incident, though Brown was needlessly officious about it, in Constantine's view.[34] The turning point came in July, 1896, when a force of police went up to Glacier Creek with the unpopular duty of upsetting an equitable miners' court decision to insist that the dispute be settled in accordance with Canadian procedures. The determination to enforce the Canadian system put miners' meetings in an untenable position, for the affair showed that their decisions could immediately be appealed to the Canadian authorities. As Constantine reported to Commissioner L. W. Herchmer on August 15, 1896, "The action taken has shown the American miner who does not care for constituted authority, that they can't run the creeks on our side, and has had a very quieting effect on gentlemen of that stamp."[35] On the eve of the gold discovery that would revolutionize the history of the Yukon, Constantine had established the pattern for his successors to pursue: through the hectic years that lay ahead, the Yukon would follow the traditional practices of Canadian authority and law.

An immediate result of the assertion of Canadian authority, the Commissioner of the N.W.M.P. reported, was that "About $300,000 worth of gold was taken out on the Canadian side, and . . . the advent of the police and proposed collection of customs, have caused a very large amount of money to be spent in Victoria, B.C., and Montreal for supplies hitherto purchased in the United States."[36] Still another was an alarmist rumour that circulated up and down the Pacific coast of the United States, just before the Anglo-American crisis over the Venezuela boundary, that the Canadian government was erecting stone fortifications and preparing to undertake aggressive action against American interests in the Northwest.[37]

From Constantine came renewed requests for an increased force of seventy-five men, a launch or patrol boat, a portable saw mill, and suggestions that summer posts should be established at strategic points along the upper Yukon to check the smuggling of liquor and dutiable goods over the passes. He advocated a civil court to register deeds and permit the collection of small debts, a court of criminal jurisdiction, a mining commissioner, and the commencement of a proper system of land survey. He was especially insistent on the need for civil courts: "The want of them creates a distrust in the administration of the government and there is an idea spreading that the country is occupied by the government solely for purposes of revenue."[38] Constantine was also concerned at the lack of control over liquor importation. Distrusting the issuance of licences by either the Ottawa or Regina governments, he suggested that control be vested in the police on the spot, as best equipped for judging the most reliable and responsible parties who should receive the licences. Besides, with this power at their command, the police would then be able to exercise effective control over the all-important saloon-keeping interest. Though this last suggestion was not approved, most of Constantine's other proposals were implemented, for besides these suggestions, his report also carried to the government authentic news of the momentous gold discovery on the Klondike.

CHAPTER 5

Klondike – The Gold Rush and After

In the middle of August, 1896,[1] the most important single event in the history of the Canadian North occurred. George Washington Carmack, an American who had lived and worked with the Stick Indians in the Yukon country for a decade, accompanied by two Indian partners, Skookum Jim and Tagish Charlie, discovered rich coarse gold on a small creek draining into a northerly tributary of the Yukon, the Tron-dec or Klondike River. Carmack had been invited to try his luck on Gold Bottom Creek (a tributary of Hunker Creek, ten miles farther up the Klondike) by Robert Henderson, a Nova Scotian who had been a prospector in Colorado since 1880 before coming to the Yukon in 1894, and who had uncovered a promising showing on Gold Bottom in July. Going out to Sixty Mile for supplies from Ladue's store, Henderson had come upon Carmack and his Indians fishing at the mouth of the Klondike for their winter's supply of salmon.

Their fishing finished, Carmack and his party proceeded towards Henderson's discovery on Gold Bottom by way of a somewhat shorter route along Rabbit (later Bonanza) Creek, panning fitfully as they went. They followed the easterly branch to its source, crossed the ridge, then descended to Henderson's camp. Carmack prospected along Gold Bottom but soon decided to return whence he had come. Perhaps he made some commitment to reciprocate by letting Henderson know if he came upon anything interesting; in any event, this was customary among prospectors. On their return back down Bonanza, the Carmack party camped at the mouth of a tributary creek flowing into Bonanza from the south. While there Skookum Jim sampled a panful of gravel – and found it rated no less than $4.00 gold value (a 10-cent pan was considered a good prospect locally). Jubilantly the men set about collecting the coarse gold. The following morning Carmack staked a double claim, 1,000 feet of the stream length by right of his discovery, flanked by two 500-foot claims, above and below it, for his two associates. Hurriedly the party turned downriver towards Forty Mile, sixty-seven miles

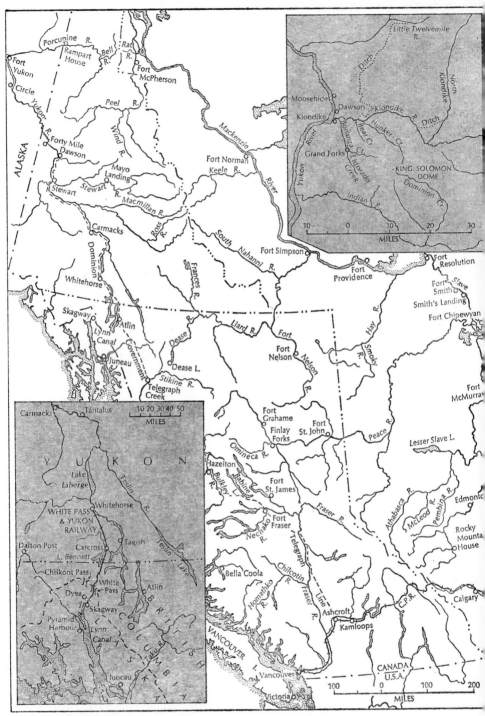

The Klondike Gold Rush and the Yukon Territory, showing the Klondike
Gold Field (upper right) and the Trail of '98 (lower left)

away, to record their claims, quite forgetting, or ignoring, Henderson and his partner at work on Gold Bottom. Carmack recounted his good fortune to every prospector he met, and they, convinced by his small stock of coarse gold, hastened to Bonanza to stake their own claims. At Forty Mile, where he proclaimed the news to an incredulous group assembled in the saloon, the camp immediately became deserted.[2]

Within a fortnight over two hundred claims were staked, mostly on Bonanza and its still richer tributary, or "pup," Eldorado. By the time Henderson learned the news from the incoming swarm of prospectors, it was too late. The rich ground had all been staked and he had to hurry to claim the most promising site he could find along Gold Bottom. Ironically, even here he was forestalled by a newcomer, Andrew Hunker, who had just staked a rich placer for which he received a double-sized discovery claim and had the creek renamed Hunker Creek after him. Henderson's own claim on Hunker Creek was no great success. Eventually, after considerable outcry from the public who felt that Henderson, a Canadian, had been badly used, the Dominion government awarded him a pension of $200 a month in recognition of his role in the gold discovery on the Klondike. He died in 1933, still searching for a strike of his own.[3]

The news of Carmack's discovery spread rapidly, first to other parts of Alaska and northern Canada, then more slowly down the Pacific coast, and finally towards the main centres of population on both sides of the Atlantic. By January, 1897, the news had reached Circle City, causing miners at Birch Creek to abandon their claims and townsmen their business to hurry to the Klondike to ply their trades. Throughout the winter of 1896-97 northerners gathered at the Klondike, staking all available ground, while the first-comers toiled below ground bringing up the precious gravel in preparation for the spring clean-up. From the south a trickle of fortune-hunters began arriving by ship and climbing the White Pass to be ready, upon the opening of navigation, to launch themselves down the Yukon to the new goldfield. The gold rush proper was only touched off in the summer of 1897 when ships arrived in San Francisco on July 15 and in Seattle on July 17, bearing the exciting news and, more dramatic, the first successful Klondikers with their winnings – $1,500,000 in gold. At once the word was flashed around a world starved for adventure and plagued by unemployment. Men, and some women, dropped everything they were doing and made preparations to go to the new El Dorado to make their fortunes by mining or other means. Some of the earliest or more experienced travellers, particularly from the American or Canadian west, succeeded in reaching the Yukon during the autumn of 1897. Most preferred to make their preparations during the winter of 1897-98 so as to reach the new gold capital in the spring of 1898. This third wave of humanity was by far the largest of the three gold rushes, containing the most diverse assortment of participants, and giving rise to most of the tragedy and ironic humour that has come to be associated with the Klondike gold rush.

Getting there was more than half the battle, particularly since the travellers had to carry their own basic supplies and equipment, as well as anything else they might require. The sheer mass of struggling humanity was much larger than could easily be funnelled into the Yukon by the existing routes or modes of transportation. The longest but easiest route was by way of St Michael's and the Yukon River, on which a number of river steamers were operating even before the stampede began. Many more vessels were brought to navigate the Yukon during the brief months of open water, while scores of ships departed from Pacific coast ports under charter for St Michael's. But only a small fraction of the most well-to-do argonauts could utilize this expensive, roundabout, restricted entry.

The vast majority of gold-seekers attempted the shorter, more direct, cheaper routes, and approached the Yukon from its headwaters. They proceeded by ship to ports on the Alaska Panhandle, some to Juneau or Wrangell, from which they worked their way up the Taku or Stikine rivers, then overland to Atlin or Teslin lakes. Most made their overland journeys from Pyramid Harbor, Dyea, or Skagway on Lynn Canal. A few travellers, wiser than most, chose the longer but more gradual northwesterly route known as the Dalton Trail, which led them to Dalton Post and the Yukon River above the future settlement of Carmacks. More adopted the route of Schwatka and Ogilvie that led from Dyea by the Chilkoot Pass to the plateau beyond. Within eighteen miles of Dyea, broken by camping areas at "Canyon City" and "Sheep Camp," the route ascended the Taiya River then mounted to the summit of the pass. From the foot of the pass, steps were cut into the steep slope that led to the 3,739-foot summit, beyond which the route descended to Lakes Lindeman and Bennett, the headwaters of Yukon navigation. Most travellers attempted the somewhat easier White Pass route Ogilvie had reported in 1887, a route that began at Skagway, followed the Skagway River a few miles, then started a dizzying six-mile climb to the 2,600-foot summit, followed by an easier descent by various rivers and streams to Lake Bennett. More than 30,000 persons traversed these two passes during the winter of 1898-99 alone. All who attempted this route found the climb up the passes their greatest trial, characterized by unremitting toil as they or their porters moved in ant-like columns up and down the icy slopes, packing their supplies in relays.

The headwaters of the Yukon having been attained, the remainder of the journey was perhaps less exhausting, though it still could be extremely dangerous for inexperienced voyagers. Particularly hazardous in the 600-mile water route between Lake Bennett and the Klondike was Miles Canyon, a five-mile section where the river raced through a narrow gorge compressed to one-third its width and cascaded over the two series of rocks, the Squaw and White Horse rapids. Dozens of scows and at least thirty lives were lost here in the early spring of 1898. Other dangerous places, Five Fingers Rapids, Rink Rapids, and off the mouth of Thirtymile River, also took their toll of lives.

The argonauts of 1898 were the last group to face most of these perils, for ambitious entrepreneurs, sniffing prospects of profits, hastened to improve travel facilities. An aerial hoist was installed at "The Scales" in 1898 to assist in hauling freight up the final slope of Chilkoot Pass. Businessmen brought in machinery over the passes and built boats; by the summer of 1898 a dozen or more small steamboats were operating along the route between Lake Bennett and the head of Miles Canyon, connecting with others that plied between the foot of White Horse Rapids and the Klondike. Miles Canyon itself was by-passed by a horse-drawn tramway operated on wooden rails. So financially successful was this that a second tramway was built on the opposite side of the river in 1899.

Finally, the summer of 1898 saw the beginning of construction of a narrow-gauge steam railway inland from Skagway – the White Pass and Yukon Railway – built without benefit of government subsidy by a group of British and American business interests under the management of Michael J. Heney. Many inbound Klondikers found employment with the railway, though progress was arrested at one stage by a mass desertion of the work force to participate in the rush to Atlin, where a rich strike was reported in 1898. Still, the line moved forward; by February, 1899, the summit of White Pass (Mile 19) had been reached, and by July 6, 1899, the line was through to Lake Bennett, so that travellers no longer had to face the difficult, hazardous climb through the passes. A year later the railway was completed to the new town of Whitehorse, at the lower end of the White Horse Rapids, circumventing the dangerous Miles Canyon section of the waterway and eliminating the need for the relay of steamships and the transhipment at the canyon. Henceforth Whitehorse became the head of navigation along the Yukon waterway and the base for winter travel by trail to the goldfields. The White Pass route also largely superseded the access route from St Michael's and became, until the completion of the Alaska Highway, the almost sole entry way into the Yukon Territory. With the construction of the railway in 1900, the Yukon became one of the most accessible sections of northern Canada, endowed with easy, safe, relatively economical year-round communications with the outside world.

The routes to the Yukon all suffered one insuperable objection from the standpoint of the Canadian nationalist – their dependence on American ports, routes, and facilities. True, under the Treaty of Washington of 1871,

Canada possessed rights of navigation on the American portions of the Stikine, Yukon, and Porcupine rivers, and Canadian traffic could flow unimpeded through Alaska into the Yukon District. But practical difficulties could, and were, imposed against such traffic for the benefit of American shipping and commercial interests. More fundamentally, the treaty had failed to foresee the place that Lynn Canal would assume as the point of departure for Yukon traffic. Hence the feverish diplomacy to negotiate concessions for the use of a port on Lynn Canal, or to secure a favourable redefinition of the boundary through re-interpretation of the Anglo-Russian Treaty of 1825. Hence, also, the strenuous efforts to develop all-Canadian routes that would end the dependence upon the United States, make Canadian rather than American interests the principal beneficiaries of the wealth generated from the Yukon discoveries, and perhaps open other portions of undeveloped northern Canada to settlement and to wealth-producing activities.

Of the alternative Canadian routes, the most immediately feasible (even though its base was situated on a river whose mouth was in Alaska) was that from Telegraph Creek, the head of navigation on the Stikine River and well inside the Canadian border. From that point it was a relatively easy traverse by land to Teslin Lake, from which uninterrupted navigation was possible to the goldfields. According to *The Klondike Official Guide*, a Canadian government publication hastily compiled during the winter of 1897-98 from various of Ogilvie's reports, the navigation from the Pacific to Telegraph Creek or from Teslin Lake down to the Klondike presented no problems. The "overland trip to Teslin Lake is over a hilly, undulating country, which offers no serious obstacle to the construction of a railway; in fact, it might be said a railway could be constructed over it almost as quickly as a waggon-road. . . . It is reported that a company is now engaged putting horses and sleighs on it, forming a continuous through line from the mouth of the Stikine to Teslin Lake."[4] With such encouragement, and backed by insistent propaganda from British Columbia interests as well as the awarding by the Laurier government of a contract to build a Canadian Yukon Railway from Telegraph Creek to Teslin Lake to the Manitoba railway builders William Mackenzie and Donald D. Mann, the route attracted some 5,000 persons by the spring of 1898. But the promised railway was never built, and the crowd added to the natural difficulties of summer overland travel through forests and muskegs that the long, hot summer days turned into quagmires.

Merging with this trail at Telegraph Creek was another from southern British Columbia that followed the valleys northwestward five hundred miles from Ashcroft. The Telegraph Trail, first traversed in the sixties by parties in the employ of the Collins Overland Telegraph Company, was also selected by Klondike-bound parties in 1898 and 1899, very few of whom persevered to their destination. Afterwards this was the route followed by the Dominion Government Telegraph system. Completed in 1901, the telegraph at last brought the Yukon Territory into immediate and direct communication with Ottawa, as well as more directly under the administrative control of the federal government.

Also publicized by *The Klondike Official Guide* were a number of routes originating east of the Rockies, all of which, it was emphasized, might be worth travelling because of the mineral and other resources of the districts traversed. These included a variety of routes commencing at the railheads of Edmonton and Prince Albert and utilizing the navigable waterways north and northwest of these communities. Parties (properly outfitted, naturally, with goods of Canadian manufacture procurable at these centres) could proceed from either of these points along good trails to Athabasca Landing and Green Lake respectively, thence with only minor breaks, by water all the way to the Peel or Porcupine rivers. From Edmonton it also was possible to travel cross-country northwest to the Peace River district and through the mountains to the headwaters of the Yukon at Pelly Banks, the route of the early explorers. Inspector J. D. Moodie of the North-West Mounted Police was ordered to blaze a trail by this route – a nightmarish ordeal that took over fourteen months (September, 1897 to November, 1898) to reach Tagish. His experience, like that of the travellers from Telegraph Creek to Teslin, or along the Telegraph Trail, conclusively demonstrated the impracticability of attempting to travel long distances overland, away from navigable water, during the summer months. Over two thousand Klondike-bound travellers started out from Edmonton; few succeeded in reaching the Klondike.

During the summers of 1897, 1898, and 1899, many parties travelled the Mackenzie River route in their own scows or on the steamers of the Hudson's Bay Company. As early as August, 1897, Charles and Fred Camsell, sons of Chief Factor Julian S. Camsell, were smitten with "the Klondike madness" by the first parties to reach Fort Simpson on their way down the Mackenzie to Fort McPherson. Such parties intended to cross to the Yukon by way of the Rat, Bell, and Porcupine rivers, a 2,700-mile journey from the end of steel at Edmonton. Some hardy souls who attained Fort McPherson attempted to ascend the Peel River and cross the divide, to the south of which lay the Klondike. A few others descended the Mackenzie River as far as the Gravel (now Keele) River, between Wrigley and Fort Norman. Their plan was to ascend the Gravel River, cross the Mackenzie Mountains, and descend the Stewart or Macmillan rivers to approach their destination from the east. Others – the Camsell brothers among them – proceeded from Fort Simpson up the Liard River to its westernmost sources, the Frances or Dease rivers, thence across to Pelly River or Teslin Lake and downstream to the Klondike. All these were mainly summertime routes, utilizing the long stretches of navigable water. But few parties succeeded in completing their journeys in a single season. Most had to winter somewhere along the route, at established posts like Fort Simpson or Fort Norman, at a remote improvised camp high up the Liard on the portage around Devil's Canyon, or, strangest of all, about "Wind City" at the headwaters of a tributary of the Peel, where George M. Mitchell's party, as well as several others totalling some ninety men in all, hunted and fraternized with the Loucheux Indians during the winter of 1898-99.

On September 2, 1896, following the Klondike discovery, Inspector Constantine outlined the need for still more federal agents, particularly to look after mining titles: "The country will have to be divided into mining districts with an agt. for each district, who must be resident on the principal creek in [the] District." Once again he complained about the lack of judicial personnel: "I don't care about being people jury & executioner which I am at present."[5] Fortunately, with the arrival of D. W. Davis (Conservative M.P., Alberta, 1887-96) as customs collector, he was relieved of some of his burdens almost at once. Later, in the spring of 1897, he was also freed from the management of mining lands and the administration of the mining regulations when the government appointed the Dominion lands surveyor, Thomas Fawcett, as gold commissioner, mining recorder, and Dominion agent. About the same time the administrative centre was transferred from Constantine's headquarters at Forty Mile to Dawson, the townsite granted to Joseph Ladue at the mouth of the Klondike River.

The federal government in August proceeded with its arrangements for the civil government of the Yukon by appointing Major J. N. Walsh, a former officer of the police, as commissioner and chief executive officer, and T. B. McGuire as justice of the Yukon Provisional District court. Walsh, who was given wide discretionary powers by Sifton, failed to reach the new headquarters before freeze-up. Departing for the Yukon in September, 1897, he wintered at Tagish and reached Dawson only in May, 1898, in time to get involved in serious quarrels with the police and the agent sent to the district by the North-West Territories government. He resigned his commission, left the district, and Fawcett had to take charge of the entire civil administration. Constantine was not much later in leaving the country. He departed on June 23, 1898, with the laconic entry in his diary: "Left Dawson per Str C H Hamilton Thank God for the release – "[6] Other agents sent to the Klondike in the gold-rush era included F. C. Wade as registrar of lands, J. D. McGregor as inspector of mines, and of course, the indispensable land surveyor, William Ogilvie.

Walsh's tenure of the commissionership coincided with a dispute between the Dominion and the government of the North-West Territories respecting the status of the Yukon. When the gold rush began, the North-West Territories endeavoured to assert its authority "in that portion of the North-West Territories called the Yukon Provisional District," particularly as regards regulation of the liquor traffic. Armed with a commission from the lieutenant-governor of the territories, a member of the executive council, G. H. V. Bulyea, proceeded to Dawson to collect fees and to license liquor distributors. Though Walsh informed Bulyea when they met at Tagish that he was without authority in the region, Bulyea went ahead and set up a local three-man board of commissioners and collected $2,000 in fees from sixteen saloons and hotels. The permits he issued for importing 61,000 gallons of liquor at a tax of $2 per gallon yielded the Regina government an unexpected $122,000 windfall—upheld by the Yukon court—before that loophole was closed.[7] For, faced by this challenge to its authority, Parliament passed the Yukon Territory Act (61 Vict., Chap. 6), separating the Yukon District from the North-West Territories and establishing it, as of June 13, 1898, as a distinct political and administrative entity with its own executive, legislative, and judicial institutions. The system was analogous to that of the older North-West Territories to the south, with the commissioner standing in the place of a lieutenant-governor. The choice of name perhaps indicated a differing concept of the nature of that officer than had been envisaged in 1875 when the North-West Territories had been organized. The appointed council (there was no elected representation as yet) included the five leading officials in the territory—the judge, gold commissioner, registrar, legal adviser, and superintendent of police.

Much in evidence in the territory, notwithstanding the establishment of civil authority there, were the police, whose numbers were increased to ninety-six by the end of 1897 and a year later to 288 officers and men. They were organized in two divisions, "B" with headquarters at Dawson, and "H" centred at Tagish (later transferred to Whitehorse). After Constantine the command devolved upon the redoubtable Superintendent S. B. Steele (February, 1898 to September, 1899) and later upon Assistant Commissioner Z. T. Wood. Moreover, in September, 1898, the police were augmented by a 203-man contingent of Canadian regulars formed into a Yukon Field Force, whose presence was further evidence of the Canadian government's determination to hold the Yukon against subversion from within or attack from without.

The police were the first symbol of Canadian authority the Klondikers encountered as they entered the Yukon, for at the summits of Chilkoot and White passes, police detachments hoisted the flag against American jingoes who tried to carry on as far as Lake Bennett. They maintained their posts through the foulest weather, checking the travellers and rendering every possible assistance. The police had been instructed not to admit any-one into the Yukon who had not brought with him "at least 1,150 pounds of solid food besides tents, cooking utensils, prospectors' and carpenters' tools." Consequently the detachments at the passes were kept busy examin-ing and checking outfits. By spring Steele reported they had checked over 30,000,000 pounds of solid food, "sufficient to feed an army corps for a year," had passed more than 30,000 persons, and collected over $150,000 in duties and fees.[8] In this fashion the Klondike was saved from starvation during the winter of 1898-99, notwithstanding the enormous increase in population. No opening was left for the United States government to inter-vene under the pretext of relieving a danger to its citizens, as it sometimes did in Alaska and was under some pressure to do in the Yukon.[9]

At Lake Bennett, where the two trails over the passes converged, the police maintained order, in striking contrast with Skagway, then in the hands of the criminal element headed by "Soapy" Smith. A careful register of all travellers was kept and each boat was given a number so that every party would be accounted for. At Miles Canyon, after a few men died trying to run the rapids, Steele took charge and ordered that all women and children disembark and portage the sector, that vessels should not be overloaded, and that a competent river man be placed in charge of each boat, with the police ruling on each case and levying fines for violations of these on-the-spot regulations. In these ways the police, acting arbitrarily, saved innumerable lives and established their role as the guardians of the public interest in the Yukon.

The North-West Mounted Police performed many other useful functions in connection with the gold rush. In cases of accidental death they im-mediately took charge, assumed the responsibility of advising next-of-kin, and settled the estates. They acted as advisers, deciding innumerable dis-putes to the satisfaction of the disputants. They supplemented the official mail service with their own system of transport by dogteam from Dawson to Skagway in 1898, sometimes hauling extremely valuable loads of gold dust without a single loss. For a time they even maintained an office at Skagway to expedite their supply system to the interior, and Soapy Smith's desperadoes knew better than to interfere with the members of the force, their supplies, or the material in their charge. By the end of the gold rush, the police had completely dispelled any lingering doubts as to their com-petence remaining from the débâcle in 1885, and their reputation had risen to its highest point.

II

And for what had so many men struggled to reach the Klondike? Gold there was in quantity, as the men who staked the first claims on Bonanza,

Eldorado, Hunker, and the other creeks demonstrated. An estimated $8,500,000 worth of gold was produced in the spring and summer of 1898 from Eldorado and Bonanza alone. Unofficial estimates give the total production for the first seven years, 1896-1903, as $95,825,000, with the maximum of $22,275,000 being achieved in 1900. In view of the richness of the placers, the operators were able to hire labourers to speed up development of their properties; the competition for men, in turn, forced wages to a very high level and raised other prices in proportion, adding to the difficulties of the police and other public servants whose wages failed to keep pace. Many owners of claims – perhaps the majority of the first-comers – leased out their holdings on "lays," arrangements whereby the men worked the claim and returned a share of the recovered gold (typically one-half or two-thirds) to the owner of the property. All sorts of variations were possible. W. S. Hamilton worked under an arrangement in the winter of 1899-1900 whereby the employer provided the men's food and lodging and gave them one-third of the gold collected during the spring cleanup. His share, $3,000, was good pay by the standards of that day.

Mining techniques continued to improve as operators adjusted to local conditions. One important innovation, introduced in 1899, was heating the gravel (for tunnelling, drifting or removing the gold-bearing sand) by means of steam rather than direct brush fires. Steam engines were installed and steam was transmitted to the face of the digging by hoses terminating in perforated iron tubes through which the steam percolated into the rock-hard sand. The head of the pipe was re-enforced to allow it to be pounded into the permanently frozen ground. After the steel was in place, steam was turned on for six to twelve hours, following which one to three cubic yards of gravel could be removed. This was faster and more economical than the former method of setting fires underground, and much safer since it reduced the chances of asphyxiation. In addition, the steam engines could be used for hoisting and other mechanical tasks, reducing the amount of labour required. Underground mining now became primarily a winter-time activity, since digging at that time did not have to cope with water seepages or the expense of props. The frozen gravel was hard enough that tunnels and even large rooms could be excavated without danger of collapse. All winter long the gravel would be collected and piled ready to be washed in the spring. The piled gravel was a commodity with recognized value, against which one could buy, sell, or borrow.

In fact, there was an extremely active market in mining claims, and properties frequently changed hands. This facilitated the disposal of property by those who wished to leave the country and enabled successful operators to accumulate more ground. These activities were made possible by the availability of credit from private sources or the local branches of two of Canada's banks. Consolidating and grouping claims made it possible to work adjoining claims as units, reducing expenses and permitting the more efficient use of machinery and equipment. The trend towards the consolidation of claims began early in the history of the Klondike.

The extraction process remained the familiar one of separating the gold particles by cradling, the only variation being in the scale of operations. The gravel was placed where it would be washed by water carried down from a dammed-up stream in a trough or flume inclined so as to impart enough momentum to the water to carry away the quartz and clay components without washing away the gold as well. The heavier metallic particles would drop to the bottom of a series of shallow sluice boxes, where they would be trapped by a succession of transverse boards or riffles and held by the liner of blanket or similar material. Separation could be achieved by scraping away the particles and adding mercury, which adsorbed the gold in an amalgam, then heating to drive off the mercury (recovered by distillation, the mercury was used again and again), leaving nearly pure gold dust or nuggets. The product of each creek differed slightly in fineness and purity, hence also the prices at which it was traded; saloon-keepers, bank tellers, miners, and policemen quickly learned to recognize the source of each sample of gold received.

Only comparatively few of the prospectors who arrived after 1897 ever succeeded in discovering paying properties, for the goldfield, for practical purposes, was restricted to the half-dozen creeks discovered in the first few months. The many would-be miners who failed to establish themselves at the Klondike diggings either turned to other work or departed to try their fortunes at the new mining camp at Atlin, British Columbia, which was developed in 1898 and after. More drifted to Alaska, particularly to Nome on the barren Arctic coast, where the discovery of gold in the beach gravels in 1898 inspired a rush that attracted almost as many men as the Klondike had done. A few later arrivals, however, did discover gold in the Klondike, for, beginning in August, 1897, certain rich gravel deposits (such as the so-called "White Channel" gravels) were uncovered on the terraces or benches of most of the original creeks. Some were as high as 450 feet above the present streambeds, where the rivers had flowed in past ages before cutting down to their present levels, and deposited even richer particles and nuggets eroded from the Dome, the 4,250-foot peak from which all the gold-bearing streams emanated. To work these hill claims successfully required adequate supplies of water under high pressure and pointed to the desirability of consolidating claims or co-ordinating operations on entire creeks as units.

The progress of mining in the Yukon was accompanied by an extraordinarily broad range of legal difficulties and policy problems. Successful operations required access to adequate supplies of water and wood fuel, both very scarce commodities, the rights to which inspired endless disputes. There were always uncertainties over boundaries because surveys were imperfect. Since a foot-wide strip of ground might contain thousands of dollars' worth of gold, there were endless encroachments upon the property of absentee or unwary operators by the holders of adjoining claims, or disputes over rights to claims. Lawsuits were often of little help. Hearings were expensive and slow, and the trespasser could evade payment of damages by simply disappearing, along with his spoils. There were perennial problems between the creek and hill claims – over how high up the slope the creek claims extended, and over the right of hill claims to intercept water from the upper courses of the creeks or dump their used gravel below. In addition, the regulations were frequently changed, giving rise to many uncertainties since they were promulgated in Ottawa and descended on the Yukon without warning.

Nor was the administration of the regulations altogether without fault, as an investigation into the management of the gold commissioner's office in 1897-98 showed. For months there were widespread complaints that records were kept closed to the public, that clerks had to be bribed to perform their ordinary duties or divulge privileged information, and that they permitted confederates to stake ground that came open in exchange for shares in claims thus secured. One particular scandal was the closing of a promising newly discovered creek, Dominion Creek, in November, 1897, and then its being suddenly thrown open for staking on July 9, 1898. It was rumoured that certain individuals had received prior knowledge of this last decision that had enabled them to leave on the previous day to stake their claims. One of these men was supposed to have been acting for the brother of Commissioner Walsh and to have agreed to turn over three-fourths of the property to him.[10]

Finally, after a considerable outcry, the federal government set up a commission of enquiry in October, 1898, and appointed William Ogilvie, the new territorial commissioner under the Yukon Territory Act, to investigate the accusations. The complainants immediately objected that the enquiry did not cover all their allegations. Their cries that it was a whitewash were renewed when Ogilvie's report found only a few minor officials guilty of actual misconduct and exonerated both Walsh and Fawcett. Fawcett, the gold commissioner, seemed personally honest but quite incapable of maintaining control over the office or of preventing misconduct by his subordinates. He had already been demoted to chief of surveys for the territory, and he left the Yukon in March, 1899, before the enquiry had got well on its way.

A sequel to the complaints was a belated order in council in 1899 prohibiting government officials from staking, purchasing, or otherwise profiting from mining claims in the territory.[11] In 1898 the Dominion government also took action on another major grievance of the miners when it exempted them from the payment of royalty on outputs of less than $5,000 per annum and lowered the royalty from 20 per cent to 10 per cent. In March, 1901, this was again reduced to 5 per cent, then it was replaced altogether in 1902 by a 2½ per cent gold export tax. The Dominion government also responded eventually to requests for proper systems of miners' and mechanics' liens, and enacted a comprehensive mining code in 1906.[12]

As time passed, most of the smaller problems of individual mining operations were resolved, but a major issue – the optimum size and type of mining land concession – continued to grow in prominence in the years after 1900. In 1898 a fantastically persuasive Englishman, A. N. C. Treadgold, visited the Yukon and perceived that mining methods were inefficient in that a considerable fraction of the gold was lost that could be recovered by more modern methods. Soon he and other engineers were proposing that certain creeks be reserved as exclusive concessions for large-scale operators using the most modern methods, rather than being thrown open to hordes of small claim-holders who might not even make wages. The federal government, on the basis of its own geological reports and opinions, also felt it might be in the public interest to grant large leases that would justify the installation of expensive machinery and permit the mining of gravels too poor to repay working by existing small-scale methods. As early as January, 1898, one such lease was granted by the Minister of the Interior for a section of Hunker Creek that had been passed over because it was too wide to prospect for a pay streak. The appearance at the end of 1898 of a set of regulations for hydraulic leases touched off efforts by many wealthy or influential persons and groups to secure concessions to the most valuable ground possible. More than forty leases were issued, most of which had to be cancelled for failing to carry out the work agreements. As defined in 1900, leases were awarded for areas up to five miles long and one mile wide, for periods of up to twelve years at an annual rental of $150 per mile of frontage, the holders being obliged to commence operations within one year and spend at least $5,000 per annum.

In theory these concessions were not supposed to interfere with the interests of the small miner, and the grants were hedged with many safeguards. The applicant had to prove that the desired ground could not be worked profitably by ordinary placer methods, and was obliged to secure certificates to that effect from the gold commissioner, the commissioner, and finally, from the Department of the Interior, which issued the provisional lease. Nevertheless there were many complaints: that leases were awarded as a result of political influence and for ground that could be worked successfully by individuals; and that the administration failed to police their operations adequately or cancel those that failed to live up to the requirements. More objectionable still were the water privileges associated with the leases, for hydraulic works required water on such a scale as to affect the operations of free miners on their own claims. The policy was bitterly opposed not merely by the free miners who feared for their own opportunities, but by all whose interest it was to cater to the individual miner, including local politicians and those who benefited from the presence in the Yukon of a large population. For these saw the modern methods used by the concessions as requiring fewer workmen, and consequently undermining the chances of the territory's acquiring a large, enterprising population.

Of all the concessions, the one that aroused the greatest public opposition was the Treadgold Concession, awarded on June 12, 1901. Treadgold had been buying up claims from 1898 onward on behalf of a group of English backers. Now he was granted the right to assume unclaimed or lapsed ground on Bonanza, Eldorado, Bear, and Hunker creeks – the most famous creeks of all – and to take water from the Klondike and other rivers. Existing holders of claims were allowed to continue operations while purchasing water from the concession at agreed prices. The scale of the grant caused alarm, as well as the obvious favouritism of the government towards Treadgold, which was attributed to Sifton's personal interest in this operation. From 1901 to 1904 the Treadgold Concession was the major political issue in the territory.[13]

Eventually, faced with widespread demands for an enquiry, the Dominion government appointed a royal commission on May 23, 1903, headed by Justice B. M. Britton of the Ontario Supreme Court. A great deal of argument and evidence was received from all sorts of interested parties, much of which the commission characterized as shallow and superficial. The report endorsed the principle of the Treadgold scheme, though it agreed that the people were strongly critical of concessions to outsiders and that their hostility by itself made implementation difficult.[14] In the meantime, faced with so much suspicion, criticism, and opposition, the syndicate surrendered the concession in the spring of 1904, prior to completion of the Britton report. But notwithstanding this setback, the inevitable trends towards consolidation could not be denied. By 1906 the supporters of the large-scale methods had emerged triumphant, and the gold-mining industry of the Yukon was on the verge of thorough-going reorganization.

Not all of Yukon society was comprised of miners. Even at the outset, would-be miners were only a fraction of the thousands who entered the territory, and their numbers dwindled with the drying up of opportunities in that area. The lure of the Klondike attracted people of every class and occupation who hoped to succeed by catering to the many varied needs of the developing community: "there were doctors enough to attend their cure . . . lawyers to settle their disputes, bank clerks to care for their money, and undertakers to bury them if death overtook them. There were men from every walk of life, all of whom had been attracted to the cold, dreary North by the greed for gold – the strongest of magnets."[15] There were also druggists, journalists, printers and photographers, auctioneers, jewellers, brokers, tailors, barbers, carpenters, and blacksmiths. There were merchants dealing in every exotic commodity, whose wares would have done credit to a large city. For the more regular supplies there were the large transportation concerns, the Northern Commercial (formerly Alaska Commercial) Company and the North American Transportation and Trading Company, whose large warehouses supplied the staple needs of the white community.

There were bakers and restaurateurs, making do with dried vegetables and local game, or imported canned or bottled luxuries. There were hotels, dance halls, saloons, and theatres where the miners whiled away their time waiting in Dawson to freight supplies out to their claims, or where they came to transact business. To finance mining and business activities in Dawson and Whitehorse there were the branches of the Bank of British North America and the Canadian Bank of Commerce. There were, in addition, the persons on the government payroll – police, mining recorders, administrators, and the like.

Above all, in the opening stages of the gold rush, came many speculators, drawn by the opportunity to make money through supplying food, equipment, or more questionable fare to the travellers, miners, or settlers. A good example is afforded by the activities of the California boy Paul Mizony and his parents, who, from supplying earlier gold rushes, knew how to capitalize on the opportunities these afforded. Between the end of 1897, when they arrived in Skagway penniless from their voyage, and the autumn of 1902 when Paul left Dawson for the last time, they made five trips into the Yukon. The first included operating restaurants in Skagway and The Scales during the winter of 1897-98, opening a store at Lake Lindeman in the spring, and finally proceeding to Dawson where, unable to find a building, they sold their produce beside the street – potatoes $1 per lb, onions 75 cents per lb, eggs $2.50 a dozen, sugar 25 cents per lb, oranges and lemons $75 a box, and the like. (Nothing, apparently, sold in smaller than 25-cent units.)

During that trip, as well as the next, between the spring of 1899 and

Laying three miles of track a day on the Grand Trunk Pacific Railway.

Grand Trunk Pacific track arriving at Tête Jaune Cache, B.C.

Temporary wooden bridge, Grand Trunk Pacific Railway,
Wolf Creek, Alberta.

Coppermine River Eskimos packing overland to Great Bear Lake, 1916.

The departure of the Stefansson Party for the journey across the ice of
Beaufort Sea, from Collinson Point, Alaska, March 16, 1914.

Captain Bernier's proclamation of sovereignty, Melville Island, July 1, 1909.

Cleaning whalebone on the whaling ship Belvedere, *October 1912.*

Last picture of the Canadian Arctic Expedition ship Karluk, *November 1913.*

the autumn of 1900, they discovered that profits were to be made in both directions—by selling goods to newcomers and buying back equipment disposed of by disgusted voyagers. Rifles, for example, could be bought at $2.50 to $7.50 apiece, and shipped back to the United States; gold dust, purchased at $15 an ounce, realized anywhere up to $19 at the assay office in Seattle. At Lake Bennett, where they remained for fifteen months in 1899-1900, they were able both to sell and to purchase the boats, tents, stoves, camping equipment of persons going to Atlin or leaving it. Each trip commonly terminated at Dawson, where the imported produce was disposed of at good prices, followed by a return passage by steamer to the United States.

This sort of operation depended on the uncertainties of supply and demand in the gold-rush era. Hence, as communications improved and the population became stabilized, the opportunities diminished. On his last trip to Dawson in 1902, Paul Mizony did poor business in an over-stocked market, and returned to Seattle with little profit. As he recalled much later, however, "Thousands of other stampeders had somewhat of the same experience, but with this difference, each trip that my parents made to the Klondike region, they made money on their ventures, while a great many other people not only lost all of their possessions, but a large number lost their lives."[16]

III

Gold-mining was the *raison d'être* of the Yukon Territory, the inspiration and driving force behind its becoming a permanent community. It also caused the territory's economic downfall when the industry failed to expand or give rise to other industries capable of becoming future main-stays of the territorial economy, as the gold rushes in California or the Fraser had done. Notwithstanding the various facilities created in the period of the gold rush, the Yukon was unable to build upon them to grow into the wealthy, populous province its pioneers had fondly imag-ined. Apart from placer gold, the region possessed few natural resources capable at that time of being developed into large industries. The Yukon was like a barren rock, deluged by a heavy shower of capital generated by its single successful industry. Unable to catch or absorb this golden rainfall, the territory remained largely unaffected and the downpour merely flowed away to nourish the vegetation growing upon remoter, more fertile soils. Nearly all the Klondike millionaires of the first phase took their winnings outside with them, while the corporations that suc-ceeded them withdrew their earnings as profits and dividends to share-holders in other parts of the world.

By reason of its success, gold-mining also inhibited the development of other industries in the early Yukon Territory. The high returns to labour from the phenomenally rich placers discouraged the development of alternative industries, for wages were raised to levels that made it difficult for other industries to compete. Even owners of claims that did not return $3.00 gold per cubic yard of gravel found it impossible to operate in the face of the high wages being offered by the rich claims. These tended to become general, making for an all-round inflation of wages and prices. At the same time the labourer was vigilant in protecting his position against forces that might reduce wages and lower the standard of living. In June, 1902, when five Chinese from Victoria arrived in Whitehorse, they were met by a delegation of townsmen who refused to permit them to pass on to Dawson, and forced them to return to Skagway on the next train.[17]

Finally, the improvements in communications, particularly the White Pass and Yukon Railway, had the effect of exposing most industries that succeeded in becoming established in the territory to outside competition. The advantage of their local situation was insufficient to offset the cost of importing alternative supplies, except, perhaps, in the case of bulky materials like coal. Even then the railway imported 10,000 tons of higher-grade coal each year from British Columbia that helped undermine the local industry. The railway also hastened the introduction of capital-intensive methods in the gold-mining industry, thereby reducing the level of employment and hampering the growth of a considerable local market for goods in the territory. It also increased the tendency of the Yukon to be served by transient labour that entered each season to meet the heavier industrial needs of the summer. This, however, may have been preferable to maintaining year-round a population large enough to meet the summer's requirements but under-employed, or unemployed, for much of the winter season. Development of transient labour upon a large scale has hampered the Yukon, like the rest of northern Canada, from evolving into a normal society based on families established in the North, having their stake in the country, and making their permanent homes there.

For forty years after the end of the gold rush, the history of the Yukon Territory was one of recession, of a shrunken economy and a society living upon facilities provided during a happier, more hopeful, more successful era. As the richest gravels reached the point that would not sustain the current high rates of wages and profits (usually after four or five seasons), the industry came under the sway of inexorable forces that held wide-ranging implications for the future of the Yukon. At first the rich gravels had been worked with profit even by inefficient, costly hand-labour methods; but when it became a matter of utilizing the less-rich sands, cheaper, more efficient methods were needed. Hydraulic mining and dredging entailed the consolidation of many claims to permit operations on as large a scale as possible, the application of large amounts of capital, and the displacement of men by machines. As early as 1901 a dredge operating on a claim on Bonanza Creek revealed the enormous potentialities of these methods: "Three men running the dredge handled 700 cubic yards of gravel in 20 hours, representing the labour of 156 men working with a shovel and pick."[18] The introduction of the new technology meant that the chief industry of the territory would become a much smaller source of employment or incentive to settle and develop the Yukon.

Small wonder, then, that the introduction of these capital-intensive methods was bitterly opposed by the free miners and was successfully resisted as long as the Yukon remained predominantly a settlement of, and for, the independent, small-scale gold-miner and prospector. But the modern methods were not to be denied, as R. G. McConnell reported in 1906:

> Mining on the Klondike creeks is at present in a transition stage. The individual claim-owner is being gradually replaced by companies owning groups of claims and working them with expensive plants. The fabulously rich placers which made Eldorado, Hunker and Bonanza Creeks famous have been mostly drifted out and the gravels which remain are too lean, as a rule, to be worked with much profit by the early pick and shovel method. The necessity for a more economic treatment of the gravels has been met by the introduction of dredges on the creek and river flats, and hydraulic plants on the hills.[19]

As the 250-foot claims were exhausted, they were acquired by wealthy organizations, and as the power of the free miner interest in the territory declined, it became politically possible to secure the all-important concessions to entire creeks. A Placer Mining Act in 1906 facilitated the grouping of claims and encouraged the investment of capital on a large scale.[20] The Yukon Gold Company (a Guggenheim subsidiary which took over the Treadgold scheme), having gained control of the claims on Bonanza Creek, arranged to mine 35,000,000 cubic yards of low-grade placer gravels from the hillsides by hydraulic methods. To secure enough water at sufficient pressure to work the uppermost deposits, a water supply was brought from Little Twelvemile River, over sixty-four miles away. Building the $7,000,000 ditch provided employment for 1,600 to 1,700 men during each of three summers. The ditch, when completed, carried up to 55,000 gallons per minute through 38 miles of ditches, 19.6 miles of elevated flumes, and 12.6 miles of pipelines, across five depressions. The water, which had descended 1,128 feet from the intake point, reached the hillside of Bonanza Creek under a head of power of 500 feet. Directed by monitors with a pressure of 100 pounds per square inch against the valley wall, the jet broke down the frozen gold-bearing aggregate and carried the material into narrow ravines or cuttings in the terrace floor, where it was made to pass through sluice boxes in which the gold was separated from the clay, sand, and gravel.[21]

An even more efficient mining method, operable on low ground on sands already in position or washed down from surrounding terraces, involved using dredges. To begin dredging operations, a large pit was dug in the midst of a patch of paying gravel and filled with water to float the dredge, which was assembled there and mounted on a scow. The dredge mined the sand in front of the pit by means of bucket belts which chewed away at its sides as they were swung from side to side. The surplus gravel, after being checked by the riffles and felt-lined sluice boxes in the body of the dredge, was spewed out to the rear into a new pile of tailings, the sand and gravel on one side, on the other the larger stones screened out and carried by conveyor belt to the rear of the dredge. Thus the dredge dug its way forward, filling in the pit behind, completely erasing the original topography of the valley by a washboard pattern of alternating ridges of fine sand and of coarser shingle and stones. The gold trapped by the felt linings of the sluice boxes was separated by the usual treatment with mercury. Thanks to these methods, it was possible to mine vast quantities of gravel from even the poorer creeks, so these expensive devices more than justified their introduction.

By 1905 dredges were coming into general use. The Canadian Klondike Mining Company installed a $300,000 dredge in that year and another two in 1908. The Bonanza Basin Gold Dredging Company followed suit in 1906, while the Yukon Consolidated Gold Fields Company completed three dredges to work their claims on Bonanza in 1907. H. M. Cadell, a mining engineer who visited the Yukon in 1913, reported that the Yukon Gold Company operated eight electric-powered dredges on Bonanza, Eldorado, and Hunker creeks with an average daily capacity of 4,000 cubic yards apiece. The Canadian Klondike Mining Company and the Bonanza Basin Gold Dredging Company properties, some forty square miles of valley lands all told, had been merged by J. W. Boyle as Boyle Concessions Limited. This company's largest dredge, newly commissioned in March, 1913, weighed approximately 2,000 tons and was capable of dredging 11,300 yards per day, with only an eleven-man crew for twenty-four-hour operation. While it cost nearly £100,000, it could check the sand at a cost of only 6 cents per cubic yard, and even though the average gold content of the gravel was only 28 cents per cubic yard, it made over £500 profit per day. To furnish the electric power and supply the water in which the dredge could operate, the company built a six-mile ditch from the north fork of the Klondike

River, providing a 228-foot head of water and powering the 10,000 horse-power hydro-electric plant of the Granville Power Company.

Gold production, which had been falling steadily since the year 1903 (itself considerably below the unofficial peak production in 1900 of $22,275,000), reached a low point in 1908, then recovered in the next few years between 1910 and 1914, before declining again in the face of higher costs and poorer grades of sands worked. The record of gold production between 1903 and 1925[22] best tells the story:

Year	Gold Production in $	Year	Gold Production in $
1903	$12,113,000	1914	$5,301,000
1904	$10,790,000	1915	$4,649,000
1905	$ 8,222,000	1916	$4,458,000
1906	$ 6,540,000	1917	$3,960,000
1907	$ 3,304,000	1918	$3,266,000
1908	$ 2,820,000	1919	$1,947,000
1909	$ 3,260,000	1920	$1,660,000
1910	$ 3,594,000	1921	$1,246,000
1911	$ 4,126,000	1922	$1,230,000
1912	$ 4,024,000	1923	$1,032,000
1913	$ 5,018,000	1924	$1,136,000
		1925	$ 625,000

This output was derived almost entirely from the creeks which had been discovered and developed around 1896, though each year small amounts of gold were secured by free miners using the familiar small-scale methods and working in many sections of the territory. Despite the strenuous efforts of prospectors, no comparably rich placer deposit was ever discovered, nor any "Mother Lode" from whence the Klondike placers must have come. Indeed, geologists concluded that the gold was derived from quartz veins carrying very low values that were concentrated over the ages by the erosive force of water into immensely rich paystreaks, either on the original creek bottoms (the hill claims), or the deeper valleys cut by the creeks following a rise in the level of the land. Owing to the district's not having been glaciated, the placers remained intact to modern times, to be mined by Carmack and his successors.

Prospecting for alluvial gold, however, did uncover at least two other metallic mineral deposits. Copper deposits discovered in the Whitehorse district in 1899 came under development after 1905. A plant was built, a small work force was recruited, a spur line was built from the railway, and in 1910 a trial shipment of 4,738 tons of ore was sent to a smelter in Tacoma, Washington. High mining costs, coupled with the low price for copper, forced the operation to close in 1921. Still later, a silver-lead deposit was discovered on the Stewart River near Mayo Landing, and a first trial shipment was made to Trail, B.C., in 1914. But neither of these held out anything like the opportunities to attract labourers, settlers, and capital that the Klondike had.

The failure of mining to maintain a high level of employment also contributed to the decline of other industries that the gold rush had inspired. Transportation facilities instituted in those years were more than sufficient for a generation to come, and only a few roads and airfields were added prior to the Second World War. The electric power plants built by the concessions served the needs of the gold-mining industry and the town of Dawson. The lumber industry, created by the demand for building materials and for mining operations, fell off as markets disappeared and readily accessible stands of timber were consumed. For a longer period, wood continued to be used as fuel for steamboats, for power plants, and for domestic heating. Coal began to be mined locally to supply the requirements of the mining companies and of the settlements. In 1907, the peak year, 7,233 tons of coal were mined at Tantalus Butte, midway between Dawson and Whitehorse, mainly for domestic users, and 5,200 tons at the Sourdough Mines, some thirty-five miles below Dawson, to generate electric power for Dawson and certain mining concerns. The coal was not of a high quality and the market was curtailed by the availability of hydro-electric power from stations built in connection with the gold-mining operations. The large local demand for fresh foodstuffs in the early days also encouraged market gardening; and garden and hothouse vegetables, as well as eggs and dairy products, were raised in the Dawson area in the early years of the present century. But all these industries faced economic difficulties, at first from an inability to compete for labour in view of the high wages of the gold-mining industry, and subsequently, from the relatively cheaper products imported from outside by way of the railway.

For business, too, the years after 1900 were characterized by decline. The exodus of miners and the reorganization of the mining industry greatly reduced the need for most professions and services, so these also were closed, further curtailing the market for goods and services. The supply businesses catering to the needs of the placer miners were adversely affected by the change-over to large-scale mining techniques, since the large companies imported their supplies direct. As business grew progressively poorer, weaker firms departed or merged, until only the stronger, or the more determined, remained to serve the needs of the shrunken market.

One industry, however, which held considerable possibilities for the future, did begin to develop shortly after the gold rush – the tourist industry. Improved communications by railway and steamer, the scenic grandeur of the train trip from Skagway to Whitehorse, the interesting trip by river steamer to Dawson, and the fascinating buildings falling into decay, soon become a strong attraction. The vast publicity attendant on the gold rush, the advertising by governments and transportation media, the continuing interest aroused by the novels of Jack London, H. A. Cody, Rex Beach, even Jules Verne, and, above all, the poems of Robert W. Service[23] – all served to attract annual streams of summer visitors to share vicariously in the adventures along the trial of '98, and feast their eyes on the scenes of Canada's most exciting modern-day adventure.

CHAPTER 6

The Yukon:
The Rise and Fall of a New Society

The Klondike gold rush was more than a dramatic moment in Canadian economic history. Increasingly, as students look below the surface, they recognize in it a most important and informative social experiment. S. D. Clark remarked that "Within this four-year period [1898-1902] the development of the Yukon passed through the full cycle of social disorganization and reorganization; for study of these social processes, few social laboratories could be more revealing."[1] The social history of the Yukon in the years to 1914 is still more complex. Proceed a few years farther, and a similarly informative period of institutional regression or disintegration is encountered. Furthermore, the social development of the Yukon reflected the highly unusual circumstances of time and place – the northern environment; a vigorous young nation seeking self-realization; and the close proximity of the powerful, aggressive American system. Again, the protagonists in the Yukon situation represented a bewildering array of social attitudes and moral codes – the largely ignored native element; the social order of the traditional mining camp of the Pacific frontier; the great variety of outlooks and attitudes carried by the Klondike-bound prospectors; the outlook of the Canadian frontier, typified by the government officials and the Canadian element among the gold-seekers, French and English; and finally, the metropolitan Canadian attitude characteristic of the older parts of Canada that directed the Dominion government's dealings with the territory. The Yukon, indeed, presents a fascinating, complicated range of differing, interacting social and political forces.

That the arrival in the Yukon of forty thousand or so Klondikers would lead to the creation of a new society is only to be expected. On the physical level, the newcomers faced problems of construction, sanitation, and providing for their accustomed amenities in the difficult northern environment. They learned how to adjust to, and work effectively in, the extreme temperatures and uneven days and nights characteristic of the region. Entering upon a primitive land, they created (or caused to be created for them) the whole apparatus of the sophisticated western civilization of their time. A complex, modern-day society in all its aspects was implanted practically overnight in the Yukon.

The Klondike gold rush also introduced the characteristic modern pattern of city and hinterland, in which the city was compelled to deal with many of the problems that have confronted northern settlements and projects of northern development since that time. The capital of Dawson – named after the diminutive geologist who had succeeded Selwyn as director of the Geological Survey in 1895 – was the full embodiment of the social and political institutions that reflected the transformed Yukon. Dawson was the heart of activity in the territory, the community whose growth from frenzied improvisation to stable, opulent, ornate city and then to decaying town mirrored the fate of the region. The city sprang up at the junction of the Klondike and Yukon rivers, on a wooded, swampy river flat, in response to the gold rush, and by the end of 1899, three years after Joseph Ladue applied for the townsite, it was a city of between fifteen and twenty thousand inhabitants, whose supporters asserted it to be the largest community in Canada west of Winnipeg.

Angelo Heilprin and Jeremiah Lynch, both of whom visited Dawson in the summer of 1898, described it as it was after the arrival of the largest wave of Klondikers.[2] The river was filled with hundreds of boats and rafts, from which horse-drawn wagons were bringing goods into town (this itself was a sign of progress; dogs had been the beasts of burden previously). The muddy main street was lined with a row of frame shacks, booths, or canvas tents, while business was also transacted from bales of goods piled on the street. The street was filled with a large number of loitering prospectors and miners, as well as uprooted men looking for a passage home. Others were building shops and houses of logs, for the one small sawmill could not supply sawn lumber quickly enough. A number of considerable buildings had already been finished – the large depots of the trading companies, sheathed in corrugated iron, the several saloons, gambling halls, and theatres or opera houses, where the men from the creeks spent their gold dust with a lavish prodigality that soon became legend.

When Lynch returned to Dawson a year later, he observed that Front Street now resembled the main street of a large city, with sewers, sidewalks, shops with plate-glass windows, and large stocks of goods, where one met scores of well-dressed men and women, while eleven steamboats lined the riverbank. Behind Front Street were Second and Third avenues with cross streets, lined with cabins, small hotels, and a few shops. The log cabins and tents were speedily being replaced with buildings of sawn lumber, and many houses possessed well-appointed, well-furnished rooms. Lynch commented that "Dawson was changed. From the winter of 1898, with its moccasins, single-roomed cabins, and tree-stumps in the streets, to the winter of 1899, with its neat felt shoes, well-appointed cottages of several rooms, and clear, straight streets."[3] J. B. Tyrrell, newly retired from the Geological Survey, had just come to Dawson to set up as a consulting geologist and mining engineer. After some delay he was able to purchase a frame house, open an office on Front Street, and invite his wife to join him in a friendly, peaceful, orderly town.

The change in buildings resulted in part from frequent fires, for large parts of the town already had been destroyed more than once. A series of stationary fire engines placed along the waterfront to pump water from the ice-covered river served as fire-fighting equipment. When an alarm was sounded, hoses were laid from the engines to the fire, but the water sometimes froze in the hoses and burst them, leaving no recourse but to dynamite buildings in the path of the flames. Not until the autumn of 1906, when a hydrant system was installed, did it become possible to combat winter fires effectively. The water was carried in wooden pipes and was kept from freezing by electric heaters attached to each hydrant.

But these were only temporary setbacks; almost before the ashes had cooled, plans for rebuilding were being laid. The steady pace of construction and improvement continued for several years. Commodious frame houses, spacious stores, and a number of roomy hotels with ample first-class accommodations made their appearance. Public buildings included a large Carnegie Library, the Dawson Amateur Athletic Association building, Masonic and Arctic Brotherhood halls, several churches, schools, and hospitals. In addition to the post office and other government buildings, an impressive administrative complex, befitting a territorial capital, arose on the government reserve: a courthouse with a three-storey Doric-columned front, the government house, and an administration building, the whole surrounded by Minto Park, planted in maples and firs, with a beautiful well-kept lawn in front, and tennis courts and recreation grounds behind. The city streets were flanked by wide, well-built sidewalks, a road was blasted around the mountainside, and a new bridge was completed across the Klondike; proper wharves eased the burden of unloading supplies and served as a reminder that Dawson was supplied mainly by water. Communications with St Michael's continued, as well as with Whitehorse, to which frequent riverboat and stage services operated to connect with the railway. From 1899, Dawson enjoyed telegraph contact with Skagway, and from 1901, with the Canadian Pacific system at Ashcroft. In 1900 telephone communication was installed in Dawson and with the mining camps, permitting miners to order and receive supplies from the city in a day.

The organization of the municipal life of Dawson proceeded more slowly than might be expected. As long as the permanence of the town was not assured, its inhabitants continued to depend on the territorial and federal governments for facilities, services, and expenditures. The territorial council, for its part, found Dawson a most burdensome responsibility. In 1898-99, council imposed a business tax, followed in 1900 with income and property taxes, this last being fixed at 12½ mills on an assessment of $11,600,000. At length, in July, 1901, after the council had passed an ordinance empowering large centres to become incorporated, a mass meeting came out in favour of an elected mayor and council, with the franchise to all ratepayers regardless of nationality. This last request was denied, and the right to vote in municipal elections was restricted to British subjects alone. After the inhabitants expressed by plebiscite a preference for an elected mayor and council rather than government by an appointed three-man commission, Dawson, with a population of 9,000 inhabitants, was incorporated as a city with powers to make local improvements and to organize and regulate local utilities. Many services continued to be furnished by the Dominion government (such as the police); by private companies which supplied utilities like water, electricity, telephones, and local railways; or by voluntary organizations, like the churches to which Dawson owed its two early hospitals. Reflecting the stabilizing quality of family life upon Dawson was the establishment, under the School Ordinance, of public elementary and high schools, as well as a Catholic separate school operated by the Sisters of Ste Anne.

The first hospital, St Mary's, was started by the Jesuit Father W. H. Judge, who followed the gold-miners from his station in Alaska, and began work in a tent on Main Street in 1897. By September, 1898, the tent had been replaced by a two-storey frame building, staffed by Sisters of Ste Anne of Lachine. Dr Andrew Grant's Good Samaritan Hospital was built in 1898 through the efforts of this Presbyterian missionary-doctor. Both institutions accepted all patients regardless of means or religious affiliation; both were financed by fees, donations, plus small *per-diem* allowances from the territorial council for indigent patients; and both were taxed to the limit by typhoid epidemics. To supplement their work, early in 1898 Lady Aberdeen arranged to send four members of the recently founded Victorian Order of Nurses to the Klondike.

Besides their hospital and educational work, the churches played a vastly important role by reminding miners and townsmen of their traditions and heritage, and binding them in fellowship with co-religionists throughout Canada and the world. Incomparably in the best position to assist the settlers was the Church of England, which alone had been active within the Yukon before the gold rush. Though Bishop Bompas's work was mainly with the Indians (Constantine said of him that "He has no use for any person unless he is an Indian"[4]), he was sufficiently concerned with the needs of the miners to strive to expand that aspect of the work. But financing mission work with the miners was difficult, for the Church Missionary Society would assist only native missions. In fact, from lack of clergy and money Bompas was not able to exploit the advantage of being first in the field. In 1895, however, he secured the Reverend R. J. Bowen for an assistant at Forty Mile and the Reverends H. A. Naylor and F. F. Flewelling in 1896, succeeded by the Reverend I. O. Stringer in 1903 and the Reverend H. A. Cody in 1904. Flewelling celebrated his first Anglican services in Dawson during the winter of 1896-97. He was followed by Bowen, who built the first St Paul's Church of logs and held the first service in it on October 24, 1897. In 1900, Bowen built the first Anglican church at Whitehorse, to which Stringer came in 1903. When Bishop Bompas resigned on November 15, 1905, Stringer was appointed in his place, moving from Whitehorse to Dawson. The two were conferring on future plans for the diocese at Carcross, Bishop Bompas's headquarters, when on June 9, 1906, the good bishop suddenly died, bringing to a close a magnificent forty-five-year record of missionary achievements.

After the heroic Father Judge died, mainly from overwork, in 1899, the Jesuits turned the work over to the Oblates and the Yukon became part of the newly formed (1901) apostolic vicariate of Mackenzie under Bishop Gabriel Breynat, O.M.I. A group of Oblates (few of them fluent in English) under the Reverend P. E. Gendreau was transferred to the region from east of the Rockies. By the first decade of the new century, Roman Catholic work in the Yukon was directed by the Reverend E. Bunoz, O.M.I., at Dawson, under whom six Oblates preached and taught in eleven centres. In addition, twelve Sisters of Ste Anne operated the school and hospital in Dawson.

Two more major Canadian churches also were represented in the gold-rush community. The Methodists did not seem particularly interested in the Yukon, perhaps because the China Mission was absorbing so much of their attention. Their effort was slow in being started, and the first missionary, the Reverend James Turner, did not arrive in the country until early in 1898, to be followed by the Reverend A. E. Hetherington, who opened a log church in Dawson in October, 1898. The Presbyterians gave a much better account of themselves, perhaps because of the interest in the Klondike of the Reverend James G. Robertson, superintendent of the home missions, who observed the beginnings of the gold rush from Victoria and took immediate action. In the summer of 1897 he sent the Reverend R. M. Dickey to Skagway, where he built a church and school. He was followed in the spring of 1898 by the Reverend A. J. Sinclair and the Reverend Dr Andrew Grant. Sinclair occupied the church at Lake Bennett, while Grant and Dickey pushed ahead to Dawson. Within a year Dr Grant built his own church there and began work on the Good Samaritan Hospital. Dickey next established a church at Bonanza, where he was joined by the Reverend John Pringle, who had worked at Telegraph Creek and Atlin during 1898 and 1899 before proceeding to Dawson in 1901. The Canadian churches contributed reasonably well towards the Yukon mission, while the Dawson Presbyterians quickly paid for the local buildings and became the first self-supporting congregation in the Yukon.

The Salvation Army also was represented in Dawson from November, 1898, serving a valuable role for the unsettled and unemployed, while Seventh Day Adventists also made occasional appearances in the territory. Thanks to its predominantly white settlement, the Yukon soon displayed the religious diversity so characteristic of Europe and America, but so different from the norm of primitive Canada.

In the ten years after 1896 the Yukon enjoyed a very lively political climate. Partly this reflected the serious need of an undeveloped region for favourable legislation to help meet its many needs. Partly it arose because control over its affairs was exercised by far-away Ottawa and it therefore became necessary to guard against the imposition of unsuitable policies through ignorance, partisan motives, or secret political influence. In the main, however, political activity arose out of the character of the settlement itself – the ebullient press; the universal confidence in the future of the Yukon as a self-sustaining, self-governing portion of the Dominion; the inhabitants' traditions of participation in government and their concern with securing the best possible future for themselves and their fellows; plus the ambitions of many individual settlers coming from political backgrounds.

Many controversies arose out of attempts at regulating the mining industry, an area of vital concern over which the federal government kept unreasonably tight control, allowing little initiative either to its own agents or to the territorial administrators. Settlers also agitated for better roads, bridges, river transport, public buildings, railway and telegraph communications with the outside world, and, after the railway was completed, for lower rates on the line. The need for assistance to deal with problems of relief, health, education, Indians, liquor, and policing powers were other predictable subjects for political agitation. The subordinate status of the territory and of its inhabitants before an all-powerful Dominion government, notably the Minister of the Interior, was an especial source of complaint and unrest in view of the partisan appointments and favouritism, or worse, in the disposal of mining lands, construction contracts, and the like. Above all, the settlers voiced complaints against Ottawa's dilatoriness in instituting representative institutions and extending the franchise to all white male residents.

Though the settlers were disfranchised under the terms of the existing Yukon Act, they were not without means of putting pressure upon the Dominion government. To begin with, they provided a large revenue for Ottawa, in return for which they expected, and felt entitled to, an adequate level of service from the federal administration. They came to the Yukon in their thousands, and carried with them the mature political attitudes of the lands they had left, particularly of the United States, with its tradition of securing favourable government decisions through political action. Regarding themselves as oppressed, they pressed for political rights for the territory and themselves, though in neighbouring Alaska American citizens alone were allowed to take out mining claims, and that territory also lacked elective institutions.

The newspapers were another potent source of intense political activity during these years. The Yukon possessed a most vigorous press, beginning with the *Klondike Nugget* and the *Yukon Midnight Sun* in June, 1898, followed by the *Klondike Miner*, and, in 1899, by the *Dawson Daily News*. For nearly three years the territorial capital continued to be served by four newspapers. When the *Miner* ceased publication in 1902, the field was left to three, and then by 1904 to two daily newspapers, the *Daily News* and the newly established *Daily World*.

The newspapers were relentless in attacking abuses and arousing the public against administrative shortcomings. They agitated against the lack of elected representatives on the territorial council, raising the old cry of taxation without representation. They fought against the closed sittings of the council and demanded that they be opened to the public, which they were in August, 1899. They led the fight against the abuses in the gold commissioner's office and defects in the mining regulations, denounced the concessions of land to friends of the administration, and spearheaded the drive against the Treadgold Concession. In fact, the newspapers were in the fore in all the popular campaigns. Their ownership changed hands as political parties sought to use them to propagate their views, while governments tried to gain their support through the judicious disbursement of printing contracts.

The means *par excellence* for political activity in the early days was the mass meeting, which in some ways was an outgrowth of the traditional miners' meeting, except that it no longer proceeded to direct action. A mass meeting, usually announced and advertised in advance by its organizers, discussed motions and passed resolutions which were then circulated or directed to some appropriate authority. In 1897 a miners' mass meeting was called to criticize the Dominion's placer-mining regulations. Instead of drawing up new regulations as a miners' meeting would have done, the mass meeting sent two delegates to Ottawa to present their views to the government. These delegates reported to a later mass meeting on how

Laurier had received their requests. Other mass meetings passed resolutions for the abolition of the royalty on gold, while one, in July, 1898, after discussing the Dominion Creek affair, appointed an eleven-man committee to draw up the petition that brought about the establishment of the Ogilvie commission.

The mass meeting had one serious defect: it was a good method for ascertaining and expressing public opinion, but it lacked a permanent organization to safeguard the people's interests. Consequently, permanent committees were required, to meet at regular intervals and call mass meetings when needed. A mass meeting of August 12, 1898, resulted in the formation of a Miners' Association, headed by a Committee of Eleven. At the same time a rival group, appealing to the tradesman as well as the miner, held meetings in support of its own particular goals – the establishment of municipal institutions and the awarding of the franchise to all property holders, regardless of nationality. This group planned to form a Citizens' Committee, but in the end the Miners' Association broadened its base and took over both programs. In 1900 a Citizens' Committee finally was formed to campaign for greater autonomy, the incorporation of Dawson, representation in Parliament, abolition of the royalty, and the recall of Commissioner Ogilvie. In view of its leadership and much of its program, this committee was suspected of being an agent of the Conservative party. The stuggle against the Treadgold Concession brought a coalition of all groups and parties and the appointment of a twenty-man committee which sent two delegates to Ottawa in February, 1902, to protest to Sifton against the concessions policy. A combination in the early months of 1903 of Miners' Association, Dawson Board of Trade, and Dawson Liberal Club probably played a major part in bringing about the appointment of the Britton commission.

The purpose of the mass meetings and of the permanent committees was to exert pressure on those who could influence the trend of affairs in the Yukon – the territorial government, federal government officials who visited the territory, and especially, the Dominion government. The Laurier administration received a succession of delegations, while the settlers also lobbied directly with the Canadian public to press those in whose hands lay the destiny of the Yukon. The newspapers were a major force in arousing public opinion within the territory and advertising its needs outside. As time passed, however, sending delegations to Ottawa became less of a necessity. Improving communications by mail and telegraph made it less likely that the government could long remain ignorant of conditions or of the true state of opinion in the Yukon. Besides, with the returning of a member to the House of Commons in 1902, he became the official territorial delegate and spokesman, the recognized channel of communication between the Yukon and the federal authorities.

Opportunities for the inhabitants to exert their influence upon the key figures of the federal government came with the surprisingly infrequent visits to the Yukon of those dignitaries. Of particular importance, in view of the timing, was a visit in August, 1900, of Lord Minto, the governor general. Minto was entertained by the leading officials, businesmen, and miners, and was presented with a casket of gold nuggets by Alex McDonald, the most successful of the early miners and reputedly the wealthiest man in the Yukon. Though Minto was careful to tell his visitors he could only receive their information, privately he informed the government that most of their recommendations were "fair and reasonable," though he considered the society still too fluid for a wholly elected council to be altogether desirable. He agreed with the criticisms of Sifton he received, and expressed the view that Ogilvie was too weak to control the situation.[5] No doubt his report, added to others, contributed to Ogilvie's retirement in February, 1901, and his replacement by J. H. Ross, a member of the executive council of the North-West Territories. Sifton, as Minister of the Interior from 1896 to 1905, presided over the destinies of the Yukon through the entire critical period, but resisted repeated pleas from the settlers to come and see for himself. His successor as minister from 1905 to 1911, Frank Oliver, M.P. for Edmonton, visited the Yukon twice – in 1905 and again in 1910 – with results that were adjudged useful from the standpoint of the territory.

Thanks to the settlers' own efforts, as well as those of their allies outside – notably the Conservative party in the Commons, which made itself the spokesman of the settlers' complaints and of their yearning for greater autonomy – the Yukon received considerable attention from the Dominion government and major complaints were gradually redressed. The mining interest eventually secured most of its requests through political action, but proved unable to prevent the trend to concentration of mining operations. Suggestions that the government should build and operate a water-gathering and supply system for the benefit of all users received no support, nor did the request for an assay office in Dawson (though one was provided in Vancouver in 1901). The settlers secured considerable outlays on roads, wharves, telegraph and public buildings, as well as on the legal and administrative system, the police, and the like. Noteworthy, too, was the impressive judicial system established with a single judge in 1897 and expanded to a bench of three judges to act as an appeal court from the police magistrates' courts and rule on constitutional questions. With the judges at the head of the legal system and police officers as justices of the peace and coroners, the territory possessed a very effective legal system, in marked contrast with that of neighbouring Alaska.

The territory achieved the beginnings of representative government principally by the residents' own efforts, re-enforced by those of the opposition in Parliament. Almost from the beginning settlers began demanding the right to elect members to the territorial council and to the House of Commons. The Dominion government was slow to accede to this demand, partly out of its desire to shape the development of the Yukon in line with national interests (as it saw them), partly because of its uncertainty as to the future of a district which had sprung up so suddenly and dramatically from nothing. Unquestionably, its hesitancy was intensified by the large number of American citizens present in the Yukon. The government was in a dilemma. It feared to give them the voice their numbers warranted lest they imperil the security of the territory in a time of difficult relations with the United States; or, alternately, to give them a grievance by keeping them disfranchised while Canadians controlled affairs, like the Boers in the Transvaal – an unhappy analogy cited more than once. Hence it moved with extreme caution and postponed its decision, using the uncertain size of the population as an excuse.

The campaign for representation, which grew in intensity because of the government's slowness, came to a head in 1900 with Yukoners' appeals for two Members of Parliament. The Conservatives seized on the question to chastise the government for disregarding the expressed will of the settlers and demanded federal representation forthwith. Laurier argued it was necessary first to await the results of the decennial census in order to determine federal representation, though he was willing to permit the immediate addition of elected representatives to the territorial council. Only in 1902 did the territory receive a Member of Parliament, elected by adult male British subjects who had twelve months' residence in the territory. The first election saw the commissioner, J. H. Ross, nominated by the Yukon Liberal Association and elected after a bitter contest.

Simultaneously, a campaign was proceeding for greater self-government on the territorial level. On May 2, 1900, when there were some 4,000 British subjects in the Yukon, Commissioner Ogilvie telegraphed Sifton that "Council sees no objection to granting local representation."[6] After Laurier expressed his willingness on this point, Parliament gave the council authority to levy new local taxes, and augmented its membership by two elected members. In 1902 the number of elected members was increased to five, equal to that of the appointed members.[7] The first territorial elections were held on October 17, 1900, the seats being contested by two candidates nominated by the Citizens' Committee, and two Independents, both of whom were known Liberals. An interesting feature was that each slate included one French-Canadian nominee. After a campaign waged mainly on the administration's record, the Citizens' Committee candidates emerged victorious. There was a significant amount of ballot-splitting along national lines, with the English-speaking candidates running well ahead of their colleagues. Shortly after the election, perhaps because of the disappointing showing of the Independents, a Yukon Liberal Association was formed, first to work for a suitable successor to Ogilvie, then later to secure Ross's election as M.P. for the Yukon.

The Yukon council found the management of the affairs of the communities – Dawson in particular – very difficult and costly, but eventually provided Dawson with an elected municipal government. At the same time the council passed an ordinance authorizing unincorporated communities of at least ten buildings to petition for limited self-government – authority to elect a paid overseer, hold an annual public business meeting to review his work, consider the estimates for the following year, and assess and levy taxes on property. The administration could then arrange for fire prevention, public works, the control of disease, regulation of stray animals, and the like.[8] Only one community adopted this form of government, the town of Grand Forks (later renamed Bonanza) at the junction of Eldorado and Bonanza creeks, and Grand Forks soon faded with the decline in mining operations and was abandoned, later to be buried under the debris of dredging operations.

A right of local self-government that had greater significance and survival power was that of establishing school districts and operating schools according to a system analogous to that of the North-West Territories. A number of boards were set up in Dawson and on the main gold creeks. To manage this and other of its functions, the council gradually acquired its own territorial civil service – including such officials as a secretary, treasurer, superintendent of works, officer of health, licence inspector, and superintendent of schools – and regulated it under the provisions of the Public Service Ordinance of 1902.[9]

But the ability of the territorial council to play a meaningful role in the development of the Yukon was hampered by its lack of control over the commissioner at the head of the territorial administration and its limited powers of authority, particularly over natural resources, which were all-important for the progress of the territory. Even though the Yukon was contributing large tax revenues to the Dominion treasury, the council, in the absence of the revenue from Crown lands or the power to borrow money, had very limited financial resources. Consequently, the territory had to rely on private enterprises to provide most public utilities – the thirty-two-mile Klondike Mines Railway from Dawson to Grand Forks and the Dome, the hydro-electric power companies, the telephone system, even the civic waterworks.

II

In establishing the permanent community of the Yukon it had been necessary to set aside the pre-existing Indian society and the self-regulating mining-camp society that had held sway in the region since placer mining began there in the eighties. The miners and the police quickly found a common interest in order and stability and the former readily accepted external controls that did not differ too radically from their own ways and facilitated their going about their business more securely. Ogilvie claimed in May, 1897, that the miners were glad to give up their meetings as a way of adjudicating disputes and that they welcomed the arrival of the rule of law – even Canadian law.

The vaster influx inspired by news of the gold strike created somewhat different problems. The newcomers were not miners accustomed to the conditions of the country, nor to accepting directions from above. Many were drawn to the Klondike by their desire to break with established conventions and to "kick over the traces" while away from home. Adventurous, chauvinistic, Americans for the most part, all were seeking a new life, a chance to achieve fame or fortune, and did not appreciate having their freedom of action cramped, regulated, or controlled by Canadian functionaries. Still, though Tappan Adney portrayed the Americans as resentful of the (to them) alien aspects of the territorial administration, he was quick to add that "if there were not serious disorders it was due less to the quality of government than to the orderly character of the population, and to the fact that men were there enduring the privations of an Arctic climate to make their fortunes and get away, not to help set in order the political household of their Canadian friends."[10]

Undoubtedly the Klondike did attract some criminal or near-criminal elements, seeking new fields where money was easily secured since it was so plentiful. When a city like Seattle cleaned house, many of the displaced tried to move on to the Yukon. Constantine reported (January 18, 1898) that "The majority of the newcomers are from the United States, many of them could well be spared in any community. The rush has brought in toughs, gamblers, fast women, and criminals of almost every type, from the petty thief to the murderer. . . . A considerable number of the people coming in from the Sound cities appear to be the sweepings of the slums and the result of a general jail delivery."[11] However, the police succeeded in keeping out such undesirables, to judge from the claim eleven years later of Assistant Commissioner Z. T. Wood that "the population has always been law abiding notwithstanding the heterogeneous mixture of the multitude of gold seekers in the rush of 1897 and 1898. There have been twelve (12) murders committed in a period of thirteen (13) years, all the murderers being convicted and executed but one who died before the day set for his execution."[12] This remarkably clean record as regards crimes of violence did not mean that the Yukon lacked its share of lesser crimes and misdemeanours. Indeed, in the latter area the record would have been much blacker had the police not decided against rigorously enforcing certain laws. In this, as in other aspects of their Yukon work, the police adopted a policy of acting in accordance with the needs of the region, as they and the settlers saw them. Just as the police had decided who could come to the Yukon or how traffic should move around the White Horse Rapids, so they used their discretion in setting up systems of social controls and law enforcement. Wood advised the commanding officer at Whitehorse that the police should not fine offenders like prostitutes or gamblers on a regular basis, as though they were collecting a kind of business tax; instead, they should be ignored altogether unless they openly infringed the laws, and only then should the police proceed to appropriate action. Ogilvie, like Wood, agreed that activities like gambling, liquor, and prostitution were inevitable under the circumstances of the Yukon, arguing that it was better if such activities were carried on openly rather than clandestinely, where they would likely proceed to far more noxious, dangerous practices.

In this they reflected the considerable discrepancy that existed between the social norms of the Yukon frontier and those of contemporary Canada. From the commencement of the gold rush a campaign was waged by the Canadian public, through the Dominion government, to impose the standards of southern Canada on the Yukon. The government in Ottawa was pressed to secure the vigorous enforcement of existing laws and the enactment of new ones to control those activities that offended Canadians' sense of propriety. The same pressures that were forcing the Laurier government to yield on the matter of the Lord's Day Act found a cause in making over the Yukon into a model frontier society. This seemed all the more worthy since it was a way of differentiating the Yukon from the United States and re-enforcing its Canadian identity. A big step was achieved during the brief stay of the North-West Territories plenipotentiary, G. H. V. Bulyea. His licensing commission worked out a system that, besides securing revenue, compelled the saloons to maintain lodgings for at least twenty guests, and no gambling tables; and to close from 2:00 to 6:00 a.m. every night, and from Saturday midnight to Monday 6:00 a.m. to observe the Sabbath. On the creeks the nightly closing was excused, but even there Sunday closing – the Canadian Sunday – prevailed.

Puritanical forces inside and outside the Yukon could not be denied. The arrival of families demanding orderly, moral conditions in the territory was strengthened by the activities of outside organizations. Roused by lurid accounts of conditions in Dawson, these pressed the Dominion government to take vigorous action against gambling, dancehalls, prostitution, and other infractions of the moral code of southern Canada. The business community of Dawson, the miners, and even Commissioner Ogilvie opposed the attempt to impose outside standards upon their society, but the pressure was unrelenting. In 1901-2 restrictions were imposed on the gambling halls, the sale of liquor in dancehalls was forbidden, and prostitutes were barred from Dawson and compelled to move across the Klondike to Klondike City. By the end of 1902 Dawson was said to be not very different from many Canadian cities of comparable size.

Still the criticism continued, notably by the Reverend J. Pringle, the Presbyterian missionary to the miners who had been elected to the territorial council in 1903. After complaining unsuccessfully in private letters to Laurier, Pringle began circularizing the eastern Canadian press with charges that immorality was not being checked and that members of the administration had an interest in such laxity. Once again the sale of liquor in the dancehalls was prohibited, with the result that the last one closed in 1908. The Presbyterian Church of Canada endorsed Pringle's action and the Conservatives took up the attack in Parliament.[13] In Dawson the commissioner protested that "the Yukon Territory and Dawson will compare favorably with any part of America and with any town in the respect paid to law and order, the regard for morality and observance of all social, commercial, legal and religious conventions, decencies and amenities."[14] The territorial council also passed a resolution regretting Pringle's campaign of calumny, slander, and vilification.

The police filled many functions besides shaping the limits of the emerging society. They investigated breaches of federal or territorial laws, made arrests, and arranged for trials of offenders. They acted as coroners, as justices of the peace, maintained jails, and supervised prisoners, mostly by setting them "to saw wood for the Queen." They patrolled and visited all parts of the territory, checked the passing of liquor to Indians, and looked after the indigent. In the early years, on behalf of other departments, they acted as mining recorders, Crown lands and timber agents, served as game wardens and fire wardens, and collected customs and other taxes. They escorted visiting dignitaries about the territory, and sometimes, to their intense disgust, found themselves conscripted as glorified batmen to minor government officials. They hauled the mail in and out of the territory at great difficulty to themselves and considerable expense to the public, and served as local postmasters and telegraph agents.

Their role was also far more fundamental: they controlled travel in and out of the country. As late as 1909 Wood observed that

> All persons leaving the Territory either via Forty Mile or Whitehorse are searched by the Police for gold on which royalty has not been paid; the Immigration Officers at both ports of entry are assisted in their efforts to keep undesirables out of the Territory; a register is kept of all boats and scows leaving White Horse for Dawson, and the names of the

occupants. Copies are forwarded the Police in Dawson who check up the arrivals as each boat reaches its destination. This register has been of great service in keeping track of suspects, and in preventing crime on the long stretch of river between White Horse and Dawson.[15]

They supervised doubtful elements who had gained entry to the territory. Steele caused a register to be made of all suspicious characters, and then set detectives to watch the movements of those people. Constantine, who had a strong fear of American conspiracies to overthrow Canadian control of the Yukon, had his detectives in the winter of 1897-98 infiltrate American organizations so as to be advised of their activities. The touchy political situation, the current high tide of imperialistic adventuring, and the many disputes over Yukon boundaries or the rights of transit through Alaska all disposed Canadian authorities to be on their guard. Frederick White, who, as comptroller of the police, was constantly in touch with the situation in the Yukon, wrote of a threat of American "Spread-Eagleism" to organize a filibuster against the Yukon from a base in Skagway in the winter of 1901-2.[16] But nothing overt ever occurred, either because of the deterrent effect of the police and the Yukon Field Force, or because there never was anything more serious behind the fears than saloon talk.

Thanks to the police, newcomers to the Yukon found a complete contrast with their experience and expectations. It was certainly no untrammelled wilderness where a man could play Caesar, but virtually a police state, in which the police wielded the widest discretionary powers. Yet they exercised this power in exemplary fashion, without causing unnecessary aggravation, and by their own clean record they quite disarmed criticism of their motives, if not of their actions. That such power was not abused and was exercised with such success must be credited to the very able, incorruptible men – notably Charles Constantine, Samuel B. Steele, Albert B. Perry, and Zachary T. Wood – who directed the force in the Yukon during the hectic years after 1894.

Backing the decisions of these doughty defenders of Canadian interests was a force that totalled about three hundred between 1898 and 1904. Besides the large divisional forces at Dawson and Whitehorse, staffs of four men or more were maintained in at least fourteen centres. Dawson itself was under patrol round the clock by four of the ten-man squad assigned to that duty, so public places were visited many times each day. The gold creeks were similarly patrolled and outlying settlements were visited in the summer by boat and in winter by dog team. The most onerous of the regular patrols was the rather needless annual four-hundred-mile trip each way executed in mid-winter between Dawson and Fort McPherson, to carry despatches between these two northernmost police posts.

The police, and the style of government administration typified by them, produced a distinctive socio-political pattern in the Yukon. It was grounded on a philosophy of the state that contrasted sharply with that of the United States, on which the American newcomers based their own conduct. Hence the Yukon was the locale of a fascinating contrast between two different North American political philosophies. The American version stressed local autonomy and the right of settlers to establish their own system of government and frame their own regulations. In the territories of the United States, federal government authority was asserted diffidently and always was likely to be challenged in the name of the citizen's right of self-determination, and by the confident assertion that he, not some distant authority, knew his own situation best. Such a system facilitated the rapid and total development of the potentialities of a frontier region. There was little or no taxation from outside to drain off the capital produced from the region, a highly individualistic and competitive local situation stimulated and encouraged local initiative to the utmost degree, and few regulations were imposed from outside to check the triumph of the most efficient producers or the speedy reorganization of industry to maximize profits.

Against this stood the tradition of Canadian administration, sprung from British roots – a tradition of authority, of rules and regulations established from outside, of development controlled and directed in the presumed general, or national, rather than the particular local, or regional, interest. The complex framework of regulations and institutions developed in Ottawa was upheld and administered on the frontiers by various federal government agencies – the police, Indian administration, Dominion Lands Branch, and the like – that sought to be first on the ground and in sufficient force to impose a pre-determined pattern of orderly development. Settlers were expected to look to these agencies – or beyond them to the central government – to implement their needs, rather than attempt to provide for their needs from their own resources or evolve their own form of government. Thus the frontier tradition of Canada was one of unspectacular, orderly, solid development under external guidance, characterized by fewer abuses and injustices than its American counterpart perhaps, but also by little of the obsessive, all-consuming drive to speedy, efficient development and exploitation of natural resources, of which the United States is mankind's supreme exponent.

The battle to shape the institutions and society of the Yukon was won for Canada by the efforts of police, administration, legal system, and the churches, shaped and sustained by the desires of the Canadian people. The administration of the Yukon was in the hands of a powerful appointed civil service who owed their places not to local elections but to the Dominion government, and were far less amenable to local pressures than locally elected officials would have been. Elective institutions came belatedly, and in so far as authority was not tightly maintained by Ottawa, care was taken to transfer it to the Canadian sector of the population. In appearance the Yukon came to resemble its Canadian more than its American heritage. Guns and gunplay were almost unheard of. The universal presence of the police deterred crimes and made for a quiet, orderly environment. The firm controls instituted over the sale of liquor, gambling, and prostitution – carried farther than the officials on the ground themselves considered advisable – were another sharp differentiation from the American West. Above all, the Sunday observance that was the hallmark of the Canadian way of life of the Edwardian era made its unlikely appearance even in this remote corner of the country. The history of the Yukon after 1896 was the triumph of the Canadian regulated frontier tradition, notwithstanding the contiguity of the Yukon to American territory and influences. The efforts of political and administrative agencies of the Canadian government were supplemented by Canadian social agencies, so that in little more than a decade the Yukon Territory was integrated within the Canadian institutional and social framework. The Canadian frontier had swept forward a thousand miles to plant on the Yukon an offshoot of Canadian civilization in the image of Winnipeg, Toronto, or Ottawa. How far the Yukon was altered may be seen in the way the territory joined most of Canada in going prohibitionist by plebiscite in 1920.

The separate but related contest for the economic control of the Yukon – for a channelling of the fruits of the mining and other industries of the region for the benefit of the country as a whole – was another matter. American control of the Yukon economy was very difficult, if not impossible, to break. The overwhelming majority of the early miners took their winnings out with them to spend in the United States, and as far as they could, also purchased their supplies there. Even when the industry moved on to the age of dredges and long-distance flumes and to the corporate level of organization, most of the companies that replaced the individual miners were American-controlled (even if sometimes largely British-financed).

The Canadian government exerted itself to cut into this trade pattern. It strove to channel imports into the Yukon to Canadian centres of supply by strict enforcement of the customs regulations. The government throughout strove to secure its own supplies from Canadian sources. G. M. Dawson encountered an interesting example on September 26, 1897, while travelling east across the prairies from Calgary: "Pass a freight train with car loads of dogs En route for Yukon. This is the third car sent out by the police for carrying mail in the winter. Dogs collected from various places, broken to harness. This lot from as far East as Missinaibi & White River."[17] Because of complaints that much of the American dominance of the trade resulted from the presence of assay offices in Seattle and San Francisco (Seattle's drew almost $17,000,000 of the $22,300,000 of gold believed to have been recovered in 1900),[18] the Dominion government was led to open an assay office in Vancouver. Perhaps the strongest card in Canada's economic hand was finance. Federal control of banking no doubt accounted for the domination of financial operations within the Yukon by branches of two Canadian banking companies.

To promote trade with the Yukon, Canadian manufacturers were urged to push products similar to those used in the contest for the trade of Klondike-bound travellers in 1897 and 1898: specialty goods, mining supplies, hardware, outdoor work clothing, fresh meat and other foods, soap or candles, and mining machinery appropriate to the new level of operations. In the Yukon itself economic nationalists had to fight powerful interests geared to the American trade, like the Northern Commercial Company which H. J. Woodside claimed had obtained his dismissal as editor of the *Yukon Sun* in 1901 in retaliation for his outspoken "Buy Canadian" policy.[19] These efforts slowly turned the economic tide, and by October, 1902, Canadian firms were reported as doing 60 per cent of the trading business of the Yukon.[20]

Transportation routes and facilities were a considerable part of the key to controlling the trade of the Yukon, and the opening of the route in 1900 via Skagway and the White Pass and Yukon Railway gave Canadian businessmen a good chance to break the American economic domination of the Yukon. Vancouver soon became the main trading centre with the Yukon, thanks to the development of frequent, speedy ship service to Skagway, and concern was expressed that the railway should keep its rates low enough to undercut the service by the Yukon River route through Alaska that played into the hands of American west coast trading interests. In 1904 the Dominion government even attempted to reduce trade by that route by ordering, in effect, that all Canadian goods shipped to the Yukon be carried to Skagway and not to St Michael's, only to be forced to rescind the move by threats of retaliatory action.[21] But increasingly the dwindling trade of the region became more strongly oriented to Canadian centres.

III

Just as Dawson City testified to the prosperity of the gold-rush years, so it also was quick to respond to the economic downturn. As early as 1904, real property could no longer find buyers even at a small fraction of the former market value. T. A. Rickard, a writer on mining subjects who visited the Yukon in 1908, described its appearance as follows:

> A stroll through Dawson gives an impression of respectability compelled by impoverishment, of the temperance that succeeds dissipation, of the bust after the boom. . . . The streets are unpaved black loam, luckily dry just now, and the wooden sidewalks, in places rickety, are weather-beaten but clean. The main street follows the water-front and the wharves are more numerous than required by the diminished traffic. . . . North-ward are many untenanted buildings, and even the centre of the town bears a bedraggled appearance, indicative of shrunken commerce. During the boom days the population was 50,000; now it is 2000. Dawson looks like a stout man who has grown very thin and yet wears the cloths made for him in his adipose days. Although it has been difficult for Dawson to accommodate itself to straitened circumstances, the adaptation has been effected heroically. The boom has gone, but business remains.[22]

Rickard was exaggerating, inasmuch as the population of Dawson never exceeded 25,000 or 30,000 even in its most crowded moments, while its population in 1908 was probably somewhat greater than 2,000. By 1912, when the population had fallen to approximately 2,500, the city was described to the Empire Club of Toronto as follows:

> Whole streets of empty houses, fast decaying, can be seen. The old building that the government used for its offices and paid, I believe, $1,700 a month rent for, is torn down and the logs used for firewood. We had 45 lawyers in 1902; today there are only four, and doctors have decreased in nearly the same proportion.[23]

Dawson's fate was shared by other Yukon communities like the village of Bonanza (formerly Grand Forks), Lake Bennett, the boat-building centre at the start of navigation down the Yukon in 1898, and "Conrad City," near Carcross, which sprang to life, then disappeared with the rise and fall of the Whitehorse copper-mining belt. On the other hand, reflecting the transportation revolution, was the rise of Whitehorse, which had its inception with the completion of the White Pass and Yukon Railway to that point. Rickard described Whitehorse as a prospering town of large railway warehouses alongside the river, steamboats busy taking on cargoes and handling a large influx downriver of 3,000 persons thus far during the spring of 1908. Businesses included a bakery, a steam laundry, a weekly newspaper, the *Star*, founded in 1900, a branch of the Canadian Bank of Commerce from 1905 (in which the poet Robert Service worked), telephone service, and street lighting. Public buildings included three churches, public and separate schools, a hospital, and the large police divisional headquarters establishment. In 1911 the town, boasting eighteen stores and ten hotels, had an approximate population of 800.

Thus the Yukon gradually settled down to a tranquil existence, punctuated by the annual seasonal rhythms of life and work – in the spring and summer the lengthening days, the return of part-time residents from outside, the opening of navigation, the arrival of the summertime workers and tourists, and the bursting of the country into full activity; in the autumn and winter the closing down of operations, the departure of the summer workers and tourists, and the permanent residents' preparations to cope with another long, cold, dark winter. There were the meetings of church organizations, the Masonic Lodge, Arctic Brotherhood, and other societies, the rounds of visits and the "at homes," the annual climbs up the mountain behind Dawson on June 21 to view the midnight sun, the Ice Derby with its wagers on when the ice would move down the Yukon River in front of Dawson. Yukoners also shared in the greater and lesser concerns of the day – in the rather absurd foray of a Klondike hockey team to Ottawa to compete for the Stanley Cup in 1905, the recruiting of a Yukon Infantry Company by the millionaire mining entrepreneur Joe Boyle, the gallant actions of this 226-man unit that went to France as the 17th Machine Gun Company, and the tragic, needless loss of 313 passengers' lives in the wreck on October 23, 1918 of the steamship *Princess Sophia*, outward bound for Vancouver.

The population figures revealed by the decennial censuses exemplify the decline of the Yukon most strikingly. From the first one, taken in 1901, which showed a population of 27,219 (unquestionably below the peak reached in 1898-99 of probably close to 40,000), the total dropped to 8,512 a decade later, then to 4,157 in 1921, a figure maintained in 1931 (4,230) and not greatly increased (4,914) even as late as 1941. Since the territory included an Indian sector of between 1,500 and 2,000 persons throughout, the white population must have fallen by 1921 to less than one-tenth the number in 1901. In spite of the boom during the Second World War and the subsequent upsurge of industry in the Yukon, its present population is still far below that of the boom years.

Despite the obvious decline in the population and prospects of the Yukon Territory, the federal government persisted for some time with its program of extending the elected membership of the territorial council. The increase to five elected members as against five appointed occurred in 1905, when Laurier conceded it was now perhaps time for this step that had been too hazardous to contemplate when the Yukon Territory was new. The final concession, a council of ten elected members, was not granted until May, 1908, when the territory at last received full representative government.

But even while the enlargement of the elected membership of the council was proceeding, an opposite, downward trend was in evidence, for the Yukon, like Newfoundland, has experienced the curtailment of its democratic institutions as a result of adverse conditions. In 1904, after a plebiscite, the ratepayers of Dawson voted to replace their elected municipal government with an appointed one, and the short-lived experiment in elective municipal government was terminated. Also at the end of 1904 the federal and territorial governments dismissed large numbers of officials in the interests of economy, while the salaries of the remainder were drastically cut on the grounds of the reduced cost of living. The extra duties fell to the police (renamed Royal North-west Mounted Police since 1904), who gradually again resumed the nearly universal functions against which Constantine had complained in 1896. They were the obvious group to take over these duties; though their numbers also were considerably reduced – from the 303-man force of 1903 to 74 men in 1909 – they covered most of the territory from their nine permanent detachments in patrols by riverboat, wagon, and dog team.

The first overt steps in the reduction of the political status of the territory were a little longer in coming. In 1912 the judicial system was reduced from three justices to a single judge. Even though the territory as late as 1917 was producing $502,000 in federal government revenues, against padded expenditures of $956,000 (including such items as the government telegraph, $218,000; postal service, $123,000; and Department of the Interior administration, $344,000),[24] the federal government in 1918 proposed to abolish the offices of commissioner, administrator, director of surveys, assistant gold commissioner, mining inspector, legal adviser, various mining recorders and clerks and to replace the elected council by an appointed one of two or more members.[25] This was too drastic, however, and in the end, the council in 1919 was reduced from ten to three elected members. The consolidation of administrative offices proceeded; the positions of commissioner and gold commissioner, after being held on an acting basis by the gold commissioner George Mackenzie since 1918, were merged in 1920.

As the Yukon began to decline to something approaching the emptiness of pre-gold-rush days, the Indian population assumed a more prominent position on the territorial landscape. Now that there was less concern with planning for an expanding white industrial community, there was time to take stock of what the changes had meant for the Indian inhabitants and what role they might play in the Yukon Territory of the post-gold-rush epoch. The changes had brought excellent economic opportunities for many Indians. From the days of the climb over the passes, Indians found employment as porters, deckhands, and unskilled labourers at the mines and in the settlements. The government's original thought, as expressed to Constantine, had simply been to encourage Indians to become assimilated into the society of the incoming settlers: "The instructions concerning Indian affairs given me when I came to this Country was that the Indians were not to be recognized in any way which would lead them to believe the Govt would do any thing for them as Indians."[26] They were therefore largely left to their own devices in the white community and sometimes adopted the worst habits of the white man. The three members of the Carmack party, who played so great a part in starting the gold rush, all came to disappointing ends. Tagish Charlie and Skookum Jim became wealthy beyond imagining from disposing of their claims, but did not long enjoy their winnings. Tagish Charlie was reported to have fallen off a bridge and drowned in 1908, barely a dozen years after the discovery, while Skookum Jim Mason, tired of trying to keep up with the whites, eventually withdrew to Carcross and the safety of the church-dominated environment where he, too, died in 1916. His sister, Klondike Kate, was deserted by Carmack, who returned to California with his wealth and remarried. For many years, till her death from influenza on March 29, 1920, Kate Carmack was a familiar figure about Carcross, selling needlework to tourists and posing for her photograph.

Other Indians were less affected by the gold rush. Some assisted the miners and settlers by bringing in considerable quantities of moose, caribou, and sheep meat from as far away as Peel River to help the whites eke out the hungry winters. Most merely continued the old life of hunting and trapping, trading their furs at outposts like Ross River (where Isaac Taylor and William Drury had one of their stores), Rampart House (where Dan Cadzow had replaced the departed Hudson's Bay Company), or in Dawson or Whitehorse. They frequently came in contact now with white men in their hunting and trapping grounds, since the prospectors, miners, and big-game hunters ranged about the hinterland, and other newcomers trapped fur to trade at the Yukon stores or to ship outside to San Francisco or London. In all these contacts the Indians of the Yukon were reported to be mild, honest, able to get along well with the whites, more often imposed upon by the whites than the reverse. Thanks to the missions, a fair number were learning to read, write, and speak English and keep gardens in a small way.

In the field of Indian-white relations, the Church of England, claiming two-thirds of the territory's Indians as adherents, represented the conscience of Canada. Its work in the Yukon pre-dated the gold rush and in its beginnings had been directed towards the Indians. Bishop Bompas had brought with him to the Yukon in 1891 the Reverend T. H. Canham, whom he placed at Selkirk, and Mr B. Totty, who was stationed as a schoolteacher at Moosehide, while the bishop himself made Forty Mile his headquarters. At these and other centres, schools were conducted for Indian and half-breed children. In 1903 the bishop selected Caribou Crossing (Carcross) on the railway as the centre of his Indian work, transferring the school from Forty Mile there and developing it into a boarding school for children from all parts of his diocese. His successor, Bishop Stringer, had also spent many years working with Indians and Eskimos, was familiar with the bands at Fort McPherson, Rampart House, Fort Yukon, and Dawson City, and was equally concerned with the impact of the gold rush upon the Yukon's first inhabitants.

Bishop Stringer's, therefore, was perhaps the strongest voice for better treatment of the Indians by the Canadian government. His first charge to his synod, in 1907, called for the recognition of the legal status of the Indians, the provision of treaties or compensation for their lands, legislation to preserve their natural rights to hunt, trap, and fish, the reservation of selected lands as band headquarters, and greater outlays on housing and medical supplies. His charge in 1911 contained an appeal for the protection of the natives, including more aid to education, and a suggestion that the government consider introducing reindeer to the Yukon to replace the caribou as a food source for the Indians.

The Canadian government's concern for the Indians of the Yukon remained very small for many years, although Constantine's attitude by no means reflected that of the entire administration. Even in November, 1896, Ogilvie was warning Constantine that "With reference to the Indian claims it is not the policy of the Government to ignore them definitely, & the Government will after due information on the subject determine what will be done."[26] But the government was very slow to act and never did go so far as to extend the treaty system to the Yukon. Relief to needy Indians (doled out often by reluctant police), and small grants to Anglican schools, were the sum total of its activities for many years. As late as 1910 these aids amounted to only $5,878 for supplies and $2,399 for schools. In 1911, however, following Minister of the Interior Oliver's visit, the Department of Indian Affairs awarded $30,000 to convert the boarding school at Carcross into the first Indian residential school in the Yukon. At long last, in 1914, the department took a belated first step by appointing as Indian superintendent for the Yukon Territory a veteran Church of England missionary, the Reverend John Hawksley, who had served at Mackenzie and Yukon posts since 1887. Thus, a central component of the primary level of Canadian frontier society was making its entry in a region that was reverting, through economic setbacks, from an advanced order of social development to one approximating much more closely that of the primitive North.

CHAPTER 7

Ontario and Quebec as Agents of Northern Development: the Late Nineteenth Century

In British Columbia and the Northwest, the problem of frontier development was to introduce the modern-day economy and society into the richest, most attractive, most accessible districts. In the older parts of Canada, however, such districts by and large were already occupied, so it was a matter of attracting settlers to marginal situations that were currently, and perhaps permanently, inferior to those already settled. The challenge facing the governments of Ontario and Quebec was to draw settlement to their frontier areas in competition with alternative attractions within their own boundaries, not to mention those of other sections of Canada or North America.

Still, arrayed against this challenge were the two most powerful regional governments in Canada, armed with the fiscal and administrative means to meet the problem, as well as with considerable political power to command the further aid of the Dominion government. Thus endowed, they proceeded to the task, bequeathed them by the former Province of Canada, of opening up the regions of lakes and rivers, forests, swamps, thin soils, and Precambrian rocks that extend north beyond the Trent waterway or in the rear of the counties lining the north bank of the Ottawa and north shore of the St Lawrence.

While promoting frontier development was an onerous responsibility, it also presented great opportunities. The settlers would produce forest, mineral, and farm products for export, and they would provide custom for the mercantile, financial, and cultural establishments of the older sections of the province. They would participate in the life of the provinces as members of churches and societies, and as taxpayers and electors. Moreover, the administration of the natural resources could yield large revenues, particularly from the bonuses and dues paid by the timber trade. Ontario derived the revenue that largely accounted for its phenomenal fiscal position in this period from its natural resources. Instead of having debts, it

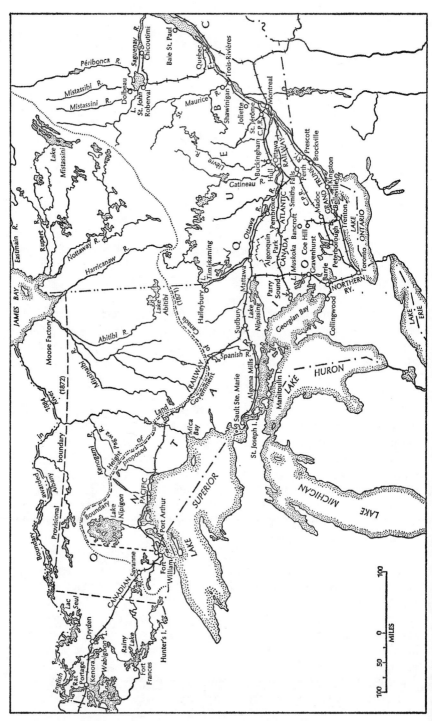

Frontier Districts of Ontario and Quebec, 1867-96

constantly had a healthy surplus of between $2,000,000 and $6,000,000 in the provincial treasury. This highly favourable financial situation made it relatively simple for Ontario to meet the needs of its developing frontier. Furthermore, Ontario was blessed with a frontier that was comparatively easy to develop. The Great Lakes afforded ready access to the interior, the hinterland was richly endowed with readily exploited natural resources, and it was handy to development by American enterprise and for American markets immediately across the lakes.

The new province began almost at once to carve out a series of new districts from pre-Confederation Nipissing and Algoma, that between them divided the country north of Lakes Huron and Superior. A District of Parry Sound was established in 1870 embracing the country fronting on Georgian Bay, followed in 1871 by a new District of Thunder Bay from the territory north and west of Lake Superior. Farther east, the junior county of Muskoka, temporarily attached to the county of Simcoe, was formed in 1869, while the county of Haliburton was established in 1874. Even though Muskoka, Parry Sound, Nipissing, and Algoma had a combined population of only 15,728 (1871), the province quickly instituted appropriate units of local administration – township councils, school districts, villages, and towns – to integrate the settlement into its system. The concern thus expressed to expand Ontario's frontiers was tested almost at once in the long contest the province waged with the Dominion for its western and northern boundaries.

For along with their other responsibilities, the new provinces also inherited the still-unresolved question of their territorial limits. The Hudson's Bay Company had claimed that Rupert's Land extended to the sources of all rivers draining into Hudson and James bays – which would have confined Canada to the St Lawrence-Great Lakes drainage basin north of the United States boundary. The former Province had begun collecting documentary evidence in 1857 to challenge this contention. The question had not been tested in the courts prior to the transfer of 1870 when the Dominion took over the Hudson's Bay Company's land and began applying its territorial claims against Ontario. To Ontario, this was a very serious matter indeed. The height of land was only a few miles west of Lake Superior, and Ontario was vitally interested in the district between the lake and the newly established province of Manitoba. To make matters worse, Ontario was appalled to discover that the Dominion sought to restrict the western limit of Ontario still farther – to a line that intersected Lake Superior just east of Thunder Bay, at longitude 89° 9′ 27″, due north of the junction of the Ohio and Mississippi rivers. Since this would separate settlements and townships at the lakehead which Ontario was already administering, the province immediately challenged the Dominion's contention.

Ontario claimed that its western limit extended to the Lake of the Woods, the longitude 95° 13′ 48″, due north of the source of the Mississippi River. As for the northern boundary, Ontario resurrected the arguments thoughtfully assembled by the former Province of Canada. Basing its case on various proclamations and instructions issued by Britain to colonial governors, as well as on the Hudson's Bay Company's readiness in 1701 to relinquish all claims to land south of the Albany River, Ontario claimed for its northern boundary the line of the English and Albany rivers to James Bay and to a point due north of the head of Lake Timiskaming, thence to that lake, and so along the existing boundary with Quebec. The dispute was referred first to a three-man arbitration board, then, when the Dominion government refused to recognize their decision in Ontario's favour, to the Judicial Committee of the Privy Council, which in a judgement of 1884 once again awarded the disputed territory to Ontario.[1] Incidentally, this ruling vindicated the older arguments of the Province of Canada that the Hudson's Bay Company's charter of 1670 held no exclusive, privileged legal status over subsequent imperial enactments.

But the Dominion, unwilling to concede, still claimed the natural resources of the disputed territory as belonging to the Dominion by virtue of its treaties with the region's Indians. This argument also went to the Privy Council in the case of the St Catherine's Milling Company, a lumbering concern operating in the district under a licence from the Dominion. The ruling of the Privy Council in July, 1888, denied the Dominion's contention that the Indians had been the absolute owners of the territory and had relinquished that ownership to the Dominion by the treaties. Instead, they found that the title to the soil rested with the Crown even before the treaties: "The Crown has all along had a present proprietary estate in the land, upon which the Indian title was a mere burden."[2] Lord Watson held that the terms of the Proclamation of 1763, on which the Dominion's case was based,

> shew that the tenure of the Indians was a personal and usufructuary right, dependent upon the good will of the Sovereign. The lands reserved are expressly stated to be "parts of Our dominions and territories;" and it is declared to be the will and pleasure of the sovereign that, "for the present," they shall be reserved for the use of the Indians, as their hunting grounds, under his protection and dominion. . . . there has been all along vested in the Crown a substantial and paramount estate, underlying the Indian title, which became a plenum dominium whenever that title was surrendered or otherwise extinguished. . . .[3]

Under Section 109 of the British North America Act, the title to the soil devolved on Ontario as the lawful agent of the Crown within the adjudicated provincial boundaries. This judgement, in what is also known as the

Indian Title Case, is a major legal ruling on the contentious question of aboriginal claims. Ontario's victory was sealed in 1889 by an imperial act – the Canada (Ontario Boundary) Act, 52-3 Vict., Chap. 28 – defining the boundaries as determined by the judgement of 1884.

That there should be so long-standing a dispute in such an important part of the country was bound to create serious problems. Province and Dominion from the outset tried to reach an agreement that would minimize dislocations arising from the eventual decision as to ownership of the territory. They agreed to act jointly in issuing mining licences and land patents, with a provisional boundary line, on the west, of longitude 90° 58′, the eastern tip of "Hunter's Island," the territory enclosed by two chains of lakes and rivers in what is now Quetico Provincial Park. For practical purposes, Ontario's control of the zone east of this line was not challenged hereafter. The Dominion, however, incorporated the western zone into the District of Keewatin when it created that district in 1876, and later, in defiance of the award of 1878, it included the territory in the extended boundaries Parliament granted to Manitoba in 1881. On the other hand, following the decision of 1878, the province began to assert its authority over the district west of the Hunter's Island line, by delegating to W. D. Lyon, the stipendiary magistrate administering the District of Thunder Bay, supervision over the territory as far west as Lake of the Woods, the future District of Rainy Lake.

Disputes between Ontario and the Dominion arose almost from the outset over resource-granting policies, particularly timber leases. The province claimed that the contractors on the Canadian Pacific Railway abused their right to gather timber from up to twenty miles on either side of the railway route, and that they and others were stripping the region of "enormous quantities" of timber. Even more, the province criticized the Dominion for its timber-granting practices, which did not secure anything like an adequate return (as little as one-one hundredth the comparable prices secured by Ontario, it was alleged), and for disposing of rights to pockets of very valuable timber that reduced to insignificance the value of the surrounding territory. Lyon reported many abuses in timber licences, trespasses which he was powerless to halt, and widespread lawlessness at Rat Portage, where "vice and immorality seemed to reign triumphant." The village was filled with violent, desperate characters who walked the village with knives and revolvers in their belts.[4]

Disputes arose over the on-the-spot administration, particularly after 1881 when Manitoba began to assert its jurisdiction. Both provinces conducted police magistrate courts and municipal governments at Rat Portage, and in September, 1883, they even held provincial elections for the same district. The situation grew more acute in 1883 after work on the Canadian

Pacific Railway was finished in the locality and the Dominion withdrew its liquor prohibition order. Both provinces then licensed their own liquor dealers and premises, and began a chain of arrests and counter-arrests that finally forced the two attorneys-general to work out the details of the suit that was carried to London and finally awarded the disputed territory to Ontario.

Meanwhile, despite the jurisdictional dispute and the highly publicized inter-governmental crises, settlement and development went ahead, apparently without great disturbance, and in spite of such alarmist predictions as Lyon's, in a letter to Premier Mowat of February 23, 1881:

> The people of the locality are suffering in many ways from the unsettled condition of affairs. There is no civil court to collect debts, no land agent to locate settlers, no registry office to record deeds, no timber agent to protect the forest. There are timber locations to be had, but there is no security for the expense of exploring and surveying them. All is uncertainty and confusion. The mineral lands will be so mixed up before long that men who own locations will not be able to recognize their own property.[5]

The Dominion government, for its part, in the years after 1870 proceeded with its program of completing the vital communications link across the district between Lake Superior and Red River on which the success of Confederation depended. The Dawson Route, investigated by the earlier Dawson-Hind expedition, was inaugurated in the spring of 1870 with the despatch of the Wolseley Expedition to Manitoba, and it was improved in subsequent years. From Fort William, by various rivers, lakes, and portages, the route proceeded to Rainy Lake, Lake of the Woods, Winnipeg River, and Lake Winnipeg. Launches were afterwards placed on navigable parts of the waterway, wagon trails were built around the twelve portages, and a road was extended from Lake of the Woods to Fort Garry. Eventually a canal lock was also built at Fort Frances to afford uninterrupted navigation over 164 miles of the water route from Rainy Lake to Lake of the Woods, and tramways were planned around certain of the longer portages. But in the meantime, the section of the Pacific railway was completed from Fort William to Winnipeg by way of Savanne, Wabigoon, and Rat Portage. This line missed the Rainy River country along the International Boundary by some eighty miles, leaving the settlements and lumber operations of the locality entirely dependent upon water communication with the railway at Kenora (formerly Rat Portage) until the turn of the century. Nevertheless, the railway greatly stimulated the lumber industry by opening up large markets in the developing towns and farms on the prairies to the west. Great sawmilling industries arose at Fort Frances, Kenora, Fort William, and

Prince Arthur's Landing to process the logs floated down the waterways from limits on either side of the border.

The years also brought the inauguration of a mining industry, high-lighted by the remarkable Silver Islet mine. Located near Thunder Bay, it was on one of the Montreal Mining Company's original locations and was prospected on the company's behalf by Thomas Macfarlane. He traced a rich silver-bearing vein along the Sibley peninsula, over to Jarvis Island, and to a rounded rock, only eighty feet in diameter, that jutted like the top of a skull a few feet above the level of Lake Superior. True to form, the company, rather than exploit the find, sold the property for $125,000 to a group of Americans, who developed a mine in the face of tremendous natural difficulties and gradually carried it by 1884 to a depth of 1,230 feet beneath the storm-tossed lake. There the mine had to be closed because of operational difficulties, after over three million dollars' worth of silver had been won from it. But though the success of the Silver Islet mine in-spired a search through the country, and several other mines were opened, all turned out disappointingly, and the district acquired a bad reputation that it was slow to overcome.

In the meantime, Ontario's stipendiary magistrate for the District of Nipissing, E. B. Borron, carried the authority of the province to the un-inhabited northern and eastern parts of the disputed territory. Borron travelled annually to Moose Factory by as many routes as possible to report on the timber, agricultural, mineral, and shipping possibilities of the region and the impact of the building of the Canadian Pacific Railway. He found the country so completely dominated by the fur-traders that he advocated ruling through them by commissioning them as provincial justices of the peace. He reported that the district seemed very law-abiding and "any attempt on my part, to meddle or interfere *unnecssarily*, would be ex-ceedingly injudicious."[6] The Ontario government should modify its liquor program in line with company practice (which he described as "involun-tary abstinence"), and not undermine its practical control of the region "until we are in a position to provide a really sufficient substitute."[7] In a later report, when he began to win the confidence of the residents of Moose Factory, he urged the province to establish a public school and hos-pital (paid for jointly by province and Dominion), and station a constable there. The province should also assume its responsibilities to the 2,500 inhabitants of the district by legislation protecting the natives' fishing and hunting rights and it should license fur-traders, enforce its liquor legisla-tion, and settle the Hudson's Bay Company's land claims. The federal gov-ernment should be pressed to bring the region's Indians under treaty and to provide some service in return for the $100,000 a year in customs duties it was collecting at Moose Factory.

Quebec had been an interested spectator throughout the contest of province and Dominion. Ontario's success in extending its borders inspired Quebec to put forward its claim to a boundary based on the Eastmain River on grounds similar to those of Ontario – that the Hudson's Bay Company had been prepared in 1701 to surrender all its territories south of that river to New France. The Quebec proposal suggested the boundary should proceed from the source of the Eastmain River to Hamilton River and follow it to the boundary of Newfoundland. The Dominion government delayed until the proposed boundary could be properly surveyed; accordingly, in 1890 William Ogilvie examined the boundary north from Lake Timiskaming to James Bay, while A. P. Low and others mapped the Eastmain and other rivers of the Labrador plateau. Finally, in 1898, Parliament passed an act (61 Vict., Chap. 3) giving Quebec the northern boundary of the Eastmain River to its source, down the Hamilton River to the boundary of Newfoundland, then south to Anse Sablon on the Strait of Belle Isle. Thus Quebec acquired an additional 122,973 square miles of territory, which it organized into three districts – Ashuanipi, Waswanipi, and Abitibi – as well as an unresolved boundary dispute with Newfoundland.

To provide a satisfactory economic base for their developing frontier districts, improved communications were required that linked those districts with existing transportation facilities. Hence, both provinces continued to construct colonization and district roads that were particularly important for opening pioneering districts, usually following the advice of land surveyors as to location. Work on roads provided settlers with welcome cash or credit that might be applied towards their land-purchase instalments or taxes. Such roads, however, were only links binding the countryside with the most efficient long-distant transportation media – navigable lakes or rivers, or more particularly, railways – by means of which the frontier districts would be connected with ambitious metropolitan centres. Hence the building of colonization railways was supported both by settlers of remote districts and by civic business interests who could throw political weight into the campaign. Quebec City, conscious of being overshadowed by Montreal, looked eagerly to developing links with the Lake St John district or the upper St Maurice valley, while Montreal sought railways into the Laurentides, along the Ottawa River, or north to James Bay. It was the same in Ontario. Toronto business interests strove to see that their existing railway to Georgian Bay, the Northern Railway, was extended to the new Canadian Pacific Railway that spanned the whole of northern Ontario. Smaller centres like Kingston or Belleville had similar ambitions, on a smaller scale, of developing hinterlands in the mineral-rich, forested districts to their north.

Both provinces responded by extending aid to promoters of desired railways, mainly in the form of cash subsidies, usually of $3,000 per mile.

Ontario spent from $200,000 to $1,500,000 each year on this form of assistance. Land grants, and more rarely, bond guarantees were also used to encourage railway construction, as were lucrative contracts for placing settlers on the lands or for performing other services. Still other developmental railways were subsidized by the Dominion government, which matched its program of aid to the Canadian Pacific Railway by offering cash subsidies for several other railway enterprises in the two central provinces. Many developmental railways also were built with ends other than serving the needs of settlers on the frontiers of Ontario or Quebec in view. Such were the Canadian Pacific, the lines Mackenzie and Mann acquired in their headlong course of throwing together a new transcontinental system, or the Canada Atlantic system, built by the millionaire lumberman J. R. Booth.

Construction of the Canadian Pacific Railway was fundamental to the opening of northern Ontario, which was such virgin territory that Sandford Fleming could say that "No civilized man, so far as known, had ever passed from the valley of the upper Ottawa through the intervening wilderness to Lake Superior. The country east and west of Lake Nepigon was all but a *terra incognita*."[8] Fleming's route, it was true, was largely discarded by the syndicate that completed the railway between 1881 and 1885 and a route closer to the lakes was adopted. As built, the railway travelled northwest from Sudbury along the height of land, then gained the north shore of Lake Superior, which it followed around to the lakehead. Still, even that route greatly facilitated lumbering and the search for minerals in those sections of Ontario. In addition, the Canadian Pacific extended a line from Sudbury to the shore of Lake Huron at Algoma Mills (used as an interim port to forward freight by ship to the lakehead) and later to Sault Ste Marie. On the east it took over the Canada Central to carry its line into Ottawa, whence it secured other connections with Brockville, Prescott, and Toronto. In response to pressures from settlers and clergy interested in opening the Lake Timiskaming region, the company also constructed a branch north from Mattawa to the foot of that lake. Moreover, the Northern Railway, aided by provincial and Dominion subsidies, was encouraged to extend branches from Barrie north to Gravenhurst and eventually, in 1886, to a link with the Canadian Pacific at Nipissing Junction. A most remarkable Ontario railway enterprise was the Central Ontario, controlled by the American industrialist S. J. Ritchie, who acquired the charter with its land grant to use as a probe to locate and gain control of desirable mineral and other properties. In the course of these endeavours, he built seventy-two miles of railway in 1884 from Trenton to Coe Hill in North Hastings, and had secured charters to build to Marmora and to Bancroft before his energies and interests became diverted to the possibilities of the new mineral discovery at Sudbury.

Thanks to its central location, Ontario fared very well in terms of development railways, which came into being without any effort on the province's part, the Canadian Pacific Railway being the prime example. Far different was the position of Quebec, which derived very little benefit of that kind from the construction of the Canadian Pacific, which barely skirted the province as it approached Montreal and crossed the Eastern Townships into Maine. Even then, the Canadian Pacific merely used the western part of the Quebec, Montreal, Ottawa and Occidental, otherwise known as the North Shore Railway, built between 1875 and 1878 with provincial backing. Two years after the Canadian Pacific acquired the Hull to Montreal section of this line in 1882, the Dominion government, following a celebrated episode in the House of Commons, paid the province a retroactive subsidy for having built the North Shore line in the first place.

Consequently, the Quebec government faced considerable pressure to assist colonization railways. The most important of these was the Quebec and Lake St John Railway, which grew out of the twenty-five-mile Quebec and Gosford Railway, built in 1869 with wooden rails mainly to carry firewood and lumber to the port of Quebec. That line soon disintegrated, but its promoters launched ten years of strenuous campaigning to construct a proper railway north to the Saguenay district. Eventually, thanks to cash grants totalling $5,000 per mile from the province and $3,200 from the Dominion government, a land grant that ultimately amounted to 1,871,950 acres, plus other bonuses from municipalities along the route, the line was completed in 1888 from Quebec to Roberval and Chicoutimi. The railway was of immense help in colonizing that fertile district, for the company management deliberately set out to aid the work with the knowledge that new settlers would provide large freight revenues for the line as well as possible purchasers of company lands.

As a result of these efforts, both central provinces by the 1890's possessed considerable railway mileages that served developmental purposes. The Ottawa-Huron tract, in fact, was over-supplied with railway lines that crisscrossed the district, facilitating the development of its timber resources and numerous small, short-lived mineral deposits, and assisting farmers to struggle a little longer on the inhospitable rocky acres to which they or their fathers had been lured. By the nineties most of these activities had ceased, and many of the lines now catered to little more than hunters and tourists coming to enjoy the recreational and scenic values of the district. As well as the Ottawa-Huron tract, settlement of the upper Ottawa valley, the north shore of Lake Huron, the Sault Ste Marie district, and west and northwest of the lakehead, was assisted and was largely made possible by the construction of railways. Similarly, in Quebec, short lines linked together farming, lumbering, and industrial communities like St Jérôme, New Glasgow, Rawdon, Joliette, and Shawinigan along the northern frontier, or penetrated deeper into the Shield country to Labelle in 1893 and eventually to Mont Laurier in 1909, or from Hull up the Gatineau valley to reach Maniwaki in 1904. But among all the Quebec developmental railways, undoubtedly the greatest achievement was bridging a barren corner of the Laurentians to give the Lake St John lowland convenient, direct links with Quebec City.

II

Ever since the mining boom north of the Great Lakes in the 1840's, hopes for important mining industries figured large in all plans for the development of Ontario's northland. These were kept alive by fitful spells of mining at Bruce Mines when the price of dressed copper ore warranted, a short-lived gold rush to the Madoc area in 1866 in the wake of a lode gold discovery, and the finding, shortly after, of the rich silver vein that became the Silver Islet mine. Contributing to the same result, too, were frequent announcements by the Geological Survey of the presence in the Shield of many large areas of Huronian rocks (greenstones) that were regarded as favourable indications of the occurrence of metallic minerals. In keeping with these hopes, the new province quickly passed a Gold and Silver Act in 1868 setting up mining divisions and a system for staking claims and securing exploring licences.[9] A General Mining Act followed in 1869, under which mining locations were to be sold in 80-, 160-, or 320-acre parcels at a flat $1.00-per-acre price, without any requirement as to prior discovery of a workable deposit or commitment respecting development of the grant; the previous royalty on gold and silver was also repealed.[10] Nothing could have been more favourable to the speculator, as results readily showed.

In spite of these generous conditions and many attempts to develop mining properties in the Precambrian rocks of the Frontenac Axis and elsewhere, the first really important discovery in northern Ontario was an accident. While the Canadian Pacific Railway was being built west from Lake Nipissing in 1883, clearing parties noted peculiar rocks a few miles northwest of Sudbury. In the following winter two Pembroke merchants, the brothers Thomas and William Murray, purchased land in the area from the government, as did other speculators reacting to news of additional finds a little to the southwest along the route of the newly begun Sudbury-Sault Ste Marie branch. Prospectors thoroughly combed the area in 1885 and discovered most of the ore bodies that were subsequently mined, the locations being acquired from the government at the standard $1 per acre, chiefly by speculating merchants of Pembroke, Ottawa, Sudbury, and Sault Ste Marie.

Developing mines from these properties required outside capital and technical skill, and was beyond the means of the owners. Many properties consequently were sold to the Canadian Copper Company, a firm organized by S. J. Ritchie, who was attracted to the district in 1885 and secured most of the lots for as little as $100,000. Mining began in 1886, but full exploitation awaited a practicable process for separating and refining the nickel content of the ore, and the development of markets for this little-known metal. Ritchie arranged with the Orford Copper Company (an American firm developing the large Eastern Townships' copper deposits) to attend to the copper refining and develop a nickel-separation process, while he lobbied with the United States Navy to purchase his company's nickel output for armour plating. Practicable refining processes were developed almost simultaneously by J. Wharton of the United States, H. H. Vivian and Sons in England, and an Anglo-German chemist, Ludwig Mond. The Orford Copper Company secured a process by hiring away an employee from the Vivian firm, while Ritchie also succeeded in his approach to the United States Navy.

By the late eighties, consequently, the prospects of the Sudbury camp became highly favourable, and in 1890, ore production amounted to 130,000 tons. The ore was roasted in the open on vast piles of wood to reduce the sulphur content and produce a rich copper-nickel matte which was exported mainly to the United States for refining. In the process the trees were cut down for miles about, while the sulphur and arsenic fumes poisoned the vegetation over a still wider area. Speculators rushed to buy up all available land, and the province belatedly increased the land price to $4.50 per acre, and in 1891 imposed a 3 per cent royalty clause for all subsequent grants. Unfortunately this was not applied retroactively, so virtually all mined ore escaped the royalty. The province tried to interest the British government in establishing a Canadian refinery to ensure its supply, and also to encourage the opening of an independent refinery, but neither effort succeeded. Ritchie played a dubious game, simultaneously working for an exclusive contract with the United States Navy (to which end he became a major contributor to the current political campaign in Canada for unrestricted reciprocity with the United States) while also negotiating, in the best protectionist tradition, for financial assistance from the Ontario government to open a nickel-steel plant near Trenton. His associates, appalled by the recklessness and double-dealing, finally dismissed him from the company. In the meantime, the Canadian Copper-Orford Copper combination secured a virtual monopoly of the American market, entered the British and European markets, and came to an agreement with the French company, Le Nickel, dividing the European market between them. Sudbury became one of the leading mining camps of its time, the world's largest nickel producer, and Canada's greatest mine. Its success stimulated prospecting and other activities that helped develop that section of northern Ontario.

The important mining industry of Quebec had little noticeable effect on the development of the northern parts of that province, since it was centred on the Eastern Townships, the site of early copper- and gold-mining industries, and from the 1880's, of asbestos-mining. There were some developments north of the Ottawa – iron, mica, and graphite mines, and especially a considerable apatite (phosphate) mining industry near Buckingham that flourished for twenty years after 1871, till its market was ruined by better, cheaper supplies in the United States. A short-lived effort in 1871 by an English company to mine titaniferous ore near Baie St Paul, along the St Lawrence between Quebec City and the Saguenay River, quickly failed from lack of local charcoal supplies. Largely as a result of the phosphate boom, the province passed a General Mining Act in 1880 and followed this by appointing a provincial mining engineer.

More important than mining as an administrative concern in both provinces was the management of the Crown lands so as to promote the development of the northern districts. By the time of Confederation, the long debate over the relative value of each industry had largely been resolved in favour of the view that agricultural settlement should enjoy primacy in governmental planning as being the more desirable social objective. But forestry, too, was seen as holding out important benefits in terms of the employment and income it generated, and encouragement to settlement, not to speak of its important contribution to governmental revenue. Hence, the objectives were to maximize settlement in the case of arable land; and to maximize public revenue in the case of forested lands.

The difficulty lay in deciding which was the more appropriate use when the land seemed suited for both forestry and agriculture, and how to weight the two objectives. Here there was a wide discrepancy between the attitudes and practices of Ontario and Quebec. Ontario from its experience with the Ottawa-Huron tract seemed to appreciate the natural difficulties in the way of farming in certain parts of the northern regions, and consequently took some care to restrict the lands thrown open to farming settlement. The province also appreciated the contribution of the lumbermen and sought to protect them in their holdings, excluding agriculture from areas it considered better suited to forestry, or not completely suitable for farming. By segregating the agricultural and forest lands in this way, the two industries remained physically apart, and did not clash too seriously. In Quebec, however, agricultural settlement had strong religious and national motives besides the usual economic ones, so the means of assessment was by no means clear cut or completely realistic. In some quarters almost any land capable of sustaining human life seemed to be considered as potential farm land. The promotion of agriculture was given complete primacy over forestry, lands were withdrawn from timber limits at any time for settlement purposes, and the two industries became hopelessly and fatally entangled as competitors for the same land.

The administration of the undeveloped northern districts of Ontario was designed to encourage the orderly development of the several resources of the region. A continuing program of land survey and subdivision was carried on in line with changing needs of the mining, forest, and farming populations, and the effort was made to earmark the land for its most appropriate use. As townships were surveyed they were classified for agricultural or other uses, and if for the former, were assigned for free grant disposal or for sale at a fixed price per acre, but still subject to settlement duties. Reports of these surveys, as well as pamphlets and books like Alexander Kirkwood and J. J. Murphy's *The Undeveloped Lands in Northern and Western Ontario*, were compiled as settlement propaganda. Local patriots also strove to attract interest and support to their particular localities. Perhaps no region had so devoted a propagandist as the Timiskaming district of Ontario possessed in C. C. Farr, a retired Hudson's Bay Company employee who settled in 1887 on the site of Haileybury and devoted the rest of his life to publicizing the attractions and opportunities of the Little Clay Belt.

The problem with agricultural settlement was to work out a system of land tenure that would not only place settlers on the land, but keep them there. Speculation was above all to be avoided. Most of the lands north of the Trent River that were open for agricultural settlement were available as free grants (homesteads) whereby the settler obtained title to his 200-acre (or 160-acre) grant in return for fulfilling such requirements as five years' occupancy, erecting a habitable house, and clearing and cultivating at least fifteen acres. The pine and the minerals of the tract were subject to separate disposal by the Crown, and did not become the property of the settler even after he secured his patent, thus further protecting the rights of the timber licensee. Land was subject to purchase in some areas where it was felt a small charge might deter too promiscuous abandonment of the holdings. Thus in Timiskaming the settler paid 50 cents per acre for his holding, but still had to fulfil settlement duties similar to the homesteader before he secured his patent to the property. At times a combination of the two was used; in the Rainy River country settlers were urged to take out 160-acre homesteads and buy adjoining 80-acre tracts at $1.00 per acre on instalments.

To dispose of its lands, the province set up several Crown lands agencies in the north and periodically opened new townships to homestead applicants. Thus 148 townships were so designated in the Districts of Muskoka, Parry Sound, and Nipissing by 1878. Other cultivable townships were opened west of the lakehead, or about Sault Ste Marie and on Manitoulin and St Joseph islands, while the completion of the Canadian Pacific Railway led to townships being opened along the north shore of Lake Huron, and west of Fort William. At Lake Wabigoon seven townships were opened, and by 1895 some six hundred settlers were occupying 20,439 acres of free grant lands there. In the Lake Timiskaming district thirty townships were surveyed, eight of which were opened to settlement in 1891.

To assist these settlers the government had to provide many customary, and some special, facilities – colonization roads, school grants, police and welfare services, grants for fairs and exhibitions, and the like. The Ontario Agricultural Commission, which examined the northern districts in 1880, suggested settlers needed to be trained in improving soils and growing better field crops, in effective use of the hardwood resources, and encouraged to expand dairy production.[11] Along these lines, the province in 1895 established a pioneer dairy farm at the Wabigoon settlement, where the village of Dryden soon grew up.

With agricultural settlement Ontario was more concerned to have the land occupied by successful farmers; securing a revenue was only a minor consideration. With the forested lands it was otherwise; the province expected to make this a major revenue source, and organized its program accordingly. Following the system evolved in the Province of Canada, Ontario auctioned the right to cut the mature pine off given tracts under renewable licences, the successful bidder paying a bonus at the time of the sale, an annual ground rental, plus stumpage dues on timber actually cut. Timber rights in most of southern Ontario had been disposed of before Confederation, and the system was extended as the northern parts came within the reach of economical development. A large timber sale, for 5,031 square miles (about seventy miles square) north of Lake Huron, was made in 1872 for a bonus of $592,601 ($117.79 per square mile, or 18 cents per acre – the statistic selected reflecting the bias of the commentator). For years the government apologized for this transaction, explaining the low price on the grounds that the region was isolated at the time and unattractive to operators, but on the other hand so exposed to destruction that any longer delay might have meant no timber would be left worth selling.[12] Later sales were far more profitable as market conditions improved and the government gained experience in timing the auctions. The average bonuses rose to $532 per square mile in 1881, then jumped to $2,859 in 1887 and $3,657 in 1892, raising the average sale price since 1871 to $1,205 per square mile. Other fees also were increased as the limits began to be developed – the ground rental from $2.00 per square mile to $3.00 in 1887, and the stumpage dues from 75 cents per thousand f.b.m. to $1.25 in 1892.

As a result, the province derived an average revenue from the Crown lands of about $646,000 per annum in the eighties, then as much as $2,252,972 in 1892 and $1,823,500 in 1893, while even a poor year like 1896 yielded a sum of $924,862. All told, the province secured from its Crown lands an average revenue of over one million dollars a year (less administration costs and expenses of about 15 per cent), a total of $40,000,000 by 1904, almost all of it from the forests. This constituted a quarter or more of the province's total revenues, was second only to Dominion grants as a source of provincial funds, and accounted in fair measure for the highly satisfactory financial position of the Ontario government in this period.

A resource that contributed so handsomely to the provincial treasury had to be properly cared for, and this the government strove to do. Timber-cullers were examined, certified, and licensed to practise their trade with accuracy and impartiality. A system of controlling damage from forest fires was instituted in 1878, under which forest rangers were hired during the forest-fire season to patrol those limits most liable to damage because of their proximity to settlement, the limit-holders being assessed half the cost of the service. The expense was small (about $4,000), but after the act was strengthened in 1885, the costs were doubled and trebled year by year in keeping with the service provided, for the patrols were quickly seen to produce a marked diminution in the number and seriousness of fires, as well as improved success in apprehending violators. Arising from the report of the Agricultural Commission of 1880-81 and, even more, from the meeting of the American Forestry Association in 1882 in Montreal, was the appointment of a new official, a clerk of forestry, to superintend the administration of this division of the public domain, take charge of enforcing the regulations, promote research in forestry, and educate the public to the importance of protecting the forests. The regulations that split off the townships devoted to agriculture from the rest of the land aided in protecting the forests, since they greatly reduced farming operations (including brush-burning) near the forests, and diminished travel in the forested lands. Prospectors remained a danger, however, since they ranged freely over the land, and were sometimes suspected of starting fires to expose the rocks. A further measure of control against this kind of practice, as well as against timber pirates, came in 1897 with an act regulating travel in unorganized territory.

Ontario's good fortune in the administration of its natural resources did not result solely from favourable resource and locational factors; it owed a good deal to the policies of the able, though annoyingly self-righteous, Mowat government that controlled the province for so great a part of the late nineteenth century. The government made management of the Crown lands a major point of its appeal to the public, and went out of its way to impress the voters with the economy, efficiency, honesty, and progressiveness of its stewardship. Election pamphlets regularly boasted about the management of the public domain by T. B. Pardee and his successors: "Nothing but a rare combination of executive ability, official integrity, and judicial fairness, could have enabled the head of the Department to avoid giving his opponents some advantage over him during his long term of administration."[13]

In its handling of the public domain, the government followed the same pattern of investigations and gradual reforms as it did in other spheres, appointing special commissions, calling in experts, taking guidance from foreign examples, and educating the public to its programs. It paraded its administration of the resources as demonstrably superior to those of the Dominion government (witness, the disputed territory), or the neighbouring province of Quebec. An effort was made to put the management of the various resources in the hands of qualified people and to improve procedures. The Agricultural Commission of 1880-81 was followed by three more notable royal commissions on natural-resource matters. That on fish and game, reporting in 1892, produced legislation that was heralded as the most advanced in America. Past regulations were consolidated, and administration was put under the Commissioner of Crown Lands (for inland fisheries, declared by the courts in 1882 to be an area of provincial jurisdiction),[14] and the Provincial Secretary (for game). The expenses of administration were largely defrayed by licence fees levied on non-residents.

Perhaps the most important commission was that on mineral resources, appointed in 1888 and reporting in 1890. The slowness in developing mines in the lakehead and Frontenac Axis districts, as well as the inability of the province to share in the Sudbury bonanza, clearly indicated the need for reform. The commission recommended that the size of mining claims be reduced to enable individuals with limited means to secure them; that no mining claim be granted unless the presence of minerals on the property was proved; and that some development-work requirement be imposed before a final patent was awarded. To promote the development of mining, the report welcomed American investment, urged the provision of better transportation facilities, and proposed steps to encourage the refining of minerals in Canada. Most of these recommendations were implemented in the following years. The size of claims was reduced, the unfortunate system of outright sale of mining lands at $1.00 an acre was replaced by one making the granting of patents conditional on seven years of satisfactory development work, and a system of ten-year renewable leases was instituted. Above all, the report resulted in the inauguration in 1891 of a Bureau of Mines to administer the regulations, inspect mines and mine fields, encourage and undertake geological and mining researches, and institute appropriate educational and training programs in the universities. The omission of any royalty on production was rectified, though this did not extend to lands already alienated. At least something could be done for the future; by the early years of the new century, mining was contributing its share to the provincial treasury. A bounty of $1.00 a ton also was instituted in 1894 for iron smelted from ore mined in the province.

Still another royal commission was appointed in 1892 to study the advisability of establishing a forest reserve and provincial park in the Ottawa-Huron tract of the District of Nipissing. This was followed in 1893 by setting up the Algonquin National Park of Ontario, comprising eighteen townships north and east of Haliburton County. It covered an area of 1,733 square miles, all of which was under the timber licence (mostly granted in the preceding five years), but had never been opened to agricultural settlement.[15] The purposes were to provide watershed protection for adjoining districts, preserve the wildlife and restock the region, and keep out settlement. The park would also provide a locale and opportunity for experimental forestry practices, protect a section of natural forest, and offer an outdoor environment for the increasing tourist population. The establishment of Algonquin Park was a bold forward step towards the introduction of a proper land-use system that took into account more than material resources.

Thanks to the combination of farming, forestry, mining, fishing, transportation, and commerce, northern Ontario attracted considerable settlement during the period after 1867. In scattered localities from Rainy River to Lake Timiskaming, agricultural pioneers took up farms in the bush. Forestry was conducted in these and other areas where the timber could be exported by way of the Great Lakes or by rail west to the prairies. Mining accounted for the population lingering at Bruce Mines, as well as that growing up around the remarkable copper-nickel deposit at Sudbury. An important commercial fishery was carried on in the upper Great Lakes and other lakes made accessible by rail transport, making it possible for the fish to gain the large urban markets of the United States. Unfortunately, there was also considerable poaching by American operators now that their own part of the lakes was growing depleted, while heavy losses were attributed also to Indians ignorant of the regulations, and to the sawdust and bark spewed out by sawmilling operations. Tourism was a growing industry, associated with sports fishing in the Nipigon area and elsewhere. Railway and shipping employment, primary industries, trading, professional and administrative functions, all combined to build several considerable communities – Port Arthur and Fort William, Kenora and Keewatin, Fort Frances, Sault Ste Marie, and Sudbury. In thirty years the population of the northern districts, which had stood at only 15,728 souls in 1871, increased ninefold to 146,309, and that at a time when slow growth in population of Canada as a whole was occasioning great concern.

III

In Quebec, national, religious, cultural, and "racial" motives both intensified and distorted the drive to develop the natural resources, and particularly to expand agricultural settlement. Agricultural pioneering was seen as affirming and fortifying the French character of the province, keeping faith with the founders of the French race in America, and protecting the position of French Canadians in Canada by maintaining their rate of population growth. As Father F. X. A. Labelle put it, "Chaque pas fait dans la forêt par le défrichement est une conquête qui fortifie nos droits, nos institutions et nos lois."[16] The drain of young people to the United States, or to western Canada, and the assimilative influence facing them there, had to be arrested. There was no desire to encourage a polyglot immigration such as the Dominion government was trying to attract to the prairie west, since the entire purpose of colonization was to strengthen the French character of the province. Even the English-speaking population, which had been attracted to the valleys of the Ottawa and its tributaries by lumbering and mining operations before the French colonization movement was properly set in train, had to be overcome.

Indeed, the propaganda credited the French Canadian with a special aptitude for contending with the challenges of the fringes of the Canadian Shield: "La vigueur de nos colons ne recule pas devant les arbres de la forêt, le climat leur est salutaire, et leur tempérament est fait à la rigueur de nos hivers."[17] Agriculture was the noblest of all callings, and the rural environment offered the opportunity to create a society in which the highest spiritual goals could be realized. Cardinal Taschereau wrote of colonization as something in which "Notre nationalité, notre réligion, et, par conséquent, l'avenir spirituel et temporel de vos enfants et de vos compatriotes, y sont profondément intéressés."[18] The drive to push back the frontiers of Quebec not only drew together the usual array of businessmen, transportation interests, publicists, and politicians, but the clergy as well.

To accommodate these pressures for pushing back the frontiers of Quebec, the province, through its Department of Crown Lands and Department of Agriculture and Public Works, undertook the usual functions of exploring and surveying the country north to the height of land that was accepted as the northern limit of the province. Explorers were followed by surveyors who prepared township and subdivision surveys in areas deemed suitable for settlement, their reports being circulated as guides for possible settlers. Land agents directed colonists to surveyed farm land, while a staff of inspectors cleared up squatter problems and saw that settlement conditions were complied with. In some areas, free homesteads were granted for fulfilling the usual conditions of occupancy, habitation, and improving the land for cultivation. Crown lands were sold to settlers on easy terms, and bonuses were even paid at times for clearing land and bringing it under cultivation. A picturesque arrangement inaugurated in 1888 was that of giving the father of twelve children a second 100-acre lot as a bonus for his services to la patrie. Before the law was repealed in 1905, 3,490 such grants had been made. Other aids included help for schools, agricultural institutes, syndicates and cercles, model demonstration farms, and a dairy school. A system of issuing awards of merit to deserving farmers was begun in 1890. Road grants provided work for settlers as well as improved access to the outside.

To recruit settlers, the government maintained colonization agencies and publicity officers in strategic centres, published brochures and articles, prepared exhibits, offered excursions at low cost, and fostered strong propaganda in the schools to nourish among impressionable youngsters "une mentalité agricole." In addition to its own efforts, the province co-operated with colonization societies, as did the federal government when work outside Canada was involved, notably with efforts to repatriate Franco-Americans from New England. The Société Générale de Colonisation et de Rapatriement de Montréal, founded in 1894 with the support of the federal government, sent 877 settlers to Canada in its first year, all but fifteen to Quebec.

The province also employed colonization societies to recruit settlers and place them on the land, a method used by the Dominion government in the West but not in Ontario, where the appeal was directed at the individual would-be settler. The traditional method of allowing companies to purchase land from the government and then to resell it to settlers at a profit was continued in Quebec. A more common method, however, was to offer a reservation (usually a township) to a society, out of which grants were made by the government in proportion to the money subscribed, until eventually the whole township was paid for. The Société de Colonisation de la Vallée du lac St Jean, which was granted the township of Normandin, consisted of fifty members, each of whom could purchase four 100-acre lots subject to the usual conditions of occupancy and improvement, for a mere twenty cents per acre (or $80), paid in instalments. A high government official, reviewing the activity of the first type of colonization society in

1903, termed it on the whole "one series of fiascos, a source of trouble, embarrassment and loss to the government, and to their members, without furthering colonization in any way."[19] However he excepted some of the companies of associates as being properly conducted and successful in placing settlers on the land.

The clergy saw the colonization movement as an opportunity to play a meaningful role in the life of French-Canadian society, as an outlet for its own energies, and as an opportunity of identifying itself with the people, of being a truly national church. Hundreds of priests threw themselves wholeheartedly into the work of recruiting and leading groups of colonists to their new homes. The bishops, concerned with "des grands intérêts" of the nation, placed themselves at the head of diocesan colonization societies, and put the machinery of the church at the service of agricultural colonization. A day was consecrated to the honour of St Isidore, the patron saint of agriculture, to bring the cause to the full attention of the faithful. In the archdiocese of Quebec, all parish priests were to direct and publicize the work at the parish level, excite public generosity, and appoint collectors to receive the proposed annual contribution of ten cents per head as well as other donations and gifts. The money was used for chapels, schools, roads, and bridges, and to establish benevolent institutions in the new settlements. The Quebec and Lake St John Railway used parish priests to recruit settlers, each year sending every priest of a rural parish railway passes for two approved parish delegates to inspect the country. The priest could also issue half-fare certificates to other farmers intending to inspect the district, and by certifying families as emigrating to the Lake St John country, secure free carriage for them to their destination.

Many priests became celebrated agents of colonization, recruiting settlers and peopling entire townships. Most famous was Father F. X. A. Labelle, who went to St Jérôme in 1868 and immediately began organizing a colonization movement in the counties along the Ottawa. A northern enthusiast who gained the title "Le Roi du Nord," his motto throughout his brilliant and busy career was: "C'est le nord qui sera un jour la force, le boulevard de notre nationalité; ça ne peut être le sud qui est trop petit et trop exposé."[20] He converted the brilliant, erratic Arthur Buies to the colonization movement, and convinced him to write a series of colonization pamphlets. His efforts powerfully assisted the building of the North Shore line along the Ottawa as well as the Gatineau valley railway. Labelle inspired the creation of a Department of Colonization in 1887 under the Mercier government, and became its deputy minister in 1888. When he died in 1891, he was said to have founded sixty settlements, and the district that saw many of his labours – the basins of the upper Rouge, Petite Nation, and Lièvre rivers – was named Labelle County for him. Similarly, the impetus to organize the

Timiskaming frontier came from two priests, Fathers Paradis and Gendreau, while several more priests devoted themselves to assisting in founding the settlements of the Lake St John country.

At the parish level, too, the role of the clergy was vital. Father Labelle had the following recipe for successful operation: "Faites vivre un prêtre dans un canton, construisez une modeste chapelle pour y dire la messe, et la colonisation de cette localité se fait comme par enchantement pourvu que l'on colonise graduellement et que l'on suive la zône des bonnes terres."[21] The priest gave leadership in communal efforts and acted as business agent for individuals or the group. He set the tone for the colony, adding uniformity of faith to the other common bonds among the settlers, kept his flock to its proper duty, and drove out undesirable or discordant elements. The uniform, rather authoritarian, aspect of the resulting communities was said to be in harmony with "less moeurs, les idées, les habitudes, et les besoins religieux et moraux des Canadiens-Français."[22] The priest's aim was to enable the settlers to lead lives of pious, faithful sons of the soil who preserved the virtues of their Catholic and *canadien* heritage, rather than being given over to mere ruthless exploitation of the land.

Other groups and orders of clergy also joined in the work. Nuns established schools, convents, and hospitals at strategic centres; the Jesuits founded a college at Lac Nominingue in the heart of the Laurentides; and the Trappists established a monastery on a 6,000-acre grant on the Mistassini River north of Lake St John in 1891, which, like some medieval abbey, opened the way to the settlement of the Dolbeau district. From 1888 a corps of agricultural missionaries was organized to promote the colonization work, while the Trappists established an agricultural school at Oka, near Montreal, in 1893.

As in Ontario, the forest industry was also recognized as an important contributor to the provincial economy. The first report of the Commissioner of Crown Lands of Quebec for 1867-68 expressed the opinion that the province would secure its chief revenues from the public domain, principally from the forests. It instanced its good fortune at selling in just six months 5,664 square miles of limits for a premium of $72,685, an average of $11.07 per square mile – a gratifying result inasmuch as never before had a bonus exceeded $8.00 per mile! (What a contrast with Ontario, where a similarly large sale only four years later that yielded ten times as large a bonus was for years the subject of recrimination and apologies!) The commissioner also proposed to protect lumbermen against being defrauded or harmed by settlers, and to set apart "well timbered lands not required for immediate settlement" as forest reserves.[23] For the next twenty years the revenue from woods and forests fluctuated between $261,182 (1879-80) to $684,743 (1882-83), while the bonuses paid for new limits reached a level of

$282.95 per square mile in 1884-85. Yet, in spite of the lumberman's not inconsiderable contribution to the provincial treasury, he was not given adequate protection. Colonists were allowed to intrude on tracts held by lumber firms, and all leases were subject to having areas withdrawn from them for purposes of settlement. A further difficulty was the fact that the title to the timber went with the land patent. Though the settler was supposed to cut timber only for clearing, building, or fencing purposes before receiving his patent, his entry into the property made it possible to plunder it under the guise of anticipating a future owner's right, then abandoning the land long before he had to pay more than the initial instalment on the purchase price. Indeed, custom lumber mills were established that relied almost exclusively on such timber. They were accused of aiding and abetting farmers to poach on Crown lands or lands under lease to companies, and of encouraging the bogus taking up of lands in order to strip them of their timber.

The stress on agricultural settlement was sometimes carried to excess by zealous promoters of settlement. Evaluation of the potentialities of marginal soils is very difficult at the best of times, and results shift with changing economic and technological conditions. Even Father Labelle's faith that settlers would flock to a new chapel in the wilderness was qualified by a realistic "provided that one follows the zone of good soil." But how many clerical or nationalist-minded colonizers allowed realism to be overborne by faith or hope? Lumbermen constantly complained against misguided efforts to colonize lands that were better suited for lumbering. As one of them told the Commission on Colonization in 1903:

> All our Laurentian range is fit for nothing but timber and all attempts to colonize it have proven a failure. In many places the people have starved out and abandoned the lots, and in the last five years although thousands of acres have been taken out of our limits by the make belief colons but little attempt has been made towards clearing land. They simply clear off all the valuable bush and then abandon the lots, then the Department rubs it in by returning them to the limit holder. We are paying rent on large tracts of such land on which there is nothing standing of any value.[24]

The same witness proceeded to give his opinion of the colonization movement in no uncertain terms:

> The devastation of the forests is very often assisted by over-zealous colonization agents as well as causing a good deal of misery and hardship to the poor simple colon, who is often induced to take up land unfit for cultivation. I find that the *curés* often make this mistake. Colonization is a very laudable ambition, but, like many good things, it is overdone. I say put the colon on a good land, use the most severe

measures to keep them off uncultivable land, and a better state of affairs will exist and we will have better and happier communities.[25]

The report of the commission instanced seventeen townships of Ottawa County that had acquired only a scattered population of 15,699 by 1901, despite all efforts to promote settlement, including over $100,000 spent for colonization roads. To put a couple of thousand families on land not fit for cultivation, a valuable forest amounting to three and a half billion feet of pine that could have produced $4,500,000 in timber dues alone had been destroyed. Senator W. C. Edwards claimed that about 95 per cent of the pine of the province had been destroyed by fires, "by far the greater portion of which was through squatting and illegitimate settlement in the limits, a considerable portion through well intended but misguided attempts at colonization."[26] The deputy minister of the department, E. E. Taché, listed the deficiencies from the administrative point of view as "lack of circumspection in selling lots for agricultural purposes; excessive tolerance in regard to the fulfilment of the settlement conditions and to the illegal cutting of timber. Proceedings for cancellation of sale are also too complicated."[27] William Price also attributed the difficulties faced by lumbermen to the lack of professionally trained people and of a fully professional attitude in the administration of the Crown lands, owing to the prevalence of political patronage.

In fact, the administration responsible for managing the natural resources of Quebec was not at all deficient in progressive plans. The idea of establishing forest reserves was broached in the first Crown lands report of 1868; the first forest reserve act was passed in 1875; and the Laurentides National Park was established in 1895. So, too, with the fire-ranger, game-warden, and other programs. However, effective implementation had to overcome political interference, the public's unconcern or distaste for administrative efficiency, and the widespread sentiment that agrarian colonization was part of some higher morality. These made it quite impossible to implement a rational system for the most effective utilization of the provincial resources. The forest reserve idea, perhaps the most fundamental step towards achieving that end, remained virtually a dead letter from its enactment, and was repealed in 1888 when the colonization *ethos* attained its highest point of power.

A result of the indulgent attitude towards agricultural pioneering was the scattered nature of the resulting colonization, reflecting the lack of adequate directing or channelling of colons to form concentrated settlements. Many districts were quite sparsely occupied, containing large areas still under timber licences, comparatively large holdings (up to 400 acres) owned by individual settlers, and land that never had been occupied or had soon been abandoned. These conditions made for poor roads, few schools long distances apart, slowness in organizing parishes, lack of manpower for common endeavours, and the like. But gradually the pioneers cleared a few acres, planted vegetables and some grain for livestock feed, and developed a mixed farming economy, producing their own requirements plus small but increasing surpluses for sale. The opening of scores of cheese factories was a good tangible indication that pioneer districts had reached the stage of becoming centres of regular commercial agriculture.

The form of social organization adopted along the Quebec frontier differed from that that in the main characterized Ontario or western Canada. There, the overwhelming majority of settlers arrived as individuals, and new districts became variegated collections of persons from differing religious, national, or occupational backgrounds. In contrast, the frontier colonies in Quebec, like some in the other provinces, were strongly homogeneous settlements. This homogeneity was often tested, for collective action was essential to meet the demands of the harsh environment – to clear forests, drain land, build roads, buy supplies and equipment, market produce, and secure and sustain local commercial and communal facilities.

Because the settlement alternatives of the frontier environment of Quebec were less attractive and more difficult than those currently available elsewhere in Canada, or the United States, the Laurentian frontier would unquestionably have attracted far fewer settlers had the national and clerical elements been absent from the movement. But certain qualities resulted from this aid. The exclusivist character of the settlement produced a narrowness, rigidity, dearth of new ideas and approaches. Many colonies were placed under a leadership that was not primarily concerned with material growth and progress. The colonization movement, blinded by its national and religious goals, could not always view realistically the best, most appropriate long-term use of the resources, or the long-range interests of the settlers and of the nation. Perhaps, on balance, the Ontario approach, which put the emphasis on economic and material objectives in its programs, and made justice rather than mercy its administrative goal, offered the better answer of the two to the problems of settling the Canadian Shield under the conditions of the late nineteenth century.

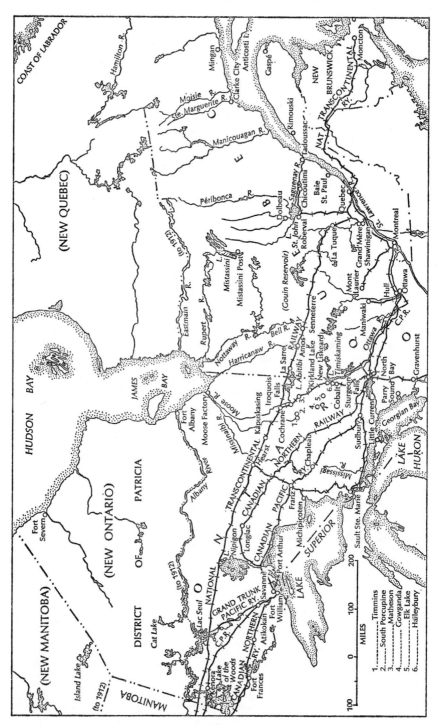

Northern Quebec and Ontario, 1896-1914

CHAPTER 8

Ontario and Quebec in the New Century

Before the mid-nineties (and to many Canadians for a long time afterwards) the Canadian Shield was regarded as the nation's particular curse, an enormous wasteland that prevented Canada from gaining the importance commensurate with its imposing geographical extent, or becoming more than a mere sliver of settlement huddled in the southern extremities of the land. Yet events were transpiring to alter this view. For suddenly, the region of rocks and lakes, of muskegs and woods, began to be recognized as possessing important economic resources worth developing. The spruce of its forests might not make good lumber, but could be turned into a superb woodpulp. The wild rivers winding across the rocky plateau from lake to lake and eventually dropping down to the St Lawrence or Ottawa could be harnessed to generate electric power. The bare rocks were among the oldest exposed anywhere, and in their aeons-long history had been invaded time and again by metallic solutions from the depths that filled their fissures with veins carrying appreciable amounts of precious and base metals. Even better, to the ideas of that day, here and there among the rocky expanses lay tracts of arable land, comparable in size with the St Lawrence valley of Quebec, or even the Ontarian peninsula. The pioneer farmers of the Lake St John district were settled on one of these, but the existence of others farther west was only gradually becoming recognized. As for utilizing the other resources, it was a matter of developing new technologies for making paper from pulpwood; for using electricity to drive motors and furnish lighting, power, or heat; for locating and mining copper or nickel ores, separating the metals from the enclosing rock, and manufacturing them into electric wire or steel alloys. Markets also had to be found for the products made possible by the new technologies.

The rise of these new industries changed the approach and course of frontier development in the older parts of Canada. In the case of Ontario, it led the government to take a new interest and develop different programs to foster the growth of new industries and settlements in the north. For Quebec, it did this and more, for it also helped lead the province somewhat reluctantly out of its pastoralist frame of mind and towards accommodation with twentieth-century industrialism.[1] The agrarian-oriented, clerical-sponsored programs of northern development were facing difficulties before the realities of the inhospitable environment. Now an alternative appeared – a way of making forestry and mining supplement farming as a means of livelihood for northern pioneers.

For the forest industry, too, the advent of the new technology was a godsend. Because of ruthless, wasteful exploitation of the pine forests and the enormous fire losses, the industry was facing a major crisis by the 1890's. The lowly spruce, hitherto neglected by the lumberman, had mostly been left to grow in profusion in the woodlands and areas of settlement and in the unexploited forests north and east of the limits of the pine. The pulp and paper industry, however, was happy to use these vast quantities of spruce for its needs. Furthermore, it was now recognized that dozens of large waterpower sites were to be found along the rim of the Precambrian Shield of Quebec, fed by rivers that rise high in the interior and fall some 1,500 feet to the St Lawrence or Ottawa, mainly in the last fifty miles of their courses. For ages these cataracts had obstructed penetration of the rocky plateau; now they were to become a major contribution to the upward progress of Quebec and Canada. The conjunction of these two new-found resources was most fortunate; as the lumber and railway magnate J. R. Booth said, "there is not likely to be found any substitute for spruce for paper making, and with our unlimited spruce forests, our greatest water power in the world and our various means for making acids, we should become the paper makers for the world."[2]

The hydro-electric power industry was also the product of many technical refinements that were achieved after 1887, as well as of the emergence of wider uses for electricity. A number of plants were installed by groups that controlled waterpower sites, for example at Chicoutimi, Baie St Paul, and on the Batiscan and St Maurice rivers. By 1900 Quebec's turbine installation of 83,000 h.p. was almost half of Canada's total.[3] New power sites were developed after 1900 on the Ottawa, Gatineau, Lièvre, North and St Maurice rivers, and on the various streams of the Saguenay watershed. The capacities of existing plants were increased by installing additional turbines and regulating the water flow by building storage dams along the watersheds, culminating with the huge Gouin Reservoir built on the upper St Maurice between 1915 and 1917 to increase the output of the downstream power sites. Quebec entrepreneurs conceived of many of these plans and obtained the sites from the government extremely cheaply, but, while some developments were financed by Canadian institutions, most were forced to borrow capital abroad, particularly in the United States. Even greater was the dependence on American managerial and engineering skills; the result was often to bring the enterprises firmly under American control.

Since the pulp and paper industry required large amounts of power and hydro plants fitted readily into company operations, the two became associated almost from the beginning of both industries. In 1890 the Laurentide Pulp Company was started at Grand'Mère to utilize the hydro-electric power to manufacture mechanical, or groundwood, pulp. By 1900 this was one of the largest plants in the country, with an investment of $3,000,000. The Chicoutimi Power Company opened a pulp mill in 1898 to consume its surplus power, create industry for the town, and take advantage of the large quantity of spruce logs available from local farmers' lots and leased limits. The Shawinigan Company attracted the Belgo-Canadian Pulp and Paper Company to establish at Shawinigan Falls by offering it a large block of power cheaply. Established forest-using companies like Price Brothers, which built hydro plants primarily for their own needs, sold the surpluses of electric power to other customers.

The use annually of hundreds of thousands of cords of spruce logs was a great boon to the rural population of Quebec, for much of the mills' requirements were purchased from farmers, who were free to dispose of the spruce timber from their lots. Unlike the lumber industry, the new industry could use small logs of from three to nine inches in diameter, so much of the forest cover could be harvested, instead of the now rather infrequent pine trees of a quality and size suitable for lumber-making. Operations in the woods, the drives, and the mills created a great deal of employment; by 1914 the forest industries in Quebec were employing 100,000 men altogether. A large mill could give rise to a considerable village, creating a permanent market for farm produce in the surrounding district. Here was an industry, then, that united the interests of frontier farmers and townsmen. Hence the joy with which it was acclaimed:

> Au Lac St-Jean, à St-Joseph d'Alma, à Roberval, au Lac Bouchette, ailleurs encore, peut-être, partout où il y a une chute d'eau, une cascade s'échelonnant aux flancs de la montagne, un pouvoir moteur économique, partout où il y a des forêts, on parle de construire des moulins pour fabriquer la pulpe. . . .
>
> La fièvre de l'activité industrielle s'est emparée de notre population. Puisse la contagion s'étendre encore et se perpétuer sur les bords du sauvage Saguenay et du grand Lac St-Jean.
>
> En avant la pulpe![4]

The clergy, too, responded to these new opportunities. At the local level, in many instances *curés* threw themselves into the work of developing new industries in their parishes, and supported the efforts of the local entrepre-

neur. In like fashion bishops collaborated with the capitalists and indus-
trialists to secure the fullest possible employment for French Canadians as
well as contributions for schools and other worthy clerical objectives, holding out the possibilities, in return, of using their good offices to promote
harmonious industrial relations.[5]

The repercussions of this technological revolution were felt even along
the North Shore below Tadoussac, heretofore the locale of the cod and
salmon fishery, the seal hunt, the fisheries patrol, and the Indian fur trade.
The major rivers between the Saguenay and the Moisie began to attract
attention, and the North Shore Power and Navigation Company, which
had just secured power rights to the Ste Marguerite River, founded the
village of Clarke City in 1908. A French syndicate obtained the power rights
to the Manicouagan River in 1906 for ninety-nine years at an annual rental
of $2,000. Neglected Anticosti Island came into the news with its acquisi-
tion in July, 1895, by an eccentric French chocolate manufacturer, Henri
Ménier, following which it began to be exploited for pulpwood.[6] Such
developments reflected the impact on the North Shore of the new economic
atmosphere. The St Lawrence made the spruce resources of the region immediately exploitable, though hydro-electric power development still was
confined to meeting limited local requirements.

The rise of the pulp industry initiated the serious phase of the Quebec-
Labrador boundary dispute. In 1902 the Newfoundland government leased
to a Grand River Pulp and Paper Company the territory on both sides of
the Hamilton River between Lake Melville and Grand Falls. Since Quebec's
boundary from 1898 was the Hamilton River, which the province claimed
to within a few miles of the Labrador coast, the lease was protested as in-
fringing on Quebec's territory and the company was told to make arrangements with Quebec or face penalties for violating Quebec law. In 1905 a
seizure of logs was made by Quebec agents, and the matter began its long
progress through the courts that culminated in the Privy Council decision
of 1927 awarding the entire Hamilton River basin to Newfoundland.

In Ontario lumbering was not quite so seriously threatened as in Quebec,
for there remained districts within the outer range of the pine that could
not be readily exploited until railways reached them, and this did not happen until early in the new century. As late as 1910 Ontario was still producing 40 per cent of all Canadian lumber, and the industry was expanding
in the district west of Lake Superior. In fact, the completion of a railway
along the Rainy River route in 1901 led American lumber interests, like the
Backus-Brooks and Shevlin-Clarke companies of Minnesota, to open some
of the largest lumber mills ever built in Ontario; the latter's plant at Fort
Frances cut 250,000 f.b.m. of lumber per shift.

The provincial government brought the industry under closer supervision.

Qualified forest rangers were placed over each forest district, and revenue was increased by raising the ground rent to $5 per square mile and timber dues from $1.50 to $2 per thousand f.b.m. in 1910. Bonuses on the 1,586 square miles auctioned between 1899 and 1902 averaged $3,243 per square mile, a total of $5,143,675. However, since few large blocks of pine timber remained, the policy was introduced of disposing of the timber in units of wood rather than on specified areas of land.[7]

In both Ontario and Quebec the needs of new industry necessitated a major revision of forest tenure practices. To justify the large investments on permanent installations, entrepreneurs required firm, long-term tenure arrangements rather than the short-term licences that were appropriate to a lumber industry that picked over a district and then moved on. Furthermore, the exploitation of the thickly concentrated, fast-growing spruce made it desirable to secure complete control of large blocks of land so as to be able to cut them over completely. Hence, in Quebec some companies began purchasing parishes and seignories to this end. But in Ontario and for the most part in Quebec, long-term leases of Crown lands was the rule. The Ontario government made a number of agreements in the final years of the nineteenth century, offering companies exclusive cutting rights over large areas, usually for twenty-one years. In return the lessees contracted to build mills of specified sizes, that cut specified quantities of wood each year, employed labour forces of agreed size, and paid the prescribed dues on the timber cut. One early agreement with the Sturgeon Falls Pulp and Paper Company resulted in a mill that processed one million spruce logs a year, created employment for six hundred men in the bush, and gave rise to a town of Sturgeon Falls, population 3,000. From 1898 Ontario, differing in this important way from Quebec, reserved water powers from all grants of land, and made them available only for leasing under separate arrangements. Pulp and paper companies, municipalities, and private companies leased such sites to supply electric power to centres like Port Arthur, Sudbury, and Cobalt.[8]

Now that the industry was contributing so mightily to rural prosperity in Quebec, it could challenge the priority over land use that agricultural settlement enjoyed. A strong debate was begun with the defenders of the colonization ethos who propounded the superiority of the agricultural way of life, the right of the individual against the soulless corporation, and of the people against foreign capitalism. The supporters of the forest industries counterattacked by pointing to the negative side of the colonization movement and to the greater benefits their industry promised. The colonization commission of 1903 was set up to deal with serious complaints against the land colonization and land-granting systems under which Quebec had lived for so long, and to investigate accusations of corruption against the administration. The hearings became an opportunity for spokesmen of lumber and pulp and paper companies to present their point of view and air their grievances against the policy of indiscriminate colonization. They complained against bogus settlers and squatters, and insisted that forest lands should be reserved exclusively for foresty purposes and closed to would-be farmers. Spokesmen for the settlers, including Henri Bourassa, upheld the freedom of the individual to choose his own vocation, denounced the speculation in lands, and urged stricter enforcement against all violations in the interests of the bona-fide settler. The commission's recommendations were mainly favourable to the forest interest. They accepted the idea of separating the public domain into areas of settlement and areas of merchantable timber, from which settlement should be excluded. They proposed strict enforcement of settlement regulations with automatic cancellation for all breaches or violations, proper protection of the forests by a good forest ranger system, effective control of burning operations on settlement lands, and the prohibition of wandering in the woods without a permit.[9]

Despite the setback before the commission, where colonization was made something of a whipping-boy, the agricultural interest was far from discomfited. Colonization continued to be promoted, for the rising pulp and paper industry added new incentives by affording opportunities to settlers of earning cash from pulpwood, from woods' employment, and from the sale of farm produce. The generally good markets and prices for agricultural produce that prevailed at the turn of the century also attracted new settlers to the frontier regions. In the Lake St John-Saguenay district, new townships were opened in the Albanel, Dolbeau, Mistassini, and Peribonca sections (the locale for Louis Hémon's classic *Marie Chapdelaine*, published in 1914), while the region's progress was reflected in the increasing numbers of schools and churches, miles of roads, acreages cleared, and cheese factories (116 by 1907) opened. A few settlers began to enter the upper St Maurice district in view of railway construction there, though the rising industrial centres of Shawinigan Falls and LaTuque were greater attractions. In the counties bordering the Ottawa, incoming French colonists, due to a combination of their high birth rate and the exodus of English-speaking settlers, began to overturn the one-time British majority; Argenteuil recorded a French-speaking majority in 1901. Now that railway communications with the outside world were assured, Timiskaming also began receiving some attention. New townships were surveyed there, and by 1911 the district claimed 8,500 people.

In Ontario, too, there was a renewed interest in agricultural settlement around the turn of the century, coinciding with the succession to the premiership in 1899 of G. W. Ross. The Crown Lands Department was reorganized and a Bureau of Colonization was set up under Thomas Southworth, the former director of forestry, who brought new vigour to the task of locating settlers in northern Ontario. The opportunities of the district were advertised in newspapers, pamphlets, exhibits at fairs, and by farmers' excursions. The merits of the territory, the easy settlement conditions, the sure rise of property values, were all held out, and the message was hammered home that "There is no other means whereby the man without other capital than the power and will to labor can so readily attain a competence and a substantial position in the community as by taking up a bush farm."[10] Southworth and other officials toured the Timiskaming district in October, 1899, and some 350 settlers moved there that year. Again in 1901 a party of 200 excursionists, farmers, and newspapermen toured the district, and many of the former actually selected farms, particularly around New Liskeard.[11]

In 1900 a most ambitious series of surveys of the agricultural potentialities of northern Ontario was carried on by exploring parties that examined the country north of the Canadian Pacific Railway between the Quebec border and Lake Nipigon. They reported the presence, hundreds of miles from the Quebec border, of a vast, fertile "Clay Belt" of some 16,000,000 acres, which they deemed suited for agriculture. The *Report of the Survey and Exploration of Northern Ontario*, 1900, touched off a flood of optimistic reports on the potentialities of this arable region, described as four-fifths as large as the area of Ontario currently devoted to agriculture. Further surveys in 1903 and 1904 confirmed these optimistic comparisons. However, occupation of the Great Clay Belt was out of the question until it could be served by railways. In the meantime the principal magnet for settlers remained the Little Clay Belt, one million acres of good soil west and northwest of Lake Timiskaming, that C. C. Farr had been boosting these many years.

II

Despite construction of the Canadian Pacific Railway system, the development of most of the Middle North of both Ontario and Quebec continued to be hampered through lack of economical transportation facilities. Though the Canadian Pacific rested content with its present railways (apart from double-tracking the Winnipeg-to-lakehead section to facilitate hauling western Canadian grain for export), other ambitious railway builders took up the challenges and the newly revealed opportunities of the land. First off the mark were the irrepressible William Mackenzie and Donald D. Mann. To supplement their growing network of lines in the prairies, they built a line to the lakehead to haul western grain to the Great Lakes for shipping, as well as to develop the resources of the country that their line would traverse. They were unequalled in their ability to sniff out good traffic prospects, and were able to create their own traffic by picking off concessions, particularly to mining properties, and developing them under one or other of their corporate aliases. By acquiring the charter of the Ontario and Rainy River Railway Company, they secured a large cash subsidy from the Dominion government for the section of their line built in Ontario, and even a bond guarantee from Manitoba to the amount of $20,000 per mile. Building from Winnipeg south of Lake of the Woods by way of Minnesota, then back to Canada at Rainy River, they tapped rich forests, mine fields, and power sites of the Rainy River section, developed an iron deposit at Atikokan, and obtained valuable concessions at the lakehead for making Port Arthur their traffic centre and for building their iron smelter there. Sault Ste Marie became another centre for new railways. F. H. Clergue was developing at the Sault possibly the broadest group of integrated companies under a single man's control in Canadian history, and needed railways to tap the rich mineral and forest resources of the region north of his base. By 1903 his Algoma Central and Hudson Bay Railway, aided by a provincial land grant was built seventy-seven miles north to the Helen Mine, and by 1914 to Hearst on the new National Transcontinental Railway. A second railway, the Manitoulin and North Shore (renamed the Algoma Eastern in 1911), aided by Ontario land and cash grants, completed a line from Little Current to Sudbury in 1912.[12]

Similarly, in Quebec provincial and federal government grants enabled short railways to be extended up the Gatineau, Ottawa, North, and St Maurice rivers to new pulp and paper, hydro-electric power, and frontier farming developments, while Mackenzie and Mann consolidated their Canadian Northern empire in Quebec by industriously buying up as many lines as they could. Still, Quebec needed railways that did something more – that tapped the forests and water powers of the upper St Maurice or the feeders of Lake St John, that brought the wealth of forest and arable land of Abitibi within range of development by and for Quebeckers, or that reached to James Bay and the rich resources (as was then believed) of Hudson Bay. Indeed, businessmen of the city of Quebec were promoting a Trans-Canada Railway project, right to the Pacific coast, that would bring the trade of a continent-wide hinterland to their city and revive its historic role as the premier seaport of the great river of Canada.[13]

Toronto business interests held very similar views regarding a hinterland along Lake Timiskaming and on to James Bay, in which they were powerfully abetted by the sympathies of Premier Ross. His response to a delegation of northerners and Toronto Board of Trade officers in February, 1901, was an announcement in the budget speech of the government's intention to build a railway from North Bay to Lake Timiskaming. The Temiskaming and

Northern Ontario Railway* was chartered in 1902 and – in keeping with the idea of public ownership of utilities – was to be built by a provincially appointed commission with money advanced by the province.[14] The first sod was turned at North Bay on May 12, 1902, in time to help the Liberals, on May 29, 1902, to win their last provincial general election in Ontario in more than thirty years. By the end of 1904 the railway was operating to New Liskeard and work was under way on the next one-hundred-mile segment.[15] In 1908 it was extended north to a junction with the new town-site of Cochrane, on the route of the National Transcontinental Railway.

Even before the railway reached New Liskeard an incredible stroke of good fortune occurred. Men employed on construction in the tangle of rocks, muskegs, and forests near Lake Timiskaming stumbled on rich silver deposits, and by 1904 thousands of prospectors were being attracted to Cobalt, swelling the railway's treasury. In fact, the railway leased three and one-half miles of its right of way through the district and for several years received over $100,000 per annum from this source. The resulting mines, farms, and forest industries provided enough traffic from the outset for the railway to be able each year to hand the province a surplus that approximated the interest on the government's investment. As the mineral discovery at Cobalt was followed by others, short branch lines were built to Charlton, Kerr Lake, Timmins, and Elk Lake. Some of these were constructed by a subsidiary acquired in 1911, the Nipissing Central Railway, which operated a successful five-mile street railway between Cobalt and Haileybury. Since that company possessed a Dominion charter, it could be used to build branches into Quebec, as was done in the mid-twenties to the Rouyn-Noranda mining camp.

The province remained anxious to extend the railway all the way to James Bay, and the government applied to the Dominion to assist construction of this part of the line. But the Laurier government, usually so generous to railway builders, objected to the railway's being owned by a provincial government, and no aid was forthcoming. Borden's victory, which owed so much to the support of the Ontario government, was followed by the introduction of a bill to grant the railway $6,400 per mile for the 300 miles constructed thus far. This plan was temporarily frustrated by the Liberal majority in the Senate, ironically led by G. W. Ross, the former premier of Ontario, whose government had started the railway. In the end

* "Timiskaming" was declared the official spelling for the lake, etc., by the Geographic Board of Canada in 1902, but "Temiskaming" was commonly used in Ontario until recent years. Quebec has officially adopted "Timiscaming" and "Témiscamingue" for the town and county. "Timiskaming" is the form followed here, except for the railway, which retained the original spelling (as above) until it became the Ontario Northland Railway in 1946.

the province did receive $2,134,000 subsidy for the railway.[16] Construction beyond Cochrane was resumed in the 1920's, eventually to reach Moosonee, at the mouth of the Moose River. The railway has been the major force in opening up the country beyond North Bay to the James Bay frontier, has largely paid its own way during most of its career, and has served the metropolitan interests of southern Ontario by linking that region with the Clay Belts and mining districts, as well as with the National Transcontinental and Hudson Bay. Few railways in Canada have been so successful.

The entirely unexpected discovery of silver at Cobalt gave Ontario a third important northern mining centre, and in 1907 carried the mineral production of the province past that of British Columbia. Ontario became by far the leading mining province of Canada, producing in 1913 over $59,000,000 of minerals, 41 per cent of the Dominion's total. Four metallic minerals won from the Canadian Shield accounted for two-thirds of this: silver, $16,900,-000; nickel, $14,900,000; gold $4,500,000; and copper $3,900,000. Mining thus constituted a major incentive in the settlement of northern Ontario that was almost absent in Quebec until the gold and base-metal resources of that province's section of the Canadian Shield began to be discovered in the twenties and thirties.

Of the three main mining camps in Ontario, Sudbury was rapidly leaving behind the wasteful pioneer days to become an important supplier of copper and the world's greatest source of nickel just when new uses were being discovered in industry and especially in the manufacture of armour plate in a world rushing on to Armageddon. Towards the end of the nineteenth century the partners Canadian Copper Company and Orford Copper Company fell out and each tried to become independent of the other. The Canadian Copper Company attempted to develop a nickel-refining process, while the Orford Company established a great furnace at Copper Cliff to secure its own ore and matte supplies from the field. Finally, they agreed to merge under the leadership of Colonel R. M. Thompson of the Orford Company, with the new title of International Nickel Company of New Jersey. The company did not long remain unchallenged. In 1902 the stubborn chemist Ludwig Mond established the Mond Nickel Company, which mined ore from its own properties and refined the matte in Wales.[17] Year by year the production of the field increased, apart from temporary setbacks, from 3,398,113 pounds to 49,676,772 pounds between 1896 and 1913.

Mining and minerals were only a part of the diversified industrial conglomerate developed at Sault Ste Marie by the remarkable entrepreneur F. H. Clergue. In 1894 he had induced the town to give him its unfinished power-development concession in return for his taking over its $225,000 debt. Raising capital in New York and Philadelphia, he completed the 20,000 horsepower plant, then, to utilize the power, established a Sault Ste

Marie Pulp and Paper Company, and thereby found a market for the un-limited supplies of spruce logs along the eastern shore of Lake Superior. His plant was producing 150 tons daily of groundwood pulp by 1896. He saw, however, that chemical pulp would be more profitable, so he went on to establish a sulphite pulp mill at the Sault which was in operation by 1902. To obtain the sulphur, Clergue acquired a nickel-copper property at Sud-bury which produced sulphur, chlorine (for bleaching the pulp), ferro-nickel for his iron and steel plant at the Sault, and a nickel-steel alloy con-tracted to Krupp's of Essen. And this was just the beginning of Clergue's classic of economic integration.

In 1897, when a high-grade hematite deposit was discovered near Michi-picoten, he purchased the location and developed it into Ontario's largest iron mine, the Helen Mine. To carry the ore from the mine to Lake Superior, he incorporated the Algoma Central Railway in 1899 and secured 7,400 acres per mile from Ontario and a cash subsidy of $591,000 from the Do-minion government. In 1901 he organized the principal component of the system, the Algoma Iron, Nickel and Steel Company, which, by 1902, was producing steel, steel alloys, and steel rails under a contract Clergue had obtained from the Dominion government to supply these to government-assisted railways. He purchased or leased twenty freighters to haul the raw materials to the Sault – iron and nickel ores, logs, coal from Pennsylvania – and to export fabricated steel products, surplus iron ore, and woodpulp. These enterprises were consolidated under a single Lake Superior Corpor-ation, with Clergue as general manager and stock held mainly in the United States. He had shown incredible daring and ingenuity in creating an enter-prise that comprised blast furnaces, steel rolling mills, iron, copper, and nickel mines, refineries, chemical plants, pulp mills, railways, and steam-ships.[18]

But the properties had been assembled without sufficient realistic analysis of benefits, costs, or markets. Clergue had no large financial stake in the properties, and he was personally extravagant and dictatorial. The inevi-table happened in the financial recession of 1903: when further borrowing became difficult the system collapsed. When hundreds of employees in the woods and mills learned that the company could not meet the payroll in September, 1903, they threatened to riot, and the provincial government intervened by persuading the banks to advance the $260,000 wage bill. About the same time, the company was unable to meet payments on a large $4,500,000 mortgage held by Speyer and Company, New York, nor could it pay $1,800,000 in other debts, about two-thirds held by Canadians. Once more the province came to the rescue to avoid the system's being taken over by the American creditors, who would perhaps close down the steel mill to prevent its competing with American companies for the Canadian market. The province made the company a $2,000,000 loan on the security of its various properties (valued at $35,000,000) as well as the 1,600,000 acres of land grant earned by the Algoma Central Railway. In the legislature, the leader of the opposition, J. P. Whitney, opposed the move as a bad precedent.[19]

The help enabled the company to weather the storm. The debts and the company were reorganized, with Clergue becoming merely a director on the board. Soon the organization was back in production, employing almost 4,000 men. By 1906, when it was busy on the 166,000-ton steel rail order, it not only met the instalments on the provincial loan but looked to a profit for the year also. In 1907 Clergue persuaded the provincial government to take back the land grant earned by the Algoma Central in return for a guarantee of $25,000 worth of bonds per mile for extending the railway north from Helen Mine. This was done, and the railway was extended to the Canadian Pacific at Franz, and eventually, in 1914, to Hearst. The industrial empire continued to have its ups and downs; in another reorganization a few years later Clergue was dropped, and control of the steel mill fell into the hands of English interests.[20]

More important even than Sudbury or the Clergue empire for the remarkable opening up of northeastern Ontario during these years was the Cobalt mine field. Silver was discovered, first by two timber cruisers, J. H. McKinley and E. J. Darragh on August 7, 1903, and a month later by Fred LaRose, a blacksmith with one of the contractors working on the Temiskaming and Northern Ontario Railway. Prospectors and speculators thronged to the vicinity, and a village, later town, of Cobalt, population 8,000, quickly sprang up. Most of the early discoveries were at or near the surface and required little equipment or investment; rich nuggets of almost pure silver could be sorted by hand and loaded on railway cars for shipment to New York for refining. Expenses were small at this stage; in two years one mine produced $2,500,000 of ore for a total outlay of only $225,000.

Soon, however, surface showings were exhausted. Then it became necessary to dig underground and install concentrating mills to treat much lower grades of ore. By 1913 the concentrators were treating 2,720 tons of ore per day that averaged only twenty to twenty-five ounces of silver per ton. Every effort was made to reduce operating expenses, to increase the margin of profitability, and to make it possible to work lower grades of mineral. Power was a major expense, so the camp quickly turned to hydro-electric power. Three plants were established on adjoining rivers, one of which in addition ingeniously developed and sold compressed air. By 1911 these were merged as the Northern Ontario Light and Power Company, supplying about 20,000 horsepower, and reducing the district's coal imports from the United States from 105,000 to 44,000 tons per annum – a considerable saving, though a hard blow to the Temiskaming and Northern Ontario Railway. From 1905 Cobalt was a million-dollar camp, and its peak output for this early period reached $17,408,000 in 1912.[21]

The significance of Cobalt was more than its impact on the railway, townspeople, farmers, and other settlers of the Timiskaming district. The reputation of the Precambrian Shield as a promising mining region was rapidly enhanced by the thousands of prospectors attracted to the district by Cobalt. These men fanned out across the country, uncovering other promising showings that gave rise to two new mining camps in the immediate future and half a dozen others subsequently. Because Cobalt – like the Klondike, but unlike Sudbury – was a "poor man's camp," many original prospectors and their local backers retained control of properties into the mining stage and grew wealthy, creating a class of successful Canadian mining men able and willing to provide risk capital for later mines. The Cobalt experience provided invaluable training for mining engineers. The large-scale, low-cost operations developed at Cobalt were admirable preparation for the future course of hard-rock mining in Canada, where most metals – gold, uranium, or others – occur in minute amounts in tons of worthless rock, or gangue. For such mines to succeed, carefully engineered plants and programs, high initial investments, and low-cost operations have been essential. Cobalt was the opening victory in the long campaign waged by Canadians to wrest mineral wealth from the Precambrian Shield.

The effects were felt farther afield. "The Precambrian Shield became a phrase to conjure with," and new institutions sprang up to mobilize capital for this and other mining booms – brokerage houses and the weekly *Northern Miner* in Toronto, as well as short-lived mining exchanges at Cobalt and New Liskeard. The Toronto mining exchange gained new prominence, and Toronto took a significant step along the road to metropolitan hegemony over northern Ontario. Public interest and concern for the development of mining along proper lines was reflected in increasing government support for mining education in the universities as well as a later school of mines at Haileybury. The usual horde of misleading promotions and frauds that accompanied the Cobalt boom encouraged reforms of those aspects of mining that were felt to contribute to the abuses. The new Mining Act of 1906 reduced the size of claims from 320 acres to a more realistic forty acres, withheld patents until development work had been done, appointed inspectors to examine properties with power to cancel claims for noncompliance with these conditions, and appointed a mining commissioner to adjudicate mining disputes. In its repercussions for the future course of Canadian development, the Cobalt bears affinities with the Klondike.[22]

By 1914 Cobalt had spawned two more gold-mining camps and a number of interesting prospects that later became important producers. The Porcupine district, ninety miles northwest of Cobalt, was prospected after 1905, but the first big discovery was made early in 1909 by an eight-man party, one of whom literally stumbled over an exposed gold vein that later became the Dome Mine. Next, B. Hollinger and A. Gillies staked a property which resulted in the Hollinger Consolidated Gold Mine, with the backing of Messrs Timmins, McMartin, and Dunlap, who had struck it rich at Cobalt. Sandy McIntyre also discovered the property that finally became the McIntyre Porcupine Mine. Development was hampered by the inaccessibility of the district until 1912, when the railway branch built to South Porcupine reached Timmins. Around 1912 gold was also discovered at Kirkland Lake, about sixty miles from Cobalt but quite close to the railway. The principal discoverers were W. H. Wright and Harry Oakes, who succeeded in hanging on until their mines, Wright-Hargreaves and Lake Shore, made them very wealthy. A mill was installed in 1912 and power became available from a hydro plant at Charlton on the Englehart River in 1914. Both camps were only becoming productive when the Great War began and did not reach their greatest days until the twenties and thirties. Still other areas of future mining activity in northern Ontario were investigated in this period.

III

In the meantime, the newly founded woodpulp industry began to encounter serious problems. Operators soon discovered that mechanical, or groundwood, pulp, which was exported in a wet state for further processing abroad, yielded very low returns and profits. Thus where a cord of exported pulpwood earned $8.00 to Canadian factors of production, its value as mechanical pulp became $25.00, and as paper $44.00. Moreover, virtually all these increments represented returns to local labour and investment, sulphur being the only material having to be imported. Once again, however, these more advanced stages entailed expensive equipment, and further resorting to foreign capital. American and British pulp- or paper-using organizations entered the field, encouraged by the guaranteed markets their integrated economies afforded, as well as by the changing production and marketing situation in the United States. Foreign ownership and control thus became ever more pronounced in the pulp and paper industry.

But a further obstacle stood in the way of upgrading the industry: the United States tariff, whose purpose it was to encourage manufacturing at home and keep imports from Canada at the pulp log stage. Unless this could be prevented, the only benefits Canada was likely to derive from the forest wealth of the Shield were the slender profits from the logs alone. Investors and operators began urging governments to place export duties on Canadian logs so as to promote their fabrication in Canada. Others advocated an embargo of the export of pulp logs from Crown lands, a step Ontario instituted in 1900 by ordering the manufacture in Canada of all pulpwood derived from Crown lands. In 1903 a manufacturers' delegation waited on the premier of Quebec to urge the imposition of export duties on pulpwood, while E. B. Eddy advised that a $4.00 export duty should be imposed on pulpwood going to the United States, for "Stop the woods from going out free to foreign countries and foreign capital will pour in to make pulp and paper in Canada, especially in the Province of Quebec."[23] American firms, responding to shortages of pulpwood at home, began investing heavily in Canadian timber limits, and by 1907 they were said to control 12,000 square miles of woodlands in Quebec alone. From these, and from logs purchased in Canada, they drew up to one million cords of pulpwood per annum for processing in United States mills.[24] The Dominion government withstood the appeals for an export duty, but was induced to prohibit the export of logs from federally controlled Crown lands in 1907. In 1910 Quebec ultimately followed suit.

Such steps reinforced the already highly favourable opportunities for profitable investment in Canadian forest and waterpower resources. In 1911 nineteen new companies, total capital $41,709,000, were incorporated in Quebec, and by the end of that year there were twenty-five pulp mills and twenty paper mills in operation in that province. Paper-making capacity was greatly increased, only to encounter another barrier to ready access to the neighbouring United States market – the $5.75 per ton duty on foreign newsprint. Soon afterwards, however, the United States, as part of the projected reciprocity agreement, agreed to grant free entry for Canadian newsprint, and a new round of newsprint plant construction was launched. In Ontario the Backus-Brooks firm developed power plants and pulp mills at International Falls and Fort Frances, while the Chicago *Tribune* built an Ontario Paper Company plant at Thorold in the Niagara peninsula that drew its logs from timber limits much farther afield. By 1914 other plants were springing up at Dryden, Mattagami, and at Abitibi on the National Transcontinental. By that time Ontario's pulpwood and woodpulp production were approximately two-thirds those of Quebec, though significantly, Ontario mills produced twice the amount of sulphite pulp as those of Quebec, more of which were still devoted to the cheaper groundwood pulp.

The expanding pulp and paper, mining, and farming economies of northern Ontario and Quebec drew inspiration and strength from the surveys and construction of two new transcontinental railway enterprises. For a dozen years after 1902 these projects captured the public imagination with plans to repeat the achievement of the Canadian Pacific Railway by building across northern Ontario, while one of them would also be the first railway to cross the Precambrian Shield of Quebec. The planning and construction of these lines in themselves provided major incentives for further settlement and development of the region's potential resources.

First off the mark was the Canadian Northern. On December 30, 1901, at the banquet held in Port Arthur to celebrate the arrival of the first train from Winnipeg, Mackenzie and Mann unveiled plans to complete a transcontinental line via northern Ontario within seven years.[25] They were frustrated in achieving their timetable, though not in the general objective, by pressures in western Canada for improved service and the completion of promised branch lines, and by the Dominion government's decision to assist the rival Grand Trunk Railway to build the nation's second transcontinental line. The Grand Trunk approached the Dominion government in 1902 with its own project to build from northern Ontario to the Pacific coast. The Laurier government, keenly aware of the concern of metropolitan, industrial, and transportation interests in Quebec for a railway that would actually open up the northern frontier of the province instead of skirting along the Ottawa River, insisted that the new project traverse Quebec and New Brunswick as well as Ontario and the West. Eventually it was arranged that the Dominion government would build the eastern half of the line from Moncton via Quebec City to Winnipeg as the National Transcontinental Railway, while the Grand Trunk Pacific, a subsidiary of the Grand Trunk, would build from Winnipeg to the Pacific coast, and, in addition, construct a branch from Fort William to the National Transcontinental at Superior Junction, near the future Sioux Lookout. On the government part of the project, the primary contracts were awarded in 1906 and 1907 in the form of a number of large (75 to 245-mile) sections to a series of contractors. Some of the sections were built expeditiously, while others were very slow and held up the progress of the work. Perhaps the most serious delay was in J. D. McArthur's 245-mile contract from Superior Junction to Winnipeg, since it immobilized the Grand Trunk Pacific's completed Fort William-Superior Junction branch, and made it impossible for that company to secure its share of grain traffic from the prairies for the line to the lakehead. Three excellent prairie harvests were lost in this way before the offending section was finished late in 1910. M. P. and J. T. Davis's 204-mile section in the Clay Belt district also was slow in being completed, and prevented regular service from Quebec City to Winnipeg before June, 1915.[26]

In the meantime Mackenzie and Mann, undeterred, were proceeding with their own plans. They acquired the charter in 1904 of the James Bay Railway with its large cash and land subsidies, and in the following year secured a charter from Parliament to build from French River to Port Arthur under the name of Canadian Northern Ontario Railway. Encouraged by bond guarantees for $20,000 per mile from the Ontario government, in 1908 they completed their 258-mile line from Toronto to Sudbury. However, the province would not help them build west to Port Arthur, so the promoters turned to the Dominion government. Eventually, in 1911, the new Dominion government, appreciative of services rendered, came to the aid of the Canadian Northern with a $35,000 per mile bond guarantee for the 1,050 miles from Montreal to Port Arthur by way of Algonquin Park, North Bay, Sudbury, Longlac, and along Lake Superior to Port Arthur.[27] Thus the unsettled, rocky, forested regions of northern Ontario became traversed by no fewer than three expensive railways – lasting monuments to the grandiose dreams of that optimistic age and to the extravagance and incompetence of the governments of the time.

Owing to its situation, the Canadian Northern mainly served established centres of North Bay, Sudbury, and the lakehead and opened little new territory in northern Quebec and Ontario apart from the border country west of Lake Superior tapped by its original road. The National Transcontinental, on the other hand, followed a route that, however poor the immediate economic returns, opened up an entirely new section of country to settlement and development extending over 800 miles from the St Maurice River to beyond Lake Nipigon. In the St Maurice sector, the building of the railway encouraged the development of forest industries, while from the Bell River west to the Ontario boundary it immediately opened the Abitibi district of the Great Clay Belt to agricultural and forestry activities. Here Father Ivanhoë Caron made himself a missionary-colonizer on the model of Father Labelle, and for thirty years Abitibi became the new frontier of colonization.[28] Township and land-classification surveys were made in 1909 and 1910 along the route of the Transcontinental. The collaboration of the provincial government was secured for a plan of settling three districts along the line, and Father Caron was authorized to recruit settlers to add to the few who had begun entering the region as early as 1909. By 1912 settlers were coming forward to Abitibi, and the town of Amos was rising on the banks of the Harricanaw River. Growth was slowed because of the Great War, but by 1921 the census gave the population of the region as 13,172, the main centres being the villages of Amos (population 1,488) and Lasarre (1,446), and the township of Senneterre (731).

Ontario, too, welcomed the National Transcontinental, and from the first announcement of the project, the provincial government made great efforts to promote settlement in the district of the headwaters of the Abitibi-Moose system of rivers. There the provincial railway serving the Little Clay Belt could connect with the national railway, which "offers a golden opportunity for settlement, extending over a distance of 750 miles through the middle of the Clay Belt North of the height of land."[29] Optimistic early reports credited the region as capable of providing as much as 288,000,000 cords of pulpwood, but the forester B. E. Fernow, who examined the country adjacent to the railway in 1913, proved much more conservative. He pointed out that the timber was not very good quality, that even in the best areas about half the country was not worth logging; and that agricultural settlement should proceed with care, paying special attention to improving the soil by fertilizers, organizing large-scale collective draining projects, and the like.[30]

Even before the National Transcontinental was completed, the provincial government had launched an ambitious program of supplying the region with colonization roads, the expenditure on the Timiskaming district alone amounting to $191,295 in 1910. By then, organized municipalities were being called on to pay half the cost of local roads, while the province built major trunk roads, colonization roads in unorganized territory, and roads in organized townships too poor to contribute their share of the cost. In 1912 the legislature passed a Northern and Northwestern Ontario Development Act that empowered the provincial government to borrow up to $5,000,000 to build roads and bridges, and to improve transportation and communication facilities in these frontier districts. In 1918 and again in 1922, two more five-million-dollar sums were allotted to the same purpose. J. F. Whitson of the Surveys Branch was appointed commissioner, and charged with constructing roads along the National Transcontinental Railway from the Quebec boundary to Hearst and south to Englehart along the Temiskaming and Northern Ontario, plus feeder roads radiating out from the main towns and railway shipping points. When building began in earnest in 1913 and 1914, four and five thousand men sometimes were employed at this work.

Thanks to these projects, as well as to the progress on the transcontinental railway, settlement began to enter the Great Clay Belt after 1910, and a Crown Lands Agency was opened in 1911 at Cochrane to be ready for the anticipated land rush. In the meantime settlers, mostly from southern Ontario, encouraged by railway publicity and assisted by free excursions as well as by special rates on settlers effects and on major export products like cordwood, continued to arrive in the District of Timiskaming to carve new homes out of the bush. Already by 1911, thanks to the mining and agricultural settlement, the census division of Timiskaming reported a total population of 37,076, a more than tenfold increase for the decade. At that time the major settlements were Cobalt, Haileybury, New Liskeard, Cochrane, Engelhart, Latchford, and Charlton, all served by the provincial railway. Ten years later, in spite of the upheavals of the war, the population had grown a further 38 per cent to 51,568. While the older centres (with the exception of Cochrane) had done no better than hold their own or had actually declined, new centres had arisen – still mainly on the provincial route – reflecting the spread of mining, agricultural settlement, and the pulp and paper industry: Timmins, 3,843; Iroquois Falls, 1,178; Kapuskasing, 926; and Matheson, 305. These advances were registered in spite of several serious holocausts, the worst of which occurred on July 11, 1911 – a careless brush fire that began near Kenogami and devastated the whole country between Cochrane and Porcupine, killing some seventy persons, twenty-two by suffocation as they huddled in the mine shaft at West Dome. In the town of Cochrane fifty stores, fifteen hotels, four churches, and two schools were destroyed. Other fires razed the towns of Timmins in 1912 and Hailey-bury in 1914.

Through the efforts of both provinces and the Dominion, the railway developers, foresters and miners, farmers and townspeople, a new section was born in northern Ontario. Quebec also experienced similar growth, but it was somewhat less than Ontario's for the period 1901-1921, especially in the decade 1901-1911, when the Ontario boom reached its peak. North-ern Quebec did not feel the impetus of the new industries quite so soon as northern Ontario; the impact of the National Transcontinental and of the newsprint paper industry began to be experienced only after 1911, and of mining in the twenties and thirties. Of the Quebec counties which con-tained appreciable parts of the Canadian Shield, the main growth occurred in Champlain on the St Maurice, where the rise of new forest industries at Grand'Mère, LaTuque, and elsewhere produced an increase from 35,159 in 1901 to 54,191 in 1921; in Labelle, where there was a similar rise from 30,931 to 46,292; in the Lake St John country, where the total population grew from 48,291 to 87,822 and the united county was split in three – Chi-coutimi, Lac St Jean, and Saguenay; and in Pontiac, which increased from 25,722 to 46,201, 26,204 of this last in the newly separated county of Témiscamingue. Taking these four main regions together, their populations rose from 140,103 in 1901 (itself nearly double the 76,235 recorded in 1871) to 175,866 in 1911, and to 234,506 in 1921. Much of this growth was in rural areas, of self-employed agricultural settlement controlled by, and in tune with, powerful clerical-nationalist forces.

In Ontario the six northern districts, which had been virtually unsettled in 1871 and had acquired a population of 100,401 in 1901 thanks mainly to the building of the Canadian Pacific Railway and its branches, experienced a period of further growth that carried their total population to 218,777 in 1911 and to 267,388 in 1921, by which time they contained 9 per cent of Ontario's total population. The most rapid growth occurred in Timis-kaming, which had only 3,378 inhabitants in 1901 but 51,568 twenty years later. Nipissing (thanks to Sudbury and to forest and railroading activities) rose from 24,931 to 58,565, and the country west of Lake Superior from 28,987 to 82,961. The two Algomas experienced a less rapid increase, from 43,105 to 74,294, mainly through forestry activities and the rise of the industrial centre of Sault Ste Marie.

Whereas northern expansion in Quebec was largely rural and self-employed, in Ontario the northern frontier was largely industrial, wage-earning, and urban, with just under half the population in 1921 reported from the incorporated cities, towns, and villages. Furthermore, railway employment, lumbering, and mining accounted for a large part of the rural population. Urban, of course, was a relative term, for of the thirty-seven communities listed in 1921, only the fourteen largest held more than 2,000 residents. Still, they included centres of national and even international significance, cities like Sault Ste Marie, Fort William, Port Arthur, and the town of North Bay, that performed very substantial industrial and transportation functions. Moreover, in Sudbury, Cobalt, Timmins, and Copper Cliff the region possessed major mining and refining centres; in Kenora, Sturgeon Falls, Fort Frances, and a dozen smaller places, important lumber and pulp industries; in Cochrane, Haileybury, and New Liskeard, the usual commercial and administrative activities.

One feature that differentiated the north from other parts of Ontario (and certainly from the new north of Quebec, which was consciously held for French settlement) was its polyglot society. Whereas Ontario in 1921 was predominantly of British extraction (78 per cent) and only about 8.5 per cent French Canadian, in the northern districts the British percentage fell to a bare 51 per cent, while the French rose to almost one-quarter of the total (23.7 per cent). Other groups comprised one-quarter of the population, nearly double their fraction in the province as a whole. They included disproportionate numbers of certain national groups not very extensively represented elsewhere in the province – over one-quarter of the Italians, about half the Scandinavians, Austrians, and Ukrainians, over half the province's Indians (whose numbers held steady at 14,200 for the twenty-year period), and almost the whole Finnish population (11,536 of 12,835 persons, comprising 4 per cent of the population of the north). French Canadians actually outnumbered English Canadians in the Nipissing and Sudbury census divisions, and comprised about 27 per cent of the total population of Timiskaming, but tapered off in the more westerly census divisions. Scandinavians were comparatively prominent in the Kenora and Rainy River districts, Italians in the cities of Algoma and Thunder Bay, Indians mainly in Kenora and Manitoulin, and Finns chiefly in Thunder Bay and Sudbury.

The new north of Ontario, therefore, had a distinctive economic, political, and social contribution to make. As it became settled, its people began insisting that their region's views be taken into account – for example, by calling for the government to adopt the principle of re-investing half the revenues derived from their district in its development.[31] Since the section now returned a dozen members to the provincial legislature, it was sedulously courted by the two evenly balanced provincial parties. Even in Parliament, with six federal representatives, its voice was not to be ignored. Indeed, the Mowat government had always given a prominent place to its developmental programs, and Premier Ross made northern development a leading feature in his political appeals in 1902 and 1905. An election pamphlet of 1905, *New Ontario: Liberal Policy to Develop its Resources, Conservative Hostility to its Development*, led off with:

> The most important question before the people of Ontario at this general election is the administration of the extensive region variously known as "New Ontario" and "Northern Ontario." . . . It depends on the development of "Northern Ontario" whether Ontario itself shall retain a place second to that of no other Province, or shall subside into a second or third rate position. Toward this region the attitude of the Liberals has always been intelligent, sympathetic, appreciative, and progressive; that of the Conservatives has been persistently obtuse, churlish, disparaging, and reactionary.[32]

Despite reminders of the Liberals' services to the north from the fight for the western boundary onward, and their attacks on the Conservatives under Whitney as being hostile to northern development, the northern electorate responded to Whitney, who campaigned in 1905 on a program of supporting northern development based on fairer administration of the public resources, including raising larger revenues from the forest and mining industries. During the campaign he also promised to appoint a mines minister from northern Ontario, and after his victory, a seat was found for Frank Cochrane, who then was appointed Minister of Lands, Forests and Mines. When Cochrane entered Borden's cabinet as Minister of Railways and Canals, Whitney chose for his successor William H. Hearst, the member for Sault Ste Marie since 1908 and the main Conservative political organizer for northern Ontario.

The interests of the region, being strongly bound up with manufacturing and with the national transportation system, were fundamentally protectionist, and also favourably disposed to a strong, directed industrial and developmental program such as seemed to come more naturally to a Conservative than to a Liberal régime. Besides, new governments meant new opportunities for further concessions and favours. After the change of government in Ottawa in 1911, Whitney appealed successfully for a mandate to treat with the new government for federal assistance and co-operation with the province on colonization, highway construction, and agricultural education, for a subsidy for the provincially owned railway and aid to carry it to James Bay, and for the northward extension of Ontario (along with Manitoba and Quebec) to the shores of Hudson Bay. He won his general election of 1911, and northern Ontario gained these and other benefits in the years after 1911. In addition, northern Ontario contributed the next provincial premier in 1914, William H. Hearst.

IV

Now that railway and other transportation facilities were being provided in both provinces the major issue of northern development was honest, rational administration of the natural resources in the interests of the general public rather than special groups or individuals. This entailed maximizing the public revenue, adopting socially desirable practices, avoiding waste, and securing the greatest possible value from the resources – value that included intangibles like fostering recreation, aesthetic appreciation, or the growth of scientific knowledge, as well as economic benefits. The movement represented a desire to apply science and reason to the important task of making the best use of the public's property, particularly since the nation's resources were increasingly being regarded as limited, not almost infinite, as once believed. In part, too, it was a political movement, attacking the vested interests, favouritism, and corruption that often accompanied the disposal of the public property to private interests. Henri Bourassa was following this traditional liberal viewpoint in his attacks on Quebec's administration of its public domain. He contrasted Ontario, which received an average of $2,524 bonus per square mile of timber limits at its auctions, with Quebec, where the government received only $111 per square mile for limits that sometimes were quickly re-sold for $5,000 per square mile. Especially he attacked the sale of waterpower resources as utterly reprehensible and indefensible ("Nous vendons pour toujours nos propriétés, dont il est impossible encore de dire la valeur"), accusing the government of giving away vast fortunes through secret deals that failed to uphold the public interest. He suggested instead that power sites should be rented out with a view to eventual public ownership, not sold "entre quatre yeux."[33]

There was good cause indeed for complaint. Down to 1884, the province included power sites as part of ordinary land sales, to be sold outright at current land prices. Thereafter they were sold separately, though between 1884 and 1908 many major sales were made (sixteen in 1906 alone) at ridiculously low prices. At first some sold for as little as $50 or $100, but even as late as 1899 major sites like Grand'Mère were sold for only $5,000, and Shipshaw for $10,000. Even after 1907 sites continued to be disposed of to private interests on fifty- and ninety-nine-year leases at comparatively low figures that guaranteed enormous profits for the developers.[34] This course has been attributed to the conservative philosophy of the people and their governments, and local conditions like the scattered nature of the resource, the apparently local character of the industry that encouraged several municipalities to build their own plants, and the historic fact that many of the sites were associated with forest-using concerns that developed them for their own needs in the first instance. In contrast, it has been said that in Ontario the presence of the great power source of Niagara Falls and the prior development on the American side of private hydro-electric generating plants encouraged the province to step in and decide to develop the resources as a public enterprise.[35] However, this does not explain the Ontario government's reserving of waterpower sites for special disposition in 1898, or such other contemporary experiments in public ownership as the Temiskaming and Northern Ontario Railway.

In any event, in 1905 the Hydro-Electric Power Commission of Ontario was established as a public utility that would eventually assume control of all generating stations in the province and co-ordinate the supply of power. Beginning with the distribution side, it soon went on to take over existing plants or build new ones. In 1909 it entered the field of power distribution in the lakehead district by making a contract with the Kaministiquia Light, Heat and Power Company for power which it used to supply the Port Arthur area, while the next year it made its first move towards public ownership in northern Ontario by taking over from private companies the lease to develop Nipigon Falls. Not only were temptations avoided by ending the sale or lease of power sites, but the Ontario system presented the possibility of managing the resource in the public interest – of developing supplies efficiently, relieving users of having to invest scarce capital to secure their own power needs, evening out costs and services to the public at large, and providing service at the lowest possible cost. Unquestionably the hydro, like railways or roads, has made an important contribution to the tasks of developing the province's northern resources and to improving the quality of life and work in the northern districts.

The drive for the state to be impartial and avoid sustaining or creating privilege in any form was a common reaction to allegations of wrong-doing. It was felt, for example, that tourist sites or townsites on government railways should be disposed of by public auction under conditions that compelled direct and immediate use, rather than be allowed to give rise to speculation or be made the spoils of friends of government. That Crown lands should be disposed of impartially, rationally, and for the greatest public benefit increasingly became the aim of reformers and reforming governments. The establishment of Algonquin Park was a great pioneering step in the way of rational land use. Another was the setting aside, in the dozen years following the passage of the Forest Reserve Act of 1898, of a number of large forest reserves – the Sibley peninsula near Thunder Bay, Lake Timagami (3,700 square miles), the upper Mississagi River (3,000 square miles), north of Lake Nipigon (7,300 square miles), Quetico Reserve (1,500 square miles), and the Cochrane Forest Reserve (19,860 square miles).[36]

The Ontario equivalent of disposing of valuable resources "entre quatre yeux" was the government's dealing with prospective pulp and paper industries. Unlike timber limits that could be leased by public auction under standard conditions, the negotiations involved in establishing a pulp and paper plant were very complicated and detailed. Consequently, they had to be carried on in privacy and resulted in agreements that were not always above criticism. In 1913 Hearst tried to promote a grandiose colonization and developmental project under which a company would be given a large land grant in return for building a railway, lumber and pulp mills, and bringing out a fixed number of settlers per annum.[37] The project was not proceeded with, but a much less pretentious experiment begun in 1912 showed the dangers of special governmental arrangements when unaccompanied by proper supervision. Two townships (154 square miles) were granted to a New Ontario Colonization Company which was to clear the timber from the grant in return for each year placing sixteen bona-fide farmers on 2,400 acres. The grantee immediately transferred title to two American lumbermen, who proceeded to strip the area of its timber while making only a half-hearted attempt to fulfil the settlement contract. By 1920, when a provincial enquiry was made, it was learned that 15,761 acres of land had been cut over, yielding 31,800,000 f.b.m. of lumber and 18,504 cords of pulpwood – all entirely free of timber dues. In return, no more than 250 acres were cleared for farming and sixty-seven acres were actually brought under cultivation, while only seven families, all of them company employees, were settled on the grant.[38]

One field in which the Whitney government achieved better control and secured a more adequate revenue was mining. In 1906, the Department of Crown Lands was reorganized as the Department of Lands, Forests and Mines, with a Mines Division that included the provincial geologist and his staff of the Bureau of Mines. This organization oversaw mining operations and collected royalties and a newly instituted tax on profits, which by 1910 were yielding the province $940,000 from mining. On the other side, it investigated the geology of new mining districts, advised miners on modes of operation or other matters, and encouraged the advance into the local processing of minerals by offering bounties in 1907 for refining nickel, copper, and other metals in Ontario. In the case of a possible radium industry, the government in 1914 played a positive role by offering a reward of $25,000 for the first authentic discovery of radium in the province, and proposed to create a state monopoly by assuming the role of sole buyer of ore, operator of plants, and fixer of prices.[39]

The increasing concern of the public for the proper use of natural resources, stimulated and guided by newly established national mining and forestry associations, received a great boost from the conservation campaign launched by President Theodore Roosevelt, for the Canadian situation, like that of the United States, was also replete with many instances of glaring abuses. In May, 1908, Roosevelt convoked a governors' conference on the subject of conservation, followed by another at which representatives of the Canadian and Mexican governments met with those of the United States. As a result of this initiative, Parliament in 1909 established a Commission for Conservation of Natural Resources, which was to bring together the federal and provincial ministers responsible for the disposal and control of natural resources, and specialists from the scientific and industrial communities.[40] Sir Clifford Sifton was appointed chairman, and James White, the Dominion geographer, secretary, along with a dozen political appointees from the various governments, and twenty individuals from academic life or other occupations. The group was to meet annually, as well as to hold special meetings to receive reports on various subjects and discuss and act on questions relating to the administration of natural resources, research possibilities, publicity, and recommendations for the several governments. At the first meeting, in January, 1910, seven committees were formed to deal with wild life, forestry, land-uses and agriculture, mining and minerals, waters and waterpowers, public health, publicity, and the work of co-ordinating agencies.

The meetings were extremely valuable, for they stimulated a creditable amount of research and study of Canada's natural resources and resource-management policies, and produced many important reports which made better known than ever before the natural wealth of Canada and proper methods of its utilization. Furthermore, since the commission consisted of cabinet ministers and other highly influential people, there was always an excellent chance of the recommendations and conclusions of reports being implemented at an early date. The commission made it simple for governments to borrow ideas and programs from one another, and by confronting the men responsible for administering the resources with their opposite numbers in other governments, inspired them to match or lead in developing and instituting new policies.

The 1913 meeting, for example, recommended in the field of forestry that all timber licences contain a clause compelling holders to remove the brush, which had heretofore been a major source of forest fires, and suggested establishing co-operative forest fire protection associations, making a systematic study of forest resources across Canada, compiling statistics of forest fire losses, and appointing qualified forestry officials.[41] Other years saw recommendations made for establishing game preserves, adopting intelligent regulations for fish and game protection, classifying lands in advance of settlement and excluding settlers from lands clearly unsuited to farming, controlling waterpowers, taking inventory of mineral reserves, improving mine-safety regulations, and the like. Since every aspect of resource policy was scrutinized in this fashion, it is apparent that the commission, so long as it endured, was an incalculable influence for good.

Unfortunately, the outbreak of the Great War once more put the emphasis on production at all costs, regardless of consequences. Then after the war, the wish to return to "business as usual" brought a reaction against all efforts at regulation, even when so beneficial and so completely voluntary as these. In the spring of 1921, after eleven years of invaluable labours, the Commission of Conservation was abolished,[42] to the discredit of the government of the day and the regrets of one of its earlier strong critics, the *Canadian Mining Journal*: "To be the keeper of the country's conscience in regard to natural resources will always be found to be a thankless task, bringing to those who keep reminding us of our economic sins, more kicks than halfpence."[43] A thoroughly admirable and promising experiment, the misfortune of the Commission of Conservation was that it was years, and maybe decades, ahead of its time.

CHAPTER 9

New Frontiers in Western Canada

In western Canada, a northward expansion similar to that in the central provinces occurred after 1896 in response to the favourable economic climate of the Laurier years. Agriculture, more than forestry or mining, was the chief incentive for expansion; the Dominion government, rather than the provinces, was the main controlling agency; and subsidized railway construction was the principal means employed. The prairie west since 1870 had been considered the region *par excellence* for exploitation in the interests of national development, and down to 1930 the federal government retained control of the resources of the prairie provinces "for the purposes of the Dominion." Settlement of this national domain before 1896 had been disappointingly slow, but from that time onward, prices for farm produce improved, many technological problems were mastered, and additional railway branch lines were built across the prairies. The Dominion government, led by the forceful Clifford Sifton, vigorously advertised the opportunities of western Canada to speed up its occupation by farmers, labourers, and businessmen from the United States, Britain, and continental Europe, as well as from eastern Canada.

By the end of the Laurier administration – the period of the "great barbecue" of the prairie west – the lands of the prairies had largely been alienated into private hands. The Dominion had disposed of 120,000,000 acres of land in the western provinces – an area almost as large as France – including 68,000,000 acres as homesteads or land sales, the remainder as grants to railways, the Hudson's Bay Company, and the like. The better lands of the prairies, extensive as they were, were becoming scarce, and newcomers faced the choice between the arid grasslands of the Palliser triangle, currently given over to ranching, or the wooded lands beyond the North Saskatchewan. The agricultural pioneers, who decided in increasing numbers to settle along the great arc extending from Portage la Prairie to Edmonton, were compelled to grapple with problems analogous

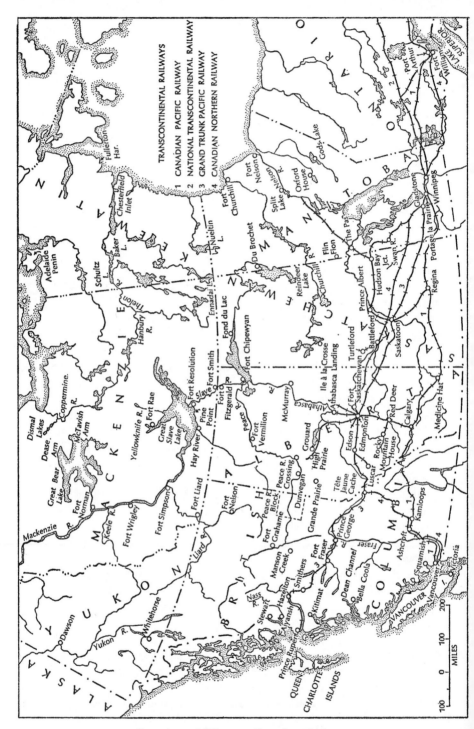

Frontiers of Western Canada, 1896-1914

to those faced by the pioneer farmers of Ontario or Quebec – clearing brush-covered land and evolving a style of farming best suited to conditions of nutrient-deficient soil, limited hours of sunlight, relatively high rainfall, and unseasonable frosts.

In fact, by the first decade of the twentieth century the conquest of the country north of the Fertile Belt had become a major new national developmental task. By 1906 the Dominion Lands agent at Edmonton – a point not so long removed from being the extreme limit of settlement – reported that the region north and west of that city could hold two million people, and that "The great Peace River country and the McKenzie River basin will prove to be the '2nd last west'."[1] A new parliamentary enquiry into the resources of the Northwest, reminiscent of Senator Schultz's of 1888, was held in 1907 by another select committee of the Senate headed by Senator T. O. Davis, a former M.P. for Saskatchewan District. From W. F. Bredin, a Peace River pioneer, the committee heard a prediction that two-thirds of the cultivable lands of Alberta would be found to lie north of Edmonton; from F. Sheridan Lawrence, of the pioneer farming family of the Fort Vermilion district, they heard the opinion that many northern muskegs could be drained and made suitable for agriculture. Other witnesses reported the successful growing of wheat as far north as Fort Providence, and potatoes at Fort Good Hope, while A. von Hammerstein discussed the mineral wealth of the Fort McMurray district where he was conducting a search for oil. J. K. Cornwall, Peace River trader, transportation promoter and legislator, reminded the committee of the 3,000 miles of navigable waterways extending to the Arctic Ocean and their hinterlands that lay open to exploitation once a railway was built from Edmonton to Fort McMurray, as well as short tramways about the Slave River rapids (above Fort Smith) and the Peace River rapids (below Fort Vermilion).[2] The highly optimistic final report of the committee was echoed in such enthusiastic government propaganda publications as E. J. Chambers' Canada's Fertile Northland (1907), The Great Mackenzie Basin (1910) – a resurrected version of the Schultz report – and The Unexploited West (1914).

Given the current emphasis upon Canada's future role as a major world granary, it is not surprising that the prairie-like Peace River district now received a good deal of notice. The Klondike gold rush had added a few more settlers to the original missionary farmers. Despite its northerly latitude of 58°24′, Fort Vermilion was the most advanced settlement because of its good soil, relatively mild climate, and, what was most unusual for the time and place, its market. The Hudson's Bay Company found it a convenient source of food supply for its northern posts and personnel, and resorted to it for cured meat and grain. By offering a standing price of $1.50

per bushel of wheat and installing an electric roller-mill in 1902, it encouraged the settlers to increase their production; in addition, farmers from other settlements higher up the Peace sent their wheat down to Fort Vermilion. After 1903, however, these settlements tended to find better local markets among newcomers to their district, for the pace of immigration into the region was accelerating. A small colony of Scandinavian Americans settled south of the Lesser Slave Lake settlement in 1903, in the vicinity of Prairie River, where they introduced modern farming practices, established the first public school north of the fifty-fifth parallel, and formed the nucleus of the community of High Prairie. Clearly the Peace River district was becoming an important focus for new settlement.

The agricultural prospects of the Peace River district were placed strongly before the public by the electrifying announcement, on November 22, 1902, made by Charles M. Hays, president of the powerful and respected Grand Trunk Railway Company, that his company intended to begin work immediately on a new railway from North Bay or Gravenhurst, west and north across New Ontario, Manitoba, Assiniboia, Saskatchewan, Alberta, and Athabasca, to a new ocean terminus at Bute Inlet or Port Simpson. In the Commons, the Prime Minister spoke enthusiastically and eloquently of the prospects of the western portion of the proposed railway,[3] while in his contribution to the debate, Frank Oliver, M.P. for Edmonton, drew attention to the value of the proposed railway for the development of the northern part of the western interior of Canada:

> Because it gives development and competition in transportation to 1,200 miles of grain growing country in the west, as compared with 400 miles of such country developed by the Canadian Pacific Railway. Because it develops vast coal fields on the Saskatchewan, Athabasca, and Peace rivers for the supply of fuel to the prairies. Because it gives the most north-westerly part of the prairie region, which is furthest from the Atlantic, a short outlet to the Pacific. Because it connects the railway system of Canada with 2,000 miles of steamboat navigation on the Athabasca, Peace, Liard and Mackenzie rivers, their great lakes, and the Arctic ocean.[4]

Eventually it was arranged that the Grand Trunk would charter a subsidiary, the Grand Trunk Pacific, which, for the section west of Winnipeg, would receive from the Dominion bond guarantees of 75 per cent of the actual cost of construction, to a maximum of $13,000 per mile for the prairie section (to Wolf Creek, Alberta), and of $30,000 per mile for the mountain division through to the coast.[5]

The Grand Trunk Pacific fastened public attention upon the Peace River district in view of the references, in its statute of incorporation, of its intention to pass through or near Dunvegan, "and by way of either the

Peace River pass, or the Pine River pass" to the coast.[6] But speedily the rail-way's surveyors decided on a route directly west from Edmonton through Yellowhead Pass (a location in which the Canadian Northern was also interested) to a completely new ocean port of Prince Rupert, near the mouth of the Skeena. Work was begun in 1909 at both the Prince Rupert and Edmonton ends by the company's contractor, Foley, Welch and Stewart. The track reached Wolf Creek in March, 1910; Fitzhugh (now Jasper) in September, 1911; Tête Jaune Cache late in 1912; Prince George early in 1914; while the final link-up with the section being pushed east from the Pacific coast was made on April 6, 1914, near Fort Fraser. By September, regular train service was in operation between Fort William and Prince Rupert, though ballasting continued into 1916.

The Grand Trunk Pacific was not unmindful of the value of the Peace River district. In 1905 the charter of the Pacific, Northern and Omineca Railway was secured, empowering the company to build from Kitimat, on the coast, to Edmonton, via Peace River Pass. A federal subsidy to assist construction of 110 miles of the western end of the route was offered in 1908, then was transferred two years later to the Edmonton end.[7] But in view of its many other commitments, the company failed to proceed farther; instead, the project was taken over by two independent companies – the Edmonton, Dunvegan and British Columbia (E.D. & B.C.), and Pacific Great Eastern (P.G.E.) railways – whose promoters were allied to the Grand Trunk Pacific interest and were to cover the proposed route and carry the line beyond Prince George to Vancouver. Through the strenuous efforts of the provincial governments concerned, both eventually were built.

While the second transcontinental project was proceeding with its various operations, Mackenzie and Mann, those guiding geniuses of the Canadian Northern system, were not idle. They had succeeded by 1905 in building a continuous system extending from Port Arthur to Edmonton, which was a major factor in settling the Parkland region of the Saskatchewan valley. But long before that, in 1899, when they had taken over the charter of the Edmonton, Yukon and Pacific Railway, with authority to build from South Edmonton to the Yellowhead or Peace River passes and the Pacific coast, they had shown an interest in extending farther west. When the Grand Trunk Pacific applied for the Yellowhead Pass route, the Canadian Northern submitted a competing plan to use the same pass en route to Prince George, then southwest to the Pacific coast at Dean Channel.[8] The Canadian Northern lost that round, but two years later the Edmonton, Yukon and Pacific received authority to build a branch from Edmonton to the headwaters of the Brazeau and McLeod rivers, somewhat south of Yellowhead Pass, together with appropriate federal government bond guar-antees. Skipping west of the mountains, the ingenious builders in 1909 won federal approval for a route from Vancouver to Tête Jaune Cache, immediately west of the Yellowhead Pass, then proceeded to secure a charter for the line (under the title of the Canadian Northern Pacific Railway) from the British Columbia legislature, together with a handsome provincial bond guarantee of $35,000 per mile.

There still was no direct alignment between these two Canadian Northern enterprises, and the Grand Trunk Pacific had been building in that vicinity since 1908. Nevertheless, Parliament rechartered the Canadian Northern interests west of Edmonton as the Canadian Northern Alberta Railway, and authorized construction from Edmonton to Yellowhead Pass, subject to the line's avoiding building between the Grand Trunk Pacific and its townsites in the duplicated section west from Edmonton. The final step came in 1911, when the Dominion government obligingly transferred the 1908 subsidy for the proposed line to the Brazeau coal field, to the Canadian Northern Alberta's link from Edmonton to Yellowhead Pass.[9] By its railway assistance program, the Dominion was helping finance construction of two railway lines that proceeded side by side west from Edmonton 280 miles through the Yellowhead Pass.

In view of the myriad projects – extending right across the country – in which the Mackenzie and Mann organization was involved, it is not surprising that completion of the transcontinental proceeded more slowly than did its rival. Besides, it did not pay the promoters to be too hasty. The work was under way in 1910, but made slow progress until 1913. By then a cash subsidy, amounting to $12,000 per mile, had been secured from the Dominion government for the entire route west from Edmonton, as well as bond guarantees for $35,000 per mile, provided by Parliament for the Alberta portion of the route and by British Columbia for the remainder of the line (raised to $45,000 per mile by that province in 1914).[10] With this assistance, the line was completed on January 23, 1915, near Basque in the Ashcroft district, though it was November before regular passenger service was begun between Edmonton and Vancouver. Somewhat like the Grand Trunk Pacific, the Canadian Northern kept open a northern route option by acquiring the charter of the Portland Canal Short Line Railway to build inland from Stewart, Canada's northernmost Pacific port at the head of Portland Channel. After Mann visited Stewart in 1910 to put the public in a properly receptive frame of mind, the provincial government rechartered the company under the name of Canadian Northeastern Railway, with authority to extend to the eastern boundary of the province.[11] But only thirteen miles of line were ever built, though the project of a Stewart to Peace River railway line across northern British Columbia was revived again and and again over the next generation.

Before the building of the Grand Trunk Pacific Railway, the northern interior of British Columbia had been a very isolated region, capable only of limited exploitation of its valuable portable commodities like gold and furs. In 1893, for example, McConnell reported that miners in Omineca paid a prohibitive 17 cents per pound on all freight. Small wonder, then, that gold production stood at a low level, with only forty miners at work on the area's creeks.[12] Nevertheless, the interior was gradually being opened up. Year by year Dominion and provincial surveyors traced out new routes among the valleys and mountains and reported on potential resources. Steamboats were placed on the rivers and lakes, while the provincial government built colonization roads and improved the trails, often simply by offering small subsidies to the interested mine-owner or fur-trader to do the work himself to his own satisfaction. In 1902, the 196-mile trail from Hazelton to Manson Creek was improved to the point where 592 tons of freight could be shipped into Omineca – 70 per cent of it machinery, supplies, and provisions for miners, the remainder goods for the Hudson's Bay Company posts at Babine, Fort St James, Fort McLeod, and Fort Grahame.[13] Miners at last were able to import hydraulic equipment to extend the precarious life of the gold-mining industry.

Announcement of the Grand Trunk Pacific project brought intensified efforts to develop resources that might now be made economical by reason of reduced transportation costs. Geological parties, for example, examined coal and base-metal occurrences in the Telkwa and Bulkley valleys, which were being made accessible by the Grand Trunk Pacific from Hazelton and Smithers. Farther north, at Groundhog Mountain, they inspected coal deposits that could be developed if the proposed Canadian Northeastern Railway was ever built. Companies began to interest themselves in these and other mineral deposits, seeking out, staking, testing, and developing mineral showings with a view to bringing mines into production.

The actual construction of the new transcontinental created much local employment on the railway grade or cutting and hauling ties and construction lumber, as well as good local markets for foodstuffs, horses, and feed. These went far to explain the rapid occupation of land in the vicinity of the routes of the new railways. End-of-steel towns like Wolf Creek or Tête Jaune Cache, which were construction headquarters for a year or two, acquired more dubious reputations from catering to the appetites as well as the needs of the railway-builders. The railway townsites, whose futures as divisional points along the line were believed assured, attracted the usual business, professional, and public amenities of potential district capitals. The Grand Trunk Pacific hoped to profit from, as well as control, the urban townsites along its right of way – a hope shared by the British Columbia government, which often held 50 per cent of the lots on the official townsites. Here, as elsewhere, rumours of future townsites attracted ambitious persons who filed for pre-emption land, or simply squatted on Crown land. At remote Finlay Forks, 150 miles north of Prince George, the surveyor F. C. Swannell encountered two stores and over a dozen new pre-emptors in 1913 occupying a presumed strategic location.

The coming of the railway immediately stimulated the forest industries along the route, at first for construction requirements of the railway, then for wider markets. In 1913, for example, railway contractors cut 56,500,000 f.b.m. for their own purposes, while commercial lumber mills operated at most major points along the line. The railway encouraged settlers to take up farming and grazing lands adjoining the route in the Fraser, Nechaco, Bulkley, and Kispiox valleys. A new Skeena Land Recording Division, with agencies at Fort George, Fort Fraser, Hazelton, and Prince Rupert, was set up to handle the large amount of business rising in the region. Notwithstanding surveyors' reports that stressed the limited amount of productive farmland and the high land-clearing costs, in the peak year, 1913, timber reserves in places like the Kitimat valley were opened to settlers, applications were received to purchase 600,000 acres, and nearly 3,900 land pre-emption claims were issued. The boom extended even to the transmontane Peace River district, where 500,000 acres were surveyed south and west of the Dominion's Peace River Block.[14] Large tracts were rumoured to be optioned to land companies here and elsewhere, the British Columbia government being prone, even at this late date, to look favourably on projects of large-scale settlement under the aegis of persons with good financial, social, or political backgrounds.

The speculative character of much of this settlement was recognized even at the time. The newly appointed pre-emption land inspectors, who examined every holding, estimated that fewer than one-third of the occupants had serious intentions. The majority, they felt, were putting minimum effort into improving their claims with a view to selling out after the anticipated rise in value accompanying completion of the railway.[15] Even more obvious were the activities of real-estate promoters who secured lands more or less adjacent to rumoured townsites which they boomed by high-pressure advertising, fleecing thousands of investors with their dubious promotions, and impairing confidence in more legitimate objects for investment. Eventually even the towns that were the objects of such attentions turned on these "benefactors." The completion of the construction phase along the railway, in fact, reduced the local markets for farm produce and settlers' labour, and caused an exodus from some districts. Next, the outbreak of the Great War even more effectively pricked the speculation bubble, not merely along the Grand Trunk Pacific route, but in other parts of the developing northland as well.

East of the Rockies, in the country between Edmonton and Yellowhead

Pass, the story of railway-induced development was much the same, except that there were two railway construction booms and two sets of townsites to promote, while the resources of the district were well known and more immediately capable of economic development by virtue of their accessibility to prairie markets. The very easy conditions of Dominion alienation of natural resources were another factor. As early as 1904 large operators (including T. A. Burrows, Sifton's brother-in-law) leased timber limits from the Department of the Interior in Athabasca, Pembina, and McLeod drainage basins against the time when railways would turn these into valuable properties, capable of commercial exploitation. The thick-seamed, bituminous coal deposits of the eastern slope of the Rockies were carefully traced by D. B. Dowling of the Geological Survey from the C.P.R. main line north to the McLeod and Athabasca basins, through which the two new transcontinentals were directing their paths. Here again came entrepreneurs staking claims, purchasing workable deposits, and forming companies financed in eastern Canada and Europe to develop mines capable of going into production as soon as railways came within shipping range. Would-be farmers were drawn into the district, even beyond the area surveyed and subdivided for settlement. From 1907 onward, Dominion Lands surveyors working in the region regularly encountered squatters on almost every favourable locality west from Edmonton to the mountains. Homesteaders commenced the long, arduous struggle to achieve an adequate livelihood from the broken, rugged, frost-prone country which the railways entered west of Edmonton.

The chief industry created by the completion of the railways west from Edmonton, however, was mining, particularly coal, a low-value commodity that could not possibly have reached western Canada or remoter markets without cheap rail transportation. Besides, the railways were large consumers of coal in their own right. Hence, as the lines approached the coal beds, companies developed their properties into mines and went into production at a number of points along the transcontinentals. More important coal districts were developed farther south by railway branches extended west of Red Deer to Rocky Mountain House, and particularly by the Alberta Coal Branch of the Grand Trunk Pacific, which was assisted by a $20,000 a mile bond guarantee from the province. Completion of the road opened half a dozen large mines in the headwaters of the McLeod River and gave rise to a new community centred on the villages of Cadomin, Luscar, and Mountain Park.[16] Lime and building-stone quarries and a cement plant also were opened in the districts west of Edmonton. Railways alone had made these industries possible; without them, equally favourable but more distant forest or mineral resources failed to be developed. A case in point is a large deposit of high-grade bituminous coking coal some eighty miles north of the transcontinentals in the headwaters of the Smoky River. Though the occurrence was discovered and a lease for 28,160 acres was granted in 1912, the deposit remained undeveloped for two generations, until the 1970's, when a railway approached the region.

By the time the new transcontinentals came to be built, the public had grown increasingly aware of the need for intelligent conservation of natural resources. Consequently, following serious destruction of northern Alberta's forests by fires in the course of railway construction and clearing operations by homesteaders, the Department of the Interior appointed many part-time fire wardens and organized forestry patrols in the threatened areas. Where surveys revealed land that was better suited for forestry than for farming, forest reserves were established. The Rocky Mountain Forest Reserve was extended north along the Alberta foothills and mountains all the way to the Peace River district, and in 1913 large new reserves were set up south and north of Lesser Slave Lake. Often this action was in the better-late-than-never category; most of the merchantable timber in the Rocky Mountain Forest Reserve by 1913 "has already passed out of the ownership of the government into the hands of owners of timber licenses."[17] Nevertheless, the reserves certainly made possible the better management of forest resources. The movements and activities of the public (including the licence-holders) could be regulated, patrolling was facilitated by building trails, roads, and cabins, and some reforestation was undertaken.

British Columbia took the first steps towards a thorough-going forestry system in 1913, though shortage of staff hampered its proper operation for many years. The province was divided into eleven great districts, each under a district forester assisted by a seasonal force of rangers, patrolmen, and railway guards. With only 114 men to supervise the four districts adjacent to the Grand Trunk Pacific, each fire guardian had to patrol an area nine to fifty times as large as his United States counterpart. Besides patrolling, the staff enforced the logging regulations, checked trespasses, and collected timber dues and royalties. They had especially to scrutinize the railway contractors, a notoriously careless class of woods' users. In addition, they classified 12,300,000 acres in 1913 in northern British Columbia for forest or agricultural uses.[18]

An important move towards the conservation of the natural resources against thoughtless exploitation and abuse was the establishment in 1908 of Jasper National Park in the scenic part of the Rockies about to be traversed by the new transcontinentals. The decision came almost too late; there already were numerous squatters and at least six timber limits within the park area. The first few years, accordingly, were spent inspecting and surveying, arranging for proper protection of natural amenities, improving trails to particular scenic features, and expelling, or buying out, licencees and squatters. One of the former, L. J. Swift, who had settled in 1892 and built up a considerable property before the park was established, eventually was allowed to maintain his holdings at Henry House, north of Jasper.[19]

II

The creation of the new prairie provinces of Saskatchewan and Alberta to take over and extend the regional governmental role of the North-West Territories government at Regina was a milestone in the development of northern and western Canada. The latter, for practical purposes, confined its operations to the three southern districts of the North-West Territories – Assiniboia, Saskatchewan, and Alberta – which alone were represented in the territorial legislature. However, in planning the new provinces, the Prime Minister, in introducing the Autonomy Bills, explained that it had been decided to incorporate in them a fourth district, Athabasca, thereby extending them north to the sixtieth parallel, inasmuch as the western part of Athabasca gave promise of becoming a centre of agricultural settlement.[20] Later speakers complained against incorporating Athabasca in the provinces, but, against this, Sifton (since February 28, 1905, out of office) even suggested the extension of the provinces "to the northern boundary of the mainland of Canada."[21]

Laurier also explained that because of the area involved, it had been decided to establish two equal-sized provinces divided along north-south lines by the 110th meridian, the Fourth Meridian of the Dominion Lands survey system. There were protests against creating two provinces rather than the single province preferred by the territorial executive headed by Premier F. W. G. Haultain, as well as over the dividing line chosen. The superior resources of Alberta, through its receiving the more valuable part of Athabasca, were commented on; so was the government's failure to make a simultaneous northward extension of Manitoba. Indeed, the easternmost part of the District of Saskatchewan was re-committed to the unorganized North-West Territories. By a Northwest Territories Amendment Act of 1905, this, as well as the District of Keewatin and the provisional districts of Ungava, Mackenzie, and Franklin, was to be administered by an appointed commissioner, assisted by an appointed four-member council, with the same powers of promulgating ordinances as those possessed by the former lieutenant-governor and legislative assembly of the pre-1905 North-West Territories.[22]

The new Northwest Territories government was far different from its predecessor. The seat of government remained in Ottawa, the appointed commissioner was the elderly comptroller of the Royal Northwest Mounted Police, Lieutenant-Colonel Fred White, and not until 1921 was a council appointed. No new ordinances were passed, nor were any inherited from the previous government repealed, and no specifically territorial administration was inaugurated. The commissioner simply exercised the limited constitutional powers of the former lieutenant-governor, and merely issued liquor import permits, made grants to remote mission schools for educating non-Indian students, paid Manitoba for treating insane patients from the territories, and received small fees from registrars or fines forwarded by the police. The expenditures for this government-in-name-only were in the order of $5,000 or less per annum, and even though White was superannuated as comptroller in 1912, the duties in connection with the by then reduced Northwest Territories were considered so slight that he retained the position with its $1,000 salary until his death on September 28, 1918.[23]

By virtue of their extended boundaries, the two new provincial governments of Saskatchewan and Alberta were committed to programs of aiding the settlement and development of the former District of Athabasca and extending their authority to the sixtieth parallel. But successive governments of Saskatchewan, which had received a seemingly unattractive northland of woods, muskegs, lakes, and rocky outcrops, displayed only a limited interest in developing this part of the Precambrian Shield. Northward expansion proceeded slowly, and only began to gain momentum after 1945.

For Alberta, the situation was very different. Its northern territory lay almost wholly within the Great Central Plain region of America, and included the arable lands of the Peace River country, the mineral wealth represented by the Athabasca tar sands, and the navigable Athabasca and Peace rivers that afforded the natural entry to the District of Mackenzie and to parts of both the adjoining provinces. Furthermore, control of the new province of Alberta was given into the hands of a party and men with a strong interest in northern expansion, for, as one Conservative M.P. during the debate charged, "The result of making these boundaries for the western province is that the further north you go the greater the Liberal majority."[24] Calgary had been the leading centre of the former District of Alberta, but the loyalty of the Edmonton district to the Liberal party – symbolized by the appointment of its M.P., Frank Oliver, as Minister of the Interior in succession to Sifton on April 8, 1905 – brought the selection of Edmonton as the capital on the grounds of its central position in the new province, while the northern half of Alberta was markedly over-represented in the legislature. These arrangements helped ensure Liberal control of the provincial administration until 1921, and gave those governments a concrete incentive to promote the needs of Edmonton and the north, among which aids to regional development took first place. A new authority had been created to give impetus to the northward extension of Canada's frontiers into one of the most promising, accessible segments of the Middle North.

The new province was immediately subjected to strong pressures to meet the transportation needs of its expanding northern frontier. From the beginning, almost half its revenues were spent on public works, with a disproportionate share on the new settlements north and west of Edmonton along the route of the Grand Trunk Pacific Railway, and in the Lesser Slave and Peace River districts. Above all, the government faced insistent clamours for more railways to link the new frontier with the transcontinental systems and permit the farm frontier to advance still farther into the wilderness. These pressures were powerfully re-enforced by interested city dwellers, notably the mercantile element of Edmonton, a city that just within three years had soared to prominence as an important railway centre. As a provincial capital, Edmonton now had power to mobilize the resources of the new province to help it achieve its long-standing metropolitan goals. The decline in 1908 of immigration into the districts beyond Edmonton was quickly blamed on the failure of railways to advance into the areas undergoing settlement. Equally, Edmonton interests were concerned for a railway to the strategic Fort McMurray district. The shipment of increasing volumes of freight and passengers by river to distant northern points was continually bedevilled by the shallows and rapids on the Athabasca below Athabasca Landing, and efforts to improve navigation along this section of the waterway proved unavailing. Only a railway to Fort McMurray could meet the situation by providing unimpeded summertime travel – apart from the single portage on the Slave River – to the vast country all the way to the Arctic Ocean.

Besides, excitement over the rich natural resources of the Fort McMurray district reached a climax just at this time. After the Geological Survey failed in its efforts to drill down to an anticipated oil-bearing formation below the tar sands, the Dominion government threw the district open to private developers.[25] By 1909 a "strike" of paying quantities of oil was reported, which was rewarded by selling outright six parcels of tar-sand lands totalling 11,405 acres for $21,913.10 to the purported discoverer.[26] Furthermore, under new regulations introduced early in 1910, 1,920-acre parcels of oil or tar-sand lands could be leased for twenty-one-year periods at 50 cents per acre annual rent and no royalties on production before January 1, 1930, the only stipulation being that $1,000 be spent on development within three years. Under this regulation, nine tar-sand leases, totalling 17,040 acres, were granted in 1910-11.[27] Resources of astronomical value thus were alienated under highly dubious circumstances that made the fortunes of a few speculators and completely failed to safeguard the public interest. The oil boom quickly faded before the difficulties of working out practicable extraction processes for the refractory bituminous sands, but while it lasted, it strongly affected the railway program of the Alberta government.

Responding to appeals from many parts of the province, the government decided to promote railway construction by extending financial assistance to builders. Among nineteen pieces of railway legislation dealt with in the spring session of 1909, three were designed to speed up the occupation of the northwestern frontier. Two were bond guarantees for Canadian Northern branches already under construction, northwest from Edmonton towards the Peace River country, and north from Edmonton to Athabasca Landing. The third was for the construction of a line between Edmonton and Fort McMurray by the Alberta and Great Waterways Railway. The arrangement with the promoter of this enterprise, a young Kansas City banker named W. R. Clarke, occasioned some surprise in view of the very generous terms: a bond guarantee for $20,000 per mile, providing for 5 per cent interest for fifty years, rather than the usual $13,000, 4 per cent, and thirty years offered the other assisted railways. Furthermore, the aid was for 350 miles, whereas the actual distance was about 300 miles, while a further $400,000 was guaranteed to cover the company's terminals at Edmonton – a total guarantee of $7,400,000 for the 300-mile railway line.[28]

There followed a provincial election in which the railway program was the main issue, though R. B. Bennett, leader of the Conservatives, also attacked the government for giving Edmonton the capital, Strathcona (South Edmonton) the university, and excessive representation to the north. He charged that the railway policy was intended to make Edmonton the railway centre of the province, and that the sole motive behind the aid to the Alberta and Great Waterways project was to appease the commercial interests of the city. The predictable result was an overwhelming government victory, and the confirming of the Liberal government in office to pursue its policies of northern development, and to superintend the work of the assisted railways.

Unfortunately, the guarantees failed miserably. The Canadian Northern had far more important concerns than building towards Athabasca Landing and Grande Prairie, and work on its two guaranteed lines proceeded exasperatingly slowly. The line ultimately reached Athabasca Landing early in 1912, confirming that centre's role for a few years longer as the jumping-off point for the north. But the so-called Peace River branch, after reaching Onoway, barely thirty miles from Edmonton, was diverted westward to become part of the builders' projected transcontinental route. Worse still was in store for the Alberta and Great Waterways project. The uneasiness occasioned by the generous terms extended to the enterprise burst into outraged fury when it was learned that Clarke had marketed the provincially guaranteed bonds in London at a 10-per-cent premium (meaning the underwriters pocketed a $740,000 bonus besides their regular commission), indicative of the extreme generosity of the financial arrangements. Charges of improvidence, negligence, and corruption produced a schism within the Liberal government, which resigned in May, 1910, and the Lieutenant-Governor went outside the legislature to select a new premier, Arthur L. Sifton, brother of Clifford Sifton and at the time Chief Justice of the Alberta Supreme Court.[29]

A royal commission appointed to investigate the contract confirmed the suspicions by disclosing that the railway's engineer considered the line could be built for $17,000 a mile, well below the $20,000 guaranteed by the province; and that the promoter apparently had received his contract without having to put up a cent of his own money. He had, it seemed, met the deposit condition with a $50,000 cheque an Edmonton bank branch manager allowed him to write as an overdraft provided it was not cashed. Once the contract was awarded, the company could carry on with bank loans secured on the strength of that contract.[30] The people of Alberta gained such close insight into the seamy side of railway financing and the perilous connection between governments and railway promoters as to undermine their faith in both. The legislature late in 1910 pronounced the Waterways company in default for failing to meet the first interest instalment on its bonds (the government having blocked its using the bond money for this purpose). It further enacted that the money borrowed on the provincial credit, repayment for which the province was responsible, should be applied to building other railways.[31] This action precipitated a lawsuit that went all the way to the Judicial Committee of the Privy Council, during which time work on the railway stood still.

In 1911, then, the effort to speed the development of northern Alberta through subsidized railway construction had been an almost unqualified failure. Louder clamours arose from the increased number of settlers drawn to the region mainly by the reports of railways already chartered to build there, and predictably, from the metropolitan planners of the cities. As early as January 24, 1911, the president of the Edmonton Board of Trade expressed alarm at the delays and his fears of encroachment by rival centres upon Edmonton's natural hinterland:

> . . . the railways projected and approved towards Fort McMurray and the Peace River districts are not yet commenced, with every evidence of the former having been abandoned for the present. The lines, if constructed, would open up a vast amount of valuable territory tributary to Edmonton, and upon which the early development of our city largely depends. I notice a charter is being applied for to build a line from Prince Albert through the Athabasca country to Fort McMurray. If this line

is built and in operation before one is constructed and operated from Edmonton, all the traffic originating in that vast territory would be diverted through the Province of Saskatchewan instead of through Alberta, which is the natural outlet for that trade.[32]

The challenge of Prince Albert or North Battleford, depending, like Edmonton, upon the vastly overcommitted Canadian Northern, was not to be taken seriously. The Canadian Northern chartered a branch line from North Battleford to Athabasca Landing and Saskatchewan gave a bond guarantee to secure its construction, but by 1914 the line was built only to Turtleford, less than sixty miles.

Far more serious was the threat from the west. The interest of Vancouver and the British Columbia government had suddenly been awakened in the Peace River country astride its boundary with Alberta, now that settlement was beginning to move into the region. Following the securing of a second transcontinental – the recently chartered Canadian Northern Pacific Railway – Vancouver businessmen began agitating for a railway connection with the Prince George and Peace River districts to bind the destinies of northeastern British Columbia more firmly with those of their city. Partly, they were reacting to Edmonton's commercial penetration of east-central British Columbia in the wake of the Grand Trunk Pacific construction, but they were also anxious to ensure that the Grand Trunk Pacific should be tapped by a feeder to divert some of its traffic south to Vancouver, notwithstanding the intention of that company to develop the port of Prince Rupert. After all, Vancouver, an established port, was considerably closer to Prince George than was Prince Rupert. By the spring of 1911, Vancouver businessmen suddenly began to take an interest in opening up this new axis of communications:

> There has been a distinct movement in Vancouver latterly towards a broader view of Vancouver's relation to the province as a whole. . . . There is a strong movement being organized in favor of building a railway from Vancouver via Pemberton Meadows and Fort George to the Peace River districts. It will be greatly to the advantage of the coast if Vancouver can get her grip on that famous and undeveloped interior which is looked on as having fabulous wealth. The opening of the Panama Canal should see the linking up of the northern interior, even perhaps as far as Dawson, with Vancouver and a steady stream of raw materials, agricultural, mineral and vegetable, flowing to the coast.[33]

Pressure mounted on the provincial government to extend financial backing to the Pacific Great Eastern Railway. The company had been formed, with the approval of the Grand Trunk Pacific, by its solicitor, D'Arcy Tate, and by its principal western contractor, Foley, Welch and Stewart, to fulfil the function of its now-defunct Vancouver-Prince George branch. The government soon capitulated. On February 20, 1912, Premier Richard McBride announced a $35,000 per mile bond guarantee to the Pacific Great Eastern to build from North Vancouver to Prince George. The project from the outset was regarded as a first step towards the Peace River country, and two years later similar aid was offered for a further section from Prince George to the eastern boundary of the province in the Peace River country.[34]

The announcement of this plan coincided almost exactly with similar action in the Alberta legislature, responding to similar pressures. In December, 1911, sixteen new branches had been chartered for the Canadian Northern Western Railway, which was clearly emerging as the favoured agent of the Alberta government to implement its policies of northern regional development. Included were branches from Athabasca Landing to Fort McMurray and Lac la Biche (replacing the Alberta and Great Waterways project), and to Peace River Crossing; from its transcontinental line to the Smoky River coalbeds and a junction with the still-unbuilt Peace River (Edmonton to Grande Prairie) branch. These were followed in February, 1912, by a new round of bond guarantees, including, for the Canadian Northern system, the branches from Athabasca Landing (315 miles at $15,000 per mile), and, for 250 miles of the vital, long-overdue Peace River branch, $20,000 per mile for construction from Onoway "in a generally north-westerly direction to a point on the provincial boundary line at or near Pine or Peace River Passes, or one of them,"[35] Another beneficiary was a little-regarded enterprise, the Edmonton, Dunvegan and British Columbia Railway, chartered by Parliament in 1907, which was afterwards acquired by J. D. McArthur, the Winnipeg contractor who had built most of the Grand Trunk's extensions between the lakehead and the Rockies. This company was offered a bond guarantee of $20,000 per mile for 350 miles, for "A line of railway from Edmonton through Dunvegan to the western boundary of the province running south of Lesser Slave Lake."[36] Obviously the government did not want to depend exclusively on the good offices of the far-spread Canadian Northern system for meeting the transportation needs of the Peace River district.

Once more the Canadian Northern did nothing to fulfil its many undertakings, apart from some work on the Peace River branch, which was carried forty miles to Sangudo in 1914, through country settled some years before. But this line went no farther until 1922, when the Canadian National Railways extended it to the important lumber centre of Whitecourt, at the junction of the McLeod and Athabasca rivers. Thus was left unfinished the much-touted railway on which so many settlers had staked their future – one of many such outcomes to be laid at the door of the overweaning ambitions of Mackenzie and Mann.

However, no real challenge materialized from the west. The Pacific Great

Eastern Railway built a few miles inland from the port of Newton (later Squamish) in 1912, but then did little for some time, owing to the pre-occupation of the builders, Foley, Welch and Stewart, with their other enterprises, as well as the scarcity of capital after 1912 that made it difficult to market the guaranteed railway bonds. None the less, like the Ross govern- ment in Ontario and the Rutherford government in Alberta, the McBride government won another term in office by the public's approval of its developmental policy, symbolized by the arrangement with the Pacific Great Eastern.

As for Alberta, the guarantee program of 1912, surprisingly, did produce considerable railway mileage in the north of the province, mainly through the efforts of J. D. McArthur. McArthur's line was to follow a rather circuitous route north from Edmonton to cross the Athabasca at Mirror Landing, then south of Lesser Slave Lake across the Peace River country to the British Columbia border. Work began in earnest in 1912, and by 1914 the track was finished to McLennan, west of Lesser Slave Lake, 261 miles from Edmonton. In 1913, McArthur also received a $20,000 per mile bond guarantee to build a branch, the Central Canada Railway, from McLennan northwest to Peace River Crossing – another example of the reassignment of a project originally given to the Canadian Northern Western. A begin- ning was made in 1914 on this important extension to a head of navigation on the Peace River. Furthermore, when the Privy Council in January, 1913, ruled that the provincial government could not divert the proceeds from the sale of Alberta and Great Waterway bonds for any other purpose, Premier Sifton induced McArthur to undertake this additional project on terms acceptable to the bondholders, the former owners, and their creditors. In 1914 this line was carried 126 miles to Lac la Biche, at the end of the forested, cultivable district, and the start of the almost unending muskeg terrain through which it would have to proceed 175 miles to reach Fort McMurray.[37]

Thus, by the end of 1914, northern Alberta was well on the way to receiving the railway arteries essential for its future growth; the city of Edmonton was realizing its metropolitan ambitions of winning an unrivalled hegemony over a vast, rich northern territory; and the Liberal government of Alberta had found an agent to redeem its railway-building commitments and heal the rifts that were the unfortunate legacy of the Waterways scandal of 1909-10. Indeed, this was confirmed when Sifton carried his record and program to the people and won a convincing victory in April, 1913, in an election in which the province was divided strongly along regional lines of south versus north.

The arrival of a railway into the Peace River district after a decade of rumours – even if it was not the anticipated direct line of the Canadian

Northern system – fulfilled the hopes of the pioneers who had settled on the expectation that these would be forthcoming within a reasonable time. Settling more than a hundred miles from a railhead was a risk that called for men willing and able to wait several years until railway facilities made it possible to begin full-scale production for outside markets. Such settlers usually were well to do. Frequently they toured the territory to examine its possibilities before bringing in their families and belongings. They came equipped with cash reserves to make a start on the land and maintain themselves through lean years of waiting. Many even were able to make considerable investments in equipment and in unlimited amounts of land purchased cheaply from the government for cash or with Half-Breed, South African Veteran, or other scrips.

As late as 1906 only forty-two occupied farms were reported for the entire Peace River district, but in the following year, a Dominion Lands sub-agency was opened at Lesser Slave Lake Settlement (soon to be renamed Grouard), and by 1909 several new settlements were taking shape – in the Swan River valley south of Lesser Slave Lake, along the Smoky River, at Spirit River, and above all, on Grande Prairie. The Grande Prairie, which contained about three hundred inhabitants in 1909, presented a picture of the bustling, confident activity of settlers building homes, importing machinery, and preparing to increase their acreage planted in crops, while a townsite was growing up at Saskatoon Lake. The planned construction of the Canadian Northern Western direct line from Edmonton made Grande Prairie the main attraction to settlers after 1910. Pending arrival of the railway, these settlers followed the roundabout route from Grande Prairie to Lesser Slave Lake, Athabasca Landing, and Edmonton, or, after the Grand Trunk Pacific built towards the Yellowhead Pass, went cross-country south to Edson, which also became the mail route for the district. On July 15, 1911, the opening day of the Dominion Lands agency at Grande Prairie, seventy-five land applications were recorded. The two agencies at Grouard and Grande Prairie recorded 942 homestead entries and 304 land-scrip certificates applied to land claims, mainly for Grande Prairie land during 1911-12, while by the autumn of 1912, the Grande Prairie agency alone was receiving approximately 100 new applications per month.[38] The tide of settlement had begun to set in for the Peace River district.

The trend, however, had the untoward effect of throwing the older settlement of Fort Vermilion into the shade. Though production continued to increase there, it came from a few long-established farms, notably that of Sheridan Lawrence, who owned 150 head of cattle, eleven teams of horses, a steam threshing machine, sawmill and small grist mill, and had 400 acres in grain crops. The district failed to attract settlers and soon it was eclipsed by the new settlements farther south. In 1911 the Hudson's Bay Company closed down its flour-milling operation and began purchasing its require-ments from the more developed farming areas in the south.[39] From the leading agricultural centre of the northern frontier, Fort Vermilion subsided into relative stagnation as a remote outpost of the Peace River farm empire.

III

Farther east, another, vastly different frontier was unfolding north of Mani-toba in the western part of the District of Keewatin, mainly inspired by the long-standing campaign of western farmers to secure a shorter rail outlet to Europe via Hudson Bay, the historic route of the fur trade. Their agitation had borne fruit in the chartering in 1880 and afterwards of a number of railway companies to build to Churchill or Port Nelson, and the holding out of land grants, bond guarantees, and transport contracts to their promoters. But the effort was in vain so far as securing construction was concerned, and prairie farmers' grain continued to follow the longer route to the lakehead ports. However, existing railway facilities could no longer cope with the immense quantities of farm produce directed to the Great Lakes and St Lawrence route as the annual Canadian wheat crop mounted from 50 million bushels in 1900 to 107 million in 1905 and 394 million by 1915. Consequently, along with the efforts to improve rail communications across central Canada went renewed pressures to realize the long-awaited Hudson Bay outlet.

It was that enterprise, in fact, that had launched Mackenzie and Mann on their meteoric twenty-year railway-building career. Having secured the charter of the Lake Manitoba Railway and Coal Company, they joined forces in 1895 with Hugh Sutherland, who controlled the Winnipeg and Hudson Bay Railway Company, and merged their two projects into the original Canadian Northern Railway, which thereby became eligible to enjoy the two lots of benefits.[40] Under the charter of the Mackenzie and Mann company, they built northwest 125 miles from Gladstone to Win-nipegosis, in return for a Manitoba government bond guarantee of $8,000 per mile and a Dominion government land subsidy of 6,400 acres per mile. Beyond Winnipegosis, under the charter and concessions of the former Winnipeg and Hudson Bay Railway (renamed Winnipeg Great Northern Railway in 1895) with an $80,000 per annum mail subsidy, they carried the line 125 miles farther to the northwest, towards the fertile Swan River and Carrot River districts and Prince Albert. For the first 250 miles of this line from Gladstone, built actually to gain access to rich farmlands of the parkland country extending all the way to Edmonton, the builders were awarded 1,897,280 acres of land for providing a so-called Hudson Bay railroad. Then they proceeded on their many enterprises in other parts of the country.

With the growth of the wheat economy and the creation of the new provinces of Saskatchewan and Alberta, pressure increased on the Dominion government to give more impetus to the Hudson Bay Railway project, in fact, to make it a public enterprise like the Intercolonial or National Transcontinental railways. So great was western farmers' concern that in the federal elections of 1904 and 1908, both Liberal and Conservative parties pledged themselves to secure the early completion of the road. The Canadian Northern was given further aid to build an eighty-mile branch from Hudson Bay Junction (the end of the portion aided under the constituent companies' charters), northeast to the Saskatchewan River crossing at The Pas. In return for 12,800 acres per mile (raising their total to 3,321,328 acres), plus the full $80,000 per annum "mail subsidy" originally promised for a railway completed to Hudson Bay, Mackenzie and Mann completed the line to The Pas by February, 1908.

Thereafter the Dominion government decided to build the Hudson Bay Railway as a public work, earmarking for the purpose money received from the sale of lands formerly reserved from homestead entry for possible selection as their earned grants by the subsidized railways. Following a survey, John Armstrong submitted a route to Hudson Bay in 1909 that separated into two branches some 150 miles from The Pas, going to Port Nelson and Fort Churchill in that order. He reported strongly in favour of Port Nelson as the terminus, arguing that the route traversed better, more promising country, and was sixty-seven miles shorter than the one to Churchill. Furthermore, he considered that dredging and building port facilities would be cheaper at Port Nelson than at Churchill. On the other hand, an investigation for the Department of the Naval Service by Captain I. B. Miles in 1910, like others before it, contended that Port Nelson was hopeless from a shipping point of view, and came out as strongly in support of Churchill as Armstrong was for Port Nelson. The Dominion government appropriated $500,000 to construct the bridge across the Saskatchewan at The Pas, and, on the eve of the general election of 1911, gave a contract to J. D. McArthur to build the 185-mile section north from The Pas that was common to either route.[41] There matters stood, when the Canadian electorate turned the Laurier government out of office on September 21, 1911, ending its sixteen years in power in one of Canada's most prosperous periods.

Manitoba voters played a considerable part in this result, for besides the unsatisfactory situation with respect to the Hudson Bay Railway, they had grown completely disillusioned by the prolonged failure of the Laurier government to extend the boundaries of their province in line with those accorded the other prairie provinces. From 1901 onward, the legislature called without success for the northward extension of Manitoba's boundaries to give it a port on Hudson Bay. The announced intention of creating two new prairie provinces with areas of 250,000 square miles apiece, northern boundaries that extended to the sixtieth parallel, and comparatively generous subsidies, gave renewed impetus to the demand. A unanimous resolution of the legislature on January 16, 1905, putting forward Manitoba's claims, was answered by an invitation to send delegates to Ottawa, couched in terms that implied a favourable reception once the Alberta-Saskatchewan legislation was disposed of. That meeting, however, broke up in recriminations and charges of bad faith against the Dominion government for coupling the settlement of Manitoba's claims with an expressed need to settle with Ontario and Quebec as well. The disappointed Manitobans asserted that Laurier, influenced by the Papal legate Msgr Donatus Sbaretti, and the Archbishop of St Boniface, L. P. A. Langevin, was making the boundary extension contingent on Manitoba's modifying its separate school legislation (based on the Laurier-Greenway Agreement of 1897) in ways acceptable to the Roman Catholic minority.[42]

These aggrieved feelings were nursed by the Conservative government of R. P. Roblin, which won a resounding electoral victory in 1907 by abusing the Laurier government for "designedly depriving Manitoba of that to which it is entitled, with barring the way to its further growth and development, with despotism and deceit."[43] The legislature in January, 1908, drew up a memorial affirming Manitoba's right to be consulted in any change of its boundaries. Following another conference with the Manitoba representatives, on July 8, 1908, Laurier announced that his government would introduce legislation in Parliament extending the boundaries of Manitoba, Ontario, and Quebec, with the dividing line between Manitoba and Ontario to run from the northeastern corner of Manitoba to the eastern point of Island Lake, thence to the shoreline of Hudson Bay at the 89th meridian (very near the easternmost limit of the Dominion's contention in the boundary dispute with Ontario). Coupled simultaneously with a northward extension to the sixtieth parallel, Manitoba would be enlarged by 178,100 square miles to an almost identical size with the other prairie provinces. Ontario would receive an additional 140,000 square miles, and Quebec no less than 350,000 square miles, including the whole of Ungava to Hudson Strait, even that part of it that extended north of the sixtieth parallel. While the larger provinces would secure full control of the resources of these added territories, the resources of the district added to Manitoba, like the rest of that province, would still remain under federal control.

Bitter disagreements over subsidies and schools, and continued political feuding between the Laurier and Roblin governments, delayed the extension of Manitoba's boundaries more than three years. On February 13, 1912, the new Borden government introduced legislation implementing the boundary arrangements of 1908 and increasing the provincial subsidy by more than $500,000 a year.[44] Other acts completed the transfer of part of Keewatin and Ungava to Ontario and Quebec with the stipulation that each should respect the Dominion government's commitments to the Hudson's Bay Company establishments and to Indian residents.[45] Quebec, whose claim was only put forward in 1908, had called for the inclusion in the province of the offshore islands in Hudson Strait and Hudson and James bays, but the acts reserved these islands for the Northwest Territories on the grounds of their possible value to the Dominion in enforcing its authority in the fields of navigation, fisheries, and defence. Instead, all three provinces were confined to the shores of James, Hudson, and other bays and straits.

A curious feature of the arrangements was an agreement of February 20 between the Conservative governments of Ontario and Manitoba, recognizing an Ontario interest in a port facility at the mouth of the Nelson River. The agreement, confirmed by a Dominion order in council, authorized Manitoba to transfer to Ontario a strip of territory five miles wide to construct a railway from a point on the Ontario boundary to the port at the mouth of Nelson River, the Ontario option to be effective until 1927.[46] Ontario voted funds in 1912 to begin the survey of the new Ontario-Manitoba boundary, and dispatched an expedition under J. B. Tyrrell to carry out a reconnaissance of the newly acquired District of Patricia, the Nelson River port, and the possible corridor through New Manitoba.[47]

The legislation of 1912 at last gave Manitoba a littoral on Hudson Bay and trebled its area to include lands rich in minerals, waterpower, forests, and, to some degree, agricultural land. To administer New Manitoba, the province later established at The Pas (incorporated as a town in 1912) a regional government headed by a commissioner, J. A. Campbell, to supervise and direct its development. The continuing presence of the federal government was represented by a mining recorder, fisheries officer, mounted police detachment, and other agents. The Pas was the major communications centre of the region, serving an ever-widening hinterland. By river, it was connected with all points on the lower part of the Saskatchewan River between Prince Albert and Grand Rapids, while as a Canadian Northern terminus it was linked with a transcontinental railway system; also, it was the point of departure for the lengthening Hudson Bay Railway to the northeast. The railways and river steamers opened up the northern lakes of Manitoba to commercial fishing and made The Pas an important fur-trading centre. They made possible the establishment of a large lumber industry and prospective pulp and paper industry, drawing on the white spruce, jackpine, and tamarack resources of the region. The transfer of New Manitoba also coincided with the beginnings of what has proved to be the region's major industry –

hard-rock mining. In 1912 and 1913 discoveries were made of massive lenses of lead-zinc-copper-bearing sulphides in the Flin Flon district and at the similar Mandy showing on Schist Lake, as well as of gold-bearing quartz veins of Amisk and Herb lakes. Railway construction greatly facilitated the exploration and development of the new properties, and before long an important mining industry was arising in New Manitoba.

The progress of the Hudson Bay Railway was the most tangible immediate evidence of the progress of the new frontier of northern Manitoba. After another halt while the Borden government reviewed the conflicting evidence as to the more desirable terminus, the order was given to proceed to Port Nelson, and J. D. McArthur received the contract to build the entire railway. By the end of 1913, when the bridge across the Saskatchewan was finished, track had been laid for 110 miles beyond. A year later the track was stopped at Mile 214 for the bridge over the Nelson River at Manitou Falls, but the line was graded 118 miles farther to Kettle Falls, only ninety-two miles from the terminus. Meanwhile, development of the facilities at Port Nelson began in 1913 at a site some twenty-two miles up the river from the open bay. The difficulties predicted by the naval experts were being realized; the resumption of work in 1914 revealed how much silt the river brought down and the real difficulties of keeping open a suitable shipping channel. In 1915 the engineer, D. W. McLachlan, decided to develop a new shipping harbour by creating an artificial island to divert the flow so the current would help scour the shipping channel. The island was built up, and another long railway bridge was built to join the harbour facility to the shore. By 1917, when the work was suspended because of wartime shortages of money, men, and materials, the government had spent $20,000,000, for which there were in operation 332 miles of railway beyond The Pas, plus the terminal facilities at Port Nelson.[48] The ill-fated, much-postponed project remained at a stand-still for another decade before construction was resumed after 1926.

By bringing the new provinces of Saskatchewan and Alberta into being and extending Manitoba, Ontario, and Quebec to their present limits, the Laurier and Borden governments rounded out the map of mainland Canada until the union with Newfoundland in 1949. Excessive optimism, careless disregard of the long-term public interest, favouritism, and corruption had characterized many of the parties who directed and participated in the expansion of those years, and a day of reckoning was soon to come for the carefree extravagance that had inspired so much of the railway-building of the time. Still, the country was the gainer. The completion of two new transcontinentals and half a dozen other important developmental railways had created economic opportunities in the North during the prosperous years of the new century. New frontiers had been opened up to give greater depth and solidity to a nation whose attentions soon were to be diverted to the challenges of a world war. The onset of that war for a time postponed the advance of the full complement of modern industries into these newly opened frontier districts, particularly in the Northwest. Not until the next period of favourable economic conditions would farm settlers and other pioneers begin occupying the lands of the Middle North made accessible to development by the railway-building boom of the Laurier era.

CHAPTER 10

Onward to the Arctic Shore

1896 – 1914

The early years of the twentieth century – "Canada's Century" – brought a remarkable surge of Canadian civilization into the southern part of the great forest belt, the Middle North of Canada. The new railways and improved water-transport facilities through this region opened up a series of modern economic and social frontiers stretching from Lake St John to Prince Rupert and the Yukon. Farther ahead, again, went other pioneers, singly or in small groups – tourists, seasonal workers, hunters and trappers, free traders, prospectors, scientists, missionaries, and government agents. These were transients or short-term residents, and most could adjust without too much difficulty to the life-style of the primitive frontier and its people. The members of the official class, however, were a force for change, since they were part of a process that was eventually to carry effective governmental control over the whole of mainland Canada.

The continent-wide advance of white settlement along the lines of the new railways was another matter. Railways meant the full range of economic development, the establishment, sooner or later, of modern industries and permanent settlements. But the arrival of considerable numbers of white settlers constituted a major threat to the native peoples of this large sector of Canada, for it introduced fundamental changes in the prevailing patterns of social organization and in the quality of every-day life. In many districts, therefore, the older fatalistic native society, which sought only to preserve or return to the natural, free environment of former days, found itself in retreat before an advancing white civilization.

The advent of white settlers imperilled the way of life of the native who depended upon fishing, hunting, and trapping fur to meet his simple wants. After 1896, the threat appeared first in Athabasca, where meat and fur were becoming noticeably more difficult to secure and even the fishery was becoming endangered, as whites, encouraged by present or impending transportation improvements, secured licences to fish the major lakes commercially. Before 1908, indeed, leases had been granted for Lesser Slave Lake and even for Lake Athabasca. As yet, however, the commercial fishery was limited by the difficulty of freighting catches many miles over crude winter trails to railheads or city markets. But the danger remained, to be turned into reality as railways approached Lesser Slave Lake, Lac la Biche, or other lakes in northern Saskatchewan and Keewatin.

It was therefore in this region that the Indian Affairs Department moved to extend the machinery of governmental protection and control embodied in the Indian treaty system. Reacting first to the advent of prospectors and settlers during and after the Klondike gold rush, the department made preparations to bring under treaty the Indians of the Athabasca and Peace River districts north of Treaty 6 and south of Great Slave Lake. The negotiations for Treaty 8 were conducted in the summer of 1899 with Cree, Beaver, and Chipewyan bands at Lesser Slave Lake, Dunvegan, Fort Smith, Fond du Lac, and other points, for cession of a 324,900-square-mile territory west and north of the Athabasca and Slave rivers to Great Slave Lake, along its southwestern shore to Hay River, then southwest along the river to the sixtieth parallel, west to the Rockies, and back to the source of the Athabasca. Only about half the Indian inhabitants were reached in 1899 when 2,217 persons accepted the treaty. Another 1,106 Indians of the Fort St John, Great Slave Lake, and Hay River districts were added in 1900,[1] and others in later years. To avoid subsequent confusion, a parallel half-breed commission – of which the poet Charles Mair was secretary – was sent around offering, in place of the annuities, reserves, and the other aids extended to Indians, the choice between 240-acre land scrips (location tickets) and $240 cash scrips. A total of 1,243 scrips were issued in 1899, about half of them at Lesser Slave Lake, and others at Fort Vermilion, Fort Chipewyan, and Peace River Crossing. In succeeding years, the Indian commissioner dealt with the Métis of the northern and western parts of the treaty area while he negotiated with the Indians. Still others came forward later to claim the bounty; in 1908, for example, Commissioner H. A. Conroy issued scrips to a large number of nomads west of Whitefish (Utikuma) Lake, north of Lesser Slave Lake. Unfortunately, despite the pleadings of their priests, in almost every case the Métis insisted on cash scrips. Few wanted to claim Indian status and join the treaty (as Conroy pleaded with the Whitefish Lake nomads to do) because of the stigma of inferiority they felt the Indian Act carried. But scarcely any accepted land scrips either; 96 per cent of the persons treated with in 1899 demanded and received money scrips. These scrips redounded almost entirely to the benefit of the swarms of traders who accompanied the commission and purchased them for resale to settlers and speculators.[2] A short spending spree, in many cases, was the only benefit the Métis secured from the government's largesse. Their money and credit exhausted, the Métis for the most part continued their traditional, nomadic, aimless way of life, without the burdens, but also without the protections and guarantees that were now available to those who adhered to the Indian treaties.

A few years later the planning of new railways, as well as the movement of settlement beyond the height of land north of Lakes Huron and Superior, which marked the limit of the Robinson Treaty with the Indians of those coasts, made it desirable to negotiate a new treaty in 1905-6 with the Indians in the remaining parts of Ontario and adjoining Keewatin. In negotiating this Treaty 9, the role of the province of Ontario had to be taken into account inasmuch as the area to be ceded included some 90,000 square miles in Ontario as well as 40,000 square miles in the portion of Keewatin lying immediately north of the Albany River. Furthermore, court decisions in the cases between Ontario and the Dominion had ruled that the province had to reimburse the Dominion the amount of the annuities paid to the Indians, as well as surrender the land required for reserves. Consequently, Ontario was approached, and nominated a representative to the treaty commission. In 1905 the commissioners dealt with the Indians along the Albany River and its tributaries, those of the James Bay coast, and south to Abitibi; in 1906 they contacted the bands more easily reached from the Canadian Pacific Railway. By the end of that season, the adherence of 2,962 Indians had been secured, the scale of payment being four dollars like the Robinson Treaty, rather than five as in the treaties farther west.[3]

Barely a year later, in 1906-7, another treaty, Treaty 10, was negotiated with the Indians of northern Saskatchewan for the territory east of Treaty 8 and north of Treaties 5 and 6 – a country of lakes, swamps, and woods likely to interest only miners, trappers, or commercial fishermen. This 85,000-square-mile tract was inhabited by nomadic Crees and Chipewyans, as well as by considerable numbers of semi-nomadic Métis, with whom Commissioner J. A. J. McKenna dealt concurrently, the Métis claims for land or cash scrips being referred to Ottawa. The inhabitants of the western part of the region at Ile à la Crosse, Portage la Loche, Buffalo Narrows, Canoe Lake, and Clear Lake were dealt with in 1906, and those in the Reindeer Lake district in the following year, 724 Indians being paid under the treaty in 1908.[4]

At the same time as these treaties were being negotiated, an effort was made to include the remaining Indians between Quebec and the Rockies under the treaties. Between 1908 and 1910, for example, the Indians north of Lake Winnipeg, in the vicinity of the much-discussed Hudson Bay Railway, were added to Treaty 5 when that treaty was extended north to places like Nelson House, Split Lake, Oxford House, God's Lake, Island Lake, "Deer's Lake East," York Factory, and Fort Churchill, adding another 2,687

Indians to the treaty by 1911. These were mainly Swampy Cree and Chipewyans; the Métis applications were sent to Ottawa for settlement. Because of the distance from existing agencies, the two bands along Hudson Bay were administered by the police detachments at those points, with the police physician attending to the treaty Indians' medical needs. Eskimos were excluded from the treaty, though the deputy superintendent-general in his report for 1910-11 referred to an increasing departmental responsibility for them as well.[5] Altogether, through the new treaties, all the Indians between the Rockies and the western border of Quebec, except those of the Mackenzie valley, had been brought into treaty relations with the government by 1914.

Even then, however, only some 60 per cent of the Indians of Canada were enrolled in such formal treaties. In the Maritimes and Quebec, and in British Columbia and the Yukon, a variety of other arrangements prevailed. Nevertheless, the Dominion, through its administrative program, tried to bring some consistency to its dealings with the Indians of all parts of Canada. The provisions of the Indian Act, for example, applied to all recognized members of Indian bands, and only through enfranchisement did an Indian become exempted from its special provisions. A system of inspectorates (or superintendencies) and agencies was developed that coincided increasingly with provincial boundaries, though the Manitoba inspectorate as late as 1914 included two Ontario agencies, those of Fort Frances, and Kenora and Savanne. New Indian agencies were established as part of the process of organizing effective control. In 1908, nine years after Treaty 8 was signed, Dr W. B. L. Donald was appointed agent for Lesser Slave Agency with headquarters at Grouard. A second agency was inaugurated for the northern district under A. J. Bell at Fort Smith in 1911, while a third agency – mainly to attend to Indian needs and supervise the spending of government funds on their behalf – was opened at Fort Simpson, still outside treaty. Soon this became an argument for bringing the Mackenzie valley Indians under treaty, as was done in 1921 by Treaty 11.[6] Unwieldy agencies like the North-West Coast Agency were also divided into smaller, more manageable units, in this case the Bella Coola, Nass, and Queen Charlotte agencies. Thus the effort began to create a uniform, effective, universal system of administrative control in the field.

This was particularly apparent in the fields of health and education, where, for the first time, attempts were made to deal with these important problems at the national level. Under the treaties, the government provided bands with medicine chests and hired medical officers on contract or on a fee basis as required, while doctors accompanied annual treaty parties to examine cases brought to their attention. Medical work on reserves, however, was mainly attended to by the missionaries or Indian agents as part of their normal functions, and only the occasional reserve possessed a hospital. What was generally known was that medical care for Indians was grossly inadequate and that their mortality rate was extremely high. They had declined greatly from their former numbers and perhaps they were doing no better than holding their own even in the enlightened twentieth century. If they were to survive, something would have to be done to arrest the ravages of tuberculosis and scrofula, of infectious diseases like smallpox (fortunately curtailed by widespread vaccination), diphtheria, measles, scarlet fever, whooping cough, and the extraordinarily high infant mortality rate.

The appointment in 1905 of Dr Peter H. Bryce as chief health officer marked the beginning of an effort to ascertain the true facts and find ways of controlling the major causes of death or disability. From his first questionnaire, covering about three-quarters of the Indian population, Dr Bryce concluded that Indians were comparatively free of many diseases – nervous disorders, cancer, and alcoholism (surprisingly so in view of the frequency with which they got into trouble for being drunk). Infectious diseases were sometimes quite serious among particular bands, though no longer were epidemics so widespread as in the past. Because of the Indians' life style, bronchial, rheumatoid, and digestive disorders were common. But the main medical problems were those diseases that were spread through contact, like eye diseases transmitted by using common wash rags, or tuberculosis and scrofula. These last were comparatively rare diseases on the prairies in the eighties, but, spawned by widespread insanitary living conditions and extended through contact in homes and schools, they reached near-epidemic proportions, to become serious killers of young and old alike by the early twentieth century.

As a result of these findings, Dr Bryce strove to change the role of medical officers from curative to preventative medicine. Doctors, he felt, should inspect school premises as well as school children, and should examine and, if necessary, condemn homes. Tubercular patients should be isolated and treated, not in regular hospitals, but in cottage or even tent hospitals staffed by volunteer nurses, whose function it should be to care for the victims and prevent them from returning to their families and spreading the diseases.

By 1909 Dr Bryce felt that the Indians had turned an important corner. Their numbers, which had remained steady around the 100,000 mark for twenty years, were beginning to show a definite increase, certainly in the eastern provinces and possibly in the four western provinces as well. But it would be a long struggle, he expected, before the Indians could become healthier, more useful members of society, success depending, partly, on an improvement in their economic status that would reduce the incidence of many debilitating and killing diseases.[7]

As early as 1909 Dr Bryce was calling for an amendment to the Indian Act permitting agents of the administration to quarantine and isolate members of the native community. He had resigned from the government service by 1914, when the desired amendment was passed empowering the superintendent-general to make and enforce health regulations.[8] Thus administrators could order the cleaning of streets and yards, the purifying, ventilating, and disinfecting of premises; could destroy buildings unfit for human habitation, limit the numbers of persons who might dwell in particular accommodations, or detain persons, conveyances, or goods where there was reason to suspect infections were being transmitted in that way. But, as with so many other reforms intended to improve the well-being of the Indian population, implementation was the difficulty. No real change occurred for many years in the management of the health services, or in the quality of Indian life. Not until 1927 did the department employ another medical superintendent, while a truly vigorous onslaught against the traditional causes of Indian disease and death had to wait for the 1950's. Dr Bryce's appointment was no more than a promising beginning.

In the field of education, too, reform was less in evidence than was the awakening of public and governmental interest in the problems of Indian schooling, heralded by the promotion in 1910 of the poet Duncan Campbell Scott as superintendent of Indian education. In most of Canada, but particularly in the west and north, the department relied on religious denominations, assisted by governmental subsidies, to operate day schools, industrial schools, or residential boarding schools. In some places in eastern Canada, in the new railway towns, and in isolated villages along the British Columbia coast, some of the Indian children were taught in provincial schools along with the local white children, the Indian department reimbursing the school board for the service. A very few young people were also aided to proceed to advanced academic and professional education. Government spending before 1910 on all these activities stood around $400,000 per annum, divided fairly evenly among the three types of schools, the money going towards teachers' salaries, construction, equipment, and maintenance of buildings. Supervision over Indian schools was relatively light, and seldom by professionally qualified persons.

The denominations found it hard to secure adequate staff for a very difficult sort of work, which demanded great skill and patience and often had to be conducted under highly unsatisfactory conditions. Furthermore, the high mortality rate from tuberculosis among children in residential schools was assuming the proportions of a national scandal. Apologists excused the schools' deplorable health record as arising from their having recruited children without proper medical examination in the early days, and predicted that with improved ventilation, water supplies, and food, the situation would right itself.[9]

In fact, official opinion, as represented by Scott, was moving back to the view that the day school was the most desirable form of education, particularly where Indians had given up the nomadic life, since the children would not be separated from their parents or divorced from their home environment through years of attendance in boarding schools. Scott therefore proposed to improve the quality of the day schools by offering better salaries and other amenities to attract superior teachers who would make school interesting and agreeable to the pupils. He also proposed to furnish children with midday meals and transportation to and from their homes. Where the Indians lived in villages, as in much of British Columbia, the day school naturally predominated.

But residential schools were needed in areas of scattered, nomadic populations such as were characteristic of the Middle North. Besides, the churches had considerable investments in them and preferred them on religious and other grounds. Every year, therefore, saw the numbers of boarding schools increased – four new ones were established in 1902 in the District of Athabasca alone. The missions' concern, therefore, was to secure government help to improve the residential schools, particularly as regards buildings and facilities. The existing system of grants – $72 per average daily attendance – did not provide enough income to allow the churches to improve the facilities and services. The system, incidentally, encouraged the securing of full attendance by sometimes accepting unhealthy pupils.

From its side, the department complained that it had no real control over the properties, and it sought a new relationship with the churches to meet this need. A conference in Ottawa on November 8, 1910, brought proposals that eventually produced a new grants system based on formal contracts, whereby the schools receiving maximum grants had to limit enrolment according to floor and air space, and to provide well-ventilated and adequately heated premises, a pure water supply and proper sewage disposal, facilities for isolating pupils with infectious diseases, and adequate buildings, farms, gardens, and industrial facilities. Schools were to be rated in three classes, with grants appropriate to each. The amounts also varied according to location – schools 200 miles or more from a railway receiving up to $125 per pupil as against up to $80 for schools in eastern Canada.[10]

The form of the new contract also regulated enrolment and teaching services. Children had to be between the ages of seven and eighteen unless permission for an exemption was secured; no student was to be admitted without a prior satisfactory physical examination, nor any child who was not a member of a recognized band of Indians. Half-breed children, however, might be accepted, provided no payment was claimed on their behalf. Teachers had to be properly qualified, be able to speak and write the English language, and to converse with pupils in English. The schools were to provide religious instruction, train boys in gardening, farming, and other arts, and girls in cooking, laundry work, domestic work, "teach all the pupils in the ordinary branches of an English education," "teach the effects of alcoholic drinks and narcotics on the human system, and how to live in a healthy manner," supply and clothe pupils, maintain sanitary standards in the school, make any changes in the buildings and remove any pupil or teacher as required, keep the building in good repair, and operate the school for eleven months, less holidays.[11]

Thus a significant degree of state control over Indian education – including a blow against French as a language of instruction – had been achieved, though management remained firmly in the hands of the churches. These last immediately set to work with a will to bring their schools up to the new requirements. Inspector Conroy reported in 1912 for Treaty 8 that a new boarding school, St Bruno's, had been opened up by the Roman Catholics at Lesser Slave Lake, a second was being completed at Fort Smith, a third was under construction at Fort Resolution, and a new wing was being added at Fort Providence, while Anglicans were planning to build at Hay River. Altogether, the new system afforded a very marked impetus to the residential school system that tended to overshadow the hoped-for improvement in day schools consequent on their also receiving increased grants. Inevitably, a very noticeable rise in expenditures on Indian education occurred. Whereas the total had amounted to only $402,542 in 1909, four years later the sum had reached $922,000. Spending on industrial schools rose only slightly, that on day schools was almost doubled, while expenditures for boarding or residential schools soared from $143,663 all the way to $491,029.[12] Hence, while the theory was beginning to favour the day-school system, the current practice served mainly to strengthen and intensify the mission-directed system of residential or boarding schools. Here again, it was the 1950's before a substantial reform was effected in the system of mission-directed Indian education.

A main purpose behind the treaties was to help the Indians live in a world dominated by white civilization, the reserves being intended as a shelter and a guarantee of their continued survival. Consequently, the speed with which reserves were taken up reflected the urgency of the local situation in the Indians' eyes, as well as the encroachment and pressure from white men upon the resources of the area. Given the situation in northern Ontario, it is no surprise that the bands decided on the localities they desired when they took treaty, or that their reserves were quite quickly selected and surveyed, even those as remote as Fort Albany and Moose Factory. On the other hand, there was far less urgency about most of the territory added to Treaty 5 or to Treaty 10, and hardly any of the bands had even made their selection by 1912. Surveying the reserves provided under Treaty 8 was also a protracted affair, with the selections being made fairly early, around 1903, in the more desired regions like Lesser Slave Lake, Swan River, and along the Peace River, but much later in other sections. By choosing reserves early, the bands secured some of the best lands in their districts from the standpoint of fish and game, timber, soil, and hay meadow resources. At Fort McMurray delay in making a selection was a serious matter, since the district was being blanketed by speculators in oil, tar sand, and railway prospects; delays simply made it more difficult to select land free of pre-existing claims.

British Columbia presented a similar situation, since white claimants quickly established themselves on the rather limited pockets of arable land, athwart strategic transportation routes, or, if they could, on the best fishing locations. At the same time, it was particularly difficult to allocate reserves because of the unwillingness of the province to make the necessary lands available, and because some bands held views on their land rights that led them to refuse to accept the reserves allotted them. Nevertheless, the work was carried forward after the difficult eighties, and most bands in New Caledonia, the Skeena, or along the coast and islands, had made, or were on the verge of making, their selections by 1905.

At the same time as new reserves were being taken up by bands under the new treaties, others, in areas of settlement strongly coveted by white men, were being relinquished as unsuitable or superfluous, with the consent of the bands. By a move that gave rise to much long, bitter controversy, the historic St Peter's Reserve, near Selkirk, Manitoba, was exchanged for another at Fisher River along the coast of Lake Winnipeg, which was deemed better suited to the Indians' occupational interests and threw fewer urban temptations in their way. Other reserves on the prairies, containing first-class agricultural land which the Indians were unwilling or unable to cultivate fully were looked at with longing by farmers, and efforts were made to secure the surrender of the lands on terms acceptable to the Indians. As the Indian commissioner for the prairies, David Laird, explained:

> Under the treaties large areas of land, in most cases the best fitted for agriculture, were set apart for the Indians. As was to be expected, the area was much in excess of that which they could, even when their maximum working power was reached, make profitable use of. The locking up of vast tracts which the Indians could not make use of was neither in their own nor in the public interest. Yet the Indians in many cases were averse to parting with any. The amendment in the new law which permits of fifty per cent of the money derived from the sale of surrendered lands being immediately used, and the investment of the returns in outfitting Indians for work and enabling them to improve the conditions in which they live, has led many of the Indians to make

surrenders. And thus with the proceeds of land that could only lie idle and unremunerative, they are being put in a position to make use of that which they still hold.[13]

Undoubtedly the surrender process was greatly accelerated by giving the Indians this immediate monetary incentive. Some reserves around Edmonton were sold in whole or in part, while more than half the Blackfoot Reserve was sold in 1910-11 for over one million dollars.[14]

Railway needs accounted for other surrenders. In 1913 the Indians of The Pas sold one of their reserves, 540 acres, for a townsite of the new railway centre.[15] The most celebrated case occurred in 1907-8, when the Grand Trunk Pacific decided to place its Pacific coast terminus at Kaien Island and applied to purchase about half the Metlakatla Reserve. In view of the great value of the location to the railway and the vast amounts of real estate money speculated on the future city of Prince Rupert, the sale of 14,160 acres of land for a price of $107,650 seems a rather inadequate return for the Metlakatla Indians (now reduced from 800, as in Duncan's day, to a band of 180 persons) and no very good protection of their interests. The negotiation and arrangement awakened a great hue and cry from the British Columbia government, which asserted its reversionary right to all reserve lands no longer needed for purposes of the Indians, and therefore its prior claim to dispose of the land to the railway. The argument between the two governments caused Dominion-provincial reserve negotiations to be suspended for a time and initiated a long series of negotiations that threatened to bring on a complete resurvey of Indian lands in the province.[16]

Moreover, the reserve question quickly merged with the broader question of aboriginal rights, the drive coming mainly in the Nass River district from among the Nishga people of Aiyansh and Lachkaltsap villages. It was apparently inspired by the Anglican missionary the Reverend J. B. McCullagh, though it had an earlier awakening on the Skeena in the eighties during the Duncan-Ridley controversies. In 1910 the aggrieved Indians formed a land committee to lay claim to their entire tribal territory as their aboriginal right. Backed by other Indian and white organizations, they instituted a long series of negotiations, hearings, a royal commission, delegations to Ottawa, and an eventual parliamentary settlement in 1927, which was proclaimed as final though it failed to satisfy the Indians. In the course of the agitation, the Indians in 1916 formed an effective native organization, the Allied Tribes of British Columbia.[17]

How did the Indians adjust practically to the widespread invasion of their formal tribal territories across the breadth of Canada? The adjustment was very uneven, but on the whole seemed quite successful at this time. In the agricultural Peace River area, the effort to encourage the Indians to cultivate their lands met with mixed results. Many work opportunities were becoming available in connection with the building of the two great transcontinental railways. At Chapleau, Ontario, the Crees were reported as having "profited largely by the advantages offered them of getting their children educated in the public school, as a result of which they speak English fluently, can read and write well, and are able to fill more or less responsible positions with the Canadian Pacific Railway Company. The women and girls are busy cleaning and doing laundry work and quite a number of the latter engage as servants, thus earning good wages."[18] The younger men of the Long Lake band "find employment as packers and guides with the Hudson's Bay Company and Revillon Bros., and also along the line of the Transcontinental railway and Canadian Northern railway construction work."[19] In northern British Columbia, from 1908 onwards, the Indians of Hazelton and other districts found plenty of work on surveys or on the right-of-way, for "On recommendation contractors did not hesitate to give contracts of clearing right of way, tie and cord-wood cutting, and freighting to the Indians, who in every case made good."[20]

In other areas the Indians found work along more traditional lines in the greater economic activity introduced by the newcomers. At Fort Frances, as in Kenora, new occupations included working in sawmills, on steam-boats or farms; river-driving, guiding, taking out dead and fallen timber on their reserves. The agent commented that "The majority of the Indians are industrious and law-abiding, and as a rule becoming richer, as they live and dress better, and have better houses, than they did a few years ago."[21]

Along the Pacific coast, where Indians were much more capable of operating their own fishing activities, many found useful work fishing, trapping, hunting, and logging, owning and operating stores, and working in the salmon fishery, the men operating their own gasoline boats, the women in the canneries. But even when Indians were successful workmen, they still were not masters of their own economic destiny; they worked mainly for wages or sold their produce to middlemen who reaped most of the benefits. As for joining fully in the better opportunities of a white society that had less understanding, tolerance, or need of the Indian, the chances of occurrences like the following were all too frequent:

> The colour line seems to me to be the greatest hindrance to the progress of ex-pupils of each class of school. Here and there one finds flashes of ambition in scholars of the best type. In many cases they desire to associate with the white people and make for the cities. They find employment as deck-hands, draymen, shop assistants and carpenters, and earn good money, which they put to good use, marrying and making

comfortable homes. They feel desirous of abandoning the reserve as much as possible – perhaps feeling a little proud of their success.

Then as Indians usually find little sympathy among the better class of white people, that is, social sympathy, they find association with the lowest type of white man an easy thing, and presently there is a case of supplying liquor to Indians, and in many cases Indian women are in this way inveigled into the habits of common prostitution. Especially is this so among ex-pupils of boarding schools, where the girls are made too smart for the Indian villages and are not fitted (because of inherent hereditary tendencies) for city environment.[22]

By 1914, for most Indians of the developing Middle North, there was only a choice between living on increasingly beleaguered reserves or trying to participate in the white man's society. In more northerly areas, however, there still was room to continue their traditional hunting, fishing, and trapping life, aided by such white man's goods as firearms, twine fish nets, and canvas tents, blankets and apparel, tea and tobacco, flour and sugar. In many remote areas, from the Naskapi of Ungava to the Slavis of Fort Nelson or the Sekanis of Fort Grahame, they could carry on as before, living mainly off the land, spending their days in the endless quest for food, trapping a little fur and meeting their few needs at the district Hudson's Bay post. Some, in fact, picked their way to less crowded, more remote hunting grounds. But even there, and still more in accessible districts in the northern parts of the provinces or along the Mackenzie waterway, they were intruded on by white prospectors, trappers, and commercial fishermen. The last of these were particularly destructive of the natives' means of livelihood, though successful commercial fishing was restricted to one hundred or 150 miles from a railway shipping point. But the competing trappers could go anywhere, and the first years of the new century saw them entering in considerable numbers in most sections of the accessible fur forest.

They presented a particularly serious threat to the native way of life. For while the Indian hunted for food and trapped some fur to meet his family's rather meagre wants, the full-time white trapper customarily devoted himself almost exclusively to trapping fur. He trapped more energetically, and strove for the maximum possible return. Since he was a transient, who could easily move on if and when the district became seriously depleted, he had no concern for conserving its wildlife; the native, on the other hand, had to concern himself with preserving as best he could the ancestral environment. The independent white trapper also threatened the established trader, since he often traded on his own account and periodically went "outside" to dispose of his fur at the best possible prices and equip himself for his next foray into the wilderness.

The opening decade of the new century was a period of rising fur prices that brought comparative prosperity to the Indians in districts where fur was still plentiful, but also encouraged an influx of white trappers and traders into those same districts. From the new centres of settlement, itinerant fur-buyers spread over the country, buying furs at higher prices since they were not hampered by overheads of maintaining regular posts and outfits or advancing credit to trappers. Being fly-by-nights, they could indulge in fraudulent or illegal practices with fair chance of escaping penalties. They undermined established traders by encouraging their clients to repudiate their debts, thereby demoralizing the regular trade. New traders entering a community were bound to have a somewhat similar effect while they strove to establish themselves by luring trade from others, though they could not afford to indulge in improper activities. The celebrated naturalist Ernest Thompson Seton went so far as to say that "it was the worst thing that ever happened [to] the region when the irresponsible free-traders with their demoralizing methods were allowed to enter and traffic where and how they pleased."[23] Not all independent traders, of course, were men of this stripe. Everyone had only praise for many long-established private traders, like Colin Fraser of Fort Chipewyan or Dan Cadzow of Rampart House, who had a real feeling for their communities and people, and took their best interests to heart.

II

The penetration by white hunters, trappers, and traders of the northern part of the great fur-producing forest belt of Canada was greatly facilitated by the improvements in transportation facilities that had gone on since the Klondike gold discovery. Thanks to the efforts to gain access to that region by Canadian routes, transport facilities along the Athabasca-Slave-Mackenzie waterway were considerably improved for future users. The years 1897 to 1899 brought enough traffic to develop the trail from Edmonton to Athabasca Landing into a wagon road with regular stagecoach service, and transformed Athabasca Landing into a substantial village. To supplement the Hudson's Bay Company fleet, new vessels, which were afterwards taken over by rival traders, were placed on the rivers, while Roman Catholic missions obtained small vessels to operate below Fort McMurray and for the Peace River as well. Both routes received other power boats and ships, and some thought was given to the possibility of making the Peace, rather than the rapid-clogged, shallow Athabasca, the true access to the northern waterway once railway connection with the outside world was achieved. However, the eventual completion of a railway from

Edmonton to the vicinity of Fort McMurray made that centre the longtime gateway to the District of Mackenzie. In the meantime, however, travellers continued to struggle year after year with the unmanageable section of the Athabasca River above Fort McMurray, entailing increasing delays and losses as traffic for points all the way to the Mackenzie delta grew. And there was no doubt about the fuller use made of this route, as the reports of travellers in successive years indicated. For, besides summertime visitors and workers, an increasing permanent settlement was arising along the waterway, as reflected by the inauguration in 1901 of official postal service that provided two mails between Edmonton and Fort Resolution at first, but by 1909 amounted to five trips to Fort Resolution and two to Fort McPherson. Deliveries were made by Hudson's Bay Company steamers in summer and by dog teams in winter, post offices being opened at Fort McMurray, Fort Smith, and Fort Resolution. From 1903 onward, when posts were opened at Fort McPherson and Herschel Island, police patrols began to be made with increasing frequency along Mackenzie River points, the detachment at Fort Chipewyan going as far downriver as Fort Simpson on occasion. Officials like Elihu Stewart, the superintendent of forestry, made a much-publicized journey by steamers down the route in 1906, crossing from Fort McPherson to the Porcupine and Yukon Rivers,[24] as did his superior, Minister of the Interior Frank Oliver, in 1910.[25]

Early off the mark was the Geological Survey. Having investigated the waterway in the eighties, the survey in 1899 began examining the country reached from the Mackenzie system by sending Robert Bell, assisted by his nephew J. Mackintosh Bell, to make a topographical and geological reconnaissance survey of Great Slave Lake, the locale of prospecting activity by Klondike-bound travellers. Bell reported on two good prospective mineralized areas – the North Arm, a region of Huronian-type rocks (where a gold-bearing specimen had already been turned up from the Yellowknife River area), and, among the younger strata west of the lake, a lead-zinc occurrence some miles southwest of Fort Resolution. Examining this Pine Point deposit, Bell concluded it would not pay development for a long time to come because of the high cost of shipping out the comparatively low-value lead and zinc ore.

J. M. Bell wintered in the country to carry on an exploration of Great Bear Lake in 1900, for which he hired a local crew that included the college-educated Charles Camsell, son of Chief Factor Julian S. Camsell, who thus began a long, celebrated career as a widely respected Canadian public servant. After tracing the northern arms and bays of Great Bear Lake, they made a sixty-mile trip overland from Dease Arm to get some idea of the long-famed copper occurrence at Coppermine River. Near Dismal Lakes they had an interesting encounter with a group of Eskimos who immediately turned and fled. They located their camp, helped themselves to some wood and meat (for they were on the verge of starvation), then resumed their trip back to Great Bear Lake. "We were evidently the first white men they had seen, as not a single article of white man's manufacture was found in their camp."[26] Years later Camsell was told they had been under surveillance for almost two days until they had definitely left the area. The Eskimos had come to the conclusion that the white men meant no harm because their involuntary guests had repaid their hospitality by leaving behind a tin plate and two steel needles, articles beyond price to these Stone Age people.

Bell and Camsell traced the eastern shore (McTavish Arm) of Great Bear Lake, then, with difficulty, made their way through the tangled chain of rivers and lakes that led south to the North Arm of Great Slave Lake and Fort Rae. Bell's report on the cliffs of McTavish Arm being stained with copper-green and cobalt-bloom was destined thirty years later to direct Gilbert LaBine to the area and his momentous radium-uranium ore discovery at Echo Bay. Other geological reconnaissances of the next five years included those by Camsell of the country west and southwest of Fort Smith to examine salt and gypsum deposits, and of the Peel River basin, which he explored by crossing the Ogilvie Mountains to the Wind River and down the Peel to its mouth, making the first satisfactory report on the geology of the region, including references to occurrences of lignite coal, indications of enormous iron deposits, and good petroleum and natural gas prospects. In 1908, too, Joseph Keele made a very arduous examination from the Yukon through the mountains to the Mackenzie by way of the Gravel River, later renamed Keele River in his honour.[27]

In the meantime, prospectors were reported year after year by police and others at work in various sectors of the region – west of the Mackenzie delta in the Richardson Mountains country, in the mountains west of Forts Wrigley and Norman, up the Liard and in the unknown Nahanni River country, and about Great Slave Lake. Perhaps the most tangible results of all their activities were the staking of the lead-zinc prospects at Pine Point in 1909, and the bringing to Athabasca Landing in 1912 of samples of a red-brown oil secured from a seepage on the east bank of the Mackenzie, twenty-five miles below Fort Norman, almost on the Arctic Circle.[28]

What with such activities proliferating here and elsewhere in the North, the non-native population of the present-day Northwest Territories rose between 1901 and 1911 from 137 to 519 persons. Among these were included the newly arriving hunters, trappers, and traders, prospectors, farmers, carpenters, boatmen, mission personnel, and teachers, a doctor or two, and numbers of governmental employees, particularly policemen and Indian agency staff. Most of these were included among the inhabitants of the growing settlements along the Mackenzie waterway. For increasing numbers of white hunters, trappers, prospectors, and scientist-observers, however, these posts provided points of departure to still more remote districts – west into the western part of the Cordillera, or east into the massive Arctic tundra extending east to Hudson Bay.

The Klondike excitement had reached even as far as the Barren Lands, in the form of a Hudson's Bay and Yukon Railway and Navigation Company, chartered in 1897, which planned to bridge navigable stretches of waterways between Chesterfield Inlet, Great Slave Lake, and the Yukon River. In 1899 an English naturalist, David T. Hanbury, completed a journey from Chesterfield Inlet to Great Slave Lake by way of Baker Lake and Thelon River. In the following year, 1900, a party of the Topographical Surveys Branch, headed by J. W. Tyrrell, made the crossing in the opposite direction, from Great Slave Lake by way of Lockhart River and Pike's Portage to the Thelon system and thence to Hudson Bay.[29] Hanbury, with another footloose Englishman, Hubert Darrell, duplicated that feat in 1901, then on his return travelled north to the Arctic coast, which he traced from west of Adelaide Peninsula to the Coppermine River, then skirted the north shore of Great Bear Lake to emerge at Fort Norman. His account of these remarkable exploring journeys of 1901-2, *Sport and Travel in the Northland of Canada*, inspired others to follow in his steps.

Adding to the incoming white hunters, trappers, and traders attracted to the still valuable fur trade of northern Canada was the most powerful and widely extended rival organization the Hudson's Bay Company had faced since 1821. This was the celebrated firm of Parisian *couturiers*, Revillon Frères, whose head, Victor Revillon, decided it would be advantageous to secure control of its own source of supply in Canada rather than purchasing its needs at Hudson's Bay Company auctions in London or at European sales and fairs. The Revillon operations in Canada were concentrated mainly in two areas – about Hudson Bay and northern Quebec, and in northern Saskatchewan and Alberta. Many of its officers were Frenchmen, and in western Canada it operated in districts where the Métis were an important element of the trapping population. Hence it was often known as the French Company, and was believed (no doubt unjustly) to enjoy the particular favour of the influential Oblate missionaries, most of whom were also French-speaking. The company opened an establishment in Edmonton in 1899 and expanded it into its main warehouse in 1905, at which time it purchased Bredin and Cornwall's stores in the Peace River district as well as their ranch to supply their posts and go after Indian treaty and police supply contracts. By 1911, the company owned thirteen posts north and west of Athabasca Landing, and from a warehouse opened at Prince Albert in 1904, another ten posts ranging all the way east to The

Pas and north to DuBrochet and Nueltin Lake, on the edge of the Arctic tundra. Similarly, it operated a string of posts in Ungava, Quebec, and James Bay, served by the company's own ships.[30]

Along the waterways of the Mackenzie basin the main competition came from Edmonton-based traders, backed by the wholesaling facilities of John A. McDougall and R. Secord of Edmonton, who in their heyday, between 1897 and 1908, were represented by many traders and buyers throughout the Northwest, whose furs were marketed mainly to the Lampson Company in London. The partnership of Hislop and Nagle, formed around 1887, continued to operate posts along the waterway from Fort Resolution to Peel River and at Fort Liard and Fort Nelson until 1911, when they disposed of their posts and vessels to the Northern Trading Company, which competed along the Mackenzie waterways until the 1930's.[31]

Faced with such rivals on so many fronts, the Hudson's Bay Company's postmasters fought back in kind, sometimes imitating their opponents' tactics of enticing trappers to ignore their other commitments. Such practices, indulged in by both sides, encouraged the worst kind of business conduct on the part of some Indian and Métis hunters, who could see only higher prices and more goods for themselves through playing off one trader against another. The trade was unsettled and many natives were turned into negligent trappers and unscrupulous, arrogant clients. The eventual result was to greatly reduce credit advances in favour of a system of cash trading, and to displace the paternalistic relationship that had been the cornerstone of the fur trade in its best days.

The Hudson's Bay Company by now was prospering as never before from the proceeds of land sales in the Fertile Belt, but it nevertheless continued to operate its fur trade much as before, with a dwindling staff of aging commissioned officers and a new breed of clerks (the apprenticeship system was abandoned in 1902) who looked realistically at the salaries and prospects offered, and readily shifted to new employers – even rival fur companies – when better opportunities presented. An age was passing, too, with the retirement in 1911 of C. C. Chipman, fur trade commissioner since 1891, and the death in 1914 of the aged governor, Lord Strathcona, the former Donald A. Smith.

As in previous decades, the Hudson's Bay Company continued to adjust to new situations, converting shops in places like Athabasca Landing, Peace River Crossing, or Prince George into general stores that catered to the needs of the new settlers as well as of the Métis, Indians, and whites who trapped the wilderness that stretched beyond these narrow bridgeheads of settlement. Even in those posts that were predominantly concerned with the fur trade, adjustments were necessary. A wider range of goods and services was called for by the growing number of tourists, prospectors, and others who entered the country, and greater stress was placed on transportation facilities or amenities. Besides, an increasing number of white settlers now resided permanently at many northern centres. Governments were putting more money into circulation in the North; more government parties entered the country that had to be equipped and served, and they hired numbers of local residents to aid them in their work. More money was reaching the inhabitants in other ways – as Indian treaty annuities, school grants, or small salaries for operating post offices, serving as customs collectors, or taking meteorological observations. There were lucrative contracts, too, for carrying the mail (which represented a subsidy for an established transportation system), and for supplying Indian relief that had once been an unavoidable company expense. The young H. S. M. Kemp had his first experience as an H.B.C. employee in 1908, when he accompanied the large Indian treaty pay party (Treaty No. 10) which the Hudson's Bay Company had contracted to supply and conduct on its 2,500-mile trip around northern Saskatchewan. The money economy thus was beginning to characterize all but the most isolated company posts. By 1906, even remote Fond du Lac had instituted a system of cash trade in place of "Made Beaver."

Improving transportation permitted the reorganization of supply systems and a regrouping of company posts. With the arrival of the railway to The Pas, most northern Manitoba posts were supplied from that point, further reducing the hinterland of the annual Hudson Bay ship to the vicinities of York Factory (Port Nelson) and Churchill. Northern Saskatchewan posts were now supplied from Prince Albert, from which supplies were freighted to Montreal Lake for distribution by York boat brigades to the northern posts. Edmonton became increasingly important as the base from which the trade of the entire Athabasca-Mackenzie basin all the way to the Mackenzie delta was conducted. Construction of the Grand Trunk Pacific redirected the trade system of New Caledonia from the difficult Hazelton-to-Omineca trail in favour of the easier trails and rivers north from the new rail centre of Prince George along the Rocky Mountain Trench. Farther west, the railway also greatly improved the transport situation for the posts of the Nechaco and Skeena districts. And in the east, from the new rail-heads north of the height of land, supplies now arrived by train to be sent by scow down rivers like the Pagwa all the way to James Bay. But all these facilities were available to rival traders too; hence the drive after 1912 to move into the Arctic coasts of northern Hudson Bay and of the mainland of Canada to develop the white fox fur trade among the tundra-dwelling Eskimos. A post was opened at Chesterfield Inlet, an outpost at Ennadai Lake on the tundra 150 miles north of du Brochet post on Reindeer Lake, and Eskimo middlemen were used to reach groups ranging over the tundra and along the coast. Furthermore, the Hudson's Bay Company was also beginning to expand along the Arctic coast east from the Mackenzie delta with a series of posts that were to be supplied by annual ships from Vancouver.

The advance of the frontier of white settlement, as well as the increasing penetration of the sub-Arctic and Arctic regions beyond, inevitably produced a serious drain on the fish and game resources that began increasingly to alarm administrators and then the public at large. In more southerly districts new industries were upsetting the natural habitats in which the wildlife flourished; in the undeveloped north, forest fires, modern weapons, and competition from migratory trappers and free traders encouraged a race to destruction. Mindful of the historic record of white penetration of America, a concerned public was beginning to demand measures that would preserve rare species from extinction and protect the well-being of native peoples depending on hunting and fishing for their livelihood. The period, therefore, was characterized by growing attention to problems of wildlife conservation. Here, as in other areas, the Commission of Conservation made a notable contribution by appointing a committee on fisheries, game, and fur-bearing animals, and sponsoring investigations, studies, and discussions that culminated in a volume of studies presented to a conference in Ottawa in November, 1915, and, after the war, in a national conference on game and wildlife conservation (1919).

These reports indicated that the depletion of game animals that had brought the virtual extinction of the bison and antelope from the western plains was beginning by 1914 to extend to the new North. Fearful of present and prospective shortages, governments passed legislation banning the sale of game (which was claimed to be the root cause of large-scale destruction of meat animals), licensed hunters and trappers, and inaugurated systems of securing accurate statistics on the annual catches. Trapping seasons were introduced to prevent useless killing of unprime animals, while several provinces instituted closed seasons to help the beaver recover from over-trapping. Unfortunately these closed seasons had often to be suspended in the interest of the native peoples, to whom the beaver was important as a source of food as well as fur. Certain practices deemed particularly destructive of game were banned, such as collecting eggs of wildfowl or using poison, except against wolves. Incidentally, the experts were far from unanimous in regarding the native as a noticeably better conservationist than his white contemporary, and efforts were made to apply the new regulations to native hunters.

In most provinces, game preserves were established where hunting and trapping were banned, and game regulations were enforced by local game wardens and guardians under the oversight of a government branch, though for many years the staffs were wholly inadequate for the purpose. In the Northwest Territories, too, steps began to be taken by this time to establish a proper system of conservation and control. Since 1894 the wood bison had been protected by statute, but the muskox and caribou, threatened by meat-hunters and traders, had no protection whatever; without a licensing system, nothing could be done to restrict the activities of interlopers. Only in 1917 was a Northwest Game Act passed, finally introducing these reforms. For lack of an effective territorial administration, enforcement of the act was put in the hands of J. B. Harkin, the superintendent of the national parks. But for practical purposes, implementation was in the hands of the only arm of government effective in the lands north of sixty – and in much of Canada besides – the Royal Northwest Mounted Police.

The police, as on earlier Canadian frontiers, played an important role in the orderly progression of this latest series of developing frontiers, overseeing the native population as wards of the Dominion government and taking cognizance of the implications of the northward influx of white settlement. In 1901 Constantine, now back on the prairies and commanding "G" Division, headquarters Fort Saskatchewan, from which he supervised virtually the entire Mackenzie basin, warned that "the time is rapidly approaching when the North should be more closely looked after, the number of men and Police stations increased and facilities for better communication improved."[32] Commissioner A. B. Perry continually complained about the need for more manpower for this and other jobs, but thanks to the rapid reduction of the staff in the Yukon, he had a considerable body of effectives available to expand activities elsewhere. A small beginning was made with the dispatching in 1903 of two units of six men, under Superintendents Constantine and Moodie, to set up bases from which to supervise the activities of foreign whalers off Canada's coasts and to commence effective policing of the Mackenzie valley and of the District of Keewatin.

Accordingly, in the summer of 1903 Constantine followed the established route from Fort Saskatchewan to Fort McPherson, the intended base from which patrols would visit Herschel Island and other centres of whaling activities. Thus his Division "G" was extended all the way to the Arctic, with a thousand-mile gap between Fort Chipewyan and Fort McPherson. Among Constantine's recommendations were two intervening detachments at Fort Resolution and Fort Simpson, an independent system of boats for patrolling the waterway plus a government revenue ship to oversee the Arctic whalers, a stipendiary magistrate resident in the district to reduce the expense of bringing persons all the way to Edmonton to stand trial, a system of local courts, and one or more jails.[33]

But, as usual, though the detachments were placed at Fort McPherson and Herschel Island, little was done about Constantine's suggestions. In 1905 he was given command of a newly created Division "N" with head-quarters at Lesser Slave Lake, whose main task was to work on the trail to the Yukon northwest from Fort St John, from which he continued to press for the extension of his division at least as far as Fort Resolution. Finally, in 1908, when the headquarters of Division "N" was shifted to Athabasca Landing, it was given control both of the westerly posts and those in the north as well. Division "G" became restricted to the Edmonton district, to which city its headquarters was moved from Fort Saskatchewan in 1910. In the meantime, the far-flung staff of Division "N", which by 1914 included the desired detachments at Fort Resolution and Fort Simpson, had been divided into three sub-districts, each under an inspector, centred at Grouard, Smith's Landing, and Herschel Island.[34]

Similarly, the other new six-man detachment, comprising the nucleus of a new Division "M", went by ship to Hudson Bay where a headquarters was established at Fullerton Harbour in the northwest corner of the bay. Superintendent J. D. Moodie came out with the ship in 1904, but returned annually with the supply ship until 1909, when he was succeeded by Superintendent Cortland Starnes. The divisional headquarters was moved to the more convenient Churchill in 1907, then by 1914 to Port Nelson, the anticipated terminus of the Hudson Bay Railway.

From all three fronts – Peace River, Mackenzie, and Hudson Bay – frequent patrols of the districts and the intervening spaces were the rule. In the winter of 1898 a patrol went from Athabasca Landing down the Mackenzie to Fort Simpson, and this, or similar patrols, became almost an annual affair. The need to link up with Division "M" on the shore of Hudson Bay inspired numerous patrols from Regina, Norway House, and later The Pas that helped police the southern part of Keewatin. In addition, Lake Winnipeg was patrolled by boat for a number of years to check on liquor being supplied the Indians, while in 1905 another patrol proceeded all the way to Cat Lake in eastern Keewatin (the future Patricia district of Ontario).

One of the most unusual assignments ever to come the way of the police was to build a wagon trail from Fort St John through the Rockies to the Yukon. Constantine had charge of this operation in the first year, 1905, during which time the two officers and thirty men built a total of ninety-four miles northwest towards Fort Grahame, along Moodie's attempted route of 1898 to the Klondike. For the following year supplies were forwarded to Fort Grahame, and by the end of the season the road had been carried 208 miles – some twenty miles beyond Fort Grahame. In 1907 the road was completed to the Telegraph Trail near Fourth Cabin, 104 miles north of Hazelton, where it was decided to use that trail for the remainder of the route, thereby ending the work. It was all to little or no purpose. When three years later, in 1910, a three-man patrol travelled from Athabasca Landing to Whitehorse by way of the trail, it experienced much difficulty from fallen timber and the like, and encountered hardly a soul along the route.[85]

An important centre of patrolling activities for Division "N" was the region west of Slave River and south of Great Slave Lake, the habitat of the rare wood bison, a few specimens of which were making their way to some of the major museums of the world. That a variety of this once so numerous species still survived was a cause of great curiosity, wonderment, and rejoicing, and there was every desire to protect the bison from extinction. Constantine reported in 1903 that the animals were not very numerous, and the paucity of calves seemed to indicate heavy destruction by wolves. A really extensive investigation was made in 1907 by Inspector A. M. Jarvis in the company of the naturalists Ernest Thompson Seton and E. A. Preble. Sweeps were made over the district from the south, east, and north to try to locate some of the animals and learn what they could about them. Since the largest herd observed was about twenty-five animals, the men considered the bison to be few in number. While they agreed wolves were a partial explanation, they found reason to suspect poaching as well. Their report, therefore, recommended steps against both predators, including detachments in the adjoining centres of Smith's Landing, Fort Chipewyan, and Fort Vermilion to patrol the district frequently and thoroughly. By 1908, it was proposed to set the area aside as a reserve closed to all hunting or trapping, and to continue paying bounties on wolves killed within a certain distance of the reserve. Patrols continued to be carried on each year from the three centres, and twenty-dollar wolf bounties were paid. Thanks to these, and to the two Indians hired to poison and otherwise destroy wolves, the situation seemed to improve, though the issuing of permits in Ottawa to shoot bison for "scientific" purposes continued to alarm the police and inspired renewed calls to hurry and establish the reserve and ban hunting of wood bison under any circumstances whatever.[86]

A good deal of long-distance patrolling was occasioned by the paucity of detachments spread over a great area. Patrols were made over the 265 miles between Fort McPherson and Herschel Island several times annually, as well as west along the coast to investigate some matter or other, or merely to see what was going on. Similarly, patrols went out from Fort Resolution to points around Great Slave Lake, and from Fort Chipewyan about Lake Athabasca or even to Fort Simpson. In 1909, Sergeant A. H. L. Mellor went by river from Fort Vermilion to Fort Liard to ascertain the fate of two brothers MacLeod who had disappeared in the South Nahanni River district. He reported back that they had presumably died of starvation. In the following year Sergeant Field returned to the Liard with a party that was bringing the Slavi and Sekani Indians of Fort Nelson under Treaty 8. Another of Mellor's patrols went to Fort Rae to investigate the report that the failure of the caribou herds to follow their usual route had caused widespread starvation and disease that killed at least seventy Dogrib Indians.

Similarly, the police noted the comings and goings of white trappers and prospectors in the country, kept close track of the men who left the whaling ships to become trappers and traders, as well as wandering scientists like Vilhjalmur Stefansson and Rudolph M. Anderson, who entered the country by way of the Mackenzie in 1908 and spent four years investigating the aborigines and natural history of the Arctic coast and Victoria Island. The police felt themselves hampered in their work by a lack of authority to compel prospectors and others to report and record their findings; or otherwise to be able (as in the Yukon) to control access or travel about the country. Their work, of course, brought them in contact with dangers everpresent in the untamed north. Each summer saw several deaths and disappearances, particularly drownings, for canoes were easily upset in dangerous waters, and few of the inhabitants could swim. Winters brought other dangers, like the "cabin fever" that resulted in a murder and suicide of two trappers in the Fort Wrigley district in 1911. One constable had the misfortune to deliver a lunatic from Fort Chipewyan to Fort Saskatchewan, which he accomplished successfully in December-January, 1904-5; on his way back, however, he became mentally unbalanced, had to be restrained, and was sent out for six months' hospitalization himself.

The worst disaster of all occurred in the course of the annual Dawson-Fort McPherson patrol, the ostensible purpose for which was to transfer messages and mail between the Yukon division and the Mackenzie sub-district. Five annual winter patrols had been made from Dawson to Fort McPherson without incident, when disaster struck the 1910-11 patrol, the first to be attempted from the Fort McPherson end. Inspector F. J. Fitzgerald, in charge of the party, had been over the route once before but that had been in the opposite direction; furthermore, the party included no competent guide, only two constables and a newly retired ex-constable. The men became lost and spent so much time in difficult weather searching for the correct route that finally it became too late to regain Fort McPherson. Their non-appearance caused a search party to be sent out from Dawson under Corporal W. J. D. Dempster, who found the four men's bodies in two separate locations, starved while apparently attempting to make their way back to Fort McPherson.[37] Thus, through over-confidence or miscalculation, a promising young officer and his three companions died, in a largely needless exercise. The men are buried at Fort McPherson, and Fitzgerald is commemorated by having Smith's Landing renamed after him. One useful result of the tragedy was a decision to set up rest cabins on this and the Fort McPherson-Herschel Island route, something that unaccountably had not been done earlier. But hereafter patrols were taken far more seriously.

An important long patrol in another direction was undertaken in the summer of 1909 by Inspector E. A. Pelletier, with a party of five policemen, to test the route from Great Slave Lake across the Barrens to Chesterfield Inlet and examine the district from a police point of view. Leaving Fort Resolution July 1, 1909, the party followed the familiar explorer's route by way of Lockhart, Hanbury, and Thelon rivers, to be met at Chesterfield Inlet on August 31 by a chartered boat from Division "M". Pelletier's report was that the region could be safely neglected, for there were few signs of native activity and none of whites along the route or its vicinity. Caribou were plentiful, some muskox were noted, and there seemed to be no undue pressure on the game resources of the region. Moreover, the route was quite difficult, particularly in the Hanbury River section, and highly uncomfortable throughout because of the lack of fuel and constant wetness. In short, there was no need for a regular patrol of this route, nor indeed for any police post north of Churchill, provided the division had proper boat facilities with which to patrol the coast and inlets.[38]

But the inspector spoke too soon, for the Arctic tundra region of the Canadian mainland, the great empty triangle with its few bands of nomadic Eskimos, its caribou, muskox, and white foxes, and the hints of mineral wealth derived from J. B. Tyrrell's limited geological reconnaissances of 1893 and 1894, was beginning to attract interest from a number of quarters. The region northeast of Great Bear Lake, explored by Bell and Camsell in 1900 and by Hanbury in 1902, for example, was occupied almost continuously from 1908 by a succession of white men who represented a veritable cross-section of motives and personalities. There were J. C. Melvill, the wealthy hunter and traveller; Jack Hornby, the romantic ill-starred misfit; Stefansson, the ambitious, headline-hunting anthropologist and Anderson, the naturalist, popping in and out; the Douglas party – George M., his brother Lionel, and the geologist August Sandberg – come to see the celebrated copper occurrence on an outing financed by the Douglases' wealthy cousin, the mining executive James Douglas; D'Arcy Arden, the hunter and trapper who settled down and made the area his home; and the Oblate priests, the agreeable Father J. B. Rouvière and the zealous Father G. LeRoux. These were advance agents of a mission to the nomadic Eskimo of the central Arctic, sent by the apostolic vicar of Mackenzie, Bishop G. Breynat, to match the parallel advance of the Keewatin missions northward along Hudson Bay to Chesterfield Inlet.[39]

The possibilities of trouble arising among such a variety of white men were minor by comparison with the explosive situation inherent in the juxtaposition of these same white men with the primitive central Arctic Eskimo, whose behaviour could instantly change through simple misapprehension from friendly co-operation to savage murder. Two incidents, occurring in 1912 and 1913, underscored this fact and demonstrated the need for full police control of the region. In 1912 an American hunter, H. V. Radford, and his companion, T. G. Street, were murdered in the Schultz Lake district by their two Eskimo guides after Radford, who apparently was bad tempered, struck one of the Eskimos with his whip.[40] Later in November, 1913, near the Bloody Falls of the Coppermine River, Fathers Rouvière and LeRoux were murdered by their two Eskimo helpers, Uluksak and Sinnisiak, apparently because LeRoux frightened them by pointing his rifle at them.[41] Long arduous police patrols were required to bring the perpetrators of these acts to justice, and these soon were followed by the opening of new posts and the extension of the regular patrol system in the region. Once again it fell to the Royal Northwest Mounted Police to play the familiar, distinctive role of introducing elements of order, authority, and stability to a remote frontier land suddenly made to undergo a difficult process of cultural change.

CHAPTER 11

Gaining the Arctic Frontier

North of the Canadian mainland lay the ice-shrouded islands of the Arctic
Archipelago, a land that British explorers of the classical age of discovery
and naval officers after 1815 had largely discovered and claimed for Britain.
Would it therefore follow the path of the Northwest, and, with Britain's
blessing, sooner or later become part of Canada? If so, when? Certainly there
was little to arouse Canadian interest in the region while a whole sub-con-
tinent cried out for development. Uncompromisingly Arctic in climate, the
islands' surface was mainly heavily glaciated rocks, treeless tundra of spongy
mosses, lichens, sedges, Arctic heath, with grasses and flowering plants only
in a few favourable localities. Influenced by polar currents and large permanent ice-sheets, the islands were cold and fog-shrouded, with about one
month's navigation possible each year in the ice-choked channels among
the islands. Yet one resource had been attracting white men from outside
to the region each summer after 1719 – the marine wealth, particularly the
Arctic Right, or Bowhead whale, *Balaena mysticetus*, that arrived early
each spring to feed on the minute shrimps, or brit, that lived off the plankton
flourishing so prolifically in those waters. The tons of blubber carried on
each whale's sixty-foot frame were rendered into an oil that was used for
fuel and lighting, as a lubricant, and in several manufactured commodities,
while the baleen, or cartilage plates, with which the whale strained the brit
from the seawater was that highly prized plastic, whalebone.

The brief, dangerous, but highly lucrative voyages were made mainly
from British ports, and were limited to Davis Strait and Baffin Bay. But the
introduction of steam power after 1850 and depletion of the more-accessible
waters caused ships to penetrate farther and farther into the archipelago,
north in Smith Sound, west in Jones Sound, along Lancaster Sound and its
side-channels, or through Hudson Strait to Foxe Basin. These were summer
voyages, taking back their catches for processing in Dundee. New England
whalers, facing a scarcity of whales in the Atlantic, began operating in

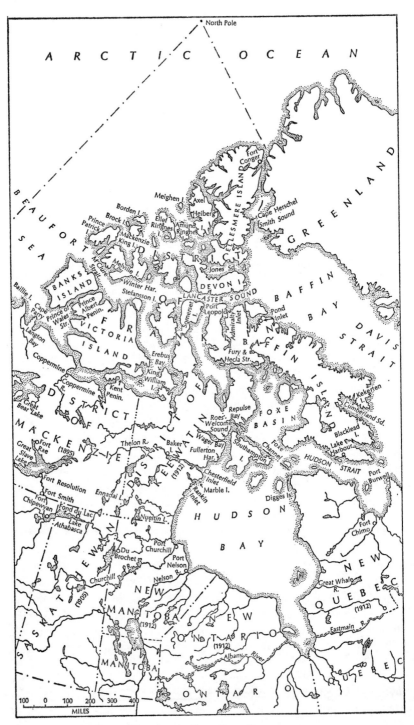

The Arctic Frontier, 1870-1914

the Gulf of St Lawrence, Hudson Bay, and Davis Strait from the mid-century onward. Equipped for lengthy voyages, these sailing vessels usually wintered off Rankin Inlet at Marble Island, or in Cumberland Sound off Baffin Island, so as to secure two fishing seasons from the one voyage; at the same time they could carry on trade with the Eskimos.

The Eskimos came regularly to known wintering centres to exchange skins, hides, whalebone, walrus ivory, dogs, and winter clothing, fresh meat and fish, and to secure work as hunters, boatcrews, and guides. Crewmen sometimes lived with them, while natives were taken on voyages around the region, or even outside. The Eskimos secured firearms and ammunition, harpoons, lances, knives, lines, whaleboats, matches, hard-tack, sugar, tea, tobacco, liquor; and the women, pots, cloth, scissors, needles, thimbles, and looking-glasses. Thus a relationship arose, analogous to that between fur-traders and woodland Indians, in which elements of the primitive civilization were adapted to the opportunities and needs of modern commercial activity. Such casual contacts with the native people of the whaling districts corresponded to the somewhat more regular relationships between the Eskimos of the Hudson Bay and western Arctic with Hudson's Bay Company traders, or the continuing connection between the Eskimos of the coast of Labrador and the missions of the Unitas Fratrem or Moravian Brethren. Through the devoted labours of generations of Moravian missionaries living in their midst since 1752, the Eskimos of Labrador not only had converted to Christianity, but had acquired the industrial and commercial skills to stand on an even footing with the white fishermen and settlers of the region.

Besides the presence of the American whalers in the region, the activities of American explorers from the 1850's onward began to cause uneasiness. Charles Francis Hall spent most of the 1860's among the Eskimos of the country beyond Repulse Bay, while a succession of explorers – Dr E. K. Kane, Dr I. I. Hayes, and Hall – pushed north along the straits between Greenland and Ellesmere Island, seeking to attain the Polar Sea. Since these expeditions were backed by important American geographical societies and were highly publicized as national triumphs, they awakened concern as to their possible consequences. The sovereignty question, in fact, was brought to the attention of the Canadian government in 1874 by the British government, which that year had received two requests for grants of land in the Cumberland Sound area, one from a British subject who wanted to erect temporary buildings in connection with a whale fishery and mining operation, the other from an American navy engineer corps lieutenant, William A. Mintzer, for a twenty-mile-square tract of land on which to mine mica. The latter request put the British government in a quandary; it did not care to assume the government of the region itself, but feared that if it disclaimed jurisdiction, the United States would immediately claim the territory for itself and interfere with future Canadian expansion in that direction. Consequently, the governor general, Lord Dufferin, was asked to ascertain whether Canada was at all interested in taking over British claims to the Arctic islands.[1] The response of the Mackenzie government was an order in council of October 10, 1874, declaring Canada's interest in including the territory within the boundaries of the Dominion.[2]

Negotiations were then begun respecting the form the transfer should take. Lord Carnarvon, the Colonial Secretary, suggested the British Parliament should pass an act providing for the annexation of Arctic territory to Canada, and proposed a boundary that embraced the territory east of the 141st meridian between the mainland and the North Pole, and west of the channels formed by Davis Strait, Baffin Bay, Smith Sound, and Kennedy Channel, plus as much of northwestern Greenland as had been discovered by British subjects, and thence north to the North Pole. The Canadian government accepted these proposals, but urged that the act be delayed until after the next session of the Canadian Parliament, since it was felt the matter should be discussed formally there, as it involved a "charge upon the revenue."[3]

Almost three years passed, and the patience of the Imperial government grew thin, particularly in 1876 when Mintzer, reportedly backed by the United States government, sent an expedition to Cumberland Sound, and shipped out a cargo of graphite and mica. Finally, in the autumn of 1877, Carnarvon urged that some action be taken "to place the title of Canada to these territories upon a clear and unmistakable footing,"[4] and the Canadian government at last was prodded into placing the matter before the next session of Parliament. Undoubtedly, the government had little or no interest in the matter; as Edward Blake observed in a report to the Colonial Office. "the object in annexing these unexplored territories to Canada is, I apprehend, to prevent the United States from claiming them, and not from their likelihood of their proving of any value to Canada."[5]

Finally, on May 3, one week before Parliament was dissolved for the general election of 1878, the correspondence was tabled before the House of Commons and the subject was opened for discussion. David Mills, the Minister of the Interior, introduced resolutions recommending that the offer be accepted, that the boundaries include all the islands between the waters west of Greenland and the 141st meridian, and that the territory come under the full and regular administration of Canada. His explanation stressed the fact that American speculators were interested in the mineral potential of the region. His severest critic was Peter Mitchell, independent Conservative M.P. from New Brunswick and Montreal businessman, who claimed that the government was acting precipitately without giving a proper explanation, and would involve Canada in a large expense for a territory of little value. He contended Canada already had more than enough territory, and that the Imperial government should simply be left to continue its responsibility until Confederation was better able to take on further commitments.[6]

The position of the official opposition was more forthright, Macdonald fully approved of Canada's accepting the territory, for, "Since this proposition was made, they would be false to their duty, as representing this great Dominion and laying the foundations of its future, if they did not at once accept it and ask the Imperial Parliament to pass an Act adjudging to the Dominion this large tract of country."[7] Unfortunately his argument was hardly more patriotic than Mitchell's. The territory, Macdonald said, would cost nothing to administer until settlement arrived, and then it should produce revenue to offset any expenses. If Canada did not wish to take it over, Britain would be entitled to abandon its sovereignty, and the United States would simply occupy the region *gratis*; at the very least Canada ought not to let this happen without securing a decent *quid pro quo*. Hector Langevin struck a stronger patriotic note by asserting that the annexation was a natural outgrowth of Confederation, a small step indeed after all the sacrifices that had been borne thus far, and Parliament must accept the commitment to remain true to the destiny of the nation. On the government side, Mackenzie and Mills spoke up a little more vigorously (though not very authoritatively) regarding the potential value of the country – the Hudson Bay navigation route, the fishery, occurrences of lead and coal on Cumberland Sound and Southampton Island, and the like. The resolutions were passed, and a humble address was forwarded to the Queen.[8]

Now further delay ensued, this time on the side of the Colonial Secretary, Michael Hicks-Beach, who wondered about the necessity for, or desirability of, an act of Parliament to effect the transfer. He suggested that unless Canada intended to form the territory into provinces, a simple Imperial order in council could suffice, and there were good reasons for following this procedure. For one thing, the hydrographer of the admiralty, Frederick Evans, had suggested that the boundaries should be limited to lands actually discovered or claimed by British subjects, and in particular should extend only to $78°30'$ N latitude, the limit of British discoveries in that sector. The Colonial Office had decided it would be best not to try to define the limits of the transfer, but simply hand over Britain's claims, whatever they might be, to Canada.[9]

The Canadian government, back in Macdonald's hands, clearly preferred an Imperial act, the better to commit the British, but the Colonial Secretary was convinced that to place the matter before Parliament would bring diplomatic repercussions: "Questions might be raised in the discussion . . . which might . . . not improbably lead to the abandonment of the project."[10] The Canadian government reluctantly acceded on November 4, 1879, made some suggestions over the wording of the order in council, and proposed the date September 1, 1880. The order was approved by the British government on July 31, and was published in the *Canada Gazette* of October 9, 1880. As there published, it repeated the vague statement of the limits of the grant preferred by the Imperial government:

> . . . all British Territories and Possessions in North America, not already included within the Dominion of Canada, and all Islands adjacent to any of such Territories or Possessions, shall (with the exception of the Colony of Newfoundland and its dependencies) become and be annexed to and form part of the said Dominion of Canada; and become and be subject to the laws for the time being in force in the said Dominion, in so far as such laws may be applicable thereto.[11]

Concern over the possible adverse reaction in the United States undoubtedly was a major reason behind the vague, innocuous statement as to the boundaries, as was the manner in which the transfer was effected. The price of this tactic, however, was that it failed to compel formal recognition by other countries either of the validity of the transfer or of the territorial extent of the Canadian claim, such as a parliamentary enactment would have entailed. At the same time, Canada's failure for many years to take any action that implied effective control over the region meant that its practical status as a *de facto* no man's land was maintained. The Canadian claim was not challenged, for what need was there to challenge it so long as the region was completely open to all comers, and Canada did nothing to obstruct activities there? Nationals of foreign powers were accorded the opportunity to establish and extend their own claims through discovery and occupation if they or their governments desired. The policy of "letting sleeping dogs lie" could well have had dangerous consequences. Fortunately it proved successful, mainly through the forebearance of other countries, notably the United States and Norway. When, in the 1920's, Canada began to take effective steps towards its permanent occupation of the region, the situation with respect to the islands was finally resolved.

In 1904, after an intensive study of the question, the chief astronomer, W. F. King, pointed out that there were other defects in the proceedings besides the failure to challenge international recognition with an act of Parliament. The British order in council itself was open to objection in failing to enumerate the islands claimed or to state how far they extended from the coast of Canada. Canada had compounded the ambiguity by failing to issue its own order in council accepting the transfer. In fact, according to King, under the terms of the British North America Act, Canada's authority to deal with the territory remained in some doubt until 1895, when a British statute regularized the alteration of colonial boundaries by simple orders in council or letters patent.[12]

Indeed, not until after the passage of this Colonial Boundaries Act did the Canadian government, on October 2, 1895, finally issue an order in council constituting the Provisional Districts of Ungava, Franklin, Macken-zie, and Yukon, which "seems to have been the first formal acceptance by Canada of the territories and islands transferred in 1880."[13] Even this action, according to King, was defective. After stating it was dividing *all* the un-organized and unnamed portions of Canada into these provisional districts, the order in council then left a possible gap between those islands included in the Districts of Yukon and Mackenzie as being within three miles of their coast, and those included in the District of Franklin, whose minimal dis-tance from the shore was not specified. This was rectified by a later order in council of December 18, 1897, which gave Yukon and Mackenzie all islands up to twenty miles from their coasts, and the remainder to Franklin.

Whether conscious or not of ambiguity in its power over the islands before 1895, Canada took no overt step until 1897 to proclaim its authority in the region itself. Indeed, after 1880 the only official sign of interest in the Arctic waters was in connection with the navigation of Hudson Bay. In response to western pressure, a House of Commons committee in 1884 enquired into the question of the Hudson Bay route, and Parliament provided money for a three-year study.[14] That summer the young deputy superintendent of the Canadian meteorological service, Lieutenant A. R. Gordon, R.N., in the chartered Newfoundland sealing ship *Neptune*, set down three-man observer teams at eight stations along the route to make meteorological observations, note tides and movements of the ice, and learn all they could about the geography, geology, wildlife, and native inhabi-tants of their areas. They were replaced by other observers brought out in the 1885 ship, who were taken home in 1886. Among the locations used were Port Burwell at the mouth of Hudson Strait, Ashe Inlet, Stupart's Bay, Nottingham Island, and Digges Island.

Since shipping to and from the prairie west was the main purpose of the exercise, the expedition also examined the west coast of Hudson Bay, notably Fort Churchill and the Nelson River estuary. Gordon was very critical of "the so-called Port Nelson," which he felt, because of prevalent fogs and shifting shoals, could not be approached closer than nine miles of the shore, or twenty-eight miles of the proposed rail terminus: "I consider that the estuary of the Nelson River is one of the most dangerous places in the world for shipping to go to . . . the Nelson River is no port, nor would the expenditure of any amount of money make it a desirable place for shipping."[15] Yet, notwithstanding this positive advice, governments persisted in pouring millions into directing the Hudson Bay Railway towards Port Nelson as more approachable from the land, before the line finally was carried, forty-five years later, to Churchill.

Gordon limited the navigation season to three months, from early July to the first week in October, for specially strengthened ships of below 2,000 tons. He mentioned, rightly, the need for careful mapping of coasts and channels, and precautions against high tides, heavy currents, interferences with compasses, and frequent fogs. From the protective point of view, he recommended a closed season on whaling, licence fees on whaling vessels, a regular patrol ship to collect customs duties, and greatly expanded surveys and investigations of the resources of the district.[16]

Meanwhile, exploration activity went on as before in the Arctic Archipelago without any official indication or acknowledgement by Canada. While the "negotiations" with Britain were in progress, a well-equipped British government expedition commanded by Sir G. S. Nares, in the two ships Alert and Discovery, proceeded in 1875 to Ellesmere Island, where the Discovery wintered in Lady Franklin Bay, while the Alert actually got through the strait to the north coast of Ellesmere Island, about 82°30', the northernmost point reached by ship to that time. During the winter of 1875-76 sledge parties from both ships explored the coasts of Greenland and Ellesmere, and travelled north over the polar ice to a new farthest north point of 83°20'. The fine record of exploration and seamanship was marred, however, by three deaths from scurvy. The expedition had failed to adopt any techniques of living off the country and put its entire faith in equipment, methods, and organization fifty years behind the times. Yet excellent work had been done in mapping the farthest extremities of the Arctic Archipelago, and in disproving Hayes' theory of an "open Polar Sea."

More annoying were certain activities of American citizens, among them a long sled journey in 1878-80 of the army lieutenant Frederick Schwatka, accompanied by a newspaper correspondent W. H. Gilder, overland from Marble Island to Repulse Bay and King William Island in search of Franklin expedition relics. A certain Captain H. W. Howgate also attempted to establish a colony near the wintering place of the Discovery, to be used for an American exploration base. He sent in supplies in 1877-78 for the purpose, and even secured an American government grant for the colony in 1880 before the plan fell through because of Howgate's peculations and subsequent disappearance.

The Canadian Arctic became the locale of an ambitious scientific operation, the International Polar Year, three of the fifteen stations established around the world being in Canada – a German base at Kekerten, Cumberland Sound; a British base at Fort Rae on Great Slave Lake; and an American base at Fort Conger on central Ellesmere Island, the locale of Howgate's erstwhile colony. All stations were to conduct elaborate environmental studies as well as meteorological observations at timed intervals. The Germans supplemented their work at Kekerten by similar readings from the Moravian mission of Nain, Labrador, by Dr C. Koch, while the noted anthropologist Franz Boas arrived at Kekerten in the relief ship of 1883, took over the facilities, and began a notable two-year study of the geography and Eskimo inhabitants of southern Baffin Island. The Fort Conger party, a military unit under Lieutenant A. W. Greely, could not resist trying to explore the interior of Ellesmere Island and the west coast of Greenland, in case something could be made of it. The expedition experienced great tragedy when relief expeditions failed to make contact with the men in 1883 and 1884 through incompetence and greed. Only seven of the original twenty-eight men survived to be eventually rescued. They brought back a gory tale of insubordination, heroism, starvation, execution, and cannibalism, but the precious records had been saved.

Meanwhile, the whaling industry continued, encouraged by very high prices for whalebone; these more than offset the declines in the value of whale oil, as petroleum products began to displace it from many of its uses. The price of whalebone reached the height of $4.75 a pound in 1883, and in the next twenty-five years seldom fell below $4.00 per pound. A full-grown whale, carrying 2,000 pounds of baleen in its jaw, became a very valuable quarry indeed. However, it was too late for the whale fishery of the eastern Arctic, where whales became very scarce after 1880. Scottish whalers now usually made an early spring seal-hunting voyage from St John's before proceeding north to the whale fishery. They also began hunting beluga or white whales, walrus, narwhals, seals, and polar bears for their skins, furs, oil, or tusks, and did some shore trading for muskox robes and white fox furs. From about 1890, copying the Americans, they established shore stations to trade with the Eskimos and to operate an early summer whale fishery. Thus, imperceptibly, the whaling industry of the eastern Arctic was being transformed into a trading operation.

The main development, though, was the expansion of the American whale fishery, based on the Pacific whaling fleet, to the waters off the northwest coast of Canada. Since the 1850's these vessels had been operating north of Bering Strait, but they were barred from going east beyond Point Barrow by the constant danger of being trapped in the polar ice-pack which the wind often jams against the north coast of Alaska. At least two fleets had been caught and destroyed there in 1871 and 1876, and government relief stations had been opened along the north coast of Alaska. In 1889, whalers learned that the water opened earlier off the mouth of the Mackenzie River than elsewhere, making for a better, longer whaling season. An ideal winter harbour. Pauline Cove, was discovered on Herschel Island; opening on the south, it was protected against heavy wave or ice action, and it was deep and capacious enough to hold several ships. Two ships went in from San Francisco in 1890 to winter there, and fished successfully in the Beaufort Sea off Baillie Island. The upshot was that four vessels wintered at Herschel Island in 1892, seven in 1893, fifteen in 1894, and eleven in 1895, and most made good returns.

The coming of so many ships to winter in the same vicinity had very adverse effects on the resources and the native inhabitants of the region. The coasts were scoured for miles around, clearing out the driftwood, and caribou were hunted over long distances inland. Runaway crew members intimidated and terrorized the Loucheux of the interior. By equipping the Eskimos with rifles and encouraging them to hunt and trap, the whalers accelerated the exhaustion of the limited wildlife resources of the region. The Eskimos grew accustomed to using white men's goods and utensils and lost some of their traditional skills for living off the land, so difficulties ensued when whalers ceased visiting their localities. The whalers depleted the whales and beluga, and in the east the walrus and muskox as well, leaving the Eskimos that much poorer an environment in which to survive.

Furthermore, the whalers unwittingly brought diseases to which the less-acclimatized Eskimos quickly succumbed. In the western Arctic, virtually all the original Eskimos of the Mackenzie district were killed off by measles and other diseases around 1900, to be replaced by other Eskimos from Alaska, introduced by the whalers to a depopulated land. In similar fashion, in Hudson Bay the Stone Age inhabitants of Southampton Island, the Sadlermiut, were said to have died off by 1903 from starvation and diseases, which followed the arrival of Eskimos from Big Island in Hudson Strait in connection with Scottish whaling operations.

What concerned the outside world, however, were reports of the carryings-on by whaling personnel at Herschel Island. Some captains kept close control over liquor on their ships, and agreed to co-operate readily with efforts "to suspend the liquor traffic, directly or indirectly as it relates to natives belonging to the vicinity of Malcolm River and to the eastward."[17] However, the crews sometimes secured liquor and supplied it to the natives on their own account. Worse still were stories of immorality spread by some missionaries, one of whom called Herschel Island "the world's last jumping-off place . . . where no law existed and no writs ran, a paradise of those who reject all restraint upon appetite and all responsibility for conduct; when a dozen ships and five or six hundred men of their crews wintered here, and scoured the coasts for Eskimo women. I do not think it extravagant to say that the scenes of riotous drunkenness and lust which this island has witnessed have probably rarely been surpassed."[18] Another reported that on his first visit to the island in 1895, many of the captains "had Eskimo women they had hired or captured from the Alaskan coast, but the petty officers depended on local women and girls for their pleasure. Intoxicants was one of the means of enticement. When girls were not obtainable, wives were enticed away from their husbands, or men induced to rent out their wives."[19] Another sort of complaint was heard from Winnipeg; Lieutenant-Governor Schultz of Keewatin complained that whalers in Hudson Bay were exhausting the whaling grounds and, by their trade with the Eskimos, were "violating the revenue laws of Canada, and injuring the trade of a Canadian-English company who traded with goods upon which duties had been paid."[20] Who could have believed that Dr Schultz would someday become concerned for the trade of the Hudson's Bay Company?

Nationalistic-minded Canadians began pouring out their feelings of outrage to the government in Ottawa. Inspector Constantine reported from the Yukon on the situation in the autumn of 1896, and called for police action to control the situation around the mouth of the Mackenzie:

> This liquor is sold or traded to the natives for furs, walrus ivory bone and their young girls who are purchased by the officers of the ships for their own foul purposes. . . .
> The presence of an armed government vessel, with a strong and disciplined crew, would do much good service in putting an end to the traffic in liquor to the natives as well as protecting the revenue, and more especially the fisheries which must be valuable or so many ships would not be in these waters.[21]

II

The new Liberal government of Sir Wilfrid Laurier took a first overt step to assert Canadian sovereignty over the Arctic islands in the summer of 1897, when it sent an expedition under William Wakeham, the veteran commander of the Gulf fisheries patrol, to Hudson Bay and Baffin Island. In the leased Newfoundland whaler *Diana*, Wakeham sailed in June, 1897, to check the duration of the shipping season and navigation conditions in Hudson Bay, which now were assuming greater importance in view of the rise of western Canadian wheat exports. His findings were similar to Gordon's, though he extended the shipping season by a fortnight, to mid-October. Afterwards Wakeham proceeded to Cumberland Sound, where he reported that whaling had declined significantly and would soon be a thing of the past. In a ceremony at Kekerten Island, the Scottish whalers' base, he formally proclaimed Canada's authority over Baffin Island and the Arctic islands generally:

Tuesday, 17th August. – Landed and hoisted the Union Jack in presence of the agent, a number of our own officers and crew, and the Esquimaux, formally declaring in their presence that the flag was hoisted as an evidence that Baffin's Land with all the territories, islands and dependencies adjacent to it were now, as they always had been since their first discovery and occupation, under the exclusive sovereignty of Great Britain. Fog all day.[22]

Unfortunately, Wakeham's proclamation coincided with the height of the Arctic exploration drive farther north from Ellesmere and other islands, which culminated in Robert E. Peary's much-publicized attainment of the North Pole in 1909. More serious from the national point of view, however, was the sixteen-man Sverdrup expedition, which spent five seasons, 1898-1902, exploring Ellesmere Island and new land to the west. That this Norwegian party worked in the Arctic Archipelago at all was somewhat accidental; they had planned to explore Greenland but had been warned off by Peary, jealous of any possible encroachment on his plans to attain the North Pole. Sverdrup determined to explore west instead.

Using Nansen's drift ship *Fram* as a stationary base, Sverdrup moored it first on the east coast of Ellesmere Island, then at two locations on the south coast. From the ship, parties of three or four men were sent exploring, particularly to districts not previously recorded or well known. Living off the country during these sledge trips, they examined and reported on all aspects of the region. Besides exploring the southern and western parts of Ellesmere, they discovered several islands farther west – notably Axel Heiberg, Amund and Ellef Ringnes islands, and the northern coast of Devon Island – mapping in all some 1,750 miles of coast and an area of about 100,000 square miles. Interested in adding to geographical and scientific knowledge rather than in self-glorification, Otto Sverdrup produced a sober, two-volume account of his explorations, *New Land*. In the hope that his expedition's discoveries would establish a national claim, he notified his sovereign, King Oscar II of Sweden, of them, apparently expecting the government to go ahead with the diplomatic steps. The Swedish government was not interested, so Sverdrup renewed his application to the new government of Norway when that kingdom was separated from Sweden in 1905. Again, however, he found little disposition to follow up his claims to Arctic territory.

The other famous explorers of the decade – Amundsen, Cook, and Peary – did not offer so much challenge to Canadian sovereignty, though Peary annoyed some Canadians by his cavalier way of pre-empting Ellesmere Island and its resources for the broad-based, wide-ranging logistical operations that underlay his dramatic solo dashes over the polar ice. Ellesmere Island was his base on his 1898, 1905, and 1908 expeditions; from Fort Conger

Peary explored west to the still-undiscovered Axel Heiberg Land, and he completed the map of the north coast of Ellesmere. Off to the northwest, he reported sighting new land, which he named Crocker Land after one of his patrons. He had Ellesmere hunted pretty thoroughly by his men for muskox and caribou to feed and clothe the large parties – up to ten whites, fifty Eskimos, and two hundred dogs – he considered essential to achieve his goal. Furthermore, since he depleted northern Greenland even more, the Eskimos of that region were compelled for years to resort to Canadian territory for their own needs. Canadian agents who examined the country – Low in 1904, Bernier in 1910 – complained about the abuse of Canadian territory by these unauthorized visitors. Low commented on the old tin cans, empty boxes, putrid walrus blubber, and the five Eskimos buried on a rocky hill, left by the Peary expedition at Payer Harbour. He acknowledged that Peary's effort was plucky and daring, but "the waste of energy, life and money in a useless and probably unsuccessful attempt to reach the pole can only be deplored, as no additional scientific knowledge is likely to be gained by this achievement."[23]

Annoyance, envy, anger – these were the reactions of Canadians, even though they admired the explorers' courage. One lone Canadian who caught the infection, and from 1898 strove to promote the exploration of the Canadian Arctic by and for Canada, was the remarkable, single-minded, French Canadian, the veteran Captain J. E. Bernier. His plan was to outfit a ship (along the lines perfected by Nansen) to drift around in the polar ice-pack until it came within a reasonable distance of the Pole. The expedition would then send a party in sleds for a quick assault over the ice to the Pole and back again to the ship.

For three years Bernier campaigned vigorously for funds and for a government grant of a ship, gaining the support of patrons like Lord Strathcona and Governor General Minto, and of geographical and scientific societies in Canada and abroad. Thousands of signatures were secured on the 3,000 subscription lists circulated across Canada, while 113 M.P.'s signed a petition to Laurier to the effect that "They feel anxious that Canada should have the credit and advertisement that would result from such an expedition under Canadian auspices."[24] Laurier, despite private misgivings, was fairly overwhelmed by the energetic, persistent Bernier, whose supporters claimed to have raised $70,000 in public subscriptions by mid-1901. Eventually, Bernier's perseverance was rewarded. Parliament voted $200,000 for Arctic exploration, with which Bernier purchased and refitted the German Arctic ship *Gauss*, renamed *Arctic*.

In the meantime, pressure began to mount for a Canadian presence in the Arctic islands. The North-West Mounted Police, who normally would be in the lead, were preoccupied with the Klondike gold rush and afterwards with the Boer War, but the annual reports of Commissioner A. B. Perry continued to call for intervention; that of 1901 referred to "Tyranny over the Indians, debauching of the Indian women, illegal trading, and lawlessness among themselves demand the assertion of our laws. . . . The cost of carrying law and order into the Arctic regions may cause hesitation, but when our territory is being violated and our people oppressed, cost should be the last consideration."[25]

Furthermore, other government agencies were anxious to examine and explore the Arctic islands as part of their regular function. The Geological Survey, for example, wanted to map and study the geology, while its museum staff desired specimens of the fauna, flora, and artifacts from the region. Morover, anthropological and ethnological interest in the Eskimo was growing. Fisheries and the meteorological service were other agencies of government with similar concerns. Their agents could be transported into the region by a government ship, even by the whaling ships; once in the country they could be supplied by this last means, as Anglican mission stations of the Reverend E. J. Peck at Blacklead Island and Lake Harbour were supplied.

By 1903 the pressure was becoming very strong, particularly in view of the unfavourable turn the Alaska Boundary arbitration had taken. Resentment against the United States was coupled with concern for Canada's control over Hudson Bay and the Arctic islands, and fears were expressed that the activities of American whalers and explorers could lead to new territorial claims being promulgated by the United States, and to Canada's encirclement on the north. On May 12, 1903, W. F. Maclean, Conservative M.P., York South, urged the government to assert its supremacy over Hudson Bay and rename it the "Canadian Sea."[26] Reports began to circulate in American and Canadian newspapers and magazines over the problem of Hudson Bay, grossly exaggerating the importance of the whale fisheries. Senator Pascal Poirier, on October 20, 1903, perhaps in league with Bernier, urged sending a Canadian expedition to try to attain the North Pole so as to head off undesirable activities of American citizens, and called for the acquisition of Greenland from Denmark. Laurier outlined his concern over Canadian sovereignty in the Arctic, as well as his own gradualist plan of action, in a letter of October 29, 1903, to Senator W. C. Edwards. That year expeditions had gone to Hudson Bay and to the mouth of the Mackenzie River to establish police posts there and "quietly assume jurisdiction in all directions." Next year, he told Edwards, these would be followed by "a cruiser to patrol the waters and plant our flag at every point." Then, "When we have covered the whole ground and have men stationed everywhere," it would be time to issue the proclamation claiming jurisdiction over the whole of Canada's northern territory.[27]

Indeed, the instructions to Superintendent J. D. Moodie, the head of the six-man police force going to Hudson Bay in the *Neptune* in 1903, had stressed this side of his activity:

> The Government of Canada having decided that the time has arrived when some system of supervision and control should be established over the coast and islands in the northern part of the Dominion, a vessel has been selected and is now being equipped for the purpose of patrolling, exploring, and establishing the authority of the Government of Canada in the waters and islands of Hudson bay, and the north thereof.
>
> In addition to the crew, the vessel will carry representatives of the Geological Survey, the Survey Branch of the Department of the Interior, the Department of Marine and Fisheries, the Royal Northwest Mounted Police and other departments of the public service. . . .
>
> It is not the wish of the Government that any harsh or hurried enforcement of the laws of Canada shall be made. Your first duty will be to impress upon the captains of whaling and trading vessels, and the natives, the fact that after considerable notice and warning the laws will be enforced as in other parts of Canada.[28]

The *Neptune* expedition, captained by S. W. Bartlett, was commanded by A. P. Low of the Geological Survey, for its role was as much scientific as national, if not more so. First the vessel proceeded to Cumberland Sound to inspect the mission and whaling stations; then it returned to the northwest corner of Hudson Bay, the whaling ground of Foxe Basin and Roe's Welcome, to winter. The police post was established near the wintering place of the lone American whaling vessel of the year, Captain George Comer's ancient whaler *Era*. In the following summer, the *Neptune* recrossed to Port Burwell for more supplies, then proceeded on a northern voyage through Baffin Bay all the way to Cape Herschel on Ellesmere Island, where the expedition landed, raised the Canadian flag, read a document taking formal possession of the island for Canada, then deposited it in a cairn built for the purpose. On the return journey the ship voyaged 300 miles west along Lancaster Sound, first following the north side of the channel to Beechey Island, Franklin's wintering place, then returning along the south side of the sound to Port Leopold, where possession of Somerset Island was proclaimed in a similar flag-raising ceremony. The *Neptune* returned to Port Burwell, checking all the establishments on Baffin Island en route, made a second quick trip to the west coast of Hudson Bay to inspect the activities of the whaling ship and relieve the police post at Fullerton Harbour, and then, at last, made its way back to Halifax.

Besides establishing the first police detachment in northern Hudson Bay, inspecting whaling, mining, and exploring activities in the region, and proclaiming Canada's sovereignty, the expedition returned with much useful information on the condition of the Eskimos, and the first comprehensive account of the geological configuration of a vast triangle of territory bounded by Port Burwell, Cape Herschel, and Fullerton Harbour, 1,200 miles a side. Low had traced the coasts of Southampton Island and other little-known sections, and gathered useful information regarding ice and navigation conditions. An important recommendation was the selection of Port Burwell, off the northernmost tip of Labrador, as the customs station and port of entry for all shipping proceeding to and from Hudson Strait and bay. A not inconsiderable result of the expedition was Low's book, *The Cruise of the Neptune, 1903-4*, which gave Canadians a full, accurate account of the little-known reaches of their country and of activities going on there, from a Canadian point of view.

As the *Neptune* was leaving the north, it met at Port Burwell the newly outfitted *Arctic*, commanded by Captain J. E. Bernier, which was bringing Moodie back to Fullerton and going to winter there (1904-5), in continuation of the program enunciated by Laurier. To Bernier's intense disappointment, he was not to be permitted to go exploring in Canada's name, but only to carry out a humdrum task of patrolling. His time would come.

Meanwhile, in Ottawa, the government was proceeding with its cautious program. For advice as to the situation, it turned to W. F. King for his report of January 23, 1904, with supplementary memorandum of May 7, 1904. The conclusion, in the first report, was that "Canada's title to some at least of the northern islands is imperfect. It may possibly be best perfected by exercise of jurisdiction where any settlements exist."[29] In the supplementary memorandum, King pointed out that British explorers, acting under official instructions to take possession in the name of the Crown, had discovered most of the Arctic coasts and islands, whereas explorations by American and other nationals had neither been undertaken with such official sanction nor been followed by the ratification of their claims by their parent governments. He expressed greater concern over the occupation of parts of the territory by nationals of other lands, particularly Americans, observing that "Though these are private adventurers, unauthorized by their government, the fact of their presence indicates the advisability of action by the Government of Canada towards asserting unequivocally their jurisdiction in these regions."[30]

He summarized the Canadian position with respect to each of seven regions regarding exploration, proclamation of possession and subsequent ratification, and occupation, the last being, in his opinion, the most important and probably ultimate determinant of sovereignty. Here Canada was in the fortunate position that "Though occupation may not have been sufficient to perfect the inchoate title by discovery, at least no opposing occupation, of a character recognized by international law as effectual, has taken place."[31] King asserted that the waters as well as the land of the northern archipelago were under Canadian jurisdiction, since navigation could only proceed with the probability that the vessels would have to winter somewhere in the region, which would require permission of the governing authority. Hudson Bay and strait were Canadian territory from the fact that Britain had asserted and never relinquished its title to them, a fact which France and later the United States had recognized by treaty. King's statement respecting territorial waters in the summary was categorical: "In accordance with accepted principles of international law, the waters of the northern archipelago and of Hudson bay and strait are to be considered territorial."[32]

The official action regarding the territorial claim to Hudson Bay came in 1906 in the form of an amendment to the Fisheries Act imposing a licence fee of $50 on every boat whaling in Hudson Bay and other waters north of 55°. The sting came in a phrase of the amendment:

> . . . and, inasmuch as Hudson Bay is wholly territorial water of Canada, the requirements of this section as to licensing, and as to the fee payable therefor, shall apply to every vessel or boat engaged in the whale fishery or hunting whales in any part of the waters of Hudson Bay, whether such vessel or boat belongs to Canada, or is registered or is outfitted in, or commences her voyage from, any other British or foreign country.[33]

During the debate, the Minister of Marine and Fisheries, L. P. Brodeur, asserted: "We claim Hudson bay as Canadian territory." But when questioned, "Has that been accepted by the United States?" he was forced to evade: "I am not in a position to inform my hon. friend as to that."[34] The British government, which, in 1904, had asked for a statement of Canada's claims in connection with the *Neptune* expedition and had received King's memorandum in reply, was similarly concerned. Ottawa was cabled for a copy of the new act and any further data or arguments explaining the Canadian government's views regarding Hudson Bay, so "we may be in a position to return an early and authoritative answer to the representations which United States Government in view of the long period during which their vessels have whaled in Bay without interference, may be expected to make."[35] Eventually the Colonial Office received a statement which it did not consider very convincing; however, the Fisheries Act amendment was not disallowed. No immediate protest ensued and the licences were collected without difficulty, though in the summer of 1910 a press report appeared to the effect that the United States government had instructed its citizens engaged in the whaling industry to disregard the demand for licences, assuring them protection if they took such action. Later, in 1912 and 1913, an

American authority, T. W. Balch, published two articles in an American law journal arguing that "the Hudsonian Sea is a great open sea."

No resistance was encountered in the Arctic by Bernier, who sallied forth in the *Arctic* from Quebec on July 28, 1906, armed with the new authority as a fisheries officer, on the first of three major voyages as upholder of Canada's Arctic sovereignty. He proceeded to Lancaster Sound, stopping at Pond Inlet, then sailed westward as far as Melville Island. He landed at fifteen places on various islands to take formal possession in the name of Canada, usually by raising the flag, reading a formal proclamation, depositing the document in a cairn, and advising the natives they were Canadians subject to Canadian law and the whalers that they must take out licences and pay customs duties on goods traded in Canada. He collected ten licence fees in his two seasons in the north. Before he returned to Pond Inlet to winter in September, 1906, Bernier sent off a report that he had taken possession "of all the Parry Archipelago Islands," including not merely those on which he had landed, but also islands north and west of Melville Island, like Prince Patrick, Eglinton, and Emerald islands, which were included in his proclamation on Melville Island.[36]

While Bernier was wintering at Pond Inlet, in Ottawa his ally, Senator Poirier, introduced a motion in the Senate on February 20, 1907, "That it be resolved that the Senate is of opinion that the time has come for Canada to make a formal declaration of possession of the lands and islands situated in the north of the Dominion, and extending to the north pole."[37] In defending his reference to the sector principle, he dilated on the potential value of the Arctic lands in the light of the northward march of civilization, Canada's need to avoid encirclement by the United States, and the convenience of the proposal as a solution for international problems; he mentioned as well Canada's rights to the territory as the successor of Britain and France. Though the resolution was not adopted, it guided Bernier's actions on his next voyage, which departed Quebec on July 28, 1908, at the height of the festivities inspired by the tercentenary of the founding of the city and to salutes from a British naval squadron in the harbour.

Since the objective this time was the western portion of the archipelago, Bernier sailed directly for Melville Island. He found the waters so completely free of ice, he reported, ". . . we were then about half-way through McClure strait, and if our instructions had included making of the Northwest passage, I feel confident that it could have been made."[38] Instead, however, he wintered in the area, exploring over the ice to Banks and Victoria islands, and observing ice and navigation conditions of McClure and Prince of Wales straits. On Dominion Day, 1909, reflecting the patriotic mood of the day, Bernier held a ceremonial unveiling of a tablet proclaiming Canadian sovereignty over the whole archipelago on the sector principle:

This Memorial,
is
Erected today to Commemorate
The taking possession for the
"DOMINION OF CANADA,"
of the whole
"ARCTIC ARCHIPELAGO,"
Lying to the north of America
from long. 60° w. to 141° w.
up to latitude 90° n.
Winter Hbr. Melville Island
C.G.S. Arctic. July 1st, 1909.
J. E. Bernier. Commander.[39]

On the return east in 1909, Bernier collected fisheries licences from the whaling ships around Baffin Island, as well as a $50 licence from the sportsman-hunter Harry Whitney, returning from a shooting expedition on Ellesmere Island. Before arriving in Quebec on October 5, 1909, the *Arctic* also made a short trip into Hudson Strait to look into navigation conditions.

Fully convinced that the truly practicable Northwest Passage route lay through McClure Strait, Bernier suggested three wintering depots should be established for safety west of Baffin Bay; besides which ships in an emergency could rely on the considerable food resources of Melville Island. He was also very apprehensive over the prospects of the Eskimo population and the considerable depletion of game resources of the Arctic islands by American explorers and hunters. During the winter of 1909-10 he wrote to Laurier to urge the passage of legislation against this threat: "Now that we have taken possession of our Arctic Archipelago, it might be advisable at this session of Parliament to pass a game law regulating hunting in this region. I hope this will be done and I will be authorized to enforce it when I go north this June."[40] Laurier agreed with the suggestion, but regretted it was too late to secure the legislation during that session of Parliament.

On his next voyage in 1910-11, Bernier had the objective of traversing the Northwest Passage if conditions were suitable, besides his usual purposes of enforcing fisheries regulations and studying the country. Hence, he proceeded to Melville Island and attempted to cross by way of McClure Strait. Frustrated this year by very heavy ice, he next tried to pass by way of Prince of Wales Strait, with the same result. Reluctantly, therefore, he made his way back to a winter location at Arctic Harbour (now Arctic Bay) near the west end of Baffin Island, where the expedition could at least explore and survey an almost completely unknown district around

Admiralty Inlet and south to Fury and Hecla Strait. After the usual task of locating and licensing vessels engaged in the whale fishery along Baffin Island, the *Arctic* returned to Quebec on September 25, 1911. In his three voyages Bernier greatly increased Canadians' knowledge of, and interest in, the Arctic islands. The presence of his ship and crew among the islands in three winters and their calls virtually every summer to points like Pond Inlet did much to bring home the fact of Canadian sovereignty in the whaling areas, though, significantly, Bernier did not venture north to Ellesmere, contemporaneously the locale of Peary's final, successful assault on the pole. Taken in conjunction with the increased surveillance of the coastline of mainland Canada by the new police detachments, Bernier's trips formed part of a considerable extension of Canadian authority.

III

Following the visit of the *Neptune* to Hudson Bay in 1903-4 and the establishment of Division "M" at Fullerton Harbour and later at Fort Churchill, police patrols were made along the coast to Wager Bay or Lyon Inlet in the north, or inland up Chesterfield Inlet to Baker Lake, usually to inspect a wintering vessel or contact the Eskimo groups. Moodie's proposal for a series of posts ringing the bay was ignored, and police activity was confined to the west coast of Hudson Bay north of York Factory. Being few in number and lacking their own ship, the police found it difficult to manage even this thousand-mile district effectively or to collect licences and customs duties from the foreign vessels, though the whalers made a show of complying whenever the police located them. There was a perennial dispute between police and captains as to what constituted dutiable goods; many of the imported goods, particularly tobacco, were given away as gratuities for services rendered, not traded at all – or so the masters argued. Moodie, like Low, urged that the whole customs administration should be systematized by compelling all ships to clear customs at Port Burwell on their way in or out of the country.

A strong concern of Moodie's was to protect the interests of the natives. He urged that whaling be halted for a period of years to enable the whales to recover, and that regulations be brought into effect compelling walrus-hunters to harpoon the animals before shooting them, to prevent the carcasses sinking and becoming lost and the kills wasted. He was particularly concerned about the large-scale trade in muskox skins, and urged that the muskox be protected in the same manner as the bison, that is, by prohibiting the sale of muskox skins or their being in the possession of any person other than a native. He imposed a ban on the export of muskox skins on

November 8, 1903, but apparently with limited success, since reports continued to come in of large numbers of skins being exported, while as late as 1908 a patrol from Fullerton to Wager Bay caught two of Comer's Eskimos redhanded with the proceeds of a recent hunt. He also felt the Eskimos were badly exploited by the traders, and that the traders, by virtue of their position, secured a dangerous ascendancy over them. Instead, he suggested, the police might take a leaf from the Greenland administration's book, where all trade was in the hands of governmental district administrators and no private trade with the natives was permitted except under special licence. This was far too daring a suggestion, and the situation had to resolve itself naturally by the eventual replacement of American and Scottish whalers by regular land-based fur-trading concerns, that could be effectively controlled on the ground or through their headquarters.

Efforts to regulate the more active whaling industry in the western Arctic fell to the northernmost district of Division "G", which Superintendent Constantine inaugurated in 1903 when he went down the Mackenzie to view for himself the situation at Herschel Island. Thereafter, as long as whaling continued, a detachment either was stationed on the island or patrolled it frequently from Fort McPherson. Herschel made a good port of entry since it lay athwart the way into, or out of, the country, but police visits did not always coincide with the coming or going of the ships, so they did not always collect the full customs duties owing on the whalers' trade in Canada. Moreover, the captains rarely took policemen with them farther east to the whaling grounds or the new wintering and trading centres along the coast, where they might have been in a position to see more of what actually went on.

As was the case in Hudson Bay, the captains made no open resistance to the payment of duties on goods they traded while in Canadian territory, and tried to satisfy the police as to their readiness to co-operate in keeping liquor out of the hands of natives, though missionaries and others often reported misconduct as soon as the police were out of the way. For their part, the police found little to complain of when they were at Herschel Island, and considered it an orderly station, whatever it might have been in years past. The apparent orderliness and co-operation may have owed something to a rapport established between the police and the captains during the hard winter of 1905-6, when the ships were unable to proceed outside and were forced to spend an involuntary winter at Herschel. At that time, the police headed off serious quarrels among the captains and protected them against their own mutinous crews. Perhaps the police, too, grew more flexible and "reasonable" on the contentious question of Eskimo-white liaisons, which were impossible to conceal. From the outset Sergeant F. J. Fitzgerald ridiculed the lurid descriptions of rampant sin when he observed the fifteen rude huts "of any old boards or packing cases, and very heavily covered with sods" which were the site of the excesses.[41] Inspector D. M. Howard, who was at Herschel in 1905-6, made excuses – "Of course their ways are not our ways" – and expressed himself as unable to reconcile the tales of Eskimos being debauched or demoralized with "the eager manner with which the Esquimaux greets the arrival of the ships and go on board shaking hands with every one they meet. If the women were ill-treated and abused as the papers say, they would surely keep away from the ships after one lesson."[42] Inspector G. L. Jennings, who was there in 1910, pictured the relationship as a regular arrangement, in which the sailors took good care of their women and children to the point of seeing the youngsters placed in schools in Alaska and the Pacific states. He did suggest, however, that these illicit unions should be discouraged in favour of proper marriages, which would provide better protection for the women and children. Many such attachments developed into lifelong unions, and a mixed society began to grow up along the western Arctic coast.

Mostly, though, the orderliness reflected the fact that Herschel Island was no longer the main centre of whaling activity or of the first, critical stages of Eskimo-white contact. When Constantine arrived at Herschel, he was told, "I was six years too late,"[43] for most whalers already wintered at Baillie Island, three hundred miles east of Herschel, or at Langton Bay, a hundred miles even farther east. The trend was still more in that direction, for in the summer of 1907 one whaling ship cruised up Prince of Wales Strait to within sight of Prince Albert Land, where a gasoline schooner, *Olga*, captained by Charles Klengenberg, was conducting a fur trade among the primitive Copper Eskimos.

Thus the years after 1903 saw an increased surveillance being exercised over the activities of Americans and other whites in the Canadian Arctic, in response to a growing demand for action on the part of the Canadian public, coupled with the greater capability of the Dominion government and its agencies to mount such operations, in part, using (and paying for) facilities provided by the objects of investigation themselves. Though their numbers were ridiculously small in view of the vast area they were intended to control, the mere presence of police and fisheries officers sufficed to demonstrate that the territory was under Canadian law, and to establish Canadian standards, even if they were honoured more in the breach than the observance.

Moreover, although the power of such small police forces was limited in practice, time was on their side, for the whaling industry was coming to an end, and being succeeded by a fur-trading industry that could be more easily and readily supervised. When Low visited Cumberland Sound, doubt was expressed whether the Scottish company could continue long in operation, and he worried that closing the stations might work hardship on the Eskimos who had come to depend on the white man's goods and employment. By 1910 the Scottish whaling and walrus-hunting station at Repulse Bay had been closed, and the other Scottish interest in the region soon followed. A lone American whaling vessel, making three-year voyages in an effort to securing a paying catch, finally gave up the effort; Comer's successor, returning in the A. T. *Gifford* in 1913, planned, instead, to concentrate on the fur trade at Fullerton. The place of the whalers was being taken after 1911 by the Hudson's Bay Company, Revillon Frères, and smaller traders, who began moving north to open new posts around the bay area and on Baffin Island.

The whaling industry still was being profitably conducted in the west so far as paying catches were concerned, when a sudden, catastrophic drop in the price of whalebone occurred in 1908. Thereafter only an occasional whaling voyage was made, and most of the ships were laid up, their masters either retiring or turning to other work. Instead, a new system began to emerge, whereby vessels from San Francisco (sometimes former whaling ships) sailed to Herschel Island to deposit supplies for, and collect country produce from, operators of yachts and gasoline schooners who engaged primarily in the fur trade with the Eskimos of the central Arctic. Former whalers like Fritz Wolki or Klengenberg carried on as traders, living among the Eskimos and rearing families there, while other ex-whaling officers, like C. T. Pederson, continued to come and go each year between San Francisco and Herschel Island, supplying these new traders as well as the few miners, missionaries and police. Here, as in the east, the disappearance of the whaling industry was followed by the entrance of major fur-trading companies, notably the Hudson's Bay Company and Northern Trading Company, which established posts in the Mackenzie delta near Aklavik in 1912 and 1913. The former company made preparations to develop a string of posts east along the coast supplied by ship from Vancouver to furnish the wants of Eskimos, who had been transformed through their contacts with the whalers into proper clients for the fur trade.

The change in government in Ottawa in the autumn of 1911 did not stop the Dominion's efforts to extend Canadian authority over the Arctic islands, though the new government followed a different approach and turned its attention to a different part of the region. The system of ceremonial flag-waving and licence-collecting expeditions was discontinued, despite Bernier's plea to be allowed to continue patrols with the *Arctic*, performing his duties as commander, fishery officer, game guardian, and customs collector on a contract basis for five years at $45,000 per annum. His offer was rejected; and though Bernier did return to the Arctic in 1912 and subsequent years, it was on private trading ventures to Baffin Island.

In 1922, under a new Liberal government with a program of establishing permanent bases in the eastern Arctic, the now-elderly Bernier resumed command of the *Arctic* and conducted the first four voyages of the annual Eastern Arctic Patrol. Following the last northern trip of the *Arctic* in 1925, Bernier made other voyages to Hudson Bay, his last in 1929, before dying in 1934.[44]

Government interest after 1911, now that the situation in Hudson Bay and the eastern Arctic was relatively stable, was diverted to the western Arctic, where considerable activity by American whalers, fur-traders, and prospectors was still under way, and furthermore, keen scientific interest was being displayed in the remaining primitive Eskimo bands not yet completely transformed by contact with the white man. The Geological Survey, under its dynamic young director R. W. Brock, was keenly interested in developing the anthropological and ethnological sides of its museum activity, as well as pushing geological mapping and studies beyond their present northerly limit of Great Bear Lake. Besides, large parts of major islands, like Victoria, Banks, and Melville, still were unexplored and there was a strong possibility of discovering other lands in the Beaufort Sea east of the 141st meridian. It would be intolerable for a proud, advanced country like Canada if such discoveries were made by foreigners, as the Sverdrup expedition had been able to do in a time when Canada was not so concerned over its northern responsibilities.

An opportunity arose in 1913 when the young Canadian-born, American-reared ethnologist Vilhjalmur Stefansson approached the government for financial support to supplement grants he had already secured from the American Museum of Natural History and from the National Geographic Society for an ambitious program of studying the Eskimos of the central Arctic (particularly a lighter-complexioned group he claimed to have encountered on Victoria Island in 1911 which newspapers had blown up into a "blond Eskimo" sensation), and exploring for new land over the ice of Beaufort Sea. Brock, who had given some small assistance to Stefansson's earlier expedition of 1908-12, eagerly recommended a substantial grant in view of the value to Canada of the proposed research: "Participation to some extent is advisable in case any new lands should be discovered, a contingency that is not beyond the range of possibility. It is practically the one remaining place in the world where great geographical discovery is possible." He added, somewhat diffidently, that "It would of course be preferable to have a purely Canadian Expedition, but on account of the cost this might not be feasible."[45] The government, however, eagerly leaped at the suggestion, offered to take over the expedition in its entirety, the American sponsors gladly withdrew their backing, and on February 22, 1913, the Canadian Arctic Expedition of 1913-18 was established.

Government support greatly enlarged the expedition's means but measurably transformed its purpose. Stefansson had wanted to conduct a nomadic anthropological and geographical expedition with ancillary scientific observations; the government, particularly Brock, wanted to use the expedition to enable specialists in the full range of the physical and natural sciences to carry out scientific mapping and collecting activities in a specific remote section of Canada. Add to this the need for haste – to secure ships and supplies and recruit staff for an operation that was to begin before the end of May, 1913 – and it is apparent that the enterprise was bound to face serious difficulties of purposes and authority.

To resolve the basic contradictions of the developed plan, the expedition was divided from the outset into two almost completely distinct parties. A northern section, led by Stefansson, would operate in the islands and Beaufort Sea, while a southern expedition, comprised mainly of specialists on the payroll of the Geological Survey and on assignment from Brock, would undertake "primarily the investigation and areal mapping of the copper-bearing and associated rocks of the mainland between Cape Parry and Kent peninsula, and for approximately one hundred miles inland, and on southern and eastern Victoria Land."[46] Their work was to be of the highest order of field reconnaissance, each member received a specific assignment, and a proper chain of authority was laid down from Brock to R. M. Anderson (Stefansson's colleague of the 1908-1912 expedition) to the various specialists. Brock was content to leave Stefansson to command the northern party and determine its scientific priorities. Further complicating the arrangements was the fact that even though the Geological Survey directed most of the scientific work of the expedition, the exploration and navigation aspects – including operating costs of the expedition – fell to the Department of the Naval Service.

The division was substantially extended to the shipping arrangements, the equipment and supplies of the northern party being transported in the purchased whaler *Karluk*, and most of the equipment of the southern party in the smaller *Alaska* and *Mary Sachs*. The final distribution of staff and supplies was to take place when the ships reached Herschel Island, from whence the sections would go their separate ways. Unfortunately, trouble arose even before that point was reached. The *Karluk* became trapped in the ice-pack near Point Barrow and was carried helplessly west some 1,000 miles, near Herald Island north of Siberia, where she sank. Led by Captain R. A. Bartlett, the passengers and crew scrambled over the ice to Wrangel Island, from whence Bartlett went on to Siberia for help, after a heroic struggle reaching St Michael's, Alaska. Eventually a rescue was effected on September 7, 1914, by an Alaskan schooner. Of the twenty-eight men on board the

Karluk, only a dozen survived, those lost including five scientists and eleven crew members.

Stefansson, however, had been lucky, or foresighted, enough to leave the stricken vessel in mid-September, 1913, when it approached the coast of Alaska, and he was off hunting caribou when the ship was finally carried away. Learning of the safe arrival of the two smaller ships at Collinson Point (west of Herschel Island), he made his way there to "get the work of Anderson's section going, and prepare for an exploration trip of my own northward over the ice of Beaufort Sea."[47] Now the ambiguity of the arrangements began to unfold. The members of the southern party took the position that they had their responsibility to carry out the program assigned them, and that the supplies and equipment on the surviving vessels (and more besides, that had been lost with the *Karluk*) had been earmarked for that purpose. Since Stefansson's program had been ruined by the loss of the *Karluk* it was incumbent on him to forgo it and not curtail their's beyond any hope of success. In this stand they had the backing of the government, which, on learning of the probable fate of the expedition, had already written Stefansson just on these lines:

> It was felt that as the greater part of expenditure for the expedition had been incurred on account of the southern party it was essential that this party should show results for the money so spent. It was, therefore, considered wise not to weaken or cripple the party in any way and to provide in the fullest way for transportation of their supplies and instruments . . .[48]

There were other, more personal factors involved. The men of the southern party resented Stefansson's turning up without the men for whom he was responsible and nonchalantly attempting to commandeer their supplies and labour. He wanted these, they felt, only for a self-dramatizing stunt of no scientific value whatever. This was Stefansson's announced plan of travelling on the drifting ice-pack north from the mainland along the line of the 141st meridian, taking soundings of the ocean depth as a clue to possible new land, and, in the event their food ran out, relying on such game as the sea ice could provide. Such an exercise had been conducted successfully north of Alaska by the Leffingwell-Mikkelsen expedition of 1906-7, which Stefansson was to have joined at a later stage, and Stefansson secured the services of Storker Storkerson, who had been on that earlier trip on the ice-pack. Eventually the members of the southern party agreed to help Stefansson get under way after he agreed not to interfere with their scientific work, and on March 22, 1914, Stefansson, Storkerson, and Ole Andreason, with six dogs and a single sled, departed on the great journey over the ice.

That done, the southern party settled down to the work of mapping the topography and geology of the Mackenzie delta country and east all the way to Bathurst Inlet, correcting the charts of some seven hundred miles of Arctic coastline. The geologist J. J. O'Neill traced the successions and formations, notably the immense but very low-grade copper occurrence that had given the Coppermine River its name. Other members observed and collected plants, animals, birds, fish, and marine life, while the anthropologist Diamond Jenness devoted two years to an intensive study of the Copper Eskimos of the mainland and Victoria Island. They were ordered home at the end of 1915 because of the war, but the instruction could not be obeyed until the summer of 1916, when they wound up the work, packed their many cases of specimens, crowded into their schooner *Alaska*, and eventually reached Ottawa, where some of the men worked on their reports while others quickly enlisted for military service overseas.

Meanwhile Stefansson continued his explorations, disappearing, then reappearing briefly in 1915 at Herschel Island to send telegrams and secure more supplies, then off again until the autumn of 1916. He was now in his element. The tragic events had put him back almost to the situation of 1908-12, when he had lived off the land by his wits and travelled about the country at will. Gone were the big ships and the ambitious programs; once again the "loner" Stefansson, with his small band of kindred spirits, could do battle with the elements, improvising their way to survival and new discoveries. In the first interval (1914-15) his party travelled north some two hundred miles on the ice, then headed east for Banks Island, which was reached after ninety-six days on the ice. For most of the distance the ocean was over 4,500 feet deep, so they concluded there was no likelihood of land in that vicinity. They spent the spring gathering meat for further explorations north beyond Melville or Prince Patrick islands and waiting for one or other of the expedition ships. But the ship sent to the rendezvous was disabled, so once again the northern party had to fend for itself. In June, 1915, they left Banks Island, traced the entire west coast of Prince Patrick Island, then landed on an unrecorded island which Stefansson named Brock Island. From it a still larger island was seen that Stefansson named Borden Island. (Later when this proved to be two islands, the larger, southern one was named Mackenzie King Island, the smaller northern one retaining the original name.) Returning to the southwest point of Banks Island, Stefansson purchased the trading ship *Polar Bear* to carry him to Herschel Island, where the news of his discovering new land in the name of Canada could be spread around the world.

Undeterred by the news of the fate of the *Karluk* or of the recall of the southern party, Stefansson returned with the *Polar Bear* to Banks Island,

and during the ensuing winter (1915-16) examined Brock and Borden islands, made another sweep over the sea ice northeast of Ellef Ringnes Island, then sighted another unmapped island west of Axel Heiberg, which he named Meighen Island. On the return journey they discovered that the maps were hopelessly inaccurate south of Ellef Ringnes Island in showing a single large Finlay Island there. The party defined the area more carefully and gave the name Lougheed Island to an especially attractive island where they encountered good hunting. They wintered (1916-17) on the northern part of Melville Island, from whence, early in 1917, Storkerson was sent east to explore and map the northern and eastern corners of Victoria Island. Stefansson in the meantime made still another search over the ice, this time north and northwest between Borden and Ellef Ringnes islands and as far north as 82°. Back at Banks Island in August, 1917, they found a ship waiting for them and returned to Herschel Island with their news and to collect supplies for still another long-distance trip over the ice which Stefansson and Storkerson planned to make, this time a long-term drift on an ice floe, sounding the ocean depth and living off the marine life they encountered.

But Stefansson was not fated to make this third expedition and Storkerson had to go it on his own. In January, 1918, Stefansson took seriously ill at Herschel Island with what was diagnosed as typhoid fever, and after being nursed a few months, was taken by sled to the nearest hospital at Fort Yukon, where he underwent a long convalescence and laid plans for a lecture tour with a professional manager to publicize his achievements in discovering new land for Canada, accomplishing the longest trips thus far over sea ice, proving (to his own satisfaction) that one could live off the country in almost any part of the Arctic, and that much could be learned from the Eskimo's philosophy and way of life. The lecture tour was inaugurated in Carnegie Hall, New York, on October 31, 1918, and Armistice Day, November 11, 1918, saw Stefansson in Toronto lecturing in Massey Hall at a meeting presided over by his first Canadian patron, Sir Edmund Walker.

In these lectures, and in his subsequent book, Stefansson did not understate his heroic role, and to heighten his achievements, he cast sometimes unnecessary and unfair aspersions on his associates. They found the book, The Friendly Arctic, in which Stefansson recounted the adventure from his own point of view in exciting prose, misleading beyond endurance. Unable as civil servants to compete with the skilled controversialist, they had to content themselves with trying to set the record straight in the scientific journals[49] and keeping the general public from taking too seriously the exaggerated, dangerous conclusions propounded by the very title.

There remained beyond the book, however, Stefansson's unquestioned achievements – that he had accomplished what he set out to do in the face of great odds and had virtually completed the discovery of the Arctic islands of Canada. He had stirred up public interest in the Far North and had extended the Canadian frontier to its ultimate limits, bringing to a fitting close the exploring phase of the Opening of the Canadian North.

CHAPTER 12

Epilogue

There exists an impression that the people and governments of Canada did not awaken to the importance of the Canadian North until the establishment in 1953 of the federal Department of Northern Affairs and National Resources; that prior to that time, in Prime Minister Louis St Laurent's words, Canada administered its North in a fit of absence of mind. This view might have been justified in the light of the situation of the previous generation, and it is undeniable that 1953 marked the beginning of closer supervision and greater expenditure on the territories. But certainly, as the foregoing pages demonstrate, a charge of governmental indifference is hard to substantiate for the period between 1870 and 1914, even in relation to the regions nowadays classed as "North," i.e., the territories north of the sixtieth parallel. The purpose of this book, however, is to examine the northward movement of Canada in a much broader sense; to see how Canadian horizons expanded from the backwoods of the Province of Canada to the northernmost Arctic islands; how governments and private enterprise in varying combinations shaped the movement; and what pressures and motives determined the progress of the northward advance.

Long before Confederation the forests of the Middle North had become a centre for the activities of fur-traders, prospectors, and missionaries following out their particular objectives. With Confederation, government assumed a more positive role, though development remained mainly a task for individuals and corporations. While the Pacific railway and the prairie region engaged the main attention of the new national government, interest continued in the current and future status of the northern parts of Canada. The Departments of Interior, Indian Affairs, Marine and Fisheries, North-West Mounted Police, and Geological Survey expanded their areas of operations as means permitted, and pressed successive administrations to undertake greater responsibilities in connection with the northern territories. The traders, missionaries, prospectors, and Arctic whalers actually carried on

278

with little change or interference, and without materially affecting either the primitive environment or the native inhabitants, except in a few localities.

The expansionist drive during the years of the Laurier boom had more profound effects on the fortunes of the North. This period, when governmental interest in the northward extension of Canadian authority suddenly burst into flame, well illustrates the roles that economic and other forces played in the developmental process. Favourable economic conditions included the availability of profitable foreign markets (and an increasingly important home market) for the natural products of Canada's mines, forests, and farms, and the well-publicized attractiveness of Canada as a home for emigrants and as a secure place for capital investment. Good prices for farm produce, the filling of the better, more accessible grain-growing territories in the prairies, the land-hunger of European and American farmers, and later, the advent of hardier, quicker-maturing grains like Marquis wheat were particular reasons that propelled the farming frontier into the forested belt north of the Saskatchewan River and the Peace River country beyond. Coincidentally, the discovery of large tracts of cultivable land in the Clay Belts, and the rise of the pulp and paper and hydro-electric power industries, permitted a remarkable expansion of settlement in the Middle North of Ontario and Quebec. Better understanding of mineral resources and of mining and refining techniques provided added incentives for the development of these and other districts.

Northward expansion was fostered by provincial and federal governments through their policies for promoting the domestic processing of raw materials, generous and lax administration of natural resources, and the reckless undertaking of communications projects. By means of tariffs, bounties, subsidies, and government contracts, the Dominion government assisted the rise of domestic resource-using industries. It countered American tariff arrangements designed to encourage the outflow from Canada of natural products in as crude or raw states as possible. Export of mineral ores and concentrates was discouraged by export duties and by steps to foster refining in Canada. A similar conflict over logs eventually resulted in a policy, in collaboration with some provinces, of embargoing the export of logs drawn from Crown lands. At the same time, the government's underlying willingness to negotiate favourable terms of trade for the produce of forest, farm, and mine was demonstrated by the imperial preference system and the abortive reciprocity agreement of 1911 with the United States.

The sunny economic climate of the period went hand in hand with the growth of national self-confidence, in which resource development assumed a more positive place than before. The Klondike rush was the first, most striking, event to kindle Canadians' confidence and fasten the eyes of the world on the potentialities of the country beyond the area of existing settlement. The announcement some years later of the second transcontinental railway project, followed closely by the silver discovery at Cobalt, gave solid proof that the northern frontier was worth expending money, energy, and science to develop. A confident sense of national destiny began to possess the people, and entrepreneurs, gambling on the promises held out by a richly endowed, growing nation, launched great and small undertakings. A bright new age – when the Dominion would have the wealth and the population to make a much greater impact on the world scene – seemed at hand. In English Canada, increasing numbers of young people saw their future in helping to extend the frontiers of Canada by settling in the new districts, or by working for government agencies concerned with investigating or managing the resources of Canada. By promoting construction of the National Transcontinental Railway, the Dominion government also helped open a valuable new frontier for French Canadians. In addition, Laurier encouraged French Canadians to look outside Quebec and to participate more fully in the developmental opportunities of the wider Canada by trying to find places for them wherever the federal government held the reins. His efforts to provide a more acceptable cultural base for them in the new territories, however, were frustrated.

Impelling government interest in the northern regions was a wide-spread public concern for, and envy of, the activities of Americans. The Klondike gold rush revived the long-standing fears for Canadian authority along the Pacific coast, while the Alaskan Boundary Arbitration of 1903 left the government and the public very sensitive to any incursions and encroachments on Canadian territory. Police detachments were stationed in the districts of American whaling operations to prevent or punish misdeeds, collect licences and taxes, and generally uphold Canadian law and sovereignty. More striking was the response to fears such as those expressed by Senator Poirier of the encirclement of Canada on the north – the somewhat farcical program of raising the flag and ceremonially proclaiming Canada's authority over empty Arctic islands, as well as the sponsoring of the Canadian Arctic Expedition of 1913-18.

Other influences also shaped the expansionist movement in the Laurier years. Improved knowledge of the various natural resources, and the increase in public concern for the proper use of resources, led to a considerable strengthening of federal and provincial bureaucracies connected with this aspect of government. In the Department of the Interior, for example, forestry, parks, waterpower, and mining branches were set up to help administer federally controlled resources, conduct research and programs of public education, and co-ordinate provincial activities in the same fields. The short-lived Commission of Conservation represented a high point in the formulation of rational programs of resource management, in keeping with the latest scientific findings to prevent waste and favouritism, and to safeguard the public interest. Scientific curiosity was an element in some of these concerns, particularly those expressed for the preservation of certain threatened species of wildlife. A major force in evidence in these and other programs, notably those relating to the Indian and Eskimo peoples, was humanitarianism.

The northward expansion of Canada between 1870 and 1914 was irregular and spasmodic, but it was represented by a succession of forward-moving frontiers of differing economic and social levels, roughly arranged with the degree of social advance diminishing from south to north. In the early stages, the frontier situation threw up on every level entrepreneurial elements in the shape of independent trappers and traders, prospectors, pioneer farmers, Klondikers, and others. But along the northern frontiers (and increasingly so the farther north one proceeded), only scattered areas possessed resource bases of a size and kind to maintain large, permanent populations, and often this was only owing to group action, government aid, or capitalistic organization. Independent prospectors were quickly followed by mining-developers who employed capital and hired labour to carry prospects forward to production. Even in the Klondike or Cobalt, where the ores were rich enough to be worked successfully by individuals in the early stages, mining operations quickly advanced to the stage of requiring heavy capital investments and production along specialized, hierarchical, managerial lines. The exploitation of forest and waterpower resources also necessitated the adoption of this capitalistic, institutional framework, as did the resulting manufacturing industries. Even modern agriculture required someone (usually the state) to make heavy investments on railways to open up long-distance markets for the produce of the frontier farms, while soil and climatic conditions compelled a measure of collective action. The Canadian North, in the main, seemed to give rise to two distinct patterns of social organization – a diffused, primitive, individualistic pattern based on the wildlife resources, which was characteristic of the early stages of development; or the pattern of the new industries, which were mainly organized on specialized, hierarchical lines and gave rise to urban communities and wage-earning labour forces. Hence, the developed northern frontier did not lend itself in any significant degree to the shaping of an egalitarian economy and society, except for those rare sections where agriculture or hand-mining on a long-term basis could be practised.

In their approaches to the problems of frontier development, Canadian governments, in line with the concept of the Crown as the ultimate source of authority and the repository of the public interest, followed authoritarian and centralizing methods. The settler was expected to look to government authority to provide his public needs, which governments in turn tried to fill. The Dominion government undertook to provide the basic transportation facility on which the opening of the frontiers depended. It kept firm control over the natural resources of the new territories, and, to administer the districts, it appointed officials who were responsible to it, and not to the local settlers. It strove to place its agents in the country and bring frontier districts under the rule of law before any appreciable amount of settlement occurred. On matters concerned with the frontiers, it made decisions according to its own convenience, in line with national rather than local interests. It determined when, and how far, to proceed with creating regional governments to attend to local needs, then set out the boundaries and powers of the resulting provinces and territories according to its will. Hence the political experience offered by the northern frontier environment of Canada, rather than affording, in the ideal, an apprenticeship in self-reliance and responsibility, tended to be limited to the acceptance of outside authority, or to more or less irresponsible agitation.

In these ways Canada's northern frontier movement did not manifest the results imputed to such movements by commentators like Frederick Jackson Turner and his successors. Equally, it failed to colour the character and quality of the political and cultural life to the degree attributed to the United States experience. Partly because of the particular frontier environment, partly because the frontier regions attracted a relatively small population, Canada's political centre of gravity never moved from the St Lawrence valley and Ontario peninsula districts of the two central provinces. The frontiers had few representatives in Parliament, and relatively little power or influence on government there, except in so far as they could gain the support of more politically powerful elements. In the provinces, their relative political weight was greater, and could become crucial when the political parties were evenly balanced. More often, too, the frontiers enjoyed the support of major urban centres, which gave them considerable power to secure their mutual desires, especially public works. In Quebec they possessed, in addition, the backing of the nationalist lobby of clergy and publicists. The powerful frontier interest that resulted from this alliance exerted itself to foster a very permissive situation that undermined effective management of the natural resources of the province.

To view the development of Canada's northern frontiers, particularly for the period of this study, the metropolitan approach affords a better perspective than Turner's frontier thesis. The drive to open the frontiers came from groups and forces outside those frontiers, more than from their few pioneer settlers. On the government side, there was an outpouring from the old Province of Canada, and afterwards from the Dominion government, of administrative policies and personnel as well as a great deal of investment

to help open up new frontiers all the way from Muskoka to Ellesmere
Island. Farmers were attracted from outside to occupy new lands, entrepreneurs to establish new industries, businessmen to serve the new countries, and churches to continue serving their communicants and gain new
adherents. Capitalists, entrepreneurs, and settlers from the older parts of
Canada shaped the educational, social, religious, and cultural life of the
new frontiers, assimilating peoples of different traditions and backgrounds
who entered the region. The Yukon Territory provides the most spectacular
example of the assimilative force of the Canadian political, social, and administrative system, deliberately applied to guarantee the Canadian identity of
the community. Elsewhere along the frontier, albeit less consciously, On-
tario-derived educational, religious, cultural, and Indian programs were
transferred to the new settlements and adopted as their own. In contrast,
the French and Catholic pattern, centred on the early Métis settlement,
quickly fell behind as immigration from Quebec failed to materialize to any
great extent, except to adjoining parts of northern Ontario, and as federal
governments remained dominated by the Anglo-Saxon ethic. However, in
1914 the new frontiers were noteworthy more for their cultural diversity
than for their uniformity; English Canadians, French Canadians, aborigines,
and "New Canadians" remained discrete elements of the social, religious,
and cultural pluralism of Canada.

A critical examination of the management of the developmental process
by which Canada extended northward in the years after 1870 reveals several
shortcomings and failings, some avoidable, others not. The greatest involved
the treatment of the native peoples, a problem whose complexity is only
being appreciated today. The entrance of the white man and his technology
into the domain of the nomadic, hunting, food-gathering aboriginal peoples
generated social and cultural revolutions. By 1914 the exploitation of the
resources by white men was beginning in many of the still-undeveloped
parts of the country. The extension of the treaties, and the expansion of
Indian agencies to include virtually all of Canada's Indians, indicated how
extensively white pioneers had intruded into the homelands of the aborigines. In many areas the primitive economy still was little changed; in others
white men had begun to participate to some extent in the wildlife industries;
while elsewhere the land itself was being occupied for transportation, farming, forestry, or mining purposes and by permanent white communities.
Deprived in this last instance from the full enjoyment of the wildlife and
other resources of their tribal territory, the Indians selected and occupied
reserves where they could try to continue their former existence or adopt
new patterns of activity along the lines of, or in conjunction with, the new
economy introduced by the whites. Though neither the divorce of the Indian
from his earlier way of life, nor the dichotomy between his present way of

life and that of the white society was so complete as both later became, serious problems of adjustment were already becoming apparent. Federal governments, for too long heedless and neglectful, were only beginning to adopt new positions in their Indian programs that tried to overcome some of the earlier shortcomings.

A second major area of frequent failures, as indicated by the numerous scandals of the period, was that of resource management. Governments sometimes treated the resources under their stewardship as if they were inexhaustible and completely valueless in their natural state; and they disposed of them as though they were their personal property, heedless of developmental priorities, or in line with every fleeting wind of public opinion. Ontario's program, though far from scandal-free, was probably the most progressive, the best administered, and the most widely copied. Successive governments of Ontario displayed a continuous progression towards a rational program. They undertook socially desirable programs like classifying resources in advance of disposal; obtaining adequate revenue for the state from alienated resources; applying progressive management programs to conserve and secure the fullest use from specific resources; guarding against speculation and failures to proceed to production; encouraging production and fabrication to the most advanced stage; and retaining ownership for the public over critical resources like hydro-electric power sites. Though much had been done in these directions, much still was required to equip governments with personnel, agencies, and policies conducive to effective resources management, and to educate the public to the importance of good management. Here again, as with Indian relations, only limited progress had been achieved by 1914.

Another failure of the resources management policies that was to create problems for the future was the trend to foreign ownership and control by American corporations. The emphasis on rapid development resulted in easy resource-granting policies that encouraged the establishment of extractive industries utilizing very large amounts of capital. Foreign control was accelerated by changes within the industries themselves, for these required capital in large amounts for construction of mills and plants, scientifically trained staffs and experienced entrepreneurs in the field of resource exploitation, and assured markets through being part of an integrated organization. American interests were in much better positions than Canadian interests on all four counts to exploit the highly favourable opportunities, and came to Canada expressly to secure control of the programs and operations of the resource-using firms. For the most part this was welcomed, for prior to the Great War Canadians were more concerned with attracting outside capital than with any perils of foreign ownership of important natural resources. Nor was such outside capital even an essential requirement – as the case of the Alberta and Great Waterways Railway demonstrated.

A major failing in the field of governmental collaboration with industry concerned governments' involvement with railway enterprises, especially in the years of the Laurier boom. This was a long-standing tradition, particularly since railways had long been recognized as the major, and sometimes the only, means of making possible the exploitation of the major resources that raised the districts above the primitive state. To secure such important facilities, governments were compelled to hold out inducements like cash subsidies, land grants, bond guarantees, or undertake construction themselves. Guaranteeing the bonds of selected railway companies was the means most frequently utilized during the opening years of the new century. Recipient companies were able to market the guaranteed bonds and construct the lines with the proceeds, while the governments, seemingly with little effort on their part, could win reputations for progressiveness that would help keep them in power.

Unfortunately, the system could be, and was, most irresponsible. While their credit lasted, provincial governments competed for the attentions of the few successful railway builders who played them off one against the other, and compelled them to increase their guarantees and other incentives. The builders, in the meantime, took on far more than they could easily perform, and proceeded with the construction slowly or not at all, to the ruin of settlers attracted by the promised lines. A dangerously intimate connection arose between governments and favoured railways over concessions by the one, and political contributions by the other. The governments, implicated in the companies' affairs, were obliged to condone extravagantly priced or substandard construction, dummy contracting subsidiaries, the use of construction funds to pay interest instalments, diversion of aid to branches more helpful to the railways' interests than to those of the government and people, and other forms of misconduct. Political scandals and the eventual calling on governments to make good their guarantees marked the débâcle of the system. Governments were trapped by debts they could not afford, sometimes for railways they did not really want or need, and the nation was left with burdens that haunted governments and held up important projects for years.

The unsatisfactory railway situation – notably the duplication reflected in parts of the second and third transcontinentals – demonstrates another major source of weakness in the developmental process of the period, one that is inherent in the federal nature of Canada. The provinces, with their own responsibilities for northern development under the constitution, faced continuing pressures to assist the expansion of their resource-based industries. Like the Dominion government, they responded by undertaking their own programs of surveys and public works, establishing municipal and judicial institutions, and furnishing social services. Frequently the Dominion and provinces clashed over their developmental programs, and even more over boundaries as the provinces strove to extend their spheres of authority. Such conflicts did not apply only to the provinces that controlled their natural resources; the retention by the Dominion of the natural resources of the prairie provinces was completely ineffectual as a means of preventing conflicts over policies and programs, while the control itself rapidly became a major source of grievance, exacerbating relations between the two levels of government.

These weaknesses and failures, however, were minor compared with the achievements of Canadians and their governments in developing their northern frontier districts – accomplishments that fill the preceding chapters. Outstanding successes had been achieved in exploring, measuring, and evaluating the qualities of the vast territories added to Canada in 1870, 1871, and 1880. Governments had worked out practical programs under which occupation and development of agricultural, forest, and mineral resources could proceed, while the direction and pace of industrial advances were set by tariff, taxation, and immigration policies, and a welcoming, respectful attitude towards the importing of capital and technology. Navigable waterways were improved, trails and roads were built, and many railways were helped to completion. By instituting their legal systems and policing agencies, governments provided an environment in which orderly development could proceed, and even the wildlife industries were gradually brought under some semblance of control.

In 1871, Canada for practical purposes barely extended beyond the Gulf of St Lawrence and the St Lawrence Lowlands region, while the Red River Settlement and British Columbia counted only a few thousand settlers apiece. By 1914, thanks to the efforts of the previous years, farmers, miners, and forest workers were advancing the industrial and social frontiers of Canada as they established themselves on the prairies, in the Cordillera, and in the forests of the Middle North from Lake St John to Dawson. Three east-to-west railways traversed the Dominion in depth, and other lines were being extended still farther north. Northward from the International Boundary stretched a band of provinces, seven hundred miles wide, and the territories beyond the sixtieth parallel were attracting activity on several fronts. Such were the achievements of these years of apprenticeship, when Canada began to come to grips with the facts of its northern nature. The task left for the next era was to respond more fully, more responsibly, and more effectively to the challenges associated with the further development of the northern frontiers of Canada.

ABBREVIATIONS

C.A.R.: *Canadian Annual Review.*
C.H.R.: *Canadian Historical Review.*
C.M.S.: Church Missionary Society.
G.S.C.: Geological Survey of Canada.
M.G.: Manuscript Group.
P.A.C.: Public Archives of Canada.
R.G.: Record Group.

NOTES TO CHAPTER ONE

1. Anna M. Wright, "The Canadian Frontier, 1840-1867," Ph.D. thesis, University of Toronto, 1943, p. 234: "To preserve a 'frontier', Canadians had been forced to build a nation."
2. Canada (Province), Crown Lands, Report, 1856, p. 6.
3. Quoted in Adam Shortt, ed., *Canada and Its Provinces* (23 vols., Toronto, 1913), V, "Indian Affairs, 1840-1867," by D. C. Scott, 339, 337.
4. Canada (Province), Legislative Assembly, *Journals*, 1854-55, Appendix L, "Report of the Select Committee on the Geological Survey," p. [2].
5. Canada, House of Commons, *Debates*, 1875, p. 656.
6. Canada, *Sessional Papers*, 1869, no. 42, "Return . . . shewing what progress has been made in opening up communication between Fort William and the Red River Settlement," p. 21.
7. *Ibid.*, 1885, no. 116, "Papers . . . in connection with the extinguishment of the Indian title preferred by Half-breeds resident in the North-West Territories," p. 65, Taché to Col. J. S. Dennis, 29 Jan. 1879.
8. Canada, Commons, *Debates*, 1884, p. 1269.
9. Canada, Department of the Interior, *Report*, 1875-76, Special Appendix, p. lxvii.
10. Canada, Secretary of State for the Provinces, *Report*, 1870, Indian Branch, p. 4.
11. Canada, Department of Indian Affairs, *Report*, 1880, p. 2.
12. *Ibid.*, 1882, p. xi.
13. Canada, Commons, *Debates*, 1884, p. 1265.
14. Marcel Giraud, "The Western Métis After the Insurrection," transl. from "Le Métis Canadien," *Saskatchewan History*, IX (1), Winter 1956, p. 5.
15. P.A.C., M.G. 29, B30, W.P.M. Street Papers, letter from A. M. Burgess, 30 March 1885.
16. Canada, Interior, *Report*, 1895, IV, p. 52.
17. Canada, Secretary of State for the Provinces, *Report*, 1870-71, p. 14.
18. Canada, Interior, *Report*, 1891, VI, "General Report of Operations from 1869 to 1889," by W. F. King and J. S. Dennis, p. 25.
19. Canada, Interior, *Report*, 1887, p. xxii.
20. Don W. Thomson, *Men and Meridians* (Ottawa, 1967), II, 26.
21. By J. Macoun and C. Horetzky, 1872; Macoun and A. R. C. Selwyn, 1875; J. Hunter, 1877; G. M. Dawson and R. G. McConnell, 1879; H. A. F. Macleod, H. J. Cambie and Rev. D. M. Gordon, 1879. See Gordon E. Bowes, comp., *Peace River Chronicles* (Vancouver, 1963), pp. 81-92, 119-45.
22. Canada, C.P.R., *Report and Documents in Reference to the Canadian Pacific Railway* (Ottawa, 1880), pp. 11-12.

NOTES TO CHAPTER TWO

1. Canada, Public Works, *British Columbia, Report of the Hon. H. L. Langevin,* C.B. (Ottawa, 1872), pp. 22, 152.
2. United Kingdom, Order in Council, 16 May 1871, cited in B.C. *Sessional Papers,* 1876, "Report of the Government of British Columbia on the Subject of Indian Reserves," p. 57.
3. Canada, Indian Affairs, *Report,* 1873-74, p. 11.
4. B.C., *Sessional Papers,* 1876, "Report on Indian Reserves," p. 58.
5. *Ibid.,* p. 60.
6. *Ibid.,* p. 60.
7. Resolution of the legislative assembly, quoted in G. E. Shankel, "The Development of Indian Policy in British Columbia," Ph.D. thesis, University of Washington, 1945, p. 143.
8. B.C. *Sessional Papers,* 1888, "Papers Relating to the Commission appointed to enquire into the State and Condition of the Indians of the North-West Coast of British Columbia," p. 424.
9. *Ibid.,* pp. 419-25.
10. Canada, Indian Affairs, *Report,* 1873-74, p. 67.
11. Marius Barbeau, *Totem Poles* (2 vols., Canada, National Museum, Bulletin No. 119, 1950), II, 825, 828.
12. P.A.C., M.G. 29, D7, Letters and Documents from the Hazelton Indian Agency, compiled by Indian Agent Mr. Loring, General Remarks, R. E. Loring, 19 Jan. 1894, p. 27.
13. Canada, Interior, Indian Affairs, *Report,* 1875-76, p. 36.
14. Canada, *Statutes,* 47 Vict. (1884), Chap. 27.
15. Canada, Indian Affairs, *Report,* 1895-96, p. 73.
16. *Ibid.,* p. 84.
17. *Ibid.,* p. 95.
18. B.C. *Sessional Papers,* 1888, "Papers Relating to the Commission...Indians of the North-West Coast," pp. 418-19.
19. Canada, British Columbia, *Report of H. L. Langevin,* p. 25.
20. Canada, G.S.C., *Report of Progress,* 1878-79, Part B, Appendix A, "On the Haida Indians of the Queen Charlotte Islands," p. 105B.
21. Canada, Indian Affairs, *Report,* 1882, p. 106.
22. Canada, Department of Fisheries, *Report,* 1888, p. 250.
23. B.C., Mines, *Report,* 1879, p. 239.
24. Canada, N.W.M.P., *Report,* 1895, Supplementary, p. 18.
25. By Term 11, United Kingdom Order in Council, 16 May 1871, quoted in B.C. *Sessional Papers,* 1880, "Correspondence with reference to the Transfer of Railway Lands to the Dominion," p. 425.
26. N. R. Hacking, "British Columbia Steamboat Days, 1870-1883," *British Columbia Historical Quarterly,* XI (2), April 1947, p. 77.
27. P.A.C., Letters and Documents from the Hazelton Indian Agency, Loring to J. R. Anderson, 2 Nov. 1893.
28. "Mining Districts of British Columbia," by A. W. Vowell and Thomas Spence, Victoria, 1878; manuscript in H. H. Bancroft Library, Berkeley, Calif., HHB/P-C 28.

NOTES TO CHAPTER THREE

1. J. S. Galbraith, "A Note on the Mackenzie Negotiations with the Hudson's Bay Company, 1875-1878," C.H.R., XXXIV (1), March, 1953, pp. 39-45.
2. C. J. Brydges reported selling $2,048,-782 worth of lots in Winnipeg, in H.B.C., *Report to Shareholders,* 22 Nov. 1883, p. 10.
3. P.A.C., M.G. 29, D9, Roderick Macfarlane Papers, v. 1, p. 335, copy of "Annual Report, Athabasca District, Portage la Loche 15 July, 1873."
4. For a good early account of the route below Athabasca Landing, see description by William Ogilvie, in Canada, Interior, *Report,* 1892, VII, pp. 3-10.
5. H.B.C. Archives, London, Letters Inland, Governor Mactavish, 1864-67, p. 362, J. A. Grahame, Norway House, 25 Nov. 1867.

6. P.A.C., Macfarlane Papers, v. 2, p. 1732, J. S. Camsell, Fort Chipewyan, 8 Aug. 1893, to Macfarlane.

7. *Ibid.*, v. 1, p. 1122, K. McDonald, Port Simpson, 7 March 1887, to Macfarlane.

8. Donald Ross, "The Athabasca Brigade," *Alberta Historical Review*, IV (2), Spring 1958, p. 21.

9. P.A.C., Macfarlane Papers, v. 1, p. 902, copy of letter from W. Armit, Secretary, H.B.C., 24 Oct., 1882.

10. *Ibid.*, p. 985, circular from W. Armit, 22 July 1884.

11. *The Beaver*, I (10), July, 1921, p. 3, however, mentions a later council of fur-trade officers held in July, 1898 at Athabasca Landing.

12. A *Charge Delivered by the Bishop of Athabasca at the First Meeting of the Synod of the Diocese of Athabasca, Held at Fort Simpson, September 4th, 1876*, p. 5, refers to the practice of baptizing all Indian children presented for the purpose by their parents, and the concomitant obligation on missionaries of instructing the children in the Christian faith as they grew up. P.A.C., microfilm, reel A-102, C.M.S., North-West America Mission (Rupertsland), C 1/o, Original Letters, Journals and Papers (Incoming), 1822-1880.

13. "Edward Sullivan," by R. J. Renison, in W. Bertal Heeney, ed., *Leaders of the*

Canadian Church, First Series (Toronto, 1918), p. 219.

14. *The Fourth Meeting of the Synod of the Diocese of Saskatchewan . . . Wednesday, August 25th, 1889* (Prince Albert, 1889), pp. 15-19.

15. P.A.C., microfilm, reel A-103, C.M.S., W. C. Bompas to C.M.S. Committee, Fort Vermilion, 18 Nov. 1878.

16. Beatrice Batty, *Forty-two Years amongst the Indians and Eskimo* (London, 1893), p. 93, quoting Bishop John Horden, 1875.

17. P.A.C., microfilm, reel A-81, C.M.S., North-West America Mission, C 1/M, Mission Books (Incoming Letters), 1868-76, p. 391, Bompas to Committee, Fort Simpson, May 1876.

18. Joseph Lofthouse, A *Thousand Miles from a Post Office* (London, 1922), pp. 77, 134.

19. P.A.C., microfilm, reel A-102, C.M.S., W. C. Bompas to Committee, Portage la Loche, 20 Aug. 1877.

20. James Woodsworth, *Thirty Years in the Canadian North-West* (Toronto, 1917), p. 193.

21. E. F. S. J. Petitot, "Géographie de l'Athabaskaw-Mackenzie et des Grands Lacs du Bassin Arctique," *Bulletin de la Société de Géographie de Paris*, Série 6, X, Juillet-Décembre 1875, pp. 5-42, 127-83, 242-90.

22. *The Fourth Meeting of the Synod of the Diocese of Saskatchewan*, p. 27.

NOTES TO CHAPTER FOUR

1. *The Wild North Land* (London, 1873 edition), p. 358.

2. Dr. Murray Campbell, "Dr. J. C. Schultz," *Historical and Scientific Society of Manitoba*, Series 3, No. 20, 1963-64, pp. 7-12.

3. Canada, Senate, *Journals*, 1888, p. 267 (phraseology varies in other references).

4. *Ibid.*, Appendix I, "Report of the Select Committee of the Senate appointed to Enquire into the Resources of the Great Mackenzie Basin," p. 11.

5. *Ibid.*

6. *Ibid.*, p. 14.

7. *Ibid.*

8. Canada, *Statutes*, 39-40 Vict. (1877), Chap. 9.

9. Douglas Leechman, "The Father of Place Names," *The Beaver*, Autumn 1954, pp. 24-28.

10. *Canadian Field Naturalist*, IV, May, 1890, 29-40.

11. Canada, G.S.C., *Annual Report*, VI (1892-93), "Summary Report, 1893," p. 4A.

12. *Ibid.*, VII (1894), "Summary Report, 1894," p. 72A.

13. *Ibid.*, pp. 78A-79A.

14. Canada, *Statutes*, 53 Vict. (1890), Chap. 11.

15. Thomson, *Men and Meridians*, II, 65.

16. United States, Congress, 48th 2nd session, *Report of a Military Reconnaissance in Alaska, made in 1883, by Frederick Schwatka* (Senate, Exec. Doc. No. 2, Washington, 1885).

17. Canada, Interior, *Report*, 1889, p. xxii.

18. Grace Lee Nute, "Down North in 1892," *The Beaver*, June 1948, pp. 42-43.

19. Canada, G.S.C., *Annual Report*, VI (1892-93), "Summary Report, 1892," p. 82A.

20. Frank Russell, *Explorations in the Far North* (Iowa City, 1898), p. iii.

21. Canada, Interior, *Report*, 1890, I, p. 21.

22. Canada, G.S.C., *Report of Progress*, 1879-80, Part B, "Report of an Exploration from Port Simpson on the Pacific Coast to Edmonton on the Saskatchewan . . ." by G. M. Dawson, p. 75B.

23. Canada, Interior, *Report*, 1892, Part VII, "Report on the Peace River and Tributaries in 1891," by William Ogilvie, p. 36.

24. Canada, N.W.M.P., *Report*, 1895, p. 5.

25. Canada, Indian Affairs, *Report*, 1895-96, p. 201.

26. Canada, Interior, *Report*, 1896, IV, p. 53.

27. Ethel G. Stewart, "Fort McPherson and the Peel River Area," M.A. thesis, Queen's University, 1955, pp. 192-98.

28. Canada, *Statutes*, 39 Vict. (1876), Chap. 21.

29. Canada, Interior, *Report*, 1882, pp. xv-xvi and map.

30. Canada, *Statutes*, 54-55 Vict. (1891), Chap. 22, Sec. 14. See also Canada, *Sessional Papers*, 1895, no. 21, "Report of the Royal Commission on the Liquor Traffic in Canada," pp. 58, 149, 175-87.

31. Canada, Fisheries, *Report*, 1895, p. 220.

32. William Ogilvie, *Early Days on the Yukon* (London, 1913), pp. 143-44.

33. *Ibid.*, p. 144.

34. P.A.C., M.G. 30, E2, Constantine Papers, v. 4, "Superintendent's Letterbook, N.W.M.P., Yukon, 1895-98," pp. 52-55. Constantine to L. Herchmer, 5 Jan. 1896, confidential.

35. *Ibid.*, p. 146, same to same, 15 Aug. 1896.

36. Canada, N.W.M.P., *Report*, 1896, p. 22.

37. *San Francisco Examiner*, 4, 5, 7 Nov., 5 Dec. 1895.

38. Canada, N.W.M.P., *Report*, 1896, pp. 235-36.

NOTES TO CHAPTER FIVE

1. The precise date of the discovery has been in doubt from early times. See *Daily Evening Star* (Whitehorse), 15 Aug. 1904. The account by Ogilvie, who was probably in the best position to know the facts, gives the discovery as coming on the evening of August 14th or 15th, the staking of the claims on the morning of the 17th, the recording at Forty Mile on the 21st. See his account in *Early Days on the Yukon*, pp. 113-36, especially 129-31. Discovery Day is celebrated annually on August 17th.

2. P.A.C., M.G. 30, C2, Ogilvie Papers, file 1, Ogilvie to James W. Wilson, 22 May 1897.

3. H. J. Woodside, "The Discoverer of the Klondike," *North*, XI (6), Nov.-Dec. 1964, pp. 1-7.

4. William Ogilvie, *The Klondike Official Guide* (Toronto, 1898), p. 112.

5. P.A.C., Constantine Papers, Yukon Superintendent's Letterbook, p. 167, Constantine to L. W. Herchmer, 2 Sept. 1896.

6. *Ibid.*, Constantine Diary, 1894-99, entry for 23 June, 1898.

7. C. E. S. Franks, "How the Sabbath came to the Yukon," *Canadian Public Administration*, X, 1967, pp. 124-36; John A. Bovey, "The Attitudes and Policies of the Federal Government Towards Canada's Northern Territories, 1870-1930," M.A. thesis, University of British Columbia, 1967, pp. 106-7.

8. Samuel B. Steele, *Forty Years in Canada* (Toronto, 1915), p. 295.

9. Canada, N.W.M.P., *Report*, 1898, III, p. 48, "Report of Inspector Z. T. Wood"; United States, 55th Congress, 3rd session, "Relief of People in the Yukon River Country" (House Doc. No. 244, Washington, 1899).

10. Canada, *Sessional Papers*, 1899, no. 87A, "Evidence Taken before the Commissioner appointed to investigate Charges of Alleged Malfeasance of the Officials of the Yukon Territory."

11. Canada, *Statutes*, 1899, pp. lxvii-lxviii (Order in Council, 29 March, 1899).

12. Canada, *Statutes*, 6 Edw. VII (1906), Chap. 39.

13. P.A.C., M.G. 27 II, D15, Sifton Papers, p. 54573, Treadgold to Sifton, 7 Sept. 1899; Canada, *Commons, Debates*, 1903, cols. 2796-2915; *Sessional Papers*, 1903, no. 63, "Correspondence, etc., relating to the Treadgold Hydraulic Mining Syndicate."

14. P.A.C., M.G. 26, G, Laurier Papers, pp. 78725-7, Minto to Laurier, 10 Nov. 1903; Canada, *Sessional Papers*, 1904, no. 142, "Report of the Britton Commission on Hydraulic Mining."

15. R. C. Kirk, *Twelve Months in the Klondike* (London, 1899), p. 91.

16. P. T. Mizony, "Gold Rush: A Boy's Impression of the Stampede into the Yukon during the Days of 1898," 1956. Typescript, H. H. Bancroft Library, HHB/P-K 221:1, p. 29.

17. *Whitehorse Semi-Weekly Star*, 28 June 1902, 2, 16 July 1902.

18. Harold A. Innis, *Settlement and the Mining Frontier* (Toronto, 1936, Canadian Frontiers of Settlement, IX), pp. 223-24.

19. Canada, G.S.C., *Summary Report*, 1906, pp. 20-21.

20. Canada, *Statutes*, 6 Edw. VII (1906-7), Chap. 39; *Sessional Papers*, 1906-7, no. 25A, "Interim Report of Commissioner of Yukon Territory," pp. 3-8. Claims were reduced to 250 feet by Order in Council of 18 Jan. 1898, and remained at this figure till 1911 (*Whitehorse Weekly Star*, 12 May 1911).

21. Jim Lotz and Allan Innes-Taylor, "The Yukon Ditch," *Canadian Geographical Journal*, LXXIV (4), April 1967, pp. 124-31.

22. Innis, *Settlement and the Mining Frontier*, p. 219. The figures vary in other works.

23. W. K. Hubbard, "The Klondike Gold Rush in Literature, 1896-1930," M.A. thesis, University of Western Ontario, 1969.

NOTES TO CHAPTER SIX

1. S. D. Clark, *The Developing Canadian Community* (Toronto, 1968 edition), p. 98.

2. A. Heilprin, *Alaska and the Klondike* (London, 1899), pp. 46-63; J. Lynch, *Three Years in the Klondike* (London, 1904), pp. 26-31.

3. Lynch, *Three Years*, pp. 177-78.

4. P.A.C., Constantine Papers, Yukon Superintendent's Letterbook, p. 58, Constantine to Herchmer, 5 Jan. 1896.

5. P.A.C., M.G. 27 II, B1, Minto Papers, vol. 24, p. 68, J. Lynch to Arthur Sladen, 17 Aug. 1900; p. 167, Laurier to Minto, 11 Oct. 1900; Lynch, *Three Years*, pp. 205-15.

6. Cited in David R. Morrison, *The Politics of the Yukon Territory, 1898-1909* (Toronto, 1968), p. 31.

7. Canada, *Statutes*, 2 Edw. VII (1902), Chap. 35.

8. Yukon, *Ordinances*, 1902, Chap. 65,

pp. 526-39, "An Ordinance Respecting Towns."

9. *Ibid.*, Chap. 5, pp. 69-76, "An Ordinance Respecting the Public Service of the Territory."

10. Tappan Adney, *The Klondike Stampede of 1897-98* (New York, 1900), p. 433.

11. Canada, N.W.M.P., *Report*, 1897, pp. 307, 309.

12. P.A.C., M.G. 30, E14, Z. T. Wood Papers, Wood to Y. Kawakami, Dawson, 15 March 1909.

13. P.A.C., Laurier Papers, pp. 130673-75, John Pringle to Laurier, 27 May 1902; pp. 130687-96, same to same, 18 Oct. 1907; Canada, *Commons, Debates*, 1907-8, cols. 9580-9693.

14. Yukon, Council, *Journals*, 1908, p. 11.

15. P.A.C., Z. T. Wood Papers, Wood to Kawakami, 15 March 1909.

16. P.A.C., M.G. 30, E13, F. C. Wade

Papers, Fred White to Wade, 15 Oct. 1901, 25 Jan., 11 Oct., 1902.

17. McGill University, Redpath Library, G. M. Dawson Papers, Diary, 1896-98, entry of 26 Sept. 1897.

18. P.A.C., Sifton Papers, p. 102692, clipping from Seattle Post Intelligencer, 1 Jan. 1901.

19. P.A.C., Laurier Papers, p. 53217, H. J. Woodside to Laurier, 5 Feb. 1901.

20. S. Morley Wickett, "Yukon Trade," Industrial Canada, III, Oct. 1902, pp. 164-72.

21. Whitehorse Semi-Weekly Star, 31 March, 2, 4 April 1904.

22. T. A. Rickard, Through the Yukon and Alaska (San Francisco, 1909), pp. 183-84.

23. J. Craig, "The Present Condition and Future Prospects of the Yukon," 4 April 1912, in Empire Club, Toronto, Speeches, 1911-12, p. 217.

24. Whitehorse Weekly Star, 26 April 1918. In 1897-98, according to Adney, Klondike Stampede, pp. 440-41, the territory contributed $1,530,000 to the Dominion treasury, against an expenditure of $647,000, leaving the Dominion government a "profit" of $883,000.

25. P.A.C., M.G. 26, H, Borden Papers, pp. 130494-96, J. P. Lithgow to Borden, 7 Jan. 1918, and p. 130498, Borden to Meighen, 21 Jan. 1918; Whitehorse Weekly Star, 5, 19, 26 April, 3, 17, 24, 31 May, 14 June, 30 Aug., 13 Sept. 1918.

26. P.A.C., Constantine Papers, Yukon Superintendent's Letterbook, p. 208, Constantine to Deputy Minister of the Interior, 19 Nov. 1896.

27. Ibid., p. 255, copy of letter, Ogilvie to Constantine,—Nov. 1896.

NOTES TO CHAPTER SEVEN

1. Ontario, Sessional Papers, 1889, no. 60, "The Proceedings before Her Majesty's Imperial Privy Council on the Special Case respecting the Westerly Boundary of the Province of Ontario"; P.A.C., R. G. 7, G21, Governor General's Numbered Files, no. 108, vol. 1 "Boundary between Ontario and Manitoba, 1872-1887."

2. Richard A. Olmsted, comp., Decisions of the Judicial Committee of the Privy Council relating to the British North America Act, 1867, and the Canadian Constitution, 1867-1954 (3 vols., Ottawa, 1954), I, 236-51, "The Queen vs. St. Catherine's Milling and Lumber Company, JC 1888, July 12, 13, 17, 19, 20, 24, 26, Dec. 12," p. 249.

3. Ibid. See also Gerard V. La Forest, Natural Resources and Public Property under the Canadian Constitution (Toronto, 1969), pp. 109-15.

4. Ontario, Sessional Papers, 1881, no. 44, "Report of Stipendiary Magistrates upon the Northerly and Westerly Parts of Ontario," p. 57.

5. Canada, Sessional Papers, 1887, no. 19A, "Return . . . respecting Timber Licenses and Crown Titles to Lands . . . within the So-Called Disputed Territory," pp. 1-2.

6. Ontario, Sessional Papers, 1887, no. 64, "Return . . . Cases brought before E. B. Borron, Stipendiary Magistrate . . . and shewing also the Other Duties performed by Him in Each Year," p. 3.

7. Ibid., 1880, no. 22, "Report of the Stipendiary Magistrates with respect to the Northerly and Westerly Parts of the Province of Ontario," p. 36; Ibid., 1881, no. 44, p. 14.

8. Canada, C.P.R., Report on Surveys and Preliminary Operations on the Canadian Pacific Railway (Ottawa, 1877), p. 46.

9. Ontario, Statutes, 31 Vict. (1868), Chap. 19.

10. Ibid., 32 Vict. (1869), Chap. 34; Ontario, Royal Commission on the Mineral Resources of Ontario, 1890, Report, pp. 267-69.

11. Ontario, Royal Commission on Agriculture, 1881, Report, pp. 539-46.

12. Liberal Party, Ontario, Ontario Elections 1879, Seven Years of Liberal Government, Electors' Guide (Toronto, 1879), pp. 49-51; A. R. M. Lower, Settlement and the Forest Frontier in Eastern Canada (Toronto, 1936, Canadian Frontiers of Settlement, IX), p. 60.

13. Liberal Party, Ontario, The Mowat Government: Fourteen Years of Liberal

Legislation and Administration, 1871-1885 (Toronto, 1886), p. 46.
14. Quebec, Crown Lands, Report, 1882-83, pp. viii-ix. Both provinces proceeded to enact regulatory legislation, but the issue was not finally resolved until 1898 when the Privy Council ruled in the provinces' favour. See R. S. Lambert, Renewing Nature's Wealth (Toronto, 1967), p. 449.
15. Ontario, Statutes, 56 Vict. (1893), Chap. 8.
16. F. X. A. Labelle, Considérations Générales sur l'Agriculture, la Colonisation, le Rapatriement et l'Immigration (Quebec, 1888), p. 10.
17. J. B. Proulx, A La Baie d'Hudson (Montreal, 1886), p. 32.
18. Le Canadien, 13 Sept. 1880, p. 2, "Mandement de Monseigneur E. A. Taschereau, Archévêque de Québec, sur la Colonisation, 1er Septembre 1880."
19. Québec, Commission de Colonisation, General Report (English version), 1904 (Quebec, 1904), p. 45.
20. Father Labelle, quoted in Georges Vattier, Esquisse Historique de la Colonisation de la Province de Québec, 1608-1925 (Paris, 1928), p. 107.
21. F. X. A. Labelle, Pamphlet sur La Colonisation dans la Vallée d'Ottawa . . . et Règlements et Avantages de la Société de Colonisation du Diocèse de Montréal (Montreal, 1880), p. 19.
22. Ibid., p. 19.
23. Quebec, Crown Lands, Report, 1867-68, p. xi.
24. Québec, Commission de Colonisation, 1904, Rapport, Appendix, Enquiry at Hull, p. 127 (evidence of R. Sissons).
25. Ibid., p. 103.
26. Ibid., pp. 171-72.
27. Ibid., General Report (English version), p. 124.

NOTES TO CHAPTER EIGHT

1. William F. Ryan, The Clergy and Economic Growth in Quebec, 1896-1914 (Quebec, 1966), p. 195.
2. Québec, Commission de Colonisation, 1904, Report (English version), Appendix, Enquiry at Hull, p. 155.
3. John H. Dales, Hydroelectricity and Industrial Development, Quebec, 1898-1940 (Cambridge, Mass., 1957), pp. 13-24, 30-1, 35.
4. La Défense, 3 Feb. 1898.
5. Ryan, The Clergy and Economic Growth, Chaps. 2 and 3.
6. Victor A. Huard, Labrador et Anticosti (Montreal, 1897), pp. 120, 164, 202-44, 421-31.
7. Lambert, Renewing Nature's Wealth, pp. 253-55, 261-63.
8. Canada, Commission of Conservation, First Report, 1910, p. 79; Merrill Denison, The People's Power, the History of Ontario Hydro (Toronto, 1960), pp. 77, 89.
9. Québec, Commission de Colonisation, 1904, Report (English version). For Bourassa, see Annexes: Enquêtes à Montréal, pp. 314-31; C.A.R., 1902, pp. 56; 1904, pp. 311-12; 1906, p. 367.
10. Ontario, Crown Lands, Land Settlement in New Ontario, A Short Account of the Advantages offered Land Seekers in Ontario (Toronto, 1903), p. 21.
11. Canadian Press Association, New Ontario, The Canadian Press Association's Excursion to Temiskaming (Welland, Ont., 1903).
12. J. Konarek, "Algoma Central and Hudson Bay Railway: The Beginnings," Ontario History, LXXII (2), June 1970, pp. 73-81.
13. J. G. Scott, Trans-Canada Railway (Quebec, 1903); C.A.R., 1902, pp. 222-24; 1903, pp. 429-30.
14. Ontario, Statutes, 2 Edw. VII (1902), Chap. 9.
15. C.A.R., 1902, pp. 47-51, 236-37; 1904, pp. 263, 274-75; 1905, p. 290; 1906, pp. 113-17, 335.
16. Canada, Commons, Debates, 1911-12, cols. 6080, 6082, 6401-49; 1912-13, cols. 11802, 11873-11906, 12181; Senate, Debates, 1911-12, pp. 894, 940-51; 1912-13, pp. 1000, 1045-59; Canada, Statutes, 3-4 Geo.V (1913), Chap. 53.
17. Ontario, Royal Ontario Nickel Commission, 1917, Report, pp. 67-68, 71-76, 79-80.
18. Margaret Van Every, "Francis Hector Clergue and the Rise of Sault Ste.

294 THE OPENING OF THE CANADIAN NORTH

Marie," *Ontario History*, LVI (3), Sept. 1964, pp. 191-202.

19. Liberal Party, Ontario, *The Ross Government and Progressive Ontario, A Brief Study of Ontario's Development under Liberal Government, Provincial Elections January 25, 1905* (n.p., n.d.), pp. 11-12; C.A.R., 1903, pp. 513-15; 1904, pp. 268-74; 1905, pp. 198, 584; Brian D. Tennyson, "The Political Career of Sir William H. Hearst," M.A. thesis, University of Toronto, 1963, pp. 7-42.

20. C.A.R., 1906, pp. 312-13; 1907, pp. 248, 501; 1909, p. 364; 1913, p. 72.

21. Innis, *Settlement and the Mining Frontier*, pp. 321-40.

22. *Ibid.*, pp. 322, 349-54, 380-85, 401-3, 409-12; C.A.R., 1906, pp. 55, 335-37; 1907, pp. 206-7, 212; 1908, pp. 270-71, 274-75; 1909, pp. 346-48.

23. Québec, Commission de Colonisation, 1904, *Rapport*, Appendix, Enquiry at Hull, p. 152.

24. C.A.R., 1907, pp. 227-33, 252; 1908, pp. 125-28, 369.

25. *Railway and Shipping World*, 1902, p. 63.

26. G. R. Stevens, *Canadian National Railways*, vol. 2, *Towards the Inevitable, 1896-1922* (Toronto, 1962), 121-71; Canada, National Transcontinental Railway Investigating Commission, *Report* (2 vols., Ottawa, 1914).

27. Canada, *Statutes*, 4 Edw. VII (1904), Chap. 60; 1-2 Geo. V (1911), Chap. 6; C.A.R., 1904, pp. 275-76; 1905, p. 556; 1906, pp. 140-41, 346; 1908, p. 563; 1909, pp. 368-69.

28. Ivanhoë Caron, *Un Nouveau Centre de Colonisation, l'Abitibi* (Quebec, 1915), pp. 59-60.

29. Liberal Party, Ontario, *The Liberal Platform discussed by Hon. G. W. Ross at Barrie* (n.p., 1904), p. 10.

30. B. E. Fernow, *Conditions in the Clay Belt of New Ontario* (Commission of Conservation, Ottawa, 1913).

31. C.A.R., 1905, p. 274; 1907, pp. 498-500, 504-5; Tennyson, "Sir William H. Hearst," Chap. 2.

32. Liberal Party, Ontario, *New Ontario: Liberal Policy to Develop Its Resources, Conservative Hostility to Its Development* (Toronto, 1904), p. 2.

33. Québec, Commission de Colonisation, 1904, *Rapport*, Annexes: Enquêtes à Montréal, pp. 324, 323.

34. Québec, Terres et Forêts, Service Hydraulique, *Tableau des Forces Hydrauliques Concédées par la Province de Québec du 1e Juillet 1867 au 30 Juin, 1923* (Quebec, 1923).

35. Dales, *Hydroelectricity and Industrial Development*, pp. 23-24, 30-32.

36. Lambert, *Renewing Nature's Wealth*, pp. 255-58, 573; C.A.R., 1906, p. 80; 1909, p. 342.

37. C.A.R., 1913, pp. 378-400; 1914, p. 438.

38. Ontario, Timber Commission, 1920, *Report* (1922), pp. 47-49, "Special Report on the New Ontario Colonization Company Limited."

39. Conservative Party, Ontario, *Splendid Record of the Whitney Government: Ontario Elections, 1911—Seven Years of the Square Deal* (Toronto, 1911), pp. 44-48; C.A.R., 1906, pp. 57, 335-36; 1907, pp. 507-9, 511; 1908, pp. 268-69, 284-87; 1909, pp. 350-51.

40. Canada, *Statutes*, 8-9 Edw. VII (1909), Chap. 27; C.A.R., 1906, pp. 81-84; 1908, p. 126; 1909, pp. 189-91, 217.

41. Canada, Commission of Conservation, *First Report*, 1910, pp. xi-xv, 1-2, 175; *Ibid.*, *Fourth Report*, 1913, pp. 178-80.

42. Canada, Commons, *Debates*, 1921, pp. 2, 875, 3146, 3739, 3958-76; Senate, *Debates*, pp. 406, 461-71, 510-20; Statutes, 11-12 Geo. V (1921), Chap. 23. See Stewart Renfrew, "Commission of Conservation," *Douglas Library Notes*, XIX (3-4), Spring 1971, pp. 17-27.

43. *Canadian Mining Journal*, XLII, May 27, 1921, p. 418.

NOTES TO CHAPTER NINE

1. Canada, Interior, *Report*, 1905-6, I, p. 18.

2. Canada Senate, *Journals*, 1906-7, Appendix I, "Report . . . as to the Value of That Portion of the Dominion lying North of the Saskatchewan Watershed

and East of the Rocky Mountains . . . ."

3. Canada, Commons, *Debates*, 1903, cols. 7658-97.

4. *Ibid.*, col. 8805.

5. Canada, *Statutes*, 3 Edw. VII (1903), Chap. 71, Sec. 28.

6. *Ibid.*, Chap. 122, Sec. 12.

7. *Ibid.*, 2 Edw. VII (1902), Chap. 90; 7-8 Edw. VII (1908), Chap. 63, Sec. 57; 9-10 Edw. VII (1910), Chap. 51, Item 40.

8. Canada, Railways and Canals, Files 4402, I and II (Grand Trunk Pacific Route Maps) and 6511 (Edmonton, Yukon and Pacific, Route Maps); Stevens, *Canadian National Railways*, II, 92-93.

9. Canada, *Statutes*, 9-10 Edw. VII (1910), Chap. 6; 2 Geo. V (1912), Chaps. 7 and 8; Canada, Commons, *Debates*, 1911-12, cols. 5162-66, 5404-5, 5841-42, 6372-73; *Railway and Marine World*, 1910, pp. 487, 649, 1031.

10. Canada, *Statutes*, 2 Geo. V (1912), Chaps. 7 and 8; 3-4 Geo. V (1913(1)), Chap. 10; 4-5 Geo. V (1914), Chap. 20; Stevens, *Canadian National Railways*, II, 90-99.

11. B.C., *Statutes*, 1 Geo. V (1911), Chap. 74.

12. Canada, G.S.C., *Annual Report*, VII (1894), Part C, "Report on an Exploration of the Finlay and Omineca Rivers," by R. G. McConnell, p. 10C.

13. B.C., Lands and Works, *Report*, 1901-2, F, p. 100-1, Report of F. W. Valleau, Omineca Division, 5 Nov. 1902.

14. B.C., Lands, *Report*, 1913, I, (Lands), pp. D8-44; IV (Survey Branch), pp. D305-6, 351-55.

15. *Ibid.*, I (Lands), pp. D25-34.

16. Canada, *Statutes*, 8-9 Edw. VII (1909), Chap. 86; Alberta, *Statutes*, 2-3 Geo. V (1912), Chap. 18; *Edmonton Bulletin*, 9 May, 28 June 1911; 29 Jan., 26 Sept., 3, 12 Oct., 12 Dec. 1912; A. A. den Otter, "Social Life of a Mining Community: The Coal Branch," *Alberta Historical Review*, XVII (4), Autumn 1969, pp. 1-11.

17. Canada, Interior, *Report*, 1912-13, VI, p. 45.

18. B.C., Lands, *Report*, 1913, II, (Forest Branch), pp. D48-84.

19. Canada, Interior, *Report*, 1907-8, III, pp. 140-50, VII, p. 18; 1908-9, V, pp. 12-

13; 1909-10, pp. xxxvii, V, 16-18,VII, 9-10; 1910-11, V, pp. 10-14, 38-40.

20. Canada, Commons, *Debates*, 1905, cols. 1425-40.

21. *Ibid.*, col. 3094.

22. Canada, *Statutes*, 4-5 Edw. VII (1905), Chap. 27; Interior, *Report*, 1904-5, p. xxxix.

23. P.A.C., R.G. 18, A2, vols. 138-39, Letterbooks, N.W.T. Commissioner's Office, 1905-8; R.G. 32, C2, Historical Personnel, vol. 480, "Frederick White"; Bovey, "Attitudes and Policies," Chap. 6.

24. Canada, Commons, *Debates*, 1905, col. 3358.

25. Canada, *Statutes*, 1905, p. xliii, "Petroleum Leases, Order in Council, 1 Oct. 1904."

26. Canada, Interior, *Report*, 1909-10, I, p. 4; 1911-12, I, p. 50; Canada, Royal Commission on the Natural Resources of Alberta (1935), Evidence, Exhibit 228A; *Edmonton Bulletin*, 23 Feb., 19 Dec. 1911.

27. Canada, Interior, *Report*, 1910-11, I, pp. 59-60; 1911-12, I, p. 50.

28. Alberta, *Statutes*, 9 Edw. VII (1909), Chaps. 14, 16, 46; *Journals*, 1908, pp. 46-47, 50; 1909, pp. 29, 31, 34, 35, 43, 55, 61, 62, 71, 81, 82, 89.

29. Alberta, *Journals*, 1910 (1), pp. 15-18, 21-23, 29-32, 37-39, 42-43, 47-54, 71-74, 75, 80, 89; *Toronto Globe*, 11, 12, 19, 21, 23, 30 March, 26, 27 May 1910; Lewis G. Thomas, *The Liberal Party in Alberta* (Toronto, 1959), pp. 70-91.

30. Alberta, Royal Commission to Investigate the Organization of the Alberta and Great Waterways Railway Company, 1910, *Report*, p. 27; Thomas, *Liberal Party*, pp. 98-102.

31. Alberta, *Statutes*, 1 Geo. V (1910(2)), Chaps. 9 and 11; *Journals*, 1910(2), pp. 23, 24, 31, 33, 37, 40-42, 45, 47, 62, 118.

32. *Canadian Finance*, II (4), 15 Feb. 1911, p. 183.

33. *Ibid.*, II (12), 21 June 1911, p. 553.

34. B.C., *Statutes*, 2 Geo. V (1912), Chaps. 34 and 36; 4 Geo. V (1914), Chap. 65; Patricia E. Roy, "Railways, Politics and the Development of the City of Vancouver as a Metropolitan Centre, 1886-1929," M.A. thesis, University of Toronto, 1963, pp. 169-84.

35. Alberta, *Statutes*, 1 Geo. V (1910(2)), Chap. 48; 2-3 Geo. V (1911-12), Chaps.

19 and 29; *Journals*, 1911-12, pp. 27, 102-18.

36. Canada, *Statutes*, 6-7 Edw. VII (1907), Chap. 85; 2-3 Geo. V (1911-12), Chap. 16.

37. Alberta, *Statutes*, 3 Geo. V (1913(1)), Chap. 46; 4 Geo. V (1913(2)), Chap. 6; J. D. Williams, "A History of the Edmonton, Dunvegan, and British Columbia Railway, 1907-29," M.A. thesis, University of Alberta, 1956; M. Zaslow, "A History of Transportation and Development of the Mackenzie Basin from 1871 to 1921," M.A. thesis, University of Toronto, 1948, pp. 289-304.

38. Canada, R.N.W.M.P. *Report*, 1909, I, pp. 120, 123, 126-27, 175-77; 1910, I, pp. 40-41; 1911, I, pp. 49, 50, 182-83; Interior, *Report*, 1909-10, I, p. 12; 1911-12, I, pp. 21-23; A. M. Bezanson, *Sodbusters Invade the Peace* (Toronto, 1954); C. A. Dawson and R. W. Murchie, *The Settlement of the Peace River Country* (Toronto, 1934, Canadian Frontiers of Settlement, VI), pp. 27-39.

39. Canada, R.N.W.M.P., *Report*, 1908, I, pp. 115-16; Interior, Topographical Survey, *Report*, 1906-7, pp. 176-77, 179-80; 1913-14, pp. 122-23; Agnes Deans Cameron, *The New North* (New York, 1912), pp. 335-44.

40. Canada, Transport, A *Statutory History of the Steam and Electric Railways of Canada, 1836-1937*, compiled by Robert Dorman (Ottawa, 1938), pp. 111-12, 319-20, 405, 644-45; Howard A. Fleming, *Canada's Arctic Outlet* (Berkeley, Calif., 1957), pp. 39-49; Stevens, *Canadian National Railways*, II. 424-31.

41. Fleming, *op. cit.*, pp. 61-69; Stevens, *op. cit.*, pp. 432-39; C.A.R., 1905, p. 556; 1906, pp. 149-51, 422; 1907, pp. 148-52;

1908, pp. 77-78, 222-25; 1909, pp. 618-19; 1910, pp. 607-8, 610-11; 1911, p. 645; Canada, *Sessional Papers*, 1911, no. 19B, "Nelson River, Report upon Reconnaissance Survey, 1909," Railways and Canals, *Report*, 1909-10, V, pp. 211-30; 1910-11, p. xv; Naval Service, *Report*, 1910-11, pp. 34-41.

42. C.A.R., 1902, pp. 69-70; 1904, pp. 345-46, 364-67; 1905, pp. 91-97, 357-65; 1906, pp. 524-27; Norman L. Nicholson, *The Boundaries of Canada* (Canada, Mines and Technical Surveys, Geographical Branch, Memoir No. 3), pp. 79-80.

43. C.A.R., 1907, pp. 573-76, 579-81.

44. Canada, *Statutes*, 2 Geo. V (1912), Chap. 32; C.A.R., 1908, pp. 465-67; 1909, pp. 502-4; 1910, p. 482; 1911, pp. 240-41, 552; 1912, pp. 220-28, 511-13; G. R. Cook, "Church, Schools, and Politics in Manitoba, 1903-12," C.H.R., XXXIX (1), Mar. 1958, pp. 1-23.

45. Canada, *Statutes*, 2 Geo. V (1912), Chaps. 40 and 45; Commons, *Debates*, 1907-8, cols. 12785-93; Nicholson, *Boundaries*, pp. 87-88.

46. C.A.R., 1912, pp. 345-46, 405-7; 1913, p. 361.

47. Ontario, Mines, *Report*, 1913, pp. 161-209, "Hudson Bay Exploring Expedition, 1912," by J. B. Tyrrell.

48. Canada, Naval Service, *Report*, 1911-12, pp. 43-57; 1912-13, pp. 51-58; 1913-14, pp. 42, 48-60; 1914-15, pp. 11, 93-94; Railway and Canals, *Report*, 1911-12, pp. xv-xvi; 1912-13, pp. 17, 335; 1913-14, pp. 379-84; 1914-15, pp. 369-74; 1915-16, pp. 173-77; 1916-17, pp. xiv-xv, 70-71; Frederick Palmer, *Report on the Selection of a Terminal Port for the Hudson Bay Railway* (Ottawa, 1927?), pp. 11-12, 15-20; Stevens, *Canadian National Railways*, II, 440-43.

NOTES TO CHAPTER TEN

1. Canada, Indian Affairs, *Report*, 1898-99, pp. xviii-xix, xxxv-xlix; 1899-1900, pp. xxxix-xlvii, and map; 1900-1, p. 201-2.

2. *Ibid.*, 1899-1900, p. xxxix; 1908-9, p. 202; Interior, *Report*, 1899, p. xxi, VIII, pp. 1-9; 1900-1, VI, pp. 3-8; Charles Mair, *Tecumseh, A Drama and Canadian Poems*, etc. (Toronto, 1926 edition), pp.

307-462, "Through the Mackenzie Basin."

3. Canada, Indian Affairs, *Report*, 1904-5, pp. xviii-xix; 1905-6, pp. 284-315; 1906-7, II, p. 68; 1910-11, II, p. 54.

4. *Ibid.*, 1907-8, pp. xxii, xl-xli; 1908-9, II, p. 55.

5. *Ibid.*, 1909-10, p. 110; 1910-11, pp. xx-xxi, 114-15, 161-62; 1912-13, p. 121.

6. *Ibid.*, 1907-8, p. xxii; 1908-9, p. 180;

1910-11, p. xx; 1911-12, pp. 125-28; 1912-13, pp. 115, 189-92; 1913-14, II, pp. 54-55, 80-84, 167; 1914-15, pp. 55, 57-58.

7. *Ibid.*, 1904-5, pp. 271-78; 1905-6, pp. 271-84; 1906-7, pp. 274-77; 1908-9, pp. 272-74, 279; 1909-10, pp. 259-68; 1910-11, pp. 281-86; C. R. Maundrell, "Indian Health, 1867-1940," M.A. thesis, Queen's University, 1941.

8. Canada, *Statutes*, 4-5 Geo. V (1914), Chap. 35; Indian Affairs, *Report*, 1908-9, p. 268; 1913-14, p. xxiv; 1914-15, p. xxv.

9. *Ibid.*, 1902-3, p. 239; 1904-5, pp. 277-78; 1906-7, p. 277; 1907-8, p. 277; 1909-10, pp. xxx-xxxi, 259, 271-75; 1910-11, pp. xxvi-xxvii, 291-96; H. J. Vallery, "A History of Indian Education in Canada," M.A. thesis, Queen's University, 1942, pp. 71-141; Maurice H. Lewis, "The Anglican Church and Its Mission Schools Dispute," *Alberta Historical Review*, XIV (4), Autumn 1966.

10. Canada, Indian Affairs, *Report*, 1910-11, pp. 294-95; Msgr. Gabriel Breynat, *Cinquante Ans au Pays des Neiges*, Vol. 2, *Voyageur du Christ* (Montreal, 1947), pp. 100, 191-92.

11. Canada, Indian Affairs, *Report*, 1910-11, pp. 439-43.

12. *Ibid.*, 1909-10, p. 271; 1913-14, pp. 113, II, pp. 186-200 ("Schedule of Establishment of Indian Boarding and Industrial Schools").

13. *Ibid.*, 1907-8, p. 196.

14. *Ibid.*, 1909-10, pp. 165-66; 1910-11, p. 187; Frederick H. Abbott, *The Administration of Indian Affairs in Canada* (Washington, 1915), p. 83.

15. Canada, Indian Affairs, *Report*, 1906-7, p. xxxiv; 1913-14, II, pp. 46-47; Luta Munday, *A Mounty's Wife* (London, 1930), p. 64.

16. Canada, Indian Affairs, *Report*, 1905-6, pp. 244-45; 1907-8, II, p. 64; 1908-9, p. 266; 1909-10, p. 252; 1910-11, pp. 234-35; C.A.R., 1906, p. 124; 1907, p. 123; 1908, pp. 526, 528; Stevens, *Canadian National Railways*, II, 200-1.

17. Shankel, "Indian Policy in British Columbia," pp. 193-235, 267-79.

18. Canada, Indian Affairs, *Report*, 1911-12, p. 3.

19. *Ibid.*, 1912-13, p. 26.

20. *Ibid.*, p. 269.

21. *Ibid.*, 1913-4, II, p. 7.

22. *Ibid.*, 1910-11, p. 387.

23. Ernest Thompson Seton, *The Arctic Prairies* (London, 1912), p. 9.

24. Elihu Stewart, *Down the Mackenzie and Up the Yukon in 1906* (London, 1913).

25. Canada, Indian Affairs, *Report*, 1910-11, p. 189; C.A.R., 1910, pp. 232-33, 520; Breynat, *Cinquante Ans*, II, 100, 186-91.

26. Canada, G.S.C., *Annual Report*, XII (1899), Part C "Report on the Topography and Geology of Great Bear Lake and of a Chain of Lakes and Streams thence, to Great Slave Lake," p. 16C.

27. *Ibid.*, XV (1902), pp. 151-69; XVI (1904), Part CC; *Summary Report*, 1905, pp. 36-46; 1908, pp. 33-37.

28. *Edmonton Bulletin*, 29 Aug., 4 Sept. 1912.

29. Canada, Interior, *Report*, 1900, pp. xxx, III, p. 6; 1900-1, III, pp. 98-131.

30. Marcel Sexé, *Two Centuries of Fur Trading, 1713-1923, Romance of the Revillon Family* (n.p., n.d.), pp. 57-83; Harold A. Innis, *The Fur Trade in Canada*, rev. ed. (Toronto, 1962), pp. 367-68.

31. Innis, *op. cit.*, pp. 366-68; Canada, N.W.M.P., *Report*, 1901, p. 55; 1903, I, pp. 44-45; 1908, I, pp. 119, 153; 1909, I, p. 185; *Edmonton Bulletin*, 16 Sept. 1897; 17 Dec. 1903; 4 May 1911; *Northern News* (Athabasca Landing), 20 May 1909; 28 April 1910; 1 June 1912.

32. Canada, N.W.M.P., *Report*, 1901, p. 56.

33. *Ibid.*, 1903, I, pp. 43-52.

34. Canada, R.N.W.M.P., *Report*, 1905, I, p. 3; 1908, I, p. 115; 1910, I, p. 71, II, p. 206; 1914, II, p. 217.

35. *Ibid.*, 1903, I, p. 41; 1905, I, pp. 3-5, 31-42; 1906, I, pp. 2-4, 141-49; 1907, I, pp. 7-10, 154-58; 1911, I, p. 58.

36. *Ibid.*, 1903, I, p. 48; 1907, I, pp. 11, 122-29; 1908, I, pp. 126-39; 1909, I, pp. 22, 178-80, 187-92; 1910, I, pp. 25, 50-51, 160, 195-200; 1912, I, pp. 134-35; Interior, *Report*, 1911-12, VI, pp. 24-25, 140-45; 1912-13, VI, pp. 109-19; 1914-15, VI, pp. 108-12.

37. Canada, R.N.W.M.P., *Report*, 1911, I, pp. 25-27, V, pp. 291-319; 1912, I, pp. 187-91.

38. *Ibid.*, 1909, I, pp. 141-68.

39. George Whalley, *The Legend of John Hornby* (Toronto, 1962), pp. 32-104.
40. Canada, R.N.W.M.P., *Report*, 1916, I,

pp. 12, 344-57; 1916-17, pp. 10-12.
41. *Ibid.*, 1915, I, pp. 13-14, 144-45, 202-12; 1916, pp. 12, 190-253.

NOTES TO CHAPTER ELEVEN

1. P.A.C., R.G. 7, G21, Governor General's Numbered Files, no. 135, "Annexation to Dominion of all British Territories ... with the Islands Adjacent Thereto," Carnarvon to Dufferin, 30 April 1874.
2. *Ibid.*, Dufferin to Carnarvon, 4 Nov. 1874, enclosing P.C. 1248, 10 Oct. 1874.
3. *Ibid.*, Carnarvon to Dufferin, 6 Jan. 1875, and Dufferin to Carnarvon, 1 May 1875, enclosing P.C. 46 D, 30 April 1875.
4. Carnarvon to Dufferin, 23 Oct. 1877.
5. Edward Blake to John Bramstrom(?), 29 Jan. 1879, in C.O. 42, vol. 759, p. 19 (P.A.C. microfilm, reel B-596).
6. Canada, Commons, *Debates*, 1878, pp. 2386-94.
7. *Ibid.*, p. 2390.
8. *Ibid.*, pp. 2391-94.
9. P.A.C., Governor General's Numbered Files, no. 296, "Status of Hudson's Bay and Hudson's Straits, 1878-1908," Hicks-Beach to Dufferin, 17 July 1878; Hicks-Beach to Lorne, 18 April 1879. See also Gordon W. Smith, "The Transfer of Arctic Territories from Great Britain to Canada in 1880 . . . ," *Arctic*, XIV (1), March 1961, pp. 55-61.
10. Hicks-Beach to Lorne, 19 April 1879, in Smith, *op. cit.*, pp. 61-62.
11. *Canada Gazette*, XIV (15), 9 Oct. 1880, p. 389.
12. Canada, Interior, *Report upon the Title of Canada to the Islands North of the Mainland of Canada*, by W. F. King (Ottawa, 1905), pp. 5-6; Smith, *op. cit.*, pp. 65-69.
13. King, *op. cit.*, p. 6.
14. Canada, Commons, *Debates*, 1884, pp. 203-7, 1379-81, 1607, 1617; *Journals*, Appendix 2, "Report of the Select Committee to enquire into the Navigation of Hudson's Bay."
15. Canada, Marine, *Report*, 1885-86, "Report of the Hudson's Bay Expedition of 1886 under the Command of Lieut. A. R. Gordon," p. 11.
16. *Ibid.*, pp. 90-92.
17. Quoted in F. A. Peake, *The Bishop Who Ate His Boots, A Biography of*

Isaac O. Stringer (Don Mills, 1966), p. 36.
18. Hudson Stuck, *A Winter's Circuit of Our Arctic Coast* (New York, 1920), p. 320.
19. C. E. Whittaker, *Arctic Eskimo* (London, 1937), pp. 234-35.
20. Canada, Interior, *Report*, 1891, IV, p. 4.
21. Canada, N.W.M.P., *Report*, 1896, p. 238.
22. Canada, Marine and Fisheries, *Report of the Expedition to Hudson Bay and Cumberland Gulf in the Steamship "Diana" under the Command of William Wakeham in the Year 1897* (Ottawa, 1898), p. 24; Canada, Commons, *Debates*, 1897, cols. 1810-35.
23. A. P. Low, *The Cruise of the Neptune*, 1903-04 (Ottawa, 1906), p. 46.
24. P.A.C., Laurier Papers, pp. 64244-50, J. E. Bernier to Laurier, 12 April 1902, enclosing signatures of 94 M.P.'s.
25. Canada, N.W.M.P., *Report*, 1901, p. 10.
26. Canada, Commons, *Debates*, 1903, cols. 2794-96.
27. P.A.C., Laurier Papers, p. 78417, Laurier to Edwards, 29 Oct. 1903, replying to Edwards' of 28 Oct. 1903, pp. 78415-16.
28. Quoted in Canada, Interior, *Southern Baffin Island, An Account of Exploration, Investigation, and Settlement During the Past Fifty Years*, compiled by A. E. Millward (Ottawa, 1930), pp. 14-15.
29. King, *Report upon the Title of Canada*, p. 8.
30. *Ibid.*, p. 24.
31. *Ibid.*, p. 26.
32. *Ibid.*
33. Canada, *Statutes*, 6 Edw. VII (1906), Chap. 13, Sec. 14.
34. Canada, Commons, *Debates*, 1906, col. 6856.
35. P.A.C., Governor General's Numbered Files, no. 296, Elgin to Grey, telegram of 24 July 1906.
36. T. W. Balch, "Is Hudson Bay a Closed

or Open Sea?" "The Hudsonian Sea is a Great Open Sea," *American Journal of International Law*, VI (1912), pp. 409-59; VII (1913), pp. 546-65.

37. Canada, Senate, *Debates*, 1906-7, p. 266.

38. Canada, Marine and Fisheries, *Report on the Dominion of Canada Government Expedition to the Arctic Islands and Hudson Strait on Board the D.G.S. 'Arctic'*, by J. E. Bernier (Ottawa, 1910), p. 38.

39. *Ibid.*, p. 195.

40. P.A.C., Laurier Papers, pp. 166833-35, Bernier to Laurier, 13 April 1910; also Laurier to Bernier, 14 April 1910.

41. Canada, N.W.M.P., *Report*, 1903, p. 53.

42. Canada, R.N.W.M.P., *Report*, 1905, I, pp. 127-28.

43. Canada, N.W.M.P., *Report*, 1903, p. 49.

44. J. E. Bernier, *Master Mariner and Arctic Explorer* (Ottawa, 1939), pp. 371-403.

45. P.A.C., M.G. 26, H, Borden Papers, p. 130237, Brock to W. J. Roche, 4 Feb. 1913.

46. P.A.C., R.G. 42, Marine, vol. 463, file 84-2-1, Brock to G. J. Desbarats, 28 May 1913.

47. Vilhjalmur Stefansson, *Discovery, the Autobiography of Vilhjalmur Stefansson* (New York, 1964), p. 156.

48. P.A.C., Marine, box 490, file 84-2-55, Desbarats to Stefansson, 5 May 1914.

49. *Ottawa Morning Journal*, 8 March 1923; Diamond Jenness, "The Friendly Arctic," *Science*, LVI, no. 1436 (7 July 1922), pp. 8-12; also the discussions by James White, F. A. McDiarmid and Stefansson in *Geographical Journal*, LXIII (6), June 1924, pp. 508-25, arising from McDiarmid's article, "Geographical Determinations of the Canadian Arctic Expedition," in *Ibid.*, LXII (4), Oct. 1923, pp. 293-302.

BIBLIOGRAPHICAL ESSAY

This work has adopted a survey approach to deal with a wide variety of governmental reports, newspaper accounts, and books and articles by participants, eyewitnesses, interviewers, and outside commentators. Extensive searches were also made into a similarly broad, scattered range of archival materials to check on the published sources or to make good the lack of such sources, to clarify particular situations, or secure appropriate illustrations of important trends or developments.

ARCHIVAL SOURCES

The following were consulted: in Ottawa, the Public Archives of Canada and other libraries of a number of departments and agencies of the Dominion government; in Montreal, the McCord Museum, McGill University (Redpath Library), and the Arctic Institute of North America; in Toronto, the Anglican Church of Canada Archives, United Church of Canada Central Archives, Toronto Public Library, University of Toronto Library, Ontario Archives, and the legislative library; in Chicoutimi, the collections of La Société Historique du Saguenay; in Kingston, Queen's University (Douglas Library); in London, University of Western Ontario (Lawson Memorial Library); in Winnipeg, the Manitoba Archives; in Regina and Saskatoon, Saskatchewan Archives; in Edmonton, Alberta Archives, the legislative library, and University of Alberta (Rutherford Library); in Calgary, the Glenbow Institute; in Vancouver, the University of British Columbia library; in Victoria, British Columbia Archives; as well as over a dozen centres in the northern parts of the provinces and territories beyond, from Cobalt to Dawson. In London the holdings of the British Museum, Church Missionary Society Archives, Hudson's Bay Company Archives, Royal Institute of International Affairs, and Royal Commonwealth Society were consulted; in Cambridge, the Scott Polar Research Institute; and in Paris the Ministère des Affaires Etrangères and the Bibliothèque Nationale. Researches in the United States included visits to the Stefansson Collection at Dartmouth College; the New York Public Library; the Library of Congress and National Archives, Washington; the University of Washington library and the National Archives (Region 10) Center in Seattle; and the Bancroft Library, Berkeley, California. The pertinent collections at each of these centres are too numerous to list here. Some have been cited in the footnotes, while others will be discussed under the appropriate headings in this essay. Fortunately for present and future researchers, it is becoming progressively easier to locate and use manuscript source materials for the topics of this study because major Canadian archives are securing copies of materials located in remote or inconvenient centres, and because an important national inventory of manuscript holdings has now been published. The appearance of this *Union List of Manuscripts in Canadian Repositories* (Ottawa, 1968) was a great forward step; but very much still remains to be done in this, as in the other, direction.

NEWSPAPERS

Newspapers were a useful type of printed source material; almost every newspaper of the time could be examined in connection with some aspect or other of this work. Those consulted included, for western Canada: the *Bulletin* and the *Journal* (Edmonton), *Saskatchewan Herald* (Battleford), *Northern News* (Athabasca Landing), *Leader* (Edson), *News* (Grouard), *Herald* (Grand Prairie), *Citizen* (Prince George), *British Colonist* (Victoria), *Star* (Whitehorse), *News* (Dawson), and *The Commercial* (Winnipeg). For eastern Canada: the *Globe, Mail, Financial Post* and *Northern Miner* (Toronto), *Temiskaming Speaker* (New Liskeard), and a wide variety of Quebec newspapers (encountered mainly as clippings in the excellent scrapbooks of La Sociéte Historique du Saguenay in Chicoutimi). Newspapers from outside Canada that were used included *The Times, New York Times,* San Francisco *Examiner;* and *Buchan Observer* and *Dundee Weekly Times* (at the newspaper library of the British Museum).

PERIODICALS AND SERIALS

Contemporary periodicals and annuals that contain information on aspects of the subject of this work include *The Canadian Annual Review of Public Affairs* (Toronto, 1901 *et seq.); Canada Year Book* (from 1905); *Canadian Mining Journal* (from 1880); *Canadian Forestry Journal* (from 1905, now *Forest and Outdoors*); *Canadian Transportation* (begun in 1898 as *Railway and Shipping World,* renamed *Railway and Marine World,* then *Canadian Railway and Marine World*); *Canadian Finance* (from 1910); *Canadian Magazine* (from 1893); *Maclean's Magazine* (from 1911; previously *Busy Man's Magazine*); *Ottawa Field Naturalist* (from 1887; renamed *Canadian Field Naturalist*); Royal Society of Canada, *Proceedings* and *Transactions* (from 1883); Société de Géographie de Québec, *Bulletin* (from 1880); and the major geographical serials, like Royal Geographical Society (London), *Journals, Proceedings,* and *The Geographical Journal;* Société de Géographie de Paris, *Bulletin;* Scottish Geographical Magazine; American Geographical Society (New York), *Bulletin;* and the familiar *National Geographic Magazine.*

Some of these periodicals and annuals also published historical accounts of early developments, but this is mainly the concern of a different group of publications, like *Review of Historical Publications Relating to Canada* (from 1896) and its successor, *Canadian Historical Review;* Canadian Historical Association, *Report; Alberta Historical Review; Saskatchewan History;* Historical and Scientific Society of Manitoba, *Papers;* British Columbia Historical Quarterly; Ontario Historical Society, *Papers and Records,* and *Ontario History; Washington Historical Quarterly* (now *Pacific Northwest Quarterly*); *Queen's Quarterly; The Beaver,* a particularly valuable source; *Canadian Geographical Journal; Cahiers de Géographie de Québec; R.C.M.P. Quarterly; Polar Record; Arctic;* and *North.*

OFFICIAL PUBLICATIONS

Governmental publications come in bewildering variety and abundance. Included are those of the Dominion and its predecessor, the Province of Canada; of six provinces extending from Quebec to British Columbia; of the first, pre-1905, North-West Territories and the Yukon Territory; of the United Kingdom, United States, and Newfoundland as they relate to Canada; and of international commissions and boards.

Official documents may be classified under the traditional legislative, administrative and judicial spheres. The last category does not figure extensively in this work, though records of court actions have been consulted on boundary and other questions. The legislative aspect is represented by:

1. *Statutes* and *Orders in Council,* published annually by the various governments, including (in the case of the Dominion) Imperial statutes and orders in council relating to Canada;

2. *Journals* of proceedings in the legislature, frequently including reports of special committees appointed to study particular questions;

3. *Debates,* published throughout the period only by the House of Commons and Senate of the Dominion, and for a time after 1879 by the legislature of Quebec. Ontario published indexes of the reports of legislative debates as printed in the major Toronto newspapers.

Administrative activities appear in the following types of publication:

1. Major orders in council and proclamations, usually printed along with the *Statutes*, arranged by departments of origination;

2. *Gazettes*, published weekly, fortnightly, or less frequently, containing more proclamations, orders in council and official announcements;

3. *Sessional Papers*, published annually, contain materials laid before the legislature during its session, including reports prepared as replies to questions in the legislature, as background material for impending legislation, or as special projects ordered for printing. Many sessional papers were not printed. Those of the Dominion previous to 1916 were lost in the Parliament Building fire of that year, but those of the provinces repose in the provincial archives or in the custody of the clerks of the legislatures.

The most important of these from the point of view of the present study are annual reports (which were also published separately) of Dominion government departments and agencies concerned with opening up and administering Canada's frontier areas:

1. *Department of the Interior*, established 1873 to take over the duties in the Northwest of the Department of the Secretary of State for the Provinces (1867-1873), notably the Dominion Lands Branch (established 1871), and Topographical Surveys, Forestry, National Parks, Water-Power and Immigration Branches, and for shorter periods of time, the Indian Affairs Branch (1873-80), Geological Survey (1873-90), and North-West Mounted Police (1878-83). The Department's reports also incorporated those of the North-West Territories, Keewatin and Yukon territorial governments for a time. Sometimes they also included special parts devoted to the half-breed (Métis) question, or to major explorations.

2. *Department of Indian Affairs*, published separately from 1880, was usually divided into parts: general report, statistics, and field reports by inspectors and agents.

3. *North-West Mounted Police* (Royal North-West Mounted Police after 1904), reports around the turn of the century began to be divided into separate parts related to statistical details of staff and operations, and to activities in special areas (Yukon, Mackenzie, Hudson Bay).

4. *Department of Mines*, created in 1907, merely issued the reports of its two branches – Mines Branch; and Geological Survey – whose annual reports were variously titled *Report of Progress* (1842-84), *Annual Report* (1885-1904), and *Summary Report* thereafter.

5. *Department of Marine and Fisheries* published a single report down to 1884 and after 1891, and separate reports for Marine and for Fisheries between 1884 and 1891. In addition, annual steamboat registers were published, as well as special reports relating to Arctic explorations, which also were issued separately.

6. *Department of the Naval Service*, established in 1910, among its other activities was a co-sponsor (with the Geological Survey) of the Canadian Arctic Expedition of 1913-18.

7. *Department of Railways and Canals* reports included those of the Board of Railway Commissioners (established 1903) and of the Hudson Bay Railway project, besides those of Railways (mainly statistical) and Canals (operations and new construction).

8. *Auditor-General* (now Public Accounts) reports are particularly helpful for specific details of government operations, like the names and salaries of persons employed by, or doing business with, the government, and of the work for which they were paid.

9. The annual reports of the Departments of Public Works, Post Office, Agriculture, Justice, and Customs, and the Census reports are also worth consulting for particular purposes.

10. Reports and evidence of royal commissions or other committees appointed to investigate specific topics. Most published only a single report, but the Commission

of Conservation, appointed for an extended term, published annual reports from 1910 to 1920, as well as numerous studies.

Besides their annual reports, many departments, notably the Departments of the Interior, Agriculture, Mines, and their several branches, issued special publications – pamphlets, bulletins or memoirs – on particular subjects. The Geological Survey, for example, had published so many of these by 1914 that the detailed list occupies 103 pages in A. G. Johnston, *Index of Publications, Geological Survey of Canada* (1845-1958) (Ottawa, 1961).

Provincial and territorial government publications followed the same pattern on a lesser scale, with *Statutes, Journals* and Appendices, *Gazettes, Sessional Papers* (of annual departmental reports and special papers); reports of boards and branches (like Ontario's Temiskaming and Northern Ontario Railway Commission, or its Hydro-electric Power Commission, or the Public Utilities Commissions of several provinces); royal commissions and commissions of inquiry; and monographs published by various departments and agencies of government. The principal departments or branches whose records were relevant for this study were concerned with the administration of lands, forests, agriculture, colonization, mines, game and fisheries, roads, railways and other public works, surveyors' reports, justice and police, municipal affairs, education, and regional development. A number of bibliographic aids list the publications of some governments, notably Olga B. Bishop, *Publications of the Government of the Province of Canada, 1841-1867* (Ottawa, 1963); Christine MacDonald, *Publications of the Government of the Northwest Territories, 1876-1905, and of the Province of Saskatchewan, 1905-1952* (Regina, 1952); Marjorie C. Holmes, *Publications of the Government of British Columbia, 1871-1947* (Victoria, 1950), and Hazel I. MacTaggart, *Publications of the Government of Ontario, 1901-1955* (Toronto, 1964). Particularly helpful in reducing the chaos of Quebec governmental publications to some semblance of order is *Répertoire des Publications Governementales du Québec de 1867 à 1964* (Quebec, 1968), by A. Beaulieu, J.-C. Bonenfant and Jean Hamelin. Those of some of the other governments are included in the regional bibliographies cited in the next paragraph.

BOOKS AND SERIES

In detailing the materials that relate to particular parts of this work, a thematic approach will be followed. For assistance with studies that can be related to specific regions, the following may be consulted: B. J. Lowther, *A Bibliography of British Columbia, 1849-1899* (Victoria, 1968); Bruce B. Peel, *Bibliography of the Prairie Provinces* (Toronto, 1955), and *Supplement* (1963); L. Spencer and S. E. Holland, *Northern Ontario, A Bibliography* (Toronto, 1968); Jim Lotz, *A Yukon Bibliography* (Northern Co-ordination and Research Centre, Ottawa, 1964); *Arctic Bibliography*, edited by Marie Tremaine for the Arctic Institute of North America, published biennially since 1953 and now extending to fourteen volumes; and W. C. Meyer, *Cumulative List of Theses in Canadian Geography* (Geographical Branch, Bibliographic Series No. 34 Ottawa, 1966). Published catalogues exist not only for the British Museum and Library of Congress holdings but also for important specialized collections like the H. H. Bancroft Library, the Stefansson Library, and the library of the Arctic Institute of North America. Other bibliographies prepared along topical lines, such as the University of Manitoba, Centre for Settlement Studies, *Bibliography – Resource Frontier Communities* (2 vols., Winnipeg, 1964), can be consulted for such subjects. Finally, another class of useful bibliographic aids is concerned with sorts of material – catalogues of manuscript collections, newspaper directories, Canadian pamphlets, periodical articles, theses, theses on microfilm, and theses in progress.

Special place among previously published scholarly work belongs to three major co-operative series whose volumes are particularly relevant to the present study. The subject matter of *Canada and Its Provinces*, edited by Adam Shortt and A. G. Doughty (23 vols., Toronto, 1914-17), corresponds closely in scope with the present work since its terminal date was almost identical with that of this study. Subtitled "A History of the Canadian People and their Institutions by One Hundred Associates," it contains no fewer than seventy-two articles by fifty-seven contributors that are relevant to the contents of his book.

The general theme of the Canadian Frontiers of Settlement Series – a product of Canadian-American scholarly co-operation during the 1930's – is also close to that of the present work. That series, however, concentrated mainly on prairie agriculture, which this study largely ignores. Besides, most of the volumes had a contemporary sociological, economic, or geographic focus and hence they do not shed much light on the period before 1914. Nevertheless, certain volumes have been of considerable value, notably C. A. Dawson, Pioneering in the Prairie Provinces (Toronto, 1940), C. A. Dawson and R. W. Murchie, The Settlement of the Peace River Country (Toronto, 1934), and the two double volumes with a historical focus: A. S. Morton and Chester Martin's A History of Prairie Settlement and "Dominion Lands" Policy (Toronto, 1936); and A. R. M. Lower, Settlement and the Forest Frontier in Eastern Canada and Harold A. Innis, Settlement and the Mining Frontier (Toronto, 1936), the latter perhaps the best single book concerned with the subjects of this study.

The third series, The Relations of Canada and the United States, was sponsored by the Carnegie Endowment for International Peace and was almost entirely historical in focus, though only some of the volumes are pertinent to this work: A. R. M. Lower et al., The North American Assault on the Canadian Forest (Toronto and New Haven, 1938); G. P. deT. Glazebrook, A History of Transportation in Canada (Toronto and New Haven, 1938); L. E. Ellis, Reciprocity, 1911 (New Haven, 1939); H. Marshall, F. A. Southard and K. W. Taylor, Canadian-American Industry (New Haven and Toronto, 1936); and especially, F. W. Howay, W. N. Sage and H. F. Angus, British Columbia and the United States (New Haven and Toronto, 1942). Several of the other volumes, especially those concerned with diplomacy and population movements, have also been helpful.

SPECIAL SUBJECTS

The West at Confederation

Two earlier volumes in this present series – E. E. Rich, The Fur Trade and the Northwest to 1857 (Toronto, 1967) and W. L. Morton, The Critical Years: The Union of British North America, 1857-1873 (Toronto, 1964) – cover the earlier history of the Canadian West, the subject of the monumental study by Arthur S. Morton, A History of the Canadian West to 1870-1 (London, 1939) that crowned that distinguished scholar's lifetime of research and writing. W. L. Morton has published an excellent provincial history, Manitoba, A History (Toronto, 1957). British Columbia is similarly served by Margaret A. Ormsby, British Columbia, A History (Toronto, 1958), which supersedes the earlier F. W. Howay, British Columbia, The Making of a Province (Toronto, 1928). Indeed, even the venerable H. H. Bancroft, History of British Columbia, 1792-1887 (San Francisco, 1887) still has value through being based on interviews with many of the makers of the colony and province. Howay, Sage and Angus, British Columbia and the United States, which deals mainly with economic development and northward expansion both before and after 1871, is very useful in these contexts.

The best contemporary account of the state of affairs in the two western communities in 1870-71 is the simply-named Red River (Montreal, 1871) by J. J. Hargrave, written expressly to set the record straight in the face of widespread misunderstandings of the situation by Canadians. A realistic statement of the condition of British Columbia at the time of Confederation is a compilation prepared for the purposes of the Dominion government: Canada, Public Works, British Columbia, Report of the Hon. H. L. Langevin, C.B. (Ottawa, 1872). Furthermore the flavour of the situation is preserved faithfully in three of the best of all Canadian travel accounts written coincidentally with the acquisition of the West by Canada: the soldier W. F. Butler's The Great Lone Land (London, 1872), his The Wild North Land (London,

1873); and Rev. George M. Grant's celebrated *Ocean to Ocean: Sanford Fleming's Expedition through Canada in 1872* (Toronto, 1873).

Frontier Experience of the Province of Canada

Anna M. Wright, "The Canadian Frontier, 1840-1867" (Ph.D. thesis, University of Toronto, 1943), an extremely useful study that deserves to be far better known, embraces both the frontier experience of the province, and Canadians' drive to expand to the West. The main contemporary sources for the first subject are the annual reports of the Commissioner of Crown Lands, which besides recording land disposal and surveys, furnishes information on agriculture, forestry, mining, fisheries, Indian affairs, and colonization roads as these became departmental responsibilities. Annual reports of the Department of Public Works and those of the Geological Survey contain other records of governmental activities in frontier districts. A comprehensive study of the government departments and their operations is J. E. Hodgetts, *Pioneer Public Service* (Toronto, 1955). Particular aspects of frontier administration are dealt with in Duncan Campbell Scott, "Indian Affairs, 1840-1867," in *Canada and Its Provinces*, vol. 6; B. J. Harrington, *The Life of Sir William E. Logan, Kt.* (London, 1883), for the early years of the Geological Survey; G. W. Spragge, "Colonization Roads in Canada West, 1850-1867," *Ontario History*, LIX (1), Winter, 1957; H. M. Morrison, "The Background of the Free Land Homestead Law of 1872," Canadian Historical Association, *Report*, 1935; and for the contest between agriculture and forestry, A. R. M. Lower, *The North American Assault on the Canadian Forest*, and his *Settlement and the Forest Frontier in Eastern Canada*. An excellent study, Florence B. Murray, ed., *Muskoka and Haliburton, 1615-1875* (Ontario Series of the Champlain Society, Toronto, 1963), offers a comprehensive study of the activities of these and other agencies on the difficult frontier of the Huron and Ottawa tract.

The drive to expand into the West is reflected in such works as Canada (Province), *Return ... Title to the Hudson's Bay Territory* (Toronto, 1857); John Ryerson, *Hudson Bay* (Toronto, 1855); Alexander Morris's nationalistic lectures, *Nova Britannia* (Montreal, 1858) and *The Hudson's Bay and Pacific Territories* (Montreal, 1859); the reports of the Dawson-Hind expeditions of 1858 and 1859; and A. J. Russell, *The Red River Country, Hudson's Bay & North-west Territories, Considered in Relation to Canada* (Ottawa, 1869). Useful later accounts are found in "Introduction" by W. S. Wallace to John McLean, *Notice of a Twenty-Five Years' Service in the Hudson's Bay Territories* (Champlain Society, Toronto, 1932); A. M. Wright, "The Canadian Frontier"; J. M. S. Careless, *Brown of the Globe* (2 vols., Toronto, 1959, 1963), as well as biographies of other major Canadian political figures. The American challenge receives a very satisfactory treatment in Alvin C. Glueck Jr., *Minnesota and the Manifest Destiny of the Canadian Northwest* (Toronto, 1965).

The Native Peoples

A long-standing and fully-merited complaint exists against the paucity of reliable historical writings on the subject of Canada's native peoples. This applies particularly to the period of this study, for anthropological writings of contemporary Indian groups did not really begin in force until the 1920's. For the years before 1914, accordingly–apart from the work of a few pioneer anthropologists whose work began in the 1880's and a few of the earliest studies by, or for, the Victoria Memorial Museum, Ottawa–accounts of the native peoples were prepared by non-specialists, and often they were only treated incidentally in the reports of government administrators, missionaries, fur-traders, policemen; or in the case of the Eskimos, of explorers and whaling captains.

Of major importance, therefore, are the annual reports of the Department of Indian Affairs, which down to the Great War provided quite full accounts of treaties, agencies, schools, health and welfare, and the economic activities of the Indian bands. Other contemporary accounts appear at frequent intervals in the reports of the North-

West Mounted Police, and occasionally, in those of topographical and geological surveyors or officers of the Department of Fisheries. Few Indian agents wrote books; one exception is W. M. Halliday, *Potlach and Totem, and the Recollections of an Indian Agent* (London and Toronto, 1953). A useful reference work for the period is F. W. Hodge, ed., *Handbook of the Indians of Canada* (Geographical Branch, Ottawa, 1913), which is an edition of the items pertaining to Canada from a larger work on the Indians of the United States prepared for the Smithsonian Institution. The most satisfactory modern account of the native people is Diamond Jenness, *The Indians of Canada* (Canada, National Museum, Bulletin No. 65, 1932, and later editions), while important works on the Indians of British Columbia include Marius Barbeau, *Totem Poles* (2 vols., Canada, National Museum, Bulletin No. 119, 1950), and Tom McFeat, ed., *Indians of the North Pacific Coast* (Toronto, 1966). An interesting thesis, Ethel G. Stewart, "Fort McPherson and the Peel River Area," (M.A., Queen's University, 1955), surveys the impact of white men and their institutions on the native inhabitants of that district over an extended period of time.

Administrative history is represented by Duncan Campbell Scott's three articles on this subject in *Canada and Its Provinces*, of which the last (in vol. 7) treats the period 1867-1912. To that time also belongs the surprisingly commendatory study by Frederick H. Abbott, *The Administration of Indian Affairs in Canada* (Washington, 1915), the work of an officer of the United States Indian service. A number of theses that fill important gaps are beginning to be written, based on the vast resources at the Public Archives of Canada. Those used in this study included C. R. Maundrell, "Indian Health, 1867-1940" (M.A., Queen's University, 1941), H. J. Vallery, "A History of Indian Education in Canada," (M.A., Queen's University, 1942), and the excellent G. E. Shankel, "The Development of Indian Policy in British Columbia" (Ph.D., University of Washington, 1945). Works relating to the important subject of the treaties include the Indian Affairs compilation, *Indian Treaties and Surrenders* (3 vols., Ottawa, 1905-12), and the well-known contemporary work *The Treaties of Canada with the Indians of Manitoba and the North-West* (Toronto, 1880), by Alexander Morris, a leading participant in some of the negotiations.

The British Columbia situation gave rise to several special reports, the dispute over reserves appearing in the *Sessional Papers* of 1874, 1875, and 1876 for the province, and on the Metlakatla and North-West Coast questions in those of 1883, 1884, and 1888. (British Columbia sessional papers were not numbered, and pagination was continuous through the volume in the early years.) Useful modern works dealing with social and economic aspects of the situation are Forrest E. LaViolette, *The Struggle for Survival: Indian Culture and the Protestant Ethic in British Columbia* (Toronto, 1961) and H. B. Hawthorn, C. S. Belshaw and S. M. Jamieson, *The Indians of British Columbia* (Berkeley, 1958).

Though works concerned with the Métis concentrate inevitably on the crises of 1869-70 and 1885, they also pay some attention to the position of this unfortunate people under Confederation. This applies to the last chapters of the gigantic Marcel Giraud, *Le Métis Canadien, Son Rôle dans l'Histoire des Provinces de l'Ouest* (Paris, 1945), A. H. de Tremaudan, *Histoire de la Nation Métisse dans l'Ouest Canadien* (Montreal, 1935), George F. G. Stanley's important *The Birth of Western Canada* (London, 1936), and his admirable *Louis Riel* (Toronto, 1963). Bearing more directly on the period of this study is Charles Mair, *Through the Mackenzie Basin* (Toronto, 1908), on the Half-Breed Claims Commission of 1899, and Mary L. Weekes, *The Last Buffalo Hunter* (New York, 1939), a biography of Norbert Welsh. For the rest, accounts of the Métis, like those of the Indians, are scattered among the writings of travellers, missionaries, surveyors, and policemen, and in the reports of the Department of the Interior.

The Eskimos, perhaps because they were a more truly primitive people at this time, received more thorough investigation in proportion to their numbers by anthropologists like Boas, Hawkes, Stefansson, Jenness, as well as by missionaries like C. E. Whittaker, *Arctic Eskimo* (London, 1937). More useful, however, are the works of

Diamond Jenness, particularly his five volumes on *Eskimo Administration*, especially vol. 2, *Canada*, vol. 3, *Labrador*, and vol. 5, *Reflections and Reconsiderations* (Arctic Institute of North America, Montreal, 1964, 1965, 1968).

Missionaries

In this area the student encounters an embarrassment of riches, what with five major denominations being active in the region and employing hundreds of individuals to whom writing letters and reports was an important activity; whose organizations were concerned to publicize their work to the utmost, and who commanded a considerable public following eager to receive reports of the work in the region. Archival collections exist at the parish, diocese, regional, and national levels, and also for particular orders or groups. The Anglican, Methodist, and Presbyterian churches are collecting scattered materials in central archives in Toronto, while the Public Archives of Canada, besides original records, has microfilms of records of many missionaries and mission organizations. A large proportion of mission records, however, remains tucked away in many local centres. A complete inventory of the holdings of missionary records in and about Canada is badly needed. The trail would lead to every part of Canada, to the United States, and to most countries of western Europe.

The published works of the several churches relating to their operations in Canada could fill a good-sized library. They include the annual catalogues of denominational activities, such as *Le Canada Ecclésiastique*, which sets out the organization and personnel of the Roman Catholic regular clergy, as well as the many special orders and institutions active in Canada (from 1887). Similar year books exist for the Anglican, Presbyterian, and Methodist churches. Every denomination published one or more magazines by, or on behalf of the work of, its various mission organizations, reports of the deliberations and decisions of synods and conferences, of the work of administrative committees, and of special agencies. A noteworthy example is the annual collection of reports of Oblate missions, published with a few interruptions since 1862: *Missions de la Congrégation des Missionnaires Oblats de Marie Immaculée*.

Few works deal with Canadian religious history in an interdenominational way. There are H. H. Walsh, *The Christian Church in Canada* (Toronto, 1956) and *Canada and Its Provinces*, vol. 11. Missionary societies of the Church of England are treated in a great four-volume *History of the Church Missionary Society* (London, 1899-1916) by E. Stock; in C. F. Pascoe, *Two Hundred Years of the S.P.G.* (2 vols., London, 1901); and W. D. A. Allan and A. McLure, *Two Hundred Years of the S. P. C. K.* (London 1898). There are the regional histories by T. C. B. Boon, *The Anglican Church from the Bay to the Rockies* (Toronto, 1962), and Frank A. Peake, *The Anglican Church in British Columbia* (Vancouver, 1959), while collective biographical works include O. R. Rowley, *The Anglican Episcopate of Canada and Newfoundland* (London, 1928), and the three series of *Leaders of the Canadian Church* (Toronto, 1918-43), edited by W. Bertal Heeney. Autobiographical and biographical works include Robert Machray, *Life of Robert Machray, Archbishop of Rupert's Land* (Toronto 1909); H. A. Cody, *An Apostle of the North* (Toronto, 1908) for Bishop W. C. Bompas, and S. A. Archer, *A Heroine of the North* (London, 1929) for Mrs. Bompas; Beatrice Batty, *Forty-two Years amongst the Indians and Eskimo* (London, 1893) for Bishop John Horden; Bishop J. Lofthouse, *A Thousand Miles from a Post Office* (London, 1922); A. J. Janvrin, ed., *Snapshot from the North Pacific* (London, 1904) for Bishop W. Ridley; Bishop W. H. Collison, *In the Wake of the War Canoe* (London, 1915); and F. A. Peake, *The Bishop Who Ate His Boots, A Biography of Isaac O. Stringer* (Don Mills, 1966). Other missionaries are commemorated in such works as A. C. Garrioch, *The Far and Furry North* (Winnipeg, 1925) and *A Hatchet Mark in Duplicate* (Toronto, 1929); John Hines, *The Red Indians of the Plains* (London, 1915); F. P. Shearwood, *By Water and the Word* (Toronto, 1943); Arthur Lewis, *The Life and Work of E. J. Peck Amongst the Eskimo* (London, 1909); and A. L. Fleming, *Perils of the Polar Pack* (Toronto, 1932). The celebrated Metlakatla experiment inspired the Church Missionary Society's *Metlahkatlah – Ten Years' Work Among the Tsimsheean Indians* (London, 1869); H. S. Wellcome,

The Story of Metlakatla (New York, 1887); K. J. W. Arctander, *The Apostle of Alaska* (New York, 1909); and a fine Ph.D. thesis, Jean Usher, "William Duncan of Metlakatla: A Victorian Missionary in British Columbia" (University of British Columbia, 1968).

The publication record of the Roman Catholic Church in general, and of the Oblates in particular, is as large as that of the Anglicans. A general work is Lionel A. Groulx, *Le Canada Français Missionaire* (Montreal, 1962), while the Canadian work of the Oblates is treated in T. Ortolan, *Les Oblats de Marie Immaculée durant le Premier Siècle . . . 1816-1916, IV: Au Canada, 1861-1892* (Paris, n.d.). The prolific controversialist A. G. Morice wrote many historical works, the most ambitious being his *Histoire de l'Eglise Catholique dans l'Ouest Canadien* (4 vols., St. Boniface, 1921-23). The work of the Church in the Northwest is also treated by P. Duchaussois in *Aux Glaces Polaires*, enlarged edition (Paris, 1928), an earlier version of which appeared as *Mid Snow and Ice* (London, 1923), *The Grey Nuns in the Far North, 1867-1917* (Toronto, 1919), and *Apôtres Inconnus* (Paris, 1924), dealing with the work of the lay brothers. Gaston Carrière, who has published widely on the role of the Oblates in eastern Canada, has in progress a massive *Histoire Documentaire de la Congrégation des Missionaires Oblats de Marie-Immaculée dans l'Est du Canada* (Ottawa), of which 8 vols. have appeared to date. Biographical and autobiographical works include Archbishop A. A. Taché, *Vingt Années de Missions dans le Nord-Ouest de l'Amérique* (Montreal, 1866), translated as *Sketch of the North-West of America* (Montreal, 1870); [Bishop Henri Faraud], *Dix Huit Ans Chez les Sauvages: Voyages et Missions de Mgr. Henri Faraud* (Paris, 1866); Bishop E. J. B. M. Grouard, *Souvenirs de Mes Soixante Ans d'Apostolat* (Montreal, 1923); Bishop Gabriel Breynat, *Cinquante Ans au Pays des Neiges* (3 vols., Montreal, 1946-48), a most important and forthright account, translated in abridged form as *The Flying Bishop: Fifty Years in the Canadian Far North* (London and Montreal, 1955); A. G. Morice, *Souvenirs d'Un Missionnaire en Colombie Britannique* (Winnipeg, 1933); Katherine Hughes, *Father Lacombe, the Black-Robe Voyageur* (Toronto, 1911); and for the northeastern frontier, V. A. Huard, *Monseigneur Dominique Racine, Premier Evêque de Chicoutimi* (Quebec, 1889); and G. Carrière, *Le Roi de Betsiamites: le Père Charles Arnaud, O.M.I.* (Ottawa, 1958), and *Explorateur pour le Christ: Louis Babel, O.M.I., 1826-1925* (Montreal, 1963).

Methodist publications include general works like Mrs. F. C. Stephenson, *One Hundred Years of Canadian Methodist Missions, 1824-1924*, vol. 1 [all published] (Toronto, 1925), J. C. Cochrane, *Trails and Tales of the North Land* (Toronto, 1934) on northern Ontario missions, and Arminius Young, *One Hundred Years of Mission Work in the Wilds of Labrador* (London, 1931). The expansion of missionary activities in the important period of western development is described in James Woodsworth, *Thirty Years in the Canadian North-West* (Toronto, 1917).

A useful collective biography is John Maclean, *Vanguards of Canada* (Toronto, 1918). The work of the McDougalls is described in a series of volumes by the son, John McDougall: *Forest, Lake and Prairie* (Toronto, 1895), *Saddle, Sled and Snowshoe* (Toronto, 1896), *Pathfinding on Plain and Prairie* (Toronto, 1898), *In the Days of the Red River Rebellion* (Toronto, 1903), and *On Western Trails in the Early Seventies* (Toronto, 1911). His career as well as his father's, is summarized in J. E. Nix, *Mission Among the Buffalo . . . 1860-76* (Toronto, 1960). Work in the country around Lake Winnipeg is described in J. Semmens, *The Field and the Work* (Toronto, 1884); in S. D. Gaudin, *Forty Four Years with the Northern Crees* (Toronto, 1942), and Nan Shipley, *Anna and the Indians* (Toronto, 1955), a biography of Mrs. Gaudin; and in a number of slight books of reminiscences by Egerton R. Young. Thomas Crosby's autobiographical *Among the An-ko-me-nums of the Pacific Coast* (Toronto, 1907) and *Up and Down the Pacific Coast* (Toronto, 1914) have a little more substance.

The Presbyterians of Canada are represented by several essays from the pen of the doughty Manitoba scholar, Dr. George Bryce; by such works as the collective biography by John McNab, *They Went Forth*, revised edition (Toronto, 1955); and C. W. Gordon ["Ralph Connor"], *The Life of James Robertson* (Toronto, 1908), superintendent of Home Missions from 1881 to 1902. For the Moravians in Labrador, see Joseph E. Hutton, A *History of Moravian Missions* (London, 1923); J. W. Davey, *The Fall of Torngak* (London, 1905); and S. K. Hutton, A *Shepherd in the Snow* (London, 1936), a life of W. W. Perrett.

The Fur Trade

Though this subject has probably received its due share of writing, this scarcely applies to the period after 1870. Perhaps the anticipated opening up of the Hudson's Bay Company archives for the period 1870-1900 will produce new insights into the company's role and other aspects of Canadian frontier development. In the meantime, there are available to the researcher the company's published *Reports to Shareholders* and *Reports of Proceedings*, Clifford Wilson, ed., "Private Letters from the Fur Trade" (extracts from the McMurray Correspondence, 1845-71), Historical and Scientific Society of Manitoba, *Papers*, Series 3, No. 5 (1950), plus several useful bodies of manuscript materials outside the company's archives. These include the Roderick Macfarlane and McIntyre Papers (Public Archives of Canada) and the Matheson Papers (Toronto Public Library).

Works that bear on the period after 1870 include H. A. Innis's great book, *The Fur Trade in Canada* (New Haven, 1930), which despite its enormous scope holds considerable value for this period of competition. Dealing directly with the years after 1870 are Gary D. Sealey, "History of the Hudson's Bay Company, 1870-1900" (M.A., University of Western Ontario, 1969); a study by G. Howard Simpson, "The Sales Organization of the Fur Trade," prepared for the University of Toronto Course in Commerce, 1925; numerous articles in *The Beaver*, notably a two-part article by G. F. G. Stanley, "The Fur Trade Party," Autumn and Winter 1953; Duane C. Tway, "The Wintering Partners and the Hudson's Bay Company," *Canadian Historical Review*, XXXIII (1), March 1952; and J. S. Galbraith, "A Note on the Mackenzie Negotiations with the Hudson's Bay Company, 1875-1878," *Canadian Historical Review*, XXXIV (1), March 1953. The company's financial history is the subject of a curious anonymous book, *The Reflections of Inkyo on the Great Company* (London, 1931). Its major rival of the period is treated in Marcel Sexé, *Two Centuries of Fur Trading, 1723-1923, Romance of The Revillon Family* (n.p., n.d.).

The considerable body of literature on or by fur-traders of the period includes the autobiographical Henry J. Moberly, *When Fur Was King* (Toronto and London, 1929); N. W. M. J. McKenzie, *Men of the Hudson's Bay Company* (Fort William, 1920); Isaac Cowie, *The Company of Adventurers* (Toronto, 1913); G. S. McTavish, *Behind the Palisades* (Sydney, B.C., 1963); J. W. Anderson, *Fur Trader's Story* (Toronto, 1961); and H. S. Kemp, *Northern Trader* (New York and Toronto 1956). Biographies include Beckles Willson, *The Life of Lord Strathcona and Mount Royal* (2 vols., London, 1915); M. L. Weekes, *Trader King* (Regina, 1948); Lowell Thomas, *Kabluk of the Eskimo* (Boston, 1932), the biography of Louis Romanet of Revillon Frères; Tom MacInnes, *Klengenberg of the Arctic* (London, 1932) on the controversial pioneer trader in the central Arctic; and J. G. MacGregor *Edmonton Trader* (Toronto, 1963), a life of John McDougall.

Surveys

Topographical, geological, hydrographic, geodetic, engineering and military surveying activities are an important part of the story of Canadian expansion. Don W. Thomson, *Men and Meridians, II: 1867 to 1917* (Ottawa, 1967), which deals with a dozen different agencies, is a useful introduction to the range and variety of such operations. A shorter account is Courtney C. J. Bond, *Surveyors of Canada, 1867-1967* (Ottawa, 1967). The early work of the Dominion Lands Branch is reviewed in the *Report* for 1891 of the Department of the Interior, Part VI, "General Report of Operations from 1869 to 1889," by W. F. King and J. S. Dennis. The administrative history of the department during the same period is described in W. E. Bauer, "The Department of the Interior and Dominion Lands, 1873-1891" (M.A. thesis, Queen's University, 1953). The activities of its distinguished member, William Ogilvie, appear in the annual reports of the department particularly from 1888 onwards, and in his own *Early Days on the Yukon* (London, 1913). The regular surveying operations are given in some detail in the annual reports of the department, while the provinces of Quebec, Ontario, and British Columbia also published similar reports, both of exploratory and subdivision surveys. Numerous land descriptions were also issued for the benefit of intending settlers. Typical of both *genres* are Quebec, *Description of the Surveyed Townships and Explored Territories of the Province of Quebec* (Quebec, 1889); or these British Columbia reports: "Exploratory Survey, Vancouver Island" (Public Works, *Report*, 1887), "Exploration of the North-Western Part of the Province, by N. B. Gauvreau" (Crown Lands, *Report*, 1893), or "Return to an Order for the Exploration Report upon the Yukon Country by Captain William Moore" (*Sessional Papers*, 1888). A very useful source of biographical and other details of surveyors is the *Annual Report* (from 1886) of the Association of Ontario Land Surveyors.

The work of the Geological Survey of Canada has produced a few historical reviews besides its great array of published reports and maps. F. J. Alcock, *A Century in the History of the Geological Survey of Canada* (Ottawa, 1947), is a popular history written along biographical lines, while a good, brief institutional history, reprinting all legislation from 1842 onward, occurs in F. H. Collins, "The National Museum of Canada" (its Bulletin No. 50, 1927). The present writer is completing a full study of this remarkable agency. A highly revealing glimpse at its organization and staff is found in House of Commons, *Journals*, 1884, Appendix No. 8 "Report of the Select Committee . . . as to Geological Surveys." Biographies of the leading personnel during the period include, besides those in Alcock, B. J. Harrington, *The Life of Sir William E. Logan, Kt.* (London, 1883); Lois Winslow-Spragge, *The Life of George Mercer Dawson, 1849-1901* (Montreal, 1962); and Charles Hallock, *One of Canada's Explorers* (Washington, 1901) on Robert Bell. J. B. Tyrrell's career is treated by W. J. Loudon, *A Canadian Geologist* (Toronto, 1930) and by William E. Eagan, "Joseph Burr Tyrrell, 1858-1957" (Ph.D., University of Western Ontario, 1971). Large collections of the personal papers of all four are extant: at McCord Museum (Logan) Redpath Library (Dawson), Public Archives of Canada (Bell), and University of Toronto Library (Tyrrell), as well as directors' letterbooks, field notebooks, etc., of these and other personnel at the Geological Survey or in the Public Archives, Ottawa. Other autobiographical works of value are T. C. Weston, *Reminiscences Among the Rocks* (Toronto, 1899), Charles Camsell, *Son of the North* (Toronto, 1954), and A. C. Lawson, "Out of Beaten Paths," *University of California Chronicle*, Jan. 1926. The reports of the expeditions, too numerous to detail here, are related in the survey publications; that of the Tyrrell brothers in 1893, was commemorated in an important book, J. W. Tyrrell, *Across the Sub-Arctics of Canada* (Toronto, 1897).

North-West Mounted Police

This important agency of northern development is represented by voluminous records at the Public Archives and R.C.M.P. headquarters, Ottawa. The published reports are also gratifyingly detailed, and they offer highly informative accounts of conditions in particular localities. The fair number of published histories, essentially rewritten versions of the reports, include A. L. Haydon, *The Riders of the Plains*, 1873-1910 (Toronto, 1910), R. C. Fetherstonhaugh, *The Royal Canadian Mounted Police* (New York, 1938), T. Morris Longstreth, *The Silent Force* (London, 1938); and the more detailed J. P. Turner, *The North-West Mounted Police*, 1873-1892 (2 vols., Ottawa, 1950), and Harwood Steele, *Policing the Arctic* (Toronto, 1935). Autobiographical accounts dealing with the pre-1914 era include J. d'Artigue, *Six Years in the Canadian North-West* (Toronto, 1882), J. G. Donkin, *Trooper and Redskin in the Far North-West* (London, 1889), C. P. Dwight, *Life in the North-West Mounted Police* (Toronto, 1892), R. B. Deane, *Mounted Police Life in Canada* (London, 1916); and bearing more directly on the northern frontiers of the time, C. E. Denny, *The*

Law Marches West (Toronto, 1939), and the outstanding S. B. Steele, Forty Years in Canada (New York, 1915). The R.C.M.P. Quarterly and Scarlet and Gold contain many useful historical articles.

Exploration and Travel in Northern Canada

A considerable literature outside governmental reports exists in contemporary and scholarly journals (listed earlier), and in the book-length accounts of the participants themselves. These last include the excellent Explorations in the Far North (Iowa City, 1898) by Frank Russell; Warburton Pike, The Barren Ground of Northern Canada (New York, 1891) and his Through the Sub-arctic Forest (London, 1896); Casper Whitney, On Snow-Shoes to the Barren Grounds (London, 1896); and Henry Toke Munn, Prairie Trails and Arctic By-Ways (London, 1932). Frederick Schwatka's expedition to the Arctic resulted in W. H. Gilder, Schwatka's Search (London, 1881), and his own Nimrod in the North (New York, 1885); his more famous expedition down the Yukon is described in Frederick Schwatka, Along Alaska's Great River (New York, 1883, and subsequent editions under different titles). The travels of the Oblate missionary E. F. S. J. Petitot are related in a succession of books: Les Grands Esquimaux (Paris, 1887), En Route Pour la Mer Glaciale (Paris, 1888), Quinze Ans Sous le Cercle Polaire (Paris, 1889), Autour du Grand Lac des Esclaves (Paris, 1891), and Exploration de la Region du Grand Lac des Ours (Paris, 1893). Later book-length accounts include D. T. Hanbury, Sport and Travel in the Northland of Canada (New York, 1904), Harry Whitney, Hunting with the Eskimos (New York, 1910), Ernest Thompson Seton, The Arctic Prairies (New York, 1911), V. Stefansson, My Life with the Eskimo (New York, 1913), George M. Douglas, Lands Forlorn (New York, 1914), and George Whalley, The Legend of John Hornby (Toronto, 1962). Travel in remote northern parts of the western provinces is described in H. S. Somerset, The Land of the Muskeg (London, 1895), Hulbert Footner, New Rivers of the North (Toronto, 1912) and P. L. Haworth, On the Headwaters of the Peace River (New York, 1917); while the northward extension of Ontario and Quebec was followed in the summer of 1912 by explorations of J. B. Tyrrell (Ontario, Mines, Report, 1913, "Hudson Bay Exploring Expedition, 1912") of New Ontario, and by W. T. Curran and H. A. Calkins, In Canada's Wonderful Northland (New York and London, 1917) of New Quebec.

These and a number of other writings provide accounts of travel by way of the improved navigation facilities along the northern rivers. Elizabeth Taylor's trip down the Mackenzie in 1892 is recounted in three articles in The Beaver, March and June 1948, and June 1951. Later trips are described in Elihu Stewart, Down the Mackenzie and Up the Yukon in 1906 (London, 1913), and Agnes Deans Cameron, The New North (New York, 1910). The facilities and amenities themselves are listed in successive editions of the famous Baedeker guidebooks, The Dominion of Canada with Newfoundland and an Expedition to Alaska (Leipzig, 1894, 1900, 1907, 1922).

Transportation Developments

A great volume and variety of source materials exist: manuscripts, published reports of government agencies and private companies, trade journals, traveller accounts, and historical studies. Though the subject includes river and oceanic navigation, trails, roads, and railways, the last has received the lion's share of study, perhaps appropriately, since the railway was the great transportation medium of the time.

Materials published by governments include those of the Dominion's Departments of Railways and Canals, Public Works, Marine and Fisheries, and Naval Service, the manuscript records for most of which repose at the Public Archives or the appropriate successor departments and agencies. The several provinces have published similar reports, based on comparable source materials, while the major companies have established archives to house their records. A particularly useful published source is the well-indexed monthly magazine begun in 1898 that went through the names *Railway and Shipping World*, *Railway and Marine World*, and *Canadian Railway and Marine World* before 1914. G. P. deT. Grazebrook, *A History of Transportation in Canada* (Toronto and New Haven, 1938) attempts to survey the whole field but deals mainly with railways. The writer's M.A. thesis, "A History of Transportation and Development of the Mackenzie Basin from 1870 to 1921" (University of Toronto, 1948), examined the roles of the several transportation media in that region.

Road transportation is poorly served by historians perhaps because of the dearth of satisfactory source materials. For details of construction one must search through reports of provincial departments of public works, public accounts, the Ontario Northern Development Branch, or an occasional consolidated work like "General Report of the Minister of Public Works, 1867-1883" (Canada, Public Works, *Report*, 1883). A few historic roads have been the subjects of articles and books, for example, R. C. Russell, *The Carlton Trail . . . 1840-1880* (Saskatoon, 1944), and Gerald L. Berry, *The Whoop-Up Trail* (Edmonton, 1953). For the Dawson Route, see Irene and K. C. A. Dawson, "The Dawson Route, 1857-1883: A Selected Bibliography with Annotations," *Ontario History*, LIX (1), March 1967.

Inland navigation is also rather poorly served, though several of the northern rivers have been made the subjects of popular books in the Rivers of America Series. John Macoun, *Manitoba and the Great North-West* (Guelph, 1882), a veritable encyclopedia of western conditions, gives a valuable description of the navigable waterways of the prairies at their fullest development on the eve of the railway age. Early steam transport on the Saskatchewan is also treated by N. Wickenden, " 'North-West' and 'Minnow,' Two Saskatchewan River Steamers," *Alberta Historical Review*, V (1), Winter 1957, and Bruce B. Peel, "Steamboats on the Saskatchewan," *The Beaver*, Autumn 1964. The northern river system is described in many travel accounts and in reports of government officials. A very good one from the beginning of steam navigation is Ogilvie's in Canada, Interior, *Report*, 1892, Part VII. For the northern rivers of British Columbia see Ronald G. Large, *The Skeena, River of Destiny* (Vancouver, 1957); Norman R. Hacking, "British Columbia Steamboat Days, 1870-1883," in *British Columbia Historical Quarterly*, XI (2), April 1947; and Mrs. C. G. Stevens, "River Boats on the Skeena," *The Beaver*, Dec. 1936. The biographies of the noted transportation entrepreneurs Captain William Moore and his son Captain William D. Moore are presented in four articles by C. L. Andrews in *Washington Historical Quarterly*, XXI (3), (4), XXII (1), (2), July, Oct. 1930 and Jan., April, 1931.

Railways are better served as regards manuscript and published materials. A basic reference work is Robert Dorman, compiler, *A Statutory History of the Steam and Electric Railways of Canada, 1836-1937* (Department of Transport, Ottawa, 1937). General railway histories, apart from Glazebrook, include O. D. Skelton, *The Railway Builders* (Toronto, 1920), and N. Thompson and J. H. Edgar, *Canadian Railway Development from the Earliest Times* (Toronto, 1933). The Canadian Pacific Railway is the subject of H. A. Innis, *A History of the Canadian Pacific Railway* (London, 1923), J. Murray Gibbon, *Steel of Empire* (Toronto, 1935), and Pierre Berton, *The Great Railway 1871-1881: The National Dream* (Toronto, 1970). Contemporary records of the governmental phase of the railway are given in Canadian Pacific Railways, *Reports of Progress* from 1872 to 1880 inclusive, and Canada, Royal Commission on the Canadian Pacific Railway, *Report* (3 vols., Ottawa, 1882), and in several sessional papers of Canada and British Columbia. Accounts by participants include Walter Moberly, *Rocks and Rivers of British Columbia* (London, 1884), and, with N. Robinson, his later *Blazing the Trail Through the Rockies* (Vancouver, n.d.); G. H. E. Secretan, *Canada's Great Highway from First Stake to the Last Spike* (London, 1924); P. Turner Bone, *When the Steel Went Through* (Toronto, 1947); John Macoun, *Autobiography* (Ottawa, 1922); and "The Canadian

Transcontinental Railway (1895)" by Marcus Smith, ms. in Marcus Smith Papers, Public Archives of Canada.

The two later transcontinentals are treated in the able account of Gerald R. Stevens, *Canadian National Railways*, vol. 2, *Towards the Inevitable, 1896-1922* (Toronto, 1962), while the Grand Trunk Pacific was the subject of the contemporary F. A. Talbot, *The Making of a Great Canadian Railway* (London, 1912). Details of the building of the National Transcontinental are given in Canada, National Transcontinental Railway Investigating Commission, *Report*, (2 vols., Ottawa, 1914). Other railways are treated in Bruce Ramsey, *PGE, Railway to the North* (Vancouver, 1962); J. D. Williams "A History of the Edmonton, Dunvegan, and British Columbia Railway, 1907-29" (M.A. thesis, University of Alberta, 1956); and Howard A. Fleming, *Canada's Arctic Outlet* (Berkeley, 1957) for the Hudson Bay Railway. Railway labouring conditions are described in E. W. Bradwin, *The Bunkhouse Man, A Study of Work and Pay in the Camps of Canada, 1903-1914* (New York and London, 1928).

Colonization in Ontario and Quebec

The efforts of governments, interested organizations, and individuals to bring to the attention of would-be settlers the opportunities available in particular districts gave rise to a considerable volume of literature. That of Ontario includes: Ontario, Crown Lands, *North Western Ontario: Its Boundaries, Resources and Communications* (Toronto, 1879), and *The Algoma District* (Toronto, 1884), Walpole Roland, *Algoma West, Its Mines, Scenery and Industrial Resources* (Toronto, 1887); Frank Yeigh, *The Rainy River District, Province of Ontario* (Toronto, 1892); C. C. Farr, *The Lake Temiscamingue District* (Toronto, 1893); D. Anderson, *The Newer Districts of Ontario* (Toronto, 1895); and at the turn of the century, Ontario, Crown Lands, *Report of the Survey and Exploration of Northern Ontario, 1900* (Toronto, 1901), and *Land Settlement in New Ontario: A Short Account of the Advantages Offered Land Seekers In Ontario* (Toronto, 1903); and Canadian Press, *New Ontario, the Canadian Press Association's Excursion to Temiskaming* (Welland, Ont., 1903). The Temiskaming and Northern Ontario Railway also published a series of pamphlets on settlement projects (1911?), while B. E. Fernow issued an important report on *Conditions in the Clay Belt of New Ontario* (Commission of Conservation, Ottawa, 1913).

A very good survey of colonization and settlement in Quebec is Georges Vattier, *Esquisse Historique de la Colonisation de la Province de Québec* (Paris, 1928). Some of the main colonization pamphlets were Canada, Agriculture, *Le Saguenay et le Lac St-Jean* (Ottawa, 1879), *Société de Colonisation du Lac Temiskaming* (Ottawa, 1885), and *La Région du Lac Saint-Jean* (Ottawa, 1890); J. B. Proulx, *A la Baie d'Hudson* (Montreal, 1886); the works of the celebrated journalist Arthur Buies, *Sur le Parcourus du Chemin de Fer du Lac St-Jean* (Quebec, 1887), *L'Outaouais Supérieur* (Quebec, 1889), and *Au Portique des Laurentides* (Quebec, 1891). The leading apostle of colonization, Father F. X. A. Labelle, whose work was eulogized by E. J. Auclair in *Le Curé Labelle, Sa Vie et Son Oeuvre* (Montreal, 1930), wrote the very influential *Pamphlet sur la Colonisation dans la Vallée d'Ottawa . . . et Règlements et Avantages de la Société de Colonisation du Diocèse de Montréal* (Montreal, 1880), and *Considérations Générales sur l'Agriculture, la Colonisation, le Rapatriement et l'Immigration* (Quebec, 1888). An equally ardent supporter of the cause, somewhat critical of Father Labelle, is B. A. Testard de Montigny, *La Colonisation – Le Nord de Montréal ou la Région Labelle* (Montreal, 1896). Later colonization literature includes C. A. M. Paradis, *From Temiskaming to Hudson Bay* (n.p., 1900), and Ivanhoë Caron, *Un Nouveau Centre de Colonisation, l'Abitibi* (Québec, 1915). The colonization drive received a very critical appraisal in Québec, Commission de Colonisation, 1904, *Rapport et Annexes*. Since then the question has received some consideration, among others, in A. R. M. Lower, *Settlement and the Forest Frontier* (Toronto, 1936); Michel Brunet, "Trois Dominantes de la Pensée

Canadienne-Francaise . . .," *Ecrits du Canada Français*, III, 1957; some of the articles in Marcel Rioux and Yves Martin, eds., *French-Canadian Society*, vol. 1 (Toronto, 1964); and Arthur I. Silver, "French-Canadian Attitudes towards the North-West and North-West Settlement, 1870-1890" (M.A. thesis, McGill University, 1966).

Beginnings of Industry in Northern Quebec and Ontario

That outstanding volume, Lower and Innis, *Settlement of the Forest and Mining Frontiers* (Toronto, 1936), offers the most comprehensive treatment of the forest, mining, and hydro-electric power industries in the pre-war period. Some articles in *Canada and Its Provinces* also deal with these subjects, notably in volume 16 (Quebec) which contains chapters on "Forest Resources," by E. T. D. Chambers, and "History of Mining in the Province," by F. D. Adams, while vol. 18 (Ontario) presents "Forest Resources and Forestry," by B. E. Fernow, and "Mines and Mining," by W. G. Miller to correspond. For Quebec there is also the useful series of studies, *Études sur Notre Milieu*, prepared in the 1940's by the Ecole des Hautes Etudes Commerciales of Montreal under the editorship of Esdras Minville, comprising a general volume, *Notre Milieu: Aperçu Général sur la Province de Québec* (Montreal, n.d.), and particular volumes on agriculture, forestry, mines, and fish and game. The volumes of the *Canadian Annual Review of Public Affairs* are invaluable for the years after 1901, while technical journals like the *Canadian Mining Journal* and the *Canadian Forestry Journal* furnish full accounts of developments in those industries.

Forest administration is treated in "A History of Crown Timber Regulations from the Date of the French Occupation to the Present Time," in Ontario, Clerk of Forestry, *Report*, 1899; and the important R. S. Lambert, *Renewing Nature's Wealth: A Centennial History of the Public Management of Lands, Forests & Wildlife in Ontario, 1763-1967* (Toronto, 1967), which also contains a most informative chapter on sources. The newly established pulp and paper industry is studied in N. Reich, *The Pulp and Paper Industry in Canada* (Montreal, 1926), J. A. Guthrie, *The Newsprint Paper Industry* (Cambridge, Mass., 1941); and G. Carruthers, *Paper in the Making* (Toronto, 1947). Histories of some major concerns include Charlotte Whitton, *A Hundred Years A'Fellin* (Ottawa, 1943), an account of the Gillies Brothers lumber firm; International Paper Company, *After Fifty Years, 1898-1948* (New York, 1948); and the very good Carl Wiegman, *Trees to News* (Toronto, 1953), on the Ontario Pulp and Paper Company.

Hydro-electric power is treated by Merrill Denison, *The People's Power, the History of Ontario Hydro* (Toronto, 1960); by John H. Dales, *Hydroelectricity and Industrial Development: Quebec 1898-1940* (Cambridge, Mass., 1957); and in the company history, Shawinigan Water and Power Company, *Fifty Years of Achievement* (Montreal, 1948). From 1908 there are published annual reports of the Hydro-electric Power Commission of Ontario, and soon afterwards, those of the Quebec regulatory agency.

An important source for the mining history of Ontario is Ontario, Royal Commission on the Mineral Resources of Ontario, 1890, *Report*, which interviewed many pioneer miners and entrepreneurs of the preceding half century. The Sudbury mining camp is dealt with in A. E. Barlow, "Report on the . . . Nickel and Copper Deposits of the Sudbury Mining District, Ontario," in Canada, Geological Survey, *Annual Report*, XIV, Part H, 1901; Ontario, Royal Nickel Commission, 1917, *Report*; and O. W. Main, *The Canadian Nickel Industry* (Canadian Studies in Economics, Toronto, 1955). The early years of Quebec mining, notably in the Eastern Townships and the Ottawa valley, are presented in R. W. Ells, "Report on the Mineral Resources of Quebec," Canada, Geological Survey, *Annual Report*, IV, Part K, 1889. The later Ontario mining fields are treated in O. T. G. Williamson, "Cobalt and Porcupine," *The Beaver*, March, 1954; and L. Carson Brown, "The Golden Porcupine," *Canadian Geographical Journal*, LXXIV (1), Jan. 1967, and S. A. Pain, *Three Miles of Gold, The Story of Kirkland Lake* (Toronto, 1958). D. M. LeBourdais,

Metals and Men (Toronto, 1957) contains chapters on the four Ontario mining districts.

The annual reports of the departments concerned with the forest, mineral, and waterpower resources provide records of production and financial results, as well as of frequently changing legislation and policies of administration. A useful source where these details may be found in more convenient, consolidated form is the election pamphlets published by governments, particularly those between 1879 and 1914, of the Ontario governments from Mowat to Whitney.

Local histories are often very informative about the rate of settlement and industrialization in particular districts, as are the publications of the longest established or most active historical societies, La Société Historique du Saguenay, La Société Historique du Nouvel-Ontario, and Thunder Bay Historical Society. For Quebec the many valuable local histories include: Raoul Blanchard, *Le Centre du Canada Français* (Montreal, 1947), *La Mauricie* (Trois Rivières, 1950), and *l'Ouest du Canada Français* (2 vols., Montreal, 1953); Gerard Filteau, *L'Epopée de Shawinigan* (Shawinigan Falls, 1944); Pierre Trudelle, *L'Abitibi d'Autrefois, d'Hier, d'Aujourd'hui* (Amos, 1937). The Lake St John district is represented by R.-Y. Pepin, *Le Royaume du Saguenay en 1968* (A.R.D.A. Project 15023, Ottawa 1969); Victor Tremblay, *Alma au Lac Saint-Jean, Son Histoire* (Chicoutimi, 1967); R. Vien, *Histoire de Roberval: Coeur du Lac Saint-Jean* (Montreal, 1953). Works dealing with the lower St Lawrence include V. A. Huard, *Labrador et Anticosti* (Montreal, 1897), J. Schmitt, *Monographie de l'Ile d'Anticosti* (Paris, 1904), E. Rouillard, *Le Côté Nord du Saint-Laurent et le Labrador Canadien* (Quebec, 1908), and N. A. Comeau, *Life and Sport on the North Shore of the Lower St. Lawrence and Gulf* (Quebec, 1909).

Ontario comes off rather less satisfactorily as regards local histories, the major ones being, for the Timiskaming country, O. T. G. Williamson, *The Northland Ontario* (Toronto, 1946) and S. A. Pain, *The Way North* (Toronto, 1964); for Sudbury, D. M. LeBourdais, *Sudbury Basin* (Toronto, 1953); Alice Marwick, *Northland Post; the Story of the Town of Cochrane* (Cochrane, 1950); and for the country west of Lake Superior, J. P. Bertrand, *Highway of Destiny* (New York, 1959), and the forthcoming *The Thunder Bay District, 1821-1892,* in the Ontario Series of the Champlain Society, edited by Elizabeth Arthur (seen in manuscript). The few social histories include Florence R. Howey, *Pioneering on the C.P.R.* (n.p., 1938), J. B. MacDougall, *Building the North* (Toronto, 1919), and Bertha M. Shaw, *Broken Threads* (New York, 1955).

New Frontiers in Western Canada

The Laurier boom gave rise to a torrent of articles and books on Canada, particularly on the new frontiers of settlement of the Middle North being opened by the transcontinental railways, including such books as F. A. Wightman, *Our Canadian Heritage; Its Resources and Possibilities* (Toronto, 1905); R. J. Barrett, *Canada's Century* (London, 1907); H. A. Kennedy, *New Canada and the New Canadians* (London, 1907); F. A. Talbot, *Making Good in Canada* (London, 1912); *The Times* (London), *The New Canada* (1912); and E. A. Victor, ed., *Canada's Future: What She Offers after the War* (Toronto, 1916). Typical, too, of the extensive governmental immigration literature of the period are the Department of the Interior's compilations *Canada's Fertile Northland* (1907) and *The Unexploited West* (1914). Again, the annual reports of this and related departments, and the *Canadian Annual Review* provide valuable information on contemporary developments. For scholarly accounts of settlement during the pre-war period, see A. S. Morton, *A History of Prairie Settlement* (Toronto, 1936), and Robert England, *The Colonization of Western Canada* (London, 1936).

The developing frontier of northern British Columbia is described in F. A. Talbot, *The New Garden of Canada* (London, 1911); M. A. Grainger, *Woodsmen of the West*

(London, 1908); C. F. J. Galloway, *The Call of the West–Letters from British Columbia* (New York, 1916); as well as pamphlets from the Department of the Interior, the provincial Department of Lands, and the Grand Trunk Pacific Railway. Later accounts include R. G. Large, *Prince Rupert, A Gateway to Alaska* (Vancouver, 1960) and *The Skeena, River of Destiny* (Vancouver, 1957); F. E. Runnalls, *A History of Prince George* (Prince George, 1946); G. R. Elliott, *Quesnel* (Quesnel, 1958); and K. E. Dalzell, *The Queen Charlotte Islands, 1774-1966* (Terrace, B.C., 1968). For the region west of Edmonton, see Mary T. S. Schäffer, *Old Indian Trails* (New York, 1911) for the district of the future Jasper Park; S. Washburn, *Trails, Trappers and Tender-feet in the New Empire of Western Canada* (London, 1912); J. B. Bickersteth, *The Land of Open Doors* (London, 1914); J. G. MacGregor's autobiographical *North West of 16* (Toronto, 1958), and his historical *Pack Saddles to Tête Jaune Cache* (Toronto, 1962); and A. A. den Otter, "Social Life of a Mining Community: The Coal Branch," *Alberta Historical Review*, XVII (4), Autumn 1969. Accounts dealing with the opening of the Peace River district include A. L. Brick, "Rev. J. Gough Brick and the Shaftesbury Mission Farm," *Alberta Historical Review*, IV (2), Spring 1955; James M. Macoun, *Report on the Peace River Region* (Geological Survey of Canada, Ottawa, 1903); A. M. Bezanson, *Sodbusters Invade the Peace* (Toronto, 1954); and these later accounts: C. A. Dawson and R. W. Murchie, *The Settlement of the Peace River Country* (Toronto, 1934); J. G. MacGregor, *The Land of Twelve Foot Davis* (Edmonton, 1952), and Eugenie L. Myles, *The Emperor of Peace River* (Edmonton, 1965). Two books dealing with the forested Middle Norths of Saskatchewan and Manitoba are A. Buchanan, *Wild Life in Canada* (London, 1920), an account of travel around the Churchill River basin during the course of a wildlife inquiry of 1914; and Luta Munday, *A Mounty's Wife* (London, 1930), portraying the life at The Pas.

Political Aspects of Northern Development

The most useful general treatment on boundaries are Norman D. Nicholson, *The Boundaries of Canada, Its Provinces and Territories* (Canada, Mines and Technical Surveys, Geographical Branch, Memoir No. 2, 1954) and James White, "Boundary Disputes and Treaties," in *Canada and Its Provinces*, vol. 8 (which also contains N. B. Wormwith, "The Fishery Arbitrations"); for broader accounts see the many histories of Canadian-American relations, or the recent H. G. Classen, *Thrust and Counterthrust* (Don Mills, 1965).

The principal domestic boundary question, of the 1870's and 1880's between Ontario and the Dominion governments, is treated in R. L. Jones, "The Ontario-Manitoba Boundary Dispute" (M.A. thesis, Queen's University, 1928); A. F. N. Poole, "The Boundaries of Ontario," *Canadian Bar Review*, XLIV (1), March 1964; and in J. C. Morrison, "Oliver Mowat and the Development of Provincial Rights in Ontario: A Study in Dominion-Provincial Relations, 1867-1896," in Ontario, Public Records and Archives, *Three History Theses* (Toronto, 1961). The details of the dispute and its history are given in Ontario, *Sessional Papers*, notably 1878, no. 42; 1882, no. 69; 1889, no. 60, and other of its publications prepared by David Mills and Charles Lindsay; and for Canada, House of Commons, *Journals*, 1880, Appendix I. For the legal aspects, see Richard A. Olmsted, comp., *Decisions of the Judicial Committee of the Privy Council relating to the British North America Act, 1867, and the Canadian Constitution, 1867-1954* (3 vols., Ottawa, 1954). The subsequent boundary adjustments of 1912 produced fewer documents. See the collections in the sessional papers of 1912: for Canada, nos. 94 and 110A; for Quebec, no. 116; and for Ontario, no. 54. The Arctic boundaries are treated under *Arctic Islands and Waters*, below.

A variety of issues were involved in the administration of different undeveloped regions. West of the Rockies the concern was with creating a system of control different from that of the United States and proof against subversion through infiltration. The contrast of systems was commented on in H. H. Bancroft, *History* of *British Columbia, 1792-1887* (San Francisco, 1887), no doubt reflecting the ms. "Mining Districts of British Columbia," by A. W. Vowell and Thomas Spence (Victoria, 1878) in the H. H. Bancroft Collection. This dichotomy was the central theme of W. J. Trimble, *The Mining Advance into the Inland Empire* (Madison, Wisc., 1914), was taken up in F. W. Howay, W. N. Sage and H. F. Angus, *British Columbia and the United States* (New Haven and Toronto, 1942) and in W. P. Morrell, *The Gold Rushes* (London, 1940), and was carried by these last two works, along with the mining frontier, into the Yukon; see below, *The Klondike Gold Rush and the Yukon.*

The principal question in the more advanced territories, of winning an adequate measure of self-government, is the central theme of L. H. Thomas, *The Struggle for Responsible Government in the North-West Territories, 1870-1897* (Toronto, 1956), and C. C. Lingard, *Territorial Government in Canada, the Autonomy Question in the Old North-West Territories* (Toronto, 1946). For the less developed territories – where the question was that of securing a voice at all – see John A. Bovey, "The Attitudes and Policies of the Federal Government towards Canada's Northern Territories, 1870-1930" (M.A. thesis, University of British Columbia, 1967), and F. B. Fingland, "Recent Constitutional Developments in the Yukon and Northwest Territories," *University of Toronto Law Journal,* XIV (2), June, 1964. The continued retention of the natural resources after provincial status was gained is discussed in Chester Martin, *The Natural Resources Question* (Winnipeg, 1920) and his *"Dominion Lands" Policy* (Toronto, 1938). A *cri de coeur* over the question was that of A. Bramley-Moore, *Canada and Her Colonies, or, Home Rule for Alberta* (London, 1911).

The problems and political issues involved in administering the frontier areas of the provinces are treated *en passant* in the previously mentioned W. L. Morton, *Manitoba, A History* (Toronto, 1957) and M. A. Ormsby, *British Columbia, A History* (Toronto, 1958), also in Lewis H. Thomas, *The Liberal Party in Alberta* (Toronto, 1959), and in Robert Rumilly's very detailed *Histoire de la Province de Québec* (Montreal, 1940-69 to date), the first nineteen volumes of which deal with the period down to 1914. The disputes over the relative roles of agriculture and the forest and hydro-electric power industries were well expressed in Québec, Commission de Colonisation, 1904, *Rapport et Annexes,* while the general issue of promoting industrialization in the northern districts is treated in William F. Ryan, *The Clergy and Economic Growth in Quebec (1896-1914)* (Quebec, 1966). Questions relative to resource management and developmental policies are aired in various Ontario departmental and commission reports, election pamphlets, and in studies like A. Margaret Evans, "Oliver Mowat and Ontario, 1872-1896: A Study in Political Success" (Ph.D. thesis, University of Toronto, 1967), and Brian D. Tennyson, "The Political Career of Sir William H. Hearst" (M.A. thesis, University of Toronto, 1963). The problem peculiar to Ontario, of administering important disputed territories, is described particularly in Ontario, *Sessional Papers,* 1880, no. 22; 1881, no. 44; 1884, nos. 53, 75; 1887, nos. 19A, 64; and especially 1890, no. 87, which is a review and summary. An aspect of development that is common to most of the provinces – the role of metropolitan ambitions in expanding frontiers of settlement and then integrating them into the body of the province – is treated in Patricia E. Roy, "Railways, Politicians and the Development of the City of Vancouver as a Metropolitan Centre, 1886-1929" (M.A. thesis, University of Toronto, 1963), and in M. Zaslow, "A History of Transportation and Development of the Mackenzie Basin from 1870 to 1921" (M.A. thesis, University of Toronto, 1948).

An extensive body of literature has sprung up recently on the subject of foreign investment and its relationship to resource development in Canada, but it is concerned mainly with events subsequent to 1914. Among the works that deal with the earlier period are E. S. Moore, *The American Impact on Canadian Mining* (Toronto, 1941), and volumes in The Relations of Canada and the United States series, notably H. Marshall, F. A. Southard and K. W. Taylor, *Canadian-American Industry* (New

Haven and Toronto, 1936) and L. E. Ellis, *Reciprocity, 1911* (New Haven, 1939). See as well the extensive writings on Canadian economic history.

Conservation of resources was only in its infancy in the years before 1914, though the growing movement was evident in the attention paid such matters in the *Canadian Mining Journal* and especially the *Canadian Forestry Journal;* in the expansion of operations (and reports of same) by the Forestry and National Parks branches of the Department of the Interior and similar agencies in provincial governments; in the numerous commissions investigating questions of resource management, like the Ontario Royal Commissions on Agriculture (1881), Mineral Resources (1890), Fish and Game (1892), and Forest Reservation and National Park (1893), or the Québec Commission de Colonisation (1904); but above all, in the early publications and reports of the Commission of Conservation, commenced in 1910. Assessments of these early beginnings may be found in Canada, Resources for Tomorrow Conference, 1961, *Background Papers* and *Proceedings* (4 vols., Ottawa, 1961); and in S. Renfrew, "Commission of Conservation," *Douglas Library Notes,* XIX (3-4), Spring, 1971.

The Klondike Gold Rush and the Yukon

The drama of the gold rush and the intense public interest it aroused are reflected in the extensive literature it has produced, as well as in the heavier-than-normal volume of material in the manuscript records of government departments, church and business, and private papers. The published works may be found listed in *Arctic Bibliography,* and in Lotz, *A Yukon Bibliography.*

The mining history of the region properly begins with the gold rushes of the northern interior, described in A. S. Trueman, "Placer Gold Mining in Northern British Columbia, 1860-1880" (M.A. thesis, University of British Columbia, 1935). The Overland Telegraph phase is treated in Grace Lee Nute, "Kennicott in the North," *The Beaver,* Sept. 1943; W. H. Dall, "Travels on the Yukon and in the Yukon Territory in 1866-1868," in F. M. Trimmer, ed., *The Yukon Territory* (London, 1898), and J. A. James, *The First Scientific Exploration of Russian America* (Evanston, 1942). The transfer of control over interior Alaska to the United States is recounted in Clifford Wilson, "The Surrender of Fort Yukon," *The Beaver,* Autumn 1969; that episode is described in C. W. Raymond, *Report of a Reconnaissance of the Yukon River, Alaska Territory* (United States, 42nd Congress, 1st Session, Senate Exec. Doc. No. 2, 1871), and in correspondence of Hudson's Bay traders and Anglican missionaries. Subsequent explorations are represented by the reports of Schwatka, of Dawson and McConnell (Geological Survey, *Annual Reports,* III and IV, 1887-88 and 1889), of Ogilvie's explorations and other activities (Interior, *Reports,* 1887-96), of Captain William Moore (British Columbia, *Sessional Papers,* 1888), and by accounts in contemporary geographical journals. Finally, for gold-mining before the gold rush, see G. M. Dawson, "Historical Notes on Events in the Yukon District," *Review of Historical Publications Relating to Canada,* II (1897), Ogilvie's reports, and his *Early Days on the Yukon* (London, 1913).

The gold rush itself is described in a great many books; the foremost general accounts are those of Pierre Berton, *The Klondike Fever* (New York, 1958); Kathryn Winslow, *Big Pan-Out* (New York, 1951); and H. A. Innis, *Settlement and the Mining Frontier* (Toronto, 1936). Among the autobiographical works are Joseph Ladue, *Klondyke Nuggets* (New York, 1897); Tappan Adney, *The Klondike Stampede of 1897-98* (New York, 1900); J. M. Price, *From Euston to Klondike* (London, 1898); W. B. Haskell, *Two Years in the Klondike and Alaskan Gold-Fields* (Hartford, 1898); J. H. E. Secretan, *To Klondyke and Back* (London, 1898); R. Auzias-Turenne, *Voyage au Pays des Mines d'Or* (Paris, 1898); R. C. Kirk, *Twelve Months in the Klondike* (London, 1899); Angelo Heilprin, *Alaska and the Klondike* (London, 1899); Jeremiah Lynch, *Three Years in the Klondike* (London, 1904); S. Tollemache, *Reminiscences of the Yukon* (London, 1912); and M. L. Davis, *Sourdough Gold* (Boston, 1933).

Travel books inspired by the rush included *The Klondike Official Guide* (Toronto, 1898), compiled from Ogilvie's reports but issued without his authorization; *Klondike, the Chicago Record's Book for Gold Seekers* (Chicago, 1897); and numerous other local productions like *Yukon Via Prince Albert,* or *The Klondike-Peace Gold Fields,* for which see M. Casey, *Catalogue of Pamphlets in the Public Archives of Canada, II: 1878-1931* (Canada, Public Archives Publication No. 13, 1932). Travel by the several interior routes is described in Charles Camsell, *Son of the North* (Toronto, 1951); Angus Graham, *The Golden Grindstone* (Toronto, 1935); and "Eben McAdam's Diary," *Alberta Historical Review,* II, 1954. The Edmonton phase of the gold rush is the subject of J. G. MacGregor's, *The Klondike Rush Through Edmonton, 1897-1898* (Toronto, 1970). Stock drives are described in Elizabeth Page, *Wild Horses and Gold* (New York, 1932), and Norman Lee, *Klondike Cattle Drive* (Vancouver, 1960).

Many, perhaps most, of the foregoing also deal with the mining and social history of the Yukon. In addition, for the former, there are J. E. Spurr, *Through the Yukon Gold Diggings* (Boston, 1900); Frederick Palmer, *In the Klondyke* (New York, 1899); A. N. C. Treadgold, *Report on the Goldfields of the Klondike* (Toronto, 1899); T. A. Rickard, *Through the Yukon and Alaska* (San Francisco, 1909); H. M. Cadell, "The Klondike and Yukon Goldfields in 1913," *Scottish Geographical Magazine,* XXX, July 1914; and good descriptions in Canada, Interior, *The Yukon Territory . . . ,* notably in the editions of 1907 and 1916. The Treadgold Concession affair is treated in Canada, *Sessional Papers,* 1903, no. 63; and 1904, no. 142, while Treadgold's amazing career is outlined in F. Cunynghame, *Lost Trail: the Story of Klondike Gold and the Men Who Fought for Control* (London, 1953). The related Atlin gold rush is described in W. W. Bilsland, "Atlin, 1898-1910, the Story of a Gold Boom," *British Columbia Historical Quarterly,* XVI, 1952. Other aspects of the economic life are treated in P. T. Mizony, "Gold Rush: A Boy's Impressions of the Stampede into the Klondike During the Days of 1898," in H. H. Bancroft Collection; "The Yukon Adventure," in V. Ross and A. S. Trigge, *The History of the Canadian Bank of Commerce,* vol. 2 (Toronto, 1920); L. D. Kitchener, *Flag Over the North, the Story of the Northern Commercial Company* (Seattle, 1954); R. A. Bankson, *The Klondike Nugget* (Caldwell, Idaho, 1935) on that flamboyant newspaper; W. D. McBride, *A Brief History of the White Pass and Yukon Route* (Whitehorse, 1945); and W. R. Curtin, *Yukon Voyage* (Caldwell, 1938), on river navigation.

Works dealing particularly with the social, religious, and cultural life of the Yukon include S. D. Clark, *The Developing Canadian Community* (2nd edition, Toronto, 1968); Andrew Baird, *Sixty Years in the Klondike* (n.p., n.d.); Laura B. Berton, *I Married the Klondike* (Boston and Toronto, 1954); Mrs. Martha Black, *My Seventy Years* (London, 1938); William E. Eagan, "Joseph Burr Tyrrell, 1858-1957" (Ph.D. thesis, University of Western Ontario, 1971); Mrs. Edith Tyrrell, *I Was There* (Toronto, 1938); W. R. Hamilton, *Yukon Story* (Vancouver, 1964); and N. A. D. Armstrong, *Yukon Yesterdays* (London, 1936). Religious history is treated in George E. Gartrell, "The Work of the Churches in the Yukon during the Era of the Klondike Gold Rush" (M.A. thesis, University of Western Ontario, 1970); G. T. Moir, *Sinners and Saints* (Victoria, 1947); C. J. Judge, *An American Missionary: Rev. William H. Judge, S.J.* (New York, 1907); G. F. Pringle, *Adventures in Service* (Toronto, 1929); and J. McNab, *They Went Forth* (Toronto, 1955). The literary side of the Klondike, represented by short stories, novels, and poems of Jack London, Rex Beach, Robert Service, Hiram A. Cody and many others, is examined in W. K. Hubbard, "The Klondike Gold Rush in Literature, 1896-1930" (M.A. thesis, University of Western Ontario, 1969).

The political-administrative side is dealt with in D. R. Morrison, *The Politics of the Yukon Territory, 1898-1909* (Toronto, 1968); J. N. E. Brown, "The Evolution of Law and Government in the Yukon Territory," *University of Toronto Studies, History and Economics,* 1902-07, II; and C. E. S. Franks, "How the Sabbath Came to the Yukon," *Canadian Public Administration,* X, 1967. The annual reports of Department of the Interior, the N.W.M.P., and special sessional papers provide much information, backed by the departmental records and the papers of such men as Laurier, Sifton, Minto, Constantine, Z. T. Wood, Ogilvie, F. C. Wade, etc., in the Public Archives of Canada. Police work is dealt with in S. B. Steele, *Forty Years in Canada* (New York, 1915); M. H. E. Hayne, *The Pioneers of the Klondike* (London, 1897); and A. L. Disher, "The March of the Yukon Field Force," *The Beaver*, Autumn 1962. Aspects of international control are treated in F. W. Howay, W. N. Sage and H. F. Angus, *British Columbia and the United States* (New Haven and Toronto, 1942); W. P. Morrell, *The Gold Rushes* (London, 1940); S. R. Tompkins, *Alaska, Promyshlennik and Sourdough* (Norman, 1945); R. Craig Brown, *Canada's National Policy, 1883-1900* (Princeton, 1964); and M. Zaslow, "The Yukon: Northern Development in a Canadian American Context," in Mason Wade, ed., *Regionalism in the Canadian Community, 1867-1967* (Toronto, 1969).

Arctic Islands and Waters

The *Arctic Bibliography* presents over 93,000 annotated items, around one-fifth of which relate to the Canadian Arctic; for specific topics, the reader is referred to that massive work. General texts on the Arctic environment include G.H.T. Kimble and D. Good, *Geography of the Northlands* (New York, 1955), or P. D. Baird, *The Polar World* (New York, 1964).

Whaling operations in northern Canada are frequently described in works on exploration and government department reports, particularly N.W.M.P. and Marine, while newspapers of whaling ports, like the *Buchan Observer* and *Dundee Weekly News* provide good sources of contemporary information from returned captains. The best general accounts are J. T. Jenkins, *A History of the Whale Fisheries* (London, 1921); F. R. Dulles, *Lowered Boats* (New York, 1934); and Basil Lubbock, *The Arctic Whalers* (Glasgow, 1937), which gives particular emphasis to the final years of whaling in the eastern Arctic. Autobiographical accounts of activities in these waters include W. Barron, *Old Whaling Days* (Hull, England, 1895); A. H. Markham, *A Whaling Cruise to Baffin's Bay, and the Gulf of Boothia* (London, 1874); D. M. Lindsay, *A Voyage to the Arctic in the Whaler "Aurora"* (Boston, 1911); Robert Ferguson, *Arctic Harpooner* (Philadelphia, 1938); and George Comer, "Whaling in Hudson Bay," in B. Laufer, ed., *Boas Anniversary Volume, Essays Written in Honor of Franz Boas* (New York, 1906). For the western Arctic there are John A. Cook, *Pursuing the Whale* (Boston, 1926); H. H. Bodfish, *Chasing the Bowhead* (Cambridge, Mass., 1936), and a useful article, J. W. Van Stone, "Commercial Whaling in the Arctic Ocean," *Pacific Northwest Quarterly*, XLIX (1), Jan. 1958.

The bibliography of Arctic exploration can be extended *ad infinitum*. Useful general accounts are Jeanette Mirsky, *To the Arctic* (New York, 1948); L. P. Kirwan, *The White Road* (London, 1959); J. E. Caswell, *Arctic Frontiers, United States Expeditions in the Far North* (Norman, 1956); and J. K. Wright, *Geography in the Making; the American Geographical Society, 1851-1951* (New York, 1952). Works relating expressly to Arctic Canada are Canada, Interior, *Southern Baffin Island*, by A. E. Millward (Ottawa, 1940), and Andrew Taylor, *Geographical Discovery and Exploration in the Queen Elizabeth Islands* (Canada, Mines and Technical Surveys, Geographical Branch, Memoir No. 3, 1964). For the individual explorations, see Sir George Nares, *Narrative of a Voyage to the Polar Sea During 1875 in H. M. Ships Alert and Discovery* (2 vols., London, 1878); and for the Greely expedition, A. W. Greely, *Three Years of Arctic Service* (2 vols., New York, 1886), W. S. Schley and J. R. Soley, *The Rescue of Greely* (New York, 1885), and the modern-day account of this lurid affair, Theodore Powell, *The Long Rescue* (London, 1961). The later expeditions are treated in Otto N. Sverdrup, *New Land, Four Years in the Arctic Regions* (2 vols., London, 1904), rewritten and carried forward by T. C. Fairley, *Sverdrup's Arctic Adventure* (London, 1959); Roald Amundsen, *The North West Passage* (2 vols., London and New York, 1908); and Ejnar Mikkelsen, *Conquering the Arctic Ice* (London, 1909). The successful campaign to achieve the North Pole and the controversies it engendered are discussed in J. E. Weems, *Race* for the Pole (New York, 1960); Leslie H. Neatby, Conquest of the Last Frontier (Athens, Ohio, and Toronto, 1966); J. Gordon Hayes, Conquest of the North Pole (New York, 1935); and W. H. Hobbs, Peary (New York, 1936). The writings of the protagonists themselves are best represented by F. A. Cook, My Attainment of the Pole (New York, 1913), and R. A. Peary, Nearest the Pole (London, 1907), The North Pole, Its Discovery in 1909 (New York and London, 1910), and Secrets of Polar Travel (New York, 1917). Excellent accounts of these men, as well as other personalities, firms, and historical events concerned with the Canadian Arctic are to be found in the unfortunately unpublished "Encyclopedia Arctica," ms. in Stefansson Library, Dartmouth College.

For the Canadian expeditions, see Millward, Taylor, and T. E. Appleton, Usque Ad Mare, A History of the Canadian Coast Guard and Marine Services (Ottawa, 1969). The Hudson Strait expeditions of 1884-86 are recorded in C. R. Tuttle, Our North Land (Toronto, 1885), and Canada, Marine and Fisheries, Report of the Second Hudson's Bay Expedition, 1885, and Report of the Hudson Bay Expedition of 1886, both by A. R. Gordon. The 1897 expedition is also treated in Report of the Expedition to Hudson Bay and Cumberland Gulf in the Steamship "Diana" under the Command of William Wakeham in the Year 1897 (Ottawa, 1898); and the expedition of 1903-4 in A. P. Low, The Cruise of the Neptune, 1903-04 (Ottawa, 1906). Bernier's three expeditions, published also by the Department of Marine and Fisheries, are: Report on the Dominion Government Expedition to the Arctic Islands and Hudson Strait on Board the C.G.S. "Arctic," in 1906-07 (1909); Report of the Dominion of Canada Government Expedition to the Arctic Islands and Hudson Strait on Board the D.G.S. "Arctic" (1908-09) (1910), and Report on the Dominion Government Expedition to the Northern Waters and Arctic Archipelago of the D.G.S. "Arctic" in 1910 (1911). His posthumous autobiography, Master Mariner and Arctic Explorer (Ottawa, 1939) is also of great interest.

The Canadian Arctic Expedition of 1913-1918 resulted in a considerable quantity of printed material besides the eventual fourteen volumes of the official report, which represents only two-thirds of the original program, and the voluminous manuscript materials at Ottawa and the Stefansson Library. Stefansson's role may be seen from his own point of view in The Friendly Arctic (New York, 1921; revised edition, 1944) and Discovery, the Autobiography of Vilhjalmur Stefansson (New York, 1964). Other important published accounts of participants are R. A. Bartlett and R. T. Hale, The Last Voyage of the Karluk (Boston, 1916); R. M. Anderson, "Report of the Southern Division of the Canadian Arctic Expedition of 1913," in Canada, Naval Service, Report, 1916-17; and Diamond Jenness, The Life of the Copper Eskimo (Canadian Arctic Expedition, 1913-18, Report, vol. 12, 1922). For an independent assessment of Stefansson's "political" career that centres on his relations with Canadian officials in the North and in Ottawa, see Richard J. Diubaldo, "The Canadian Career of Vilhjalmur Stefansson" (Ph.D. thesis, University of Western Ontario, 1971).

Arctic sovereignty has given rise to a considerable volume of literature, mainly in the field of international law. A very limited selection dealing particularly with the Canadian side of the record in the period under discussion includes Canada, Interior, Report upon the Title of Canada to the Islands North of the Mainland of Canada, by W. F. King (Ottawa, 1905); Millward and the other works cited in the previous paragraphs; V. K. Johnston, "Canada's Title to the Arctic Islands," Canadian Historical Review, XIV (1), March 1933, and "Canada's Title to Hudson Bay and Hudson Strait," British Yearbook of International Law, 1934; Yvon Beriault, Les Problèmes Politiques du Nord Canadien (Montreal and Ottawa, 1942); and the scholarly articles of Gordon W. Smith, "The Transfer of Arctic Territories from Great Britain to Canada in 1880 . . . ," Arctic, XIV (1), March 1961, and "Sovereignty in the North: The Canadian Aspect of an International Problem," in R. S. Macdonald, ed., The Arctic Frontier (Toronto, 1966).

INDEX

A HISTORY OF CANADA IN EIGHTEEN VOLUMES

The Canadian Centenary Series is a comprehensive history of the peoples and lands which form the Dominion of Canada.

Although the series is designed as a unified whole so that no part of the story is left untold, each volume is complete in itself. Written for the general reader as well as for the scholar, each of the eighteen volumes of *The Canadian Centenary Series* is the work of a leading Canadian historian who is an authority on the period covered in his volume. Their combined efforts have made a new and significant contribution to the understanding of Canada and of Canada today.

W. L. Morton, Vanier Professor of History, Trent University, is the Executive Editor of *The Canadian Centenary Series*. A graduate of the Universities of Manitoba and Oxford, he is the author of *The Kingdom of Canada; Manitoba: A History; The Progressive Party in Canada; The Critical Years: The Union of British North America, 1857-1873;* and other writings. He has also edited *The Journal of Alexander Begg and Other Documents Relevant to the Red River Resistance.* Holder of the honorary degrees of LL.D. and D.LITT., he has been awarded the Tyrrell Medal of the Royal Society of Canada and the Governor General's Award for Non-Fiction.

D. G. Creighton, former Chairman of the Department of History, University of Toronto, is the Advisory Editor of *The Canadian Centenary Series*. A graduate of the Universities of Toronto and Oxford, he is the author of *John A. Macdonald: The Young Politician; John A. Macdonald: The Old Chieftain; Dominion of the North; The Empire of the St. Lawrence* and many other works. Holder of numerous honorary degrees, LL.D., and D.LITT., he has twice won the Governor General's Award for Non-Fiction. He has also been awarded the Tyrrell Medal of the Royal Society of Canada, the University of Alberta National Award in Letters, the University of British Columbia Medal for Popular Biography, and the Molson Prize of the Canada Council.